D0937279

Thomas R.R. Cobb

THE MAKING OF A SOUTHERN NATIONALIST

Portrait of Thomas R. R. Cobb at age 38 or 39
ca. 1861 or 1862

Thomas R.R. Cobb
(1823-1862)

THE MAKING OF A SOUTHERN NATIONALIST

by

William B. McCash

MERCER
UNIVERSITY
PRESS
Macon, Georgia

ISBN 0-86554-049-7

All books published by Mercer University Press are produced on acid-free paper that exceeds the minimum standards set by the National Historical Publications and Records Commission.

LIBRARY OF CONGRESS CATALOGING IN PUBLICATION DATA

McCash, William B., 1931-
Thomas R. R. Cobb (1823-1862)

Bibliography: p. 329.
Includes index.
1. Cobb, Thomas Reed Rootes, 1823-1862.
2. Georgia—Politics and government—1775-1865.
3. Politicians—Georgia—Biography. 4. Lawyers—Georgia—Biography. 5. Generals—Southern States—Biography. 6. Confederate States of America. Army—Biography. I Title.

F290.C67M37 1983 975.8'03'0924 [B] 82-22925
ISBN 0-86554-049-7

TABLE OF CONTENTS

DEDICATION

To my parents who gave me life

To my wife who inspired and rejuvenated it

To my children who have made it worth living

LIST OF ILLUSTRATIONS

PREFACE

Many years ago Dr. E. Merton Coulter suggested to me that Thomas R. R. Cobb might make a fit subject for study. At that time nothing had been written about the man beyond a few laudatory sketches and brief mention in a variety of books on Civil War, Georgia, and southern history. Based on what was then known, however, he seemed worthy of investigation. Dr. Coulter's suggestion was subsequently seconded by Dr. Joseph H. Parks, a distinguished biographer of southern figures, who encouraged me to pursue the matter to fruition.

Following the advice of these eminent scholars, I began to piece together the details of Cobb's life. As the research progressed, it became increasingly evident that Cobb reflected to a remarkable degree the world view of the section in which he lived and that, despite having many unique qualities which set him apart from the average man, he came very close to being a representative southerner, if such can be said of anyone.

For purposes of analysis and cohesion, I have divided Cobb's life into several topics: formative years, law, religion, educational reform, slavery and politics, secession, and Civil War. Running through these chapters are three interrelated, unifying themes: first, the impact of southern evangelicalism and slavery on Cobb's attitudes and actions; second, the manner in which his manifold public interests, many of them national in scope (for example, revivalism and the codification, Sunday school, common school, and temperance movements), manifested a distinctly southern point of view; and finally, how continued stress on southern distinctiveness led inevitably to the concept of southern nationalism. This biography, then, is the story of how one representative Georgian evolved from a southern unionist to a southern nationalist, why he became one, and what he contributed to the cause of southern nationhood.

ACKNOWLEDGMENTS

I would like to thank the staffs of the following depositories and organizations for their assistance in locating material for this study: the University of Georgia Libraries (especially Mrs. Susan Tate, now retired); Perkins Library, Duke University; Southern Historical Collection, University of North Carolina; Georgia Department of Archives and History; Emory University Library; Library of Congress, Manuscripts Division; Henry E. Huntington Library and Art Gallery; The Virginia Historical Society; The Historical Society of Pennsylvania, and the First Presbyterian Church of Athens, Georgia. I also wish to thank *The Georgia Historical Quarterly* for granting permission to reprint portions of my articles appearing in that journal, volume 60 (Spring 1976) and volume 62 (Spring 1978).

I am deeply indebted to the late Dr. E. Merton Coulter for the use of letters in his private collection and to Dr. Joseph H. Parks, who has been a kind and helpful mentor to me over the years. I am also indebted to my friends and colleagues, Dr. James K. Huhta and Dr. William T. Windham, both of whom read early versions of the manuscript and offered timely moral support. A special word of thanks goes to my typist, Sue Wrather, who, despite provocations, always remained cheerful and got the work done. Finally, I must fondly recognize the love and support of my wife, June, who listened perceptively to my ideas, and the patience of my children, Pamela, Vicki, and Rodney, who endured this project too long.

The publication of this volume was made possible in part by a grant from the Watson-Brown Foundation Inc., Atlanta, Georgia.

CHAPTER 1

Early Life

Thomas R. R. Cobb as a young man
(date unknown)

Thomas Cobb's ancestors on both sides of his family had lived in Virginia for generations; but, about the year 1769, his grandfather, John Cobbs,[1] moved to Granville County, North Carolina, where he apparently resided until shortly after the American Revolution. At no time, however, did he lose contact with the Old Dominion. In fact, in 1784 he joined several Virginia friends—John Lewis, Francis Willis, Thomas Napier, and George Mathews—in a vast land speculation in Georgia and some years later went there permanently to capitalize on the venture. Once in Georgia, he developed an extensive plantation near Louisville and purchased large tracts in the counties of Franklin, Jackson, Clarke, Baldwin, and Camden. Besides owning land in Georgia, he amassed thousands of acres in the states of North Carolina, South Carolina, Tennessee, and Kentucky.[2]

Landed wealth and an alliance with George Mathews, who was

---

[1]The "s" was dropped from the name in the early 1800s. The Cobb lineage has been traced with discrepancies in "Cobb and Cobbs Family," *William and Mary College Quarterly* 19 (July 1910); "Genealogy," *Virginia Magazine of History and Biography* 4 (October 1896); Lucian Lamar Knight, "Genealogy of the Knight, Walton, Woodson, Lamar, Daniel, Benning, Cobb, Jackson, Grant, and Other Georgia Families," (bound, typed volume) Library of Congress, Washington DC.

[2]Allen D. Candler, comp., *The Revolutionary Records of the State of Georgia*, 3 vols.

elected governor in 1787 and again in 1793, assured Cobbs of a position of prominence at least at the local level. Unfortunately, politics and speculative endeavors eventually embroiled him in disagreeable controversies which undermined old friendships and led, on one occasion, to an attempted assault on two newspaper editors who had printed an article detrimental to his ambitions.[3] Defeated for a seat in the state legislature in 1800 and plagued by lawsuits and repeated financial losses, his reputation suffered and he was subjected to all sorts of "threats and insulting duns," causing him to complain in exasperation that he was "harrassed perhaps more than any other man ever was or will be again in this Country."[4]

By the fall of 1807 Cobbs's ruin was complete. So deeply in debt had he fallen that upon the insistence of a creditor he was imprisioned in the Jefferson County jail for a period of four months. Only after presenting a schedule of his assets in court and swearing an oath that he no longer possessed any real or personal property was he released.[5] A few years later (the exact date is unknown) he died and was survived by six children—three daughters, all of whom married local men, and three sons, Howell, Henry Willis, and John Addison.

The eldest son, Howell, after a career in the army (1793-1806), was elected to Congress three consecutive times. In 1810, during his second term in office, he married Martha Jacqueline, daughter of Thomas Reade Rootes, an affluent Virginia planter, lawyer, and politician who owned a large plantation named White Marsh in the vicinity of Yorktown, a second estate called Gould Hill in Hanover County, and an attractive town house on Federal Hill in Fredericksburg. Resigning from Congress in 1812 due to ill health, Howell Cobb retired to his plantation in Jefferson County where he remained until his death in 1818.[6]

(Atlanta: Franklin-Turner Co., 1908), 3:281, 432, 2:791-93; Jefferson County GA, "Schedule of Property, Inferior Court Minutes," 1807, pp. 84-87. Hereinafter cited as "Schedule of Property."

[3]John Cobbs to Horatio Marbury, [no date], Telamon Cuyler Collection, University of Georgia Libraries, Athens GA; Thomas Carr to John Cobbs, 17 August 1792, John Cobbs to Thomas Carr, 17 August 1792, Thomas Carr to John Cobbs, 17 August 1792, Carr Collection, University of Georgia Libraries; *The Louisville Gazette*, 30 September 1800.

[4]John Cobbs to Seaborn Jones, 5 July 1803, Seaborn Jones Papers, Perkins Library, Duke University, Durham NC.

[5]"Schedule of Property," pp. 77-78, 81-82, 87-88. See also Nicholas Ware to Thomas Carr, 25 September 1807, Carr Collection.

[6]*Biographical Directory of the American Congress 1774-1961* (Washington DC:

Far less successful than either of his two brothers was Henry Willis. Addicted to alcohol, his health deteriorated and he became so irresponsible and abusive that he was excluded from his brother's will. The bulk of Congressman Cobb's estate went to his wife with the proviso that should she ever remarry everything would go to John Addison, who might, in turn, give it all to his son, Howell, "if . . . the said John A. Cobb think him truly worthy of it." When Martha married again in 1819 the property fell, as stipulated, into the hands of her brother-in-law.[7]

Colonel John Addison Cobb, who inherited all this wealth, was born on 5 January 1783, in Granville County, North Carolina, where he spent his early boyhood years before moving to Georgia with his father. He grew up to be a tall, kindhearted, heavy set man with a multiplicity of interests. Captivated by politics, he was several times elected to the state legislature and served as a road commissioner, justice of the peace, and aide-de-camp to Governor David B. Mitchell. He supported George M. Troup for governor in 1821, but later broke with the Troup faction over the nullification issue and ran unsuccessfully for the state senate on the Union Party ticket in 1834 and 1835. Although his sons became Democrats, the Colonel (a great admirer of Henry Clay) drifted in the direction of the Whig camp and voted for the Kentuckian in 1844.[8]

Planting, however, rather than politics was Cobb's chief occupation. His Cherry Hill plantation in Jefferson County—ultimately embracing 6,000 acres and worked by 150 slaves—and a farm nearby, named Rootesville, absorbed much of his attention and provided most of his income, but he was also responsible for administering the estate of a certain Dr. John Sayre, deceased. The latter obligation turned out to be a disaster. In 1810

Government Printing Office, 1961), p. 711; Will of Thomas R. Rootes, 25 July 1822, Jackson-Prince Papers, Southern Historical Collection, University of North Carolina, Chapel Hill NC.

[7]Jefferson County GA, Will of Major Howell Cobb, "Court of Ordinary, Wills," Book A. For references to Henry Willis Cobb's drunken behavior see Sarah R. Cobb to Martha J. Jackson, 30 October 1819, L. Thornton to Martha J. Jackson, 1 March 1820, Sarah R. Cobb to Martha J. Jackson, 24 March 1820, Jackson-Prince Papers. Martha's second husband was Dr. Henry Jackson, a professor at Franklin College in Athens, Georgia.

[8]The date of Colonel Cobb's birth is recorded on his gravestone in the Oconee Hill cemetery in Athens, Georgia. A. L. Hull, *Annals of Athens 1801-1901.* (Athens GA: Banner Job Office, 1906), p. 61, claimed that Cobb weighed nearly three hundred pounds, a fact which probably accounts for the portliness of some of his children. His eldest son, Howell, for example, was so stout that college chums called him "Fatty."

he was accused of negligence in supervising the estate and was ordered by the court to submit a statement of his managerial conduct. Eight months later, on 27 July 1811, he asked to be relieved of his administrative duties. The request was granted but not before a creditor of the late Dr. Sayre again accused him of mismanagement and demanded "the benefit of the bond given . . . for the faithful administration of said Estate." In the end he was held accountable for all of Sayre's debts, and, according to his wife, it came "very near ruining him entirely."[9]

John A. Cobb's difficulties with Dr. Sayre's property coincided with a happier set of circumstances which no doubt bolstered his spirits. Prior to the spring of 1811 he had begun to pay court to eighteen-year-old Sarah Robinson Rootes, the third daughter of Thomas Reade Rootes, whose eldest daughter, it will be remembered, had married Howell. Welcomed to the "charming social fire-side comfort . . . at Federal Hill," he was soon carrying on an intimate correspondence with Sarah.[10]

> I arrived home after a tiresome journey and found my plantation going on extremely well[,] indeed[,] much better than my more imagined calculations had anticipated.
>
> I want here but the society of my dear Sarah to make me happy as any person can be in this world. I look forward to the time when our fate will be one with the greatest pleasure and anxiety.[11]

John and Sarah were married in Fredericksburg on 11 April 1812, and shortly thereafter set up housekeeping at Cherry Hill. The young bride was short, plump, pious, blindly devoted to her family and exceedingly defensive where their interests were concerned. In later years she became increasingly dumpy, hard of hearing, and smoked a pipe to ease her dyspepsia. Although her father had once admonished her for her extravagance, she quickly learned the need for frugality because her husband,

---

[9]Sarah R. Cobb to Martha J. Jackson, 24 March 1820, Jackson-Prince Papers. See also Jefferson County, GA, "Court of Ordinary, Minutes," Book A, pp. 155, 220, 232; *Southern Banner* (Athens GA), 4 September 1840.

[10]The quotation is from L. Thornton to Miss Rootes, 1799, Jackson-Prince Papers. Rootes had seven children: five daughters (Martha, Mary, Sarah, Laura, and Serena) and two sons (Thomas and Edward). The Rootes family tree is traced in "Genealogy," *Virginia Magazine of History and Biography* 4 (October 1896): 207-11.

[11]John A. Cobb to Sarah R. Rootes, 7 May 1811, Cobb-Erwin-Lamar Collection, University of Georgia Libraries.

despite owning a great deal of property, was, like his father before him, chronically in debt and not always able to afford as many luxuries as the family desired.[12]

Her husband's financial plight, however, was minor when compared with that of her father and oldest brother. The latter was incompetent, drunken, and dishonest, and, as a direct consequence, sank into total ruin, dragging his father with him. Federal Hill and White Marsh, along with other property, had to be sold to satisfy creditors, leaving little or nothing to divide among the heirs of Thomas Rootes. Sarah's father died in 1824, bankrupt and embittered toward his dissolute son. His anguish would have been intensified had he lived to witness the similar downfall of his second son.[13]

By the time of her father's death Sarah Cobb had suffered one miscarriage and given birth to four children: Howell (1815), Laura (1818), Mildred (1820), and Thomas Reade Rootes, who was born at Cherry Hill on 10 April 1823, and named for his maternal grandfather.[14] Announcing the arrival of the fourth child, soon to be nicknamed Tom, the proud father wrote:

> Sally was yesterday at 8 o Clock in the morning delivered of a fine boy, I say fine, because in reality he is so, a few minutes since I weighed him, you will hardly know how to believe me, when I tell you that he weighed 21 1/2 lbs, the delivery was almost too much for Sally.[15]

About a year after the birth of their second son, the Cobbs left Cherry Hill in the care of an overseer and moved to Athens in Clarke County

---

[12]Colonel Cobb's indebtedness is mentioned in Sarah R. Cobb to Martha J. Jackson, 30 October 1819, Sarah R. Cobb to Martha J. Jackson, 24 March 1820, Sarah R. Cobb to Dr. Henry Jackson, 6 December 1821, E. J. Rootes to Martha J. Jackson, 21 February 1824, Jackson-Prince Papers.

[13]For the financial, spiritual, and physical ruin of Thomas Rootes and his two sons see Thomas Rootes to Martha, 23 March 1817, 20 August 1819, 2 June 1820, 15 September 1821, John Tabb to Henry Jackson, 13 January 1820, J. Rootes to Martha, 19 July 1823, 10 January 1824, 24 February 1824, 17 March 1827, Henry C. Lea to Martha Jackson, 19 July 1840, Serena [Lea] to Martha J. Jackson, 5 July 1840, ibid.

[14]Thomas R. Rootes to Martha J. Cobb, 18 March 1814, ibid. mentions the loss of Sarah's first child. Laura, named for one of Sarah's sisters, married Williams Rutherford, Jr., who combined farming and teaching for a livelihood. Mildred, named for one of her father's sisters, married Luther Judson Glenn, a lawyer, legislator, and mayor of Atlanta.

[15]John A. Cobb to Friend, 11 April 1823, ibid. In 1864 Sarah recorded that her second

where the Colonel owned a large tract of land on the northwestern side of town, an area subsequently denominated Cobbham, which developed into the most aristocratic section of Athens.

Viewed from almost any perspective, the decision to take up town life made sense. Between 1820 and 1860 Athens had expanded rapidly. The population increased, businesses of every description multiplied, a lucrative upcountry wagon trade developed, a rail connection with other points in Georgia was established, rival newspapers competed to shape public opinion, male and female academies sprang up, Franklin College (the University of Georgia) grew in size and prestige, churches flourished, itinerant entertainers made regular appearances, saloons, houses of prostitution, and gambling halls found a ready clientele as well as reform-minded opponents, and "a complex and highly differentiated occupational structure" evolved. In brief, as one student of comparative social systems has explained: "Athens was no metropolis, but it offered a variety of urban services and a self-consciously urban ethos, a strong sense of its urban character, which separated it from the surrounding countryside."[16]

The Cobbs fit easily and comfortably into Athenian society and contributed significantly to the town's development as an economic, cultural, and political center. Colonel Cobb variously served as town commissioner, chairman of the board of the local grammar school, and director of both the Georgia Railroad Company and the Athens branch of the Bank of the State of Georgia. His wife, meanwhile, became a fixture in the Trail Creek Baptist Church and gave birth to three more children: John Boswell in 1826, Mary Willis in 1828, and Sarah Martha (Matty) in 1831.[17]

---

son weighed seventeen pounds at birth. See Henry Rootes Jackson Scrapbook, Georgia Department of Archives and History, Atlanta GA.

[16]Frank J. Huffman, Jr., "Town and Country in the South, 1850-1880: A Comparison of Urban and Rural Social Structures," *The South Atlantic Quarterly* 76 (Summer 1977): 369, 373. A more detailed description of the growth of Athens is in Ernest C. Hynds, *Antebellum Athens and Clarke County* (Athens GA: University of Georgia Press, 1974), pp. 22-67. For references to Cobbham see *Southern Banner*, 26 July 1834, 20 October 1853.

[17]John Boswell was the least prominent of the Cobb brothers. He attended Franklin College briefly but never graduated. For a time he worked as a clerk, first in Athens and later in New York. Dissatisfied with his New York position, he returned to Athens and opened a fairly profitable wholesale-retail store. In 1853 he married his cousin, Mary Athena Lamar, nee Jackson, the widow of Andrew Lamar who had been Howell Cobb's

Church and family were the most vital elements in the life of Sarah Cobb. The salvation of a loved one was ever a cause of rejoicing, and, when her husband belatedly joined the Baptist faith in 1841, it undoubtedly brought her an enormous sense of relief. Proper Christian conduct, of course, was expected of all the children. Once, in 1847, upon hearing that her daughter Mary Willis had attended the theatre, she expressed marked disapproval and implored her "not to do what is unbecoming a Christian and bringing disgrace upon the cause of her master." Particularly susceptible to Sarah's religious influence was young Tom, who would be caught up in the revivals of the 1840s and would become an effective lay revival leader in the 1850s. The Cobbs were clearly part of the southern evangelical tradition described by Anne C. Loveland and Donald G. Mathews.[18]

During the last month or so of his mother's pregnancy with Matty, eight-year-old Tom was sent to live on his Uncle Henry Jackson's farm a few miles outside of town. Concerning the youngster's behavior, Dr. Jackson reported: "Tom seems as yet unwearied with his stay here.... He has some habits which it will take some time to be remedied and removed—however I find him perfectly tractable and attentive to what I mention to him.[19] Whatever his faults, Thomas R. R. Cobb enjoyed a normal childhood, one that was healthy, active, and happy. He played all the usual juvenile games, rode horseback regularly with his sister, Laura, owned a variety of pets, attended the Athens grammar school, took private French lessons, and made occasional trips with his father, who traveled often to Louisville, Augusta, and Savannah on business.

The colonel's business, unfortunately, was not always good. His cotton crop failed in 1832 and it was necessary to remind the family of the

---

brother-in-law. Mary Willis married Frank Irwin, a widower and substantial businessman in 1851, and Matty, the youngest of the Cobb children, married John C. Whitner of Tallahassee, Florida in 1853 and moved to West Point, Georgia, where her husband bought part ownership in a mercantile firm.

[18]Sarah R. Cobb to Howell Cobb, 18 September 1847, Howell Cobb Collection, University of Georgia Libraries. Anne C. Loveland, *Southern Evangelicals and the Social Order 1800-1860* (Baton Rouge: Louisiana State University Press, 1980). Hereinafter cited as Loveland, *Southern Evangelicals*. Donald G. Mathews, *Religion in the Old South* (Chicago: University of Chicago Press, 1977). Thomas Cobb's evangelicalism will be explored in chapter 3.

[19]Henry Jackson to Martha Jackson, 10 August 1832, Jackson-Prince Papers.

need for economy. Nevertheless, life was anything but hard for the Cobbs who took full advantage of the social and educational opportunities open to the southern upper class. Howell, for instance, graduated from Franklin College, married the daughter of a wealthy Baldwin County planter, opened a law office in Athens, and by 1842 had embarked upon a highly successful political career that would lead to Congress and the cabinet of James Buchanan.

Following in the footsteps of his elder brother, Tom Cobb entered Franklin College on 29 July 1837.[20] He was fourteen at the time, a bright, eager, piously sentimental youth with a passion for work and a driving ambition to get ahead. From the first he promised to be an outstanding student.

The College was then under the direction of Dr. Alonzo Church, a tall, dignified Presbyterian minister from Vermont. Suspicious of educational innovations, Church valued discipline, tradition, and conformity more than originality and freedom of thought. Joseph LeConte, one of Cobb's classmates and later a teacher at Franklin College, remembered the president as a "bigoted, dogmatic, and imperious old man."[21] Despite acrimonious relations with members of the faculty, prompting some of the best professors to resign and despite a certain narrowness of outlook, Dr. Church administered Franklin College to the satisfaction of a majority of the trustees and offered the students a diversified curriculum.[22] Cobb mastered the course of study with exceptional facility, receiving a solid grounding in Latin and French and a knowledge of the classics which proved invaluable to him in his subsequent research on the history and law of Negro slavery. His fine academic record and exemplary personal conduct were complemented by his enthusiastic role as a member of the Phi Kappa Society, one of two debating fraternities on the campus. Every Saturday morning the brothers met to argue sundry questions, ranging in content from the merits of monasticism to whether a man should be "compelled by law to marry the victim of his seduction."[23] The debates

---

[20]"Minutes of the Faculty of Franklin College," 29 July 1837, University of Georgia Libraries.

[21]Joseph L. LeConte, *The Autobiography of Joseph LeConte*, ed. William D. Armes (New York: D. Appleton and Company, 1903), pp. 155-56.

[22]E. Merton Coulter, "Why John and Joseph LeConte Left the University of Georgia, 1855-1856," *The Georgia Historical Quarterly* 53 (March 1969): 18-40.

[23]The Demosthenian Society was the rival organization. For some unknown reason

might be perfunctory or uproarious depending upon the topic and mood of the members. This facet of Cobb's education had a certain practicality. In connection with courses in forensic disputation, rhetoric, and logic, it developed skills that were later useful to him as a courtroom attorney.

The privilege of nominating a commencement speaker alternated annually between the Phi Kappa and Demosthenian societies. In 1841 the choice fell to the former, and Cobb, who had been elected president of the society, appears to have assumed chief responsibility for making the necessary arrangements near the close of his senior year. Between March and the last of May he called five special meetings each time to inform the members that a chosen dignitary had rejected an invitation to speak. The Society finally secured the services of Francis Bartow, a young Whig lawyer from Savannah, Georgia, whose lifelong esteem for Cobb was already evident. "He is my beau ideal of a *young* man," Bartow declared shortly after the graduation ceremonies. "I trust and hope he will be a model of a man."[24]

Cobb finished first in his class and, on 5 August delivered the valedictory address to a commencement audience which Albon Chase, editor of the Athens *Southern Banner,* seemed to think was larger and "more attentive . . . than usual."[25]

After graduation Cobb read law for approximately five months under the tutelage of William L. Mitchell, an Athens attorney, staunch Presbyterian, and partisan Democrat. Completing his studies prior to January 1842, Cobb was admitted to the practice of law in the Western Circuit of Georgia on 22 February at the age of eighteen.[26]

His admission to the bar coincided with a severe economic depression, the worst effects of which were felt in Georgia during the period 1839-1843. It was an inopportune time to begin in the legal profession,

---

Cobb had been inducted into the Phi Kappa Society on 1 August 1836, a full year before his admission to Franklin College. See "Minutes of the Phi Kappa Society," 1 August 1836, 8 September 1838, University of Georgia Libraries.

[24]Francis Bartow to Howell Cobb, 20 September 1841, Howell Cobb Collection.

[25]"Minutes of the Faculty," 28 June 1841; *Southern Banner*, 6 August 1841.

[26]"Application for admission to the bar," Thomas R. R. Cobb folder, Original Manuscripts File no.2, Georgia Department of Archives and History. Because of his youth, a special legislative act was required to admit him to the bar. *Acts of the General Assembly of the State of Georgia,* 1841 (Milledgeville, 1842), pp. 19-20; hereinafter cited as *Acts of the General Assembly.*

but Cobb had a wide circle of friends and relatives whose advice and assistance were of material benefit in the early years of his career.

In May 1842, he was employed by Albon Chase who notified patrons of the *Southern Banner* that Cobb would "attend the Superior courts of the Western Circuit, during the present riding, and will act as our agent in procu[ring] subscriptions, advertising patronage, and in the settlement of debts due the Banner Office."[27]

Even before Cobb's admission to the bar, his brother Howell had been looking out for Tom's interests. Writing to Francis Bartow, Howell had inquired about legal prospects in Savannah and the possibility of a partnership for his younger brother. Bartow promptly replied:

> My views are in all respects enlarged upon the subject of Tom's professional course. You know my affection for him. It would delight me to serve him and to aid in his advancement for I am confident he will shoot far ahead of my mark. As a friend his society would be most valuable. I have no doubt of his professional abilities and I think this a good field for their exercise.[28]

For obscure reasons, an alliance with Bartow was never realized; in fact, Cobb rejected all offers of partnership until 1849, when he formed an association with his brother-in-law, Joseph Troup Lumpkin.[29]

From one source—namely his father—Cobb could expect no help of any kind. In the 1830s Colonel Cobb had speculated in North Georgia gold lands and had invested heavily in the stock of various banking, railroad, and insurance companies. These were costly ventures involving an enormous personal indebtedness. When the depression came the colonel's creditors pressed for immediate payment. In a vain effort to extricate himself, Cobb offered Cherry Hill for sale in September 1840. To refute a rumor that the plantation would not be sold as indicated, he again advertised that *"the sale will positively take place,"* and added, "I . . . invite all my creditors to be present . . . as I am determined to dispose of all the property I possess, with a view to get out of debt, if it should take it all."[30] In December, his sons, Howell and Thomas, went to Jefferson

---

[27]*Southern Banner*, 13 May 1842.

[28]Francis Bartow to Howell Cobb, 18 December 1841, Howell Cobb Collection.

[29]*Southern Recorder* (Milledgevelle GA), 1 May 1849.

[30]*Southern Banner*, 4 September, 6 November 1840; S. A. Lamar to John B. Lamar, 30 December 1840, Howell Cobb Collection.

County to witness the sale, but managed, at the last minute, to save the plantation. All other property and investments belonging to their father were lost, however.

Faced with total financial disaster, Colonel Cobb's morale sagged. In a matter of months he was incapable of conducting his own affairs, developed physical ailments, and suffered a mental collapse. Once an active civic leader, business promoter, and wealthy property owner, he was now a broken man, completely dependent on his eldest son for support.[31]

To maintain his destitute parents, Howell Cobb bought a farm in the Cowpens District of Walton County, between Athens and Monroe, and persuaded his brother-in-law, Williams Rutherford, Jr., to pay a portion of the purchase price in exchange for part ownership and full management of the place. The arrangement was never very satisfactory, but it lasted until Rutherford traded the farm to Judge Junius Hillyer in 1847 and moved to Athens, bringing Cobb's parents with him.

Howell Cobb also had been hurt badly by the depression. Liable for many of his father's debts, he was forced to sell his house and furniture in 1843 to meet some of his obligations, and, for nearly a decade, he allocated a portion of his income to meet the demands of creditors. In addition he paid the last two years of his brother's college tuition and provided room and board until the latter's legal practice was large enough to sustain him.[32]

Thomas Cobb was forever grateful for these benefits and did what he

---

[31]Mary Ann Cobb to Howell Cobb, 18 April 1840, John B. Lamar to Howell Cobb, 5 May 1840, R. D. Moore to Howell Cobb, 14 December 1840, Howell Cobb Collection; Joseph W. Jackson to Martha Jackson, 22 September 1840, Sarah Cobb to Martha Jackson, 3 February 1842, Jackson-Prince Papers. In the context of the Cobb family Eugene Genovese's contention that planters were precapitalist, distrustful of urban life, and devoid of habits of thrift and hard work would seem to be inaccurate. Genovese, *The Political Economy of Slavery: Studies in the Economy and Society of the Slave South* (New York: Random House, 1965; Vintage ed., 1967), pp. 19-28. For a contrary interpretation viewing southerners as part of the national mainstream but with some distinctiveness see Carl N. Degler, *Place Over Time. The Continuity of Southern Distinctiveness* (Baton Rouge: Louisiana State University Press, 1977); Edward Pessen, "How Different from Each Other Were the Antebellum North and South?" *The American Historical Review* 85 (February 1980): 1145-49.

[32]C. F. McCay to Howell Cobb, 3 October 1840, John B. Lamar to Howell Cobb, 14 February 1841, Mary Ann Cobb to John B. Lamar, 21 September 1843, Howell Cobb to [?] Thomas, 26 October 1846, Thomas R. R. Cobb Collection, University of Georgia Libraries; *Southern Banner*, 7 September 1843.

could to share some of the burdens. Playing the role of father figure while his brother was away, he outlined a course of study for his younger sister and lectured her on the subject of filial duty.

> You do not know [how] pleased I was to hear that you were doing all [in] [y]our power to make your father and mother happy [&] [com]fortable. Keep on . . . [&] every body [will] love so affectionate a daughter and God will [reward] you ten-fold in the end. We should be [than]kful too, my dear Sister that Heaven has [give]n us such parents . . . and [thou]gh we never can repay them for the care and love [they] have expended upon us, yet every act of . . . kindness, every word of affection, and every [smi]le of gratitude is a balm to their wounded [brea]sts much greater than we can realize.

In concluding, he instructed her to "Tell Ma [tha]t I have plenty always to get any thing [she] may want, and that she must never hesitate [to] write me. Am I not her child?"[33]

If Cobb was generous toward his parents and later toward poorer relations, he was not personally extravagant. Very early he vowed to avoid the financial mistakes which had ruined his father and grandfather and seriously compromised his brother. In the first lean years of law practice he was especially frugal, refusing even to buy cloth for a shirt on credit. "I [can]not bear the idea of going in debt," he told his sister. Later, in 1846, when the nation was on the verge of hostilities with Mexico, he warned: "Should there be war, there will be a terrible revulsion in money matters, and wo[e] to the man who [is] then found in debt." And, in 1861, with the Civil War breaking out, he refused to lend money to a close friend because of the uncertainty of the times. "I wish I could aid him," he apologized, "but I am sure I did right."[34]

Many traits of character—of which solicitude for his parents and financial prudence were but two—Cobb shared with his mother. In fact, he resembled her in looks, piety, and temperament. Short of stature, as she was, his weight tended to fluctuate between 155 and 196 pounds depending on the amount of nervous energy he happened to expend during any given period. When overworked, which was often, he looked lean and haggard, but he filled out fast and was normally solid without

---

[33]Thomas Cobb to Mary Willis Cobb, 26 October 1842, Jackson Scrapbook.

[34]Ibid.; Thomas Cobb to Howell Cobb, 25 April 1846, Howell Cobb Collection; Thomas Cobb to Marion Cobb, 11 May 1861, Thomas R. R. Cobb Collection.

appearing fat. His most prominent feature apparently was the nose, which one man described as "large." "He is a handsome man," wrote an admiring lady, "with a pale intellectual cast of feature [and] with a particularly sharp nose which I am disposed to admire."[35] Overall there was a boyish quality to his appearance, a quality accentuated by his clean shaven face and long hair. So young did he still look in 1853, after nine years of married life and three children, that a stranger mistook him for a "mere lad just married with his first child."[36]

His youthful looks carried over to his personality. He was impulsive, volatile, and exceedingly active. Alexander H. Stephens seemed to think that, "notwithstanding . . . his strong and manly traits," Cobb "would always be a boy," lacking judgment and guided by the whims of the instant.[37] All agreed that he was preeminently a man of action, an enthusiast for every cause he espoused, and an indefatigable worker capable of the most prodigious labor. The Reverend W. R. Bell, who later served with him in the Georgia secession convention, averred that Cobb could "dispatch more business in a given time than any man he ever met."[38] His boundless energy and keen mind encouraged those who knew him well to predict his future success. He "is very industrious and studious," remarked a family friend, "and has a plain, open path before him to distinction and wealth."[39]

For a number of years, however, fame and fortune eluded him altogether. Young and inexperienced, his cases were still too insignificant to boost his reputation, and, although he budgeted expenses carefully and worked hard to build his practice, fees were barely sufficient to meet his

---

[35]"Journal of Ella Gertrude (Clanton) Thomas," p. 19, Perkins Library, Duke University. See also William J. Rheney to Father, 29 August 1861, William J. Rheney Letters, Georgia Department of Archives and History; J. J. Flournoy to Howell Cobb, 27 December 1857, Howell Cobb Collection; Thomas R. R. Cobb to Marion Cobb, 19 June 1862, Thomas R. R. Cobb Collection; *Montgomery Weekly Post* (Montgomery AL), 27 February 1861.

[36]Sarah Cobb to Mary Ann Cobb, 20 January 1853, Howell Cobb Collection.

[37]Alexander H. Stephens to Linton Stephens, 16 January 1863, Alexander H. Stephens Correspondence, microfilm copy, Southern Historical Collection, University of North Carolina Library.

[38]*Southern Banner*, 30 January 1861. See also *Southern Watchman* (Athens GA), 17 December 1862.

[39]H. Hull to Howell Cobb, [1844], Howell Cobb Collection. For a similar prediction see John B. Lamar to Howell Cobb, 14 February 1841, ibid.

needs. Hoping to enlarge his income, Cobb turned to politics, a field in which the influence of kinsmen and acquaintances again proved extremely valuable. His first experience in political life began in the fall of 1842, when his cousin, James Jackson, became a Democratic candidate for the post of secretary of the Georgia senate. Jackson promised that, if elected, he would appoint Cobb to a clerkship.

On 8 November the legislature convened in Milledgeville, the state capital, and, on the same day, Jackson was voted into office by the senate. Jubilantly, Cobb spread the news to his sister-in-law. "Cousin James is elected," he reported. "I am his head clerk by which operation we will both make a pretty sum of money and Cousin James reap considerable honor. All are well and in fine spirits."[40]

For about a month Cobb performed the routine duties assigned him, during which time his good health and "fine spirits" gradually vanished. Ill with a cold, discontented with living accommodations in Milledgeville, and depressed by the receipt of only one letter from his fiancée, Marion McHenry Lumpkin, he gladly left the capital in December to spend the Christmas recess at her home in Lexington, Georgia.

Cobb had been engaged to Marion Lumpkin for nearly a year.[41] She was fourteen months his senior, blue-eyed, small of stature, and sweet tempered. Her father, Judge Joseph Henry Lumpkin, was a very wealthy Whig attorney and Old School Presbyterian who abhorred debt and "made it the rule of . . . life to owe no man anything but love," or so he declared in his will. A much respected orator and jurist, he was well known for his advocacy of educational and temperance reforms and served with distinction on the Georgia Supreme Court.[42] From the outset of his courtship of Marion Lumpkin, Cobb felt a deep admiration for her father and was treated like a son in return. His ultimate acceptance of the Presbyterian faith, his beginning interest in temperance reform, his continuing determination to stay clear of debt, and his early ambivalence

---

[40]Thomas Cobb to Mary Ann Cobb, 8 November 1842, Cobb-Erwin-Lamar Collection; *Southern Banner*, 11 November 1842.

[41]Thomas Cobb to Joseph H. Lumpkin, 5 January 1842, private possession of Miss Callie Hull, Washington DC.

[42]Clarke County, GA, "Court of Ordinary, Wills," vol. D. p. 213. For brief sketches of Lumpkin see Warren Grice, *The Georgia Bench and Bar. The Development of Georgia's Judicial System* (Macon GA: The J. W. Burke Co., 1931), pp. 127-28; William F. Northern,

about party politics were all attributable, in some measure, to the influence of Judge Lumpkin.

Christmas at the Lumpkins was always a festive occasion. The house was usually filled with guests and stockings were filled for all the children, slave and white alike. The December 1842 season was not an exception to the general trend. "I have heard many complain of having spent a very 'dull Christmas,' " wrote Marion Lumpkin, "but could they have . . . caught a glimpse of our 'little world' I think that 'dull care' would have been driven completely away." Naturally, the presence in Lexington of Tom Cobb, who exuded such love for his bride-to-be that his mother jokingly remarked that "Tom will lose what little sense he ever had, if they are not married soon," was sufficient guarantee that the holiday would be anything but dull for Marion.[43]

After Christmas Cobb returned to Milledgeville for the final days of the legislative session and upon adjournment in January 1843 hastened to Athens to prepare his cases for the winter term of court. In February and March he traveled to every county seat in the Western Circuit, defending clients and collecting fees, and repeated the cycle in the spring and again in the fall. By November, with his marriage to Marion Lumpkin only two months away, he was more than ever conscious of the need to augment his income. Since his practice was still not large enough to sustain a high standard of living, he again resorted to politics as the most immediate means of improving his financial condition.

The fall elections had given the Whigs a majority in the General Assembly. Democrats seeking legislative patronage fared badly as a consequence. For instance, James Jackson, in a bid to succeed himself as secretary, was defeated by Whig Benjamin F. Hardeman, a friend and neighbor of Judge Lumpkin. In fact, the only Democrat to escape defeat was Thomas Cobb. His election to the office of assistant secretary of the Georgia senate was due mainly to his connection with such Whigs as Bartow, Lumpkin, and Hardeman, plus, of course, the votes marshalled

---

ed., *Men of Mark in Georgia*, 6 vols. (Atlanta, A. B. Caldwell, 1911), 2:302-303; *Southern Watchman*, 17 May 1860, which reprints a piece from the *Temperance Crusader* written by Thomas R. R. Cobb.

[43]Marion Lumpkin to Mary Ann Cobb, 2 January 1843, Sarah Cobb to Mary Ann Cobb, 25 January 1843, Howell Cobb Collection.

on the Democratic side by his brother, Howell, who arrived in Milledgeville to direct party strategy.[44]

While his Democratic relatives were aggrieved by the overwhelming success of the Whigs, Cobb was not. "I have never used *one* bitter expression against them," he asserted, and he seemed rather proud that his victory had been bipartisan.[45]

Cobb was a very popular young assistant secretary. Numerous senators flattered him, Whigs rather more so than Democrats; and one legislator with Whig leanings offered him two valuable lots if he would move to Cass County. "I have thus made many acquaintances," he bragged, "(and excuse my vanity—favorable acquaintances) in all parts of Georgia and these will be an assistance to me in my profession[.]"[46]

Cobb was more susceptible to Whig than Democratic blandishments, in part, because of his intimacy with several prominent Whigs whose interest in him had no obvious political overtones and, more importantly, because he suspected a few unnamed Democrats of scheming to ensnare him in politics against his will for the sole purpose of aggrandizing themselves. In retrospect, his suspicions appear somewhat absurd. Certainly no one had coerced him to run for office either in 1842 or 1843; and only once, in December of the latter year, while serving as assistant secretary, had he been called upon to act in a party capacity. On that occasion a group of Clarke County Democrats elected him in absentia to a general convention in Milledgeville. Attending the meeting on 11 December, Cobb delivered one of the few purely political speeches of his career, a speech of no great import, but one that won the praise of a politician whom he described as being "rather a Whig."[47]

After a heated debate on whether to endorse Martin Van Buren or

---

[44]*Southern Banner*, 16 November 1843; *Journal of the Senate of the State of Georgia*, 1843, p. 414. Hereinafter cited as *Georgia Senate Journal.*

[45]Thomas Cobb to Marion Lumpkin, 14 December [1843], Jackson Scrapbook.

[46]Ibid. A year earlier several Whig politicians had urged him to move to Augusta and run for solicitor general. He resisted the temptation. Sarah Cobb to Martha J. Jackson, 10 November 1842, Jackson-Prince Papers; Northen, ed., *Men of Mark*, 3:156.

[47]Thomas Cobb to Marion Lumpkin, 14 December [1843], Jackson Scrapbook; John B. Cobb to Howell Cobb, 15 December 1843, Howell Cobb Collection; *Southern Banner*, 7 December 1843. Cobb made another speech, probably in support of his brother's candidacy for the Congress, in Athens on 1 October 1842. Sarah R. Cobb to Mary Ann Cobb, 1 October 1842, Howell Cobb Collection.

John C. Calhoun for the presidential nomination in 1844, the convention agreed to send uninstructed delegates to the national Democratic conclave in Baltimore and to campaign loyally for the party nominees. Though committed to Van Buren in the early stages of the Milledgeville meeting, Cobb and the rest of the Clarke County contingent supported the compromise. According to Albon Chase, the action of the convention had the effect of quashing Calhoun's hopes while affirming the nomination of Van Buren.[48] The point was academic, for Calhoun withdrew from the contest on 21 December 1843, and a few months later Van Buren wrecked his chance for the Democratic nomination by publicly proclaiming his opposition to the annexation of Texas. Commenting on Van Buren's blunder, Cobb correctly surmised that "His letter has killed him here, almost entirely. A terribly bad step, and I don't see how it can be retraced."[49]

Actually, by this time Cobb not only had lost interest in the national campaign of 1844 but had become thoroughly disillusioned with the whole political process. "I am done with politics," he declared emphatically. "I see the cup is sparkling, but the dregs I must drink with it . . . are misery[,] disappointment[,] and hate. . . ."[50] His affiliation with the Lumpkins, a family as solidly Whig as the Cobbs were Democratic, was a key factor in his decision to abandon politics. With his brother complaining in November 1843 that the "Whigs have no regard for us or our concerns," and Judge Lumpkin asserting in December that "Democrat and Demagogue are now synonymous," his reluctance to take a strong party stand was understandable.[51]

But there was another element in Cobb's political ambivalence—antipartyism. According to Ronald Formisano, two types of antipartyism prevailed in the antebellum period: "evangelical, with its roots in Puritanism; and a general antiparty prejudice common to a wide variety of men," a prejudice inspired, no doubt, by a feeling that partisanship was somehow unsavory. The former "drew sustenance from the evangelical, moral

---

[48]*Southern Banner*, 21 December 1843.

[49]Thomas Cobb to Howell Cobb, 11 May [1844], Howell Cobb Collection.

[50]Thomas Cobb to Marion Lumpkin, 14 December [1843], Jackson Scrapbook.

[51]Howell Cobb to Mary Ann Cobb, 11 November 1843, Joseph H. Lumpkin to Howell Cobb, 19 December 1843, Howell Cobb Collection.

reform, benevolent and Christianizing strains lacing Whiggery in many social and geographic sectors. Men who had a strong tendency toward devotionalism" lacked "organizational malleability" and "the knack for compromise."[52] Cobb exhibited both types of antiparty behavior. By 1843 his religious temperament coupled with a penchant for moral reform had become very pronounced and fed his evident distaste for party politics. Yet, whenever his evangelical bent—reenforced by the Whiggery and Presbyterian piety of the Lumpkins—pointed down the road to antipartyism, personal needs and ambitions together with his brother's commitment to the Democratic party forced him in the opposite direction. For a number of years he tried to ease this internal tension by paying lip service to an unworkable nonpartisan approach designed to enable him to seek office and support Howell without blatant identification with either party. Failing in this, he openly admitted in 1847 to being a Democrat, but then recoiled almost immediately from so extreme a stance. The real turning point in determining his future political posture came in 1848, the year in which he experienced a profound spiritual awakening, and from that date forward he refused to take part in any form of political activity save to vote and to help his brother.

In mid-December 1843, as the legislative session drew to a close, Cobb's thoughts turned from political matters to his forthcoming marriage. "I am so happy I can talk about nothing else," he related to his fiancée.

> Tomorrow for the news. Today to that all engrossing theme—*ourselves*. Is there not more *unity* more *identity* in that word now than formerly? Sincerely I do feel that you are *mine* now—mine beyond any casualty save a providential interference[.] *If I did not* always love you with my whole heart, that love would be increased. As it is, it is confirmed.[53]

This romantic outburst was inspired by a letter from Marion, in

---

[52]Ronald Formisano, "Political Character, Antipartyism and the Second Party System," *American Quarterly* 21 (Winter, 1969): 685-86. The concept of antipartyism as applied to southern politics has yet to be analyzed fully; consequently, it is impossible to do more than suggest that Cobb may have reflected the existence of such an attitude in Georgia. For antipartyism in Michigan see Formisano, *The Birth of Mass Political Parties Michigan, 1827-1861* (Princeton, NJ: Princeton University Press, 1971).

[53]Thomas Cobb to Marion Lumpkin, 14 December [1843], Jackson Scrapbook.

which she discussed the details of their approaching wedding and proposed 5 January 1844, as a suitable time for the ceremony. Cobb impetuously endorsed the date; then, recalling that the fifth fell on a Friday, he changed his mind. "You know I am not superstitious nor believe in signs," he hedged, but "I confess I do not like the day. Any other will meet my most hearty approbation."[54] In spite of his disclaimer, Cobb was superstitious. He never questioned the reality of supernatural occurrences, never dismissed premonitions lightly, and was impressed by signs and portents much more than he was ever willing to admit. Since there was something about Friday that disturbed him, the wedding was finally scheduled for Tuesday, 9 January.

Completing his secretarial duties on 23 December 1843, Cobb departed Milledgeville in a mood of eager anticipation. Arriving in Athens he found wedding preparations in full swing. Every seamstress in town was engaged in sewing dresses, and post-nuptial receptions were being arranged by a number of prominent families. In Lexington, where the ceremony was to be held, plans were also in progress. Here both the Lumpkins and the family of former Governor George Gilmer were busily getting ready to entertain. From Athens Cobb went to the Cowpens for a day and two nights to be with his parents and to pick up the wedding attire which his mother had made for him. Despite the presence there of a large number of relatives, he discovered that all seemed disinclined to attend his wedding. Their excuses ranged from lack of acceptable apparel to poor health. So pained did he look upon hearing the reasons that the family conscience was pricked, and, at last, his mother and several others agreed to go. Sarah dreaded the trip to Lexington. It had been so long since she had mingled in the "gay world" that only to gratify her son would she venture out. "God grant this union may be for the happiness of my beloved," she wrote to Howell in Washington, D. C. "it [sic] is a solemn thing, and I cannot help feeling downcast as the time approaches. . . . I know how much real pleasure it would give Tom to have you with him, never did a brother love another . . . [as] he does you. . . ."[55]

---

[54]Ibid.

[55]Sarah R. Cobb to Howell Cobb, 3 January 1844, Howell Cobb Collection. Besides his mother, those who finally attended were: two sisters, Mary Willis and Laura, two brothers-in-law, Williams Rutherford, Jr. and Luther Judson Glenn, and a cousin, James Jackson, who was to serve as an attendant. Cobb's father was eager to go to the wedding but was prevented from doing so by his health.

Returning to Athens in early January 1844, Cobb transferred a wagon load of new furniture from the railroad depot to a large two-story house located in Cobbham. The house, which became Cobb's permanent residence, was a gift from Judge Lumpkin, whose generosity prompted Junius Hillyer to inquire, in mock astonishment, "when this new order of things had been instituted, that a man that was to be married to another man's daughter should have a right to pick and choose from his property such as he liked best and walk into possession of it without further ceremony."[56]

Lumpkin's generosity also extended to the furniture, purchased in Augusta, Georgia, with Cobb's approval. "As to the furnishing of the house," Cobb had written, "assure your Father he shall have full scope to gratify his own taste, for I will leave it entirely to him."[57] In all things his faith in Lumpkin's judgment was unbounded.

On 9 January 1844, Thomas Cobb and Marion Lumpkin were married in Lexington by the Reverend Nathan Hoyt, minister of the Athens Presbyterian Church. For the next six days the newlyweds visited relatives and attended a round of parties given in their honor. Marion was an instant hit with the Cobbs, young and old. Speaking for the entire clan, Sarah Cobb exclaimed: "we are all delighted with Marion, she is a sweet little creature, and a warm and affectionate one. she [sic] seemed . . . anxious to be one of the family. . . . Tom is as much in love as ever."[58]

The post-wedding festivities ended on 15 January. Settling into their new home, the young couple tried to establish some sort of normal routine. Relatives observed their efforts to adjust to married life with affectionate amusement and family friends called frequently to pay their respects. "Tom is perfectly happy," reported a sister-in-law, "and talks about arrangements for housekeeping as if he had been married 7 years."[59]

Long before the honeymoon was over Cobb had to begin preparations for court. In addition to his own practice, he was required to act as counsel for his brother's clients during the congressman's absence in Washington. This proved to be a vexatious trust. "In preparing for

---

[56]Mary Ann Cobb to Howell Cobb, 31 December 1843, ibid.

[57]Thomas Cobb to Marion Lumpkin, 14 December [1843], Jackson Scrapbook.

[58]Sarah R. Cobb to Mary Ann Cobb, 25 February 1844, Howell Cobb Collection.

[59]Mary Ann Cobb to Howell Cobb, 14 January 1844, ibid.

Court," he noted, "my greatest botheration has been finding on docket several cases of which I know not the least item[!] This is the case in several Counties. I suppose these are of no great importance, and I shall presume enough to make up for my ignorance."[60]

Despite such handicaps, Cobb conducted his brother's business with efficiency and some degree of success. As he pointed out, "considering my perfect ignorance even of the faces of most of your clients, I have much cause to congratulate myself on the result of my efforts."[61]

Aside from the law, politics was the primary topic of conversation at every term of court. Although still determined to remain aloof from party affairs, Cobb never intended to be non-committal in political situations involving the future of his brother, who was up for re-election in 1844. "Need I tell you my Dear Brother of my devotion to your interest[s]," he declared,

> and that I will watch over them with vigilance. Thus far and no farther do I intend to mingle in political warfare[.] [Any]thing honest and honorable promotive of your interests you may demand of me[.] General partisanship for the present I must eschew.[62]

During the course of the congressional campaign, Cobb consulted regularly with local politicians throughout the Western Circuit, assisted in the organization of political rallies, answered urgent correspondence directed to his brother in Athens, served as the secretary at a Democratic meeting in Watkinsville, which went on record as favoring Howell Cobb for a second term, and periodically reported on Whig campaign tactics.

His efforts in this race, restricted though they were to the Sixth Congressional District, typed him as a full-fledged Democrat in the eyes of the Clarke County Whigs. This faction of the Whig Party, led by William W. Clayton and Charles Dougherty, had always been extremely hostile to the aspirations of the Cobb family and demonstrated its antagonism on every possible occasion. Thomas Cobb was not to be spared political rancor merely because he happened to be the son-in-law of Judge

---

[60]Thomas Cobb to Howell Cobb, 1 February 1844, ibid.

[61]Thomas Cobb to Howell Cobb, 1 March [1844], ibid.

[62]Ibid. At the end of the month he reiterated his commitment to his brother's cause as well as his determination to stay out of politics. See Thomas Cobb to Howell Cobb, 31 March [1844], Thomas R. R. Cobb Collection.

Lumpkin, or because he refused to campaign for the general run of Democratic candidates.

At court, in February, he was singled out and constantly harassed by Charles Dougherty, a former nullifier who had opposed Cobb's father for the state senate in the 1830s and who was currently an opponent of his brother. "Dougherty has made it a rule . . . ," Cobb complained, "to run over me everywhere. He missed his game, for I have, without forgetting his age, given his own fire in return and generally have kept the sympathy [of the bar] with me."[63]

More serious was the confrontation with John W. H. Underwood, solicitor general of the Western Circuit. At Jackson County superior court late that same month, Cobb was defending a man named Ogle who had been charged with stealing a cow. During the interrogation of a witness, Cobb interjected an aside which infuriated Underwood. Instantly, Cobb sat down, but it took a second reprimand from Judge Hillyer to halt the solicitor's tirade. When all the testimony had been recorded, Cobb moved for a dismissal on the ground that the allegation against his client had not been proved. Hillyer granted his motion despite immoderate objections from Underwood, who afterwards left the courthouse in a huff.

In describing the episode to his brother, Cobb aired his opinion of the solicitor: "John Underwood, *your* friend, thank Heaven I never called him *mine*[,] has missed no opportunity in public or *private* to . . . abuse me. . . . He got [into] [a] wrath with Hillyer for sustaining me and . . . made a fool of himself. . . . He is a scoundrel and to convince you of it is doing all he can to have you beaten."[64]

Embittered by what he deemed judicial favoritism arising from Hillyer's social and political affinity with the Cobbs, Underwood consented to run against Howell Cobb for the Sixth District Congressional seat. On election day the voting returns followed a traditional pattern. Cobb lost Clarke County, which, except for the town of Athens, had been a Whig stronghold for years, but carried enough precincts elsewhere in the district to win by a comfortable margin.[65]

Now that his brother had been safely re-elected, Thomas Cobb was theoretically devoid of an excuse for continuing in politics. Yet, new

---

[63]Thomas Cobb to Howell Cobb, 1 March [1844], Howell Cobb Collection.

[64]Ibid. See also Junius Hillyer to Howell Cobb, 6 March 1844, ibid.

[65]*Southern Banner*, 11 July, 9, 17 October 1844.

reasons for political activity were easy to find, and old vows to give it up were quickly forgotten. Revealing the emptiness of his earlier pledge to quit politics, Cobb took sides in a local patronage controversy which began in December 1844. The predominant motive for his actions was monetary gain. Court was adjourned from November to February, and during this slack season Cobb was invariably short of funds. Moreover, the birth of his first child, Lucy, on 7 October, had greatly intensified the feeling of financial insecurity which usually came upon him in the late fall and early winter months. Thus, alarmed by his monetary deficiencies, Cobb seized at the first remedy that presented itself.

Sometime prior to December, the Athens postmaster, a Whig, had been removed from office, and eight Democrats had begun to vie for the vacancy. Cobb vigorously backed his old mentor William L. Mitchell for the position in the expectation of receiving the deputy postmastership.[66] The customary method of applying for the postal appointment was to circulate a petition and forward it to a congressman for endorsement. As a personal friend of Congressman Howell Cobb, Mitchell had a distinct advantage over his seven opponents, an advantage made greater by Thomas Cobb's energetic support.

Aware of their dilemma, Mitchell's rivals formed a coalition under the leadership of Hopkins Hosley—an ambitious former congressman from Harris County who had recently moved to Athens—and demanded that a party caucus be held in lieu of the usual petition-recommendation procedure. Their aim was to dominate the meeting, cancel the influence of Howell Cobb, and manipulate Mitchell's defeat.

Agreeing reluctantly to the caucus, Mitchell sent Thomas Cobb and others to canvass Clarke and Jackson counties to ensure a full and sympathetic representation. On 14 December, approximately one hundred Democrats answered the call to meet at the Athens town hall. Realizing that a large majority favored Mitchell, Holsey tried to disrupt the proceedings in an effort to forestall official action. Some of Mitchell's supporters walked out in disgust, but enough remained to thwart the attempt. At last, a motion to adjourn and let each aspirant seek office in the traditional manner was introduced. Holsey objected. The Democratic Party, he alleged, was about to surrender control of the patronage to one

[66]Thomas Cobb to Howell Cobb, 2 December [1844], Howell Cobb Collection.

man, Howell Cobb, a potential "monarch, and he did not like monarchs."[67]

Ignoring Holsey's objections, the caucus approved the motion by a vote of sixty to thirty, and by nightfall Mitchell had seventy signatures on a petition. On the morning of 18 December, Thomas Cobb mailed the petition to his brother with an explanation of what had transpired. Holsey, he wrote, "made a tremendous flourish . . . hitting at you and endeavoring to raise a prejudice against you all the time." Mitchell's opponents, he added, "are grumbling, but I do not think any of their friends *even* go with them."[68]

Ensconced in the Athens post office on 1 January 1845, Cobb and Mitchell jointly discharged their not too onerous duties for five months. In June, for no apparent reason, Mitchell suddenly decided to resign and offered the post to his young assistant. Cobb was tempted to accept, especially since the compensation of deputy postmasters had recently been reduced. Before committing himself, however, he solicited his brother's advice.[69]

The response was evidently negative. Wary of his brother's part in the post office dispute from the start, Howell Cobb could not have been reassured by the criticism of his brother-in-law, Andrew Lamar, who had branded Mitchell's appointment a "poor stroke of policy," productive of bitterness and calculated to diminish the congressman's popularity in the vicinity of Athens. Although informed by others that animosity was subsiding, he undoubtedly foresaw the possibility of renewed enmity if Thomas Cobb was now elevated to the postmastership. To preclude further friction, not to mention charges of nepotism, John Crawford was chosen to succeed Mitchell, a choice, commented the *Southern Banner,* "which we doubt not will please all parties."[70]

Thomas Cobb's quest for political preferment did not end in disappointment. Denied the postmastership, he became a candidate for the

---

[67]William L. Mitchell and Thomas R. R. Cobb to Howell Cobb, 14 December 1844, ibid.

[68]Thomas Cobb to Howell Cobb, 18 December 1844, ibid.

[69]Thomas Cobb to Howell Cobb, 5 June [1845], ibid.

[70]Andrew Lamar to Howell Cobb, 11 Janaury 1845, ibid; *Southern Banner*, 10 July 1845.

office of secretary of the Georgia senate in October 1845. As in the past, his only interest in the position was the salary.

Cobb did not have the field entirely to himself. His competitor was Milton H. Gathright, a Democratic stalwart from Dahlonega, Georgia. Gathright was influential in the northern part of the state where much of Howell Cobb's political strength was centered, and his record of party loyalty was far superior to that of his young adversary, whose repudiation of partisan activity in the campaign of 1844 hardly entitled him to Democratic favors. Based on any objective criterion, Gathright was the more deserving of the two candidates. The Dahlonega politician obviously thought so. Upon learning that Thomas Cobb planned to oppose him, he lodged a protest. "Howell!" he exclaimed, "you must tell Tom that he is too much my junior to interfear [sic] in this matter[.] He is young yet . . . [while] I am an old vetran [sic] in the wars of politics and have never . . . received the first crown."[71] Yet, it was the "old veteran" who was obliged to withdraw from the race, leaving the "crown" to Cobb who was easily elected secretary of the Georgia senate on 3 November 1845.[72]

The prestige of Howell Cobb was largely responsible for this victory. Had he not been present in Milledgeville to mollify Gathright, the result might have been different; as it was, two of Cobb's brothers-in-law failed of election.[73] It was also fortunate that Gathright was such a firm ally. Otherwise, the congressman's political solidarity in North Georgia might have been impaired. This possibility had caused his wife some anxious moments. "We were much gratified to hear . . . that Tom had succeeded in getting the office he desired," she wrote to her husband,

> and I was glad to learn that Mr[.] Gathright did not oppose him, as I was fearful that such an occurrence would interrupt the good feeling existing between him [Gathright] and yourself, and thereby check your increasing popularity in the Up Country. You know I am ever willing for you to aid in all matters of politics[.] Still I wish you to bear in mind that . . . it is necessary to keep *one eye at least* upon *your own interest* and not sacrifice it wholly to that of others.[74]

---

[71]Milton Gathright to Howell Cobb, 26 October 1845, Howell Cobb Collection.

[72]*Georgia Senate Journal*, 1845, p. 5; *Southern Banner*, 11 November 1845.

[73]Luther Judson Glenn and Williams Rutherford, Jr. both sought political positions, but, despite the efforts of Howell Cobb, they were defeated. Howell Cobb to Mary Ann Cobb, 4 November 1845, Howell Cobb Collection.

[74]Mary Ann Cobb to Howell Cobb, 6 November 1845, ibid.

Thomas Cobb would never have willfully jeopardized his brother's popularity simply to advance himself financially. On the contrary, he had done his best to further the congressman's political career. Nonetheless, in the span of a year, he had twice contributed to situations which were politically embarrassing to his brother and had done so, rather ironically, at a time when he professed to be a nonpartisan, at least in the general sense.

In December 1845, during Cobb's tenure as secretary, the Georgia legislature passed a long delayed and much needed law creating a State Supreme Court composed of three judges. Joseph H. Lumpkin, Hiram Warner, and Eugenius A. Nisbet were elected to serve on the bench for terms of six, four, and two years respectively.[75] Lumpkin's election had an important bearing on Cobb's future. First, it was a decisive factor in his appointment as assistant reporter of the Georgia Supreme Court and in his subsequent promotion to reporter upon the death of James M. Kelly, who previously filled the post. Second, in the capacity of reporter, he gained a special familiarity with the decisions of the Supreme Court, which knowledge was useful to him both as a lawyer and in the work of digesting the laws of Georgia. Finally, it brought an immediate increase in the size of his legal practice.

As presiding justice of the Georgia Supreme Court, Lumpkin had no time left to pursue a private practice, nor had he the physical stamina to carry on both functions. Hence, much of his legal business devolved on Thomas Cobb, who continued to represent many of his brother's clients as well as his own.

At the conclusion of his secretarial term in January 1846, Cobb faced a busy year in the courts of not less than seventeen counties spread over two judicial circuits and part of a third. Disclosing the arduous nature of his

---

[75]Lumpkin and Nisbet were both Whigs; Warner was a Democrat. *Southern Banner*, 23 December 1845; Thomas R. R. Cobb to Howell Cobb, 12 December 1845, Howell Cobb Collection. For nearly half a century the Georgia judiciary had functioned under an archaic system wherein each superior court had exclusive and final jurisdiction in its own circuit. As a result, there were conflicting interpretations of the law, and only a convention of superior court judges, meeting annually to define rules of procedure, prevented a total lack of uniformity. Not until 1835 was the Georgia Constitution of 1798 amended to provide for a supreme court empowered to correct errors in law and equity, and still another decade had lapsed before the legislature finally took action as noted above. There is no good history of the Georgia Supreme Court. However, see John B. Harris, ed., *A History of the Supreme Court of Georgia* (Macon GA: The J. W. Burke Company, 1948).

schedule, he wrote to his brother in April: "I have been away from home all the time since the commencement of the Courts, for between our own Circuit and Col[.] Lumpkin's, I have had no *rest* [in] weeks. I got home last night and leave again in the morning for Lincoln."[76]

Amidst this feverish routine, requiring constant travel, regular attendance at court, and long hours in the law office adjacent to his house, Cobb kept abreast of political developments in the Sixth District and paid particular attention to two issues of national significance: the Oregon question and the imbroglio with Mexico over the annexation of Texas.

In July 1845, Richard Pakenham, the British minister to the United States, had rejected an offer from the American government to divide the Oregon territory along the 49th parallel. In retaliation President James K. Polk had suspended negotiations, belligerently reiterated a claim to the whole region, and requested congress to give Great Britain notice that the Anglo-American treaty of joint occupation would be terminated in twelve months.

Advocates of "fifty-four forty or fight," including Howell Cobb, rallied behind the administration's policy. The Whigs and many southern Democrats, however, coalesced under the leadership of John C. Calhoun to combat the ultra-expansionists and prevent what appeared to be an almost certain clash with England.

After reading the published text of a speech by his brother on the Oregon question, Thomas Cobb declared it to be comprehensive and "decidedly the best you have delivered in Congress."[77] Nevertheless, he was much more moderate on this issue than his brother, as were most of the congressman's constituents. "I am still of the opinion . . . ," wrote Cobb,

> that the decided wish of the people . . . is for peace. The idea is with them that voting for the notice is voting for war. So that while not a voice have I heard proposing to surrender our right to Oregon, or to continue negociations [sic] when negociations are of no avail, yet the hope is on every one's lips that war may not be the final issue.[78]

Personally, he favored a notification of twelve months coupled with

---

[76]Thomas Cobb to Howell Cobb, 25 April 1846, Howell Cobb Collection.

[77]Thomas Cobb to Howell Cobb, 29 January 1846, ibid. For the speech see *Southern Banner*, 27 January 1846.

[78]Thomas Cobb to Howell Cobb, 29 January 1844, Howell Cobb Collection. Cobb's

continued diplomatic talks during the entire period. "If we fight," he agreed, "Let us fight for 54.40, but compromise at 49 if we can."[79]

The forces of conciliation ultimately succeeded in softening the president's bellicose policy, and, in June 1846, the Oregon question was resolved peacefully by establishing a boundary line at the 49th parallel. The settlement pleased Cobb, but, even so, he was not certain that war with Great Britain could be averted. The British had been meddling in the affairs of Texas for years, and Cobb, among others, was convinced that they were directly involved in the Mexican crisis, which by May 1846, completely overshadowed the Oregon controversy.

"Nobody talks of Oregon now," he asserted. "It is Mexico and War. I never saw the people more excited [.] A volunteer Company could be raised in every county in Georgia."[80] As to the causes of this impending conflict, Cobb was no more enlightened than the average Georgian, and his reaction was no less emotional.

> Our Government has permitted itself to be insulted long enough. The blood of her citizens has been spilt on her own soil. It appeals to us for vengeance [.] Can we hesitate to deal out a just retribution? It is the general opinion here that England is pulling the wires. The quicker we know it the better. Let Congress act and that quickly.[81]

Congress was already acting. On 12-13 May, a war bill was passed in the House and Senate and signed by the president. With war now a reality, the martial spirit in Athens and Clarke County rapidly evaporated. Officers and men of the local cavalry company began resigning as soon as the governor ordered the unit to hold itself in readiness for possible military service. Cobb's ardor also cooled considerably. Though a member of the Clarke County cavalry, he had no intention of going with the company if it were called to active duty. Mexican provocations might, in his mind, have dictated a war of revenge, but he did not plan to join in meting out the punishment. Moreover, he was not in sympathy with those extreme expansionists who wanted to seize all of Mexico. Aggression in the guise of Manifest Destiny struck him as being contrary to the

---

view was shared by others. See, for example, William H. Hull to Howell Cobb, May 1846, ibid.

[79]Thomas Cobb to Howell Cobb, 16 June 1846, ibid.

[80]Thomas Cobb to Howell Cobb, 12 May 1846, ibid.

[81]Ibid.

principles of American democracy. "I am opposed to this Government dismembering Mexico," he remarked.

> Let us whip her decently and give her a good government such as the *people* wish. If they *afterwards wish* to be annexed we can do it. I am for extending the area of freedom but not by *war*. The odious doctrine upon which Britain acts of taking territory for the expenses of the war is anti-democratic. Let the glory of our government be that *not one* citizen lives under its laws that is not there by *choice*.[82]

Shortly after the outbreak of hostilities, Cobb received a long, ill-tempered letter from his brother alluding to the fact that John C. Calhoun had abstained from voting on the war bill and, in league with various Whigs, had fought against it "with all the fury of a desperate gamester. . . ." Venturing the surly guess that he would be abused for daring "to array himself in opposition to the great southern statesman," Howell Cobb implied that his Democratic friends had been very lax in defending him on the Oregon issue and wondered if his stand on the Mexican War would also go unjustified. He had heard that William L. Mitchell was "preaching Calhounism in the streets and upon the house tops and that . . . others are very free in their censure of my course upon Oregon." This led him to suspect that a coalition between the Whigs and the Calhoun Democrats had been formed in the Sixth District. Any such coalition, he warned, "shall meet with no quarter at my hands."[83]

In reply to this letter and to a later communication transmitted via his sister-in-law, Thomas Cobb countered his brother's complaints. "Your position on the Oregon question," he explained, "altho differing from many democrats, raised opposition from only a handful, and here you have done your friends great injustice in supposing you have gone *unvindicated*." It had been politically inexpedient, he went on, to call attention to the criticisms of the few by publicly condemning them. And to have made the acquisition of all of Oregon a question of party loyalty would have split the Democracy and solidified the opposition. Under the

---

[82]Thomas Cobb to Howell Cobb, 25 June [1846], ibid. Cobb's opposition to an expansionist policy of partition approximated the "no territory" platform of the Georgia Whigs. See Royce C. McCrary, "Georgia Politics and the Mexican War," *The Georgia Historical Quarterly* 60 (Fall, 1976): 218-19.

[83]Howell Cobb to Thomas Cobb, 12 May 1846, Howell Cobb Collection.

circumstances silence seemed to be the most sensible strategy, and subsequent events had proved the correctness of this policy.

"Those who hinted opposition to you," continued Cobb, "were obliged to throw themselves upon Calhoun's neck, and his course upon the war bill have rendered his embraces rather rough and hot. . . . Never was there a man so completely dead." Only Charles Dougherty and one or two other Whigs tried to defend the South Carolinian and "Mitchell gives him up." Insofar as Cobb could discover, there was no combination of Whigs and Calhoun Democrats to contend with in the Sixth District. Indeed, he concluded that there was no serious opposition to his brother of any kind.[84]

His realistic and accurate appraisal of the situation was corroborated by at least two other Athens Democrats, and it apparently soothed the ruffled feelings of his brother, who retained a tight hold on the Sixth District Democracy and even composed old differences with Hopkins Holsey. In September 1846, Holsey bought the *Southern Banner* from Albon Chase and vigorously backed Howell Cobb's re-election to Congress.[85]

It was not politics and foreign problems, but the law which occupied most of Thomas Cobb's time during the latter half of the 1840s. The establishment of the Georgia Supreme Court, which held its first official session in January 1846, had added a new dimension to his practice. Besides attending the lower courts, he was forced to travel to Macon, Milledgeville, Decatur, and several other towns scattered throughout the state to argue cases on appeal.

In his initial case before the Georgia Supreme Court, tried in the September term at Gainesville, Cobb won a favorable verdict. While not always so successful, his competence as a lawyer attracted an increasing number of clients, and his financial status improved proportionately. In 1843 he had been virtually without property. Four years later he owned a large house, a carriage, fourteen slaves, forty acres of land in Cobb County,

---

[84]Thomas Cobb to Howell Cobb, 21 May 1846, ibid.

[85]Albon Chase to Howell Cobb, 20 May 1846, William H. Hull to Howell Cobb, 22 May 1846, U. B. Phillips, ed., *The Correspondence of Robert Toombs, Alexander H. Stephens, and Howell Cobb, American Historical Association Annual Report* (Washington, 1913), 2:77-79. Hereinafter cited as Phillips, ed., *Correspondence. Southern Banner*, 8 September 1846.

sundry town lots valued at $3,000 and a tract of timber about three miles from Athens.[86]

In spite of a sound and obviously lucrative practice, Cobb still felt that his income was inadequate. To supplement a budget based primarily on legal fees, he decided to seek public office once more. In the fall of 1847 he formed an alliance with Benjamin F. Hardeman of Lexington, a member of the Whig Party. Hardeman was to run for secretary of the Georgia senate with Cobb as his assistant. This appeared to be a wise move on Cobb's part, for the Whigs had a majority in the upper house of the legislature, and his alignment with Hardeman would pull the necessary votes from that side. These votes together with Democratic support would ensure victory.

Late in October 1847, Cobb arrived in Milledgeville, perfectly confident of election. He was not prepared for what happened next. Word of his bargain with Hardeman had preceded him and, as the report circulated, resentment grew. As Cobb later explained it, the "cry of *coalition*" was raised and "loudest in the chase" was State Senator William W. Clayton, an Athens Whig.[87] Hardeman was thoroughly unnerved and rather than risk his party standing timidly withdrew from the contest.

Left to his own devices, Cobb gambled on winning the secretaryship. To secure this office, he needed the backing of all the Democrats plus a few Whigs. In the beginning all went well. He had the lead on the first two ballots but lost it on the third and was defeated on the fourth. Only two Whigs voted for him, and both votes were canceled when two Democrats were bribed, according to Cobb, to oppose him. Another Democrat upon whom he depended was absent. "So it is," he commented afterwards. "I was beat and I am not sorry for it. I *know* I am a *better* party man than I ever was.[88]

Members of the Whig Party had evidently reached the same conclusion. They could hardly be blamed, therefore, for refusing to award the

---

[86]For a summary of Cobb's first case see James M. Kelly, reporter, *Reports of Cases in Law and Equity Argued and Determined in the Supreme Court of the State of Georgia in the Year 1846* (New York: The Franklin Printing and Publishing Co., 1847), 10: 514-18. The Clarke County, GA, "Tax Digest," 1843, lists Cobb as owning eighty acres of land in Cherokee County, Georgia. This land, however, belonged to his brother. See also ibid., 1847; Thomas R. R. Cobb to Sarah R. Cobb, 22 January 1847, Jackson Scrapbook.

[87]Thomas Cobb to Howell Cobb, 25 November 1847, Howell Cobb Collection.

[88]Ibid.; *Southern Recorder*, 2 November 1847.

secretaryship of the Georgia senate to Cobb, a self-professed Democrat, or for interpreting his candidacy, as undoubtedly they did, as an effort to use family ties, Whig and Democrat, to grab an unwarranted share of the patronage. Judge Lumpkin, it was reported, was deeply chagrined by the treatment accorded his son-in-law by the Whig Party, and Marion was so furious that she threatened to change her political allegiance. Cobb, on the other hand, accepted the defeat with uncharacteristic stoicism. In all probability the set back helped to resurrect his antiparty sentiment for he never again sought election to any legislative office. Indeed, by 1860 he had so far forgotten his previous partisanship that he prefaced a speech to the General Assembly with this remarkable statement: "Those of you who know me can bear witness that I have never in the slightest degree interfered in past political contests, and hence I have no disappointed ambition to satisfy—no personal wrongs to avenge—no party animosity to appease."[89]

To dismiss Cobb's disclaimer of partisanship as mere hypocrisy or political rhetoric would be much too simple. Contradictory though it may seem, he sincerely believed himself to be above the pettiness of party politics, and, notwithstanding the frequency of his attempts to obtain public office, a political career was never his aim in life. A seat on the United States Supreme Court, he once told Alexander H. Stephens, "is the *only office* in the world for which I have ever had a desire."[90]

After 1847 Cobb spent most of his time and energy on such nonpolitical activities as the law, religion, and education. He not only refrained from running for elective office, but seldom manifested great interest in politics unless slavery or the ambitions of his brother were directly involved, and nothing could induce him to campaign openly for any party candidate regardless of the issues at stake. His claim to political impartiality, at least during the last fifteen years of his life, was not, therefore, a sham.

---

[89]"Substance of Remarks Made by Thomas R. R. Cobb, Esq., before the General Assembly of Georgia, November 12th, 1860," Allen D. Candler, comp., *The Confederate Records of the State of Georgia*, 6 vols. (Atlanta, Franklin Printing and Publishing Co., 1909-1911), 1:157. Hereinafter cited as Candler, comp., *Confederate Records*. Judge Lumpkin's reaction is mentioned in Sarah R. Cobb to Mary Ann Cobb, 5 November 1847, Howell Cobb Collection.

[90]Thomas Cobb to Alexander H. Stephens, 23 June 1860, A. H. Stephens Papers, Library of Congress, Washington DC.

In any case, it had not been plain greed nor a desire to climb higher on the political ladder that had stimulated Cobb's interest in the financial rewards of politics; rather he had been motivated by an honest concern for the material well-being of his family, whose comfort he was bent upon securing and whose needs, wants, and size had kept pace with the growth of his law practice.

His first child, as noted, had been born in October 1844. "You have a grandaughter [sic]," he had announced to his parents, "and a sweeter and prettier little girl never breathed. . . . Marion has named it 'Lucy' after her Sister in Mississippi who named her first 'Marion' after her." A relative who witnessed the antics of the happy parents declared that "it was a real show to be with Tom and his wife and *baby*" and suggested that A. B. Longstreet's famous *Georgia Scenes* might have been improved had he been able to see "some of the fanciful ones . . . transacted there."[91] A second daughter, Sally, was born on 4 July 1846, followed in 1848 by a third, named Callender. "My little girls," boasted Cobb three weeks after Sally's birth, "are the finest in Georgia." He was fondest of Lucy, however, and more than once confessed: "I am sometimes afraid I love her too much. She is the smartest and sweetest child in Ga."[92]

Though inordinately proud of his daughters, Cobb longed for a son to carry on his name. He longed in vain, for his sons, one born in June 1850 and the other in August 1852 both died in infancy, and his last offspring, born in 1860, was another daughter, who was named for her mother.

Frequent pregnancies impaired the health of Marion Cobb and necessitated many trips northward to consult physicians and to visit various resorts noted for their restful surroundings and healthy climate. None of the excursions seemed to do much good, however, and, during one such trip in June 1853, she suffered a miscarriage which required a two week recuperation period at Niagara Falls before the Cobbs could journey home.

Cobb worried constantly about his wife's debilities and word that one of the children was ill could bring him rushing home from court in alarm. Few men were more devoted to their families than he was. He liked

---

[91]M.L.R. Glenn to Mary Ann Cobb, 4 February 1845, Howell Cobb Collection.

[92]Thomas Cobb to Parents, 9 October [1844], Thomas Cobb to Sarah R. Cobb, 27 July 1846, Jackson Scrapbook; Thomas Cobb to Howell Cobb, 25 July 1846, Howell Cobb Collection.

nothing better than quiet evenings at home reading the Bible and listening to his daughters sing and recite. He took charge of their religious upbringing, carefully supervised their education, and, with their welfare in mind, contributed much to the improvement of female education in Athens. Toward his wife he always felt the greatest love and on every anniversary composed long, sentimental poems to her. In brief, he was a model husband and father.

By the winter of 1847-1848, the formative years of Cobb's life and career were over. He was well established in the legal profession, and while his achievements had been as yet less than spectacular, he was still young and the most important and productive phase of his life lay ahead.

CHAPTER 2

Georgia Lawyer

St. Joseph's Catholic Church with priest in foreground
(originally Thomas R. R. Cobb's law office)

Cobb's defeat for the office of secretary of the Georgia senate in 1847 came as a rude shock. Deprived of a salary and momentarily short of funds at the beginning of the normally slack winter season, his first thought upon returning to Athens was to offset this unexpected reverse. "To be usefully employed this winter," he informed his brother, "I am preparing a Digest, supplementary to 'Prince's', of the laws since 1837. I think I can make something out of it. If you have any useful suggestions to make me I should be glad to have them."[1]

Simultaneously Cobb attempted to collect an overdue fee from the Post Office Department for certain legal services performed at the request of his cousin, Henry R. Jackson, the federal district attorney. Estimating that his proficiency had saved the government several thousand dollars, Cobb urged his brother to press the postmaster general for payment . "Now the money would be a Godsend to me this winter," he explained, "and perhaps a word or two from you to old Cave [Johnson]

---

[1]An abbreviated and somewhat altered version of this chapter appeared originally as an article by the author entitled "Thomas Cobb and the Codification of Georgia Law," *The Georgia Historical Quarterly* 62 (Spring 1978): 9-12. The first edition of Oliver H. Prince's *Digest of the Laws of Georgia* was published in 1822. The second edition to which Cobb alludes appeared in 1837. Thomas Cobb to Howell Cobb, 25 November 1847, Howell Cobb Collection.

would expedite the matter."[2] Within two months the bill was settled, thus easing his financial worries somewhat.[3]

His worries were further reduced in January 1848, when he was appointed to the newly created post of assistant reporter of the Georgia Supreme Court. Although the salary was small, the promise of promotion was great. James M. Kelly, who then occupied the office of reporter, was expected to retire at the end of the year, and it was tacitly understood that Cobb would inherit his position.[4]

In the meantime, Cobb assisted Kelly in the compilation of volumes four and five of the Georgia Supreme Court decisions embracing all cases argued and determined between January and December 1848. In the preface to the former volume, the reporters announced that the title was being altered from *Kelly's Reports* to the more descriptive *Georgia Supreme Court Reports* "in order that a change of Reporters may not interfere with the series." This sensible modification reflecting a similar change in several other states was continued by subsequent reporters. The necessity of starting a new sequence of volume numbers with each change of reporters was thus eliminated.[5]

Before the fifth volume was published Kelly died, and Cobb was chosen to fill the vacancy on 25 January 1849. For the next eight years Cobb functioned with efficiency and dispatch, compiling fifteen volumes of decisions, a *Supreme Court Manual* (Athens 1849), setting forth the proper procedures for appealing cases to the highest state tribunal, and *A General Digested Index to Georgia Reports* (Athens 1852). The *Index,* compiled in collaboration with his brother-in-law, William Wilberforce

---

[2]Thomas Cobb to Howell Cobb, 25 November 1847, Howell Cobb Collection.

[3]Thomas Cobb to Howell Cobb, 27 January 1848, ibid.

[4]An amendment to the Act of 1845 was approved on 24 December 1847, authorizing the appointment of an assistant reporter. *Acts of the General Assembly of the State of Georgia,* 1847, p. 82; Joseph H. Lumpkin to Howell Cobb, 21 January 1848, Phillips, ed., *Correspondence,* p. 95.

[5]James M. Kelly and Thomas R. R. Cobb, reporters, *Reports of Cases in Law and Equity Argued and Determined in the Supreme Court of the State of Georgia From Savannah Term, to Hawkinsville Term,* 1848. *Inclusive; Being a Continuation of Kelly's Reports* (Athens GA: Franklin Printing & Publishing Co., 1848), p. v. Hereinafter cited as *Georgia Reports.* For similar changes in other states see Erwin C. Surrency, "Law Reports in the United States," *The American Journal of Legal History* 25 (January 1981): 58. Hereinafter cited as Surrency, "Law Reports."

Lumpkin, was a useful guide not only to the opinions of the Supreme Court but also to several earlier compilations of superior court decisions.[6]

For his services Cobb received an annual salary of $1,000 and a copyright on all volumes of *Georgia Reports* published under his name. A more liberal, if belated, bounty was bestowed almost four years after his resignation (effective 1 January 1857) when the legislature granted him three dollars per volume "for all the Reports furnished to the State without compensation, under the Act of 1845." This represented a substantial benefit amounting to $6,532.[7]

The dual role of attorney and reporter, though absorbing most of Cobb's time, had not prevented the completion of his proposed supplement to Prince's *Digest.* As the work progressed Cobb decided to broaden the scope of the project. His own experience at the bar and advice from various colleagues convinced him that a new and revised digest of all state laws currently in force from the colonial period to the present was needed rather than a mere supplement.

In 1849, there were three digests in general use: Prince's *Digest* (1837); a *Codification of the Statute Law of Georgia* (1845) by William A. Hotchkiss; and an *Analysis of the Statutes of Georgia* (1846) by Howell Cobb of Houston County.[8] In addition to these, six volumes of Georgia Supreme Court decisions had been published, plus numerous pamphlets containing the laws of Georgia passed since the second edition of Prince's *Digest.* This plethora of authorities was confusing and inconvenient. One lawyer complained that court proceedings were frequently interrupted

---

[6]Cobb's appointment was confirmed by Governor George Towns on 2 February 1849. See "Commission of Thomas R. R. Cobb," Cobb folder, Original Manuscripts File no. 2, Georgia Department of Archives and History; Sarah Cobb to Sarah M. R. Jackson, 30 January 1849, Jackson-Prince Papers; John B. O'Neall to Joseph Henry Lumpkin, 17 October 1849, Joseph Henry Lumpkin Papers, University of Georgia Libraries.

[7]*Acts of the General Assembly*, 1845, p. 23, 1860, p. 68. Beginning with volume 6, Cobb's *Georgia Reports* were bound and distributed for sale in the North by the Philadelphia firm of T. & J. W. Johnson. See Cobb to T. & J. W. Johnson, 23 October, 6 December 1849, 8 February, 16 December 1850, 11 August 1855, Simon Gratz Collection, The Historical Society of Pennsylvania, Philadelphia, Pennsylvania; *Annual Report of the Comptroller General of the State of Georgia*, 1861, p. 149. Cobb's compensation, though perhaps slightly on the low side, was generally in line with that of reporters from other states. See Surrency, "Law Reports," p. 59.

[8]Howell Cobb of Houston County, Georgia, is sometimes mistaken for Howell Cobb of Athens, Clarke County, Georgia. For a discussion of this confusion, see Horace

for as long as an hour while the judge searched for a law in one of the several digests, then consulted the pamphlets for subsequent amendments, and finally turned to the reports of the state Supreme Court for a judicial interpretation of the act in question.

Many other members of the legal profession, if not a majority, were dissatisfied with the three existing digests as well as with the profusion of sources. Prince's *Digest* was considered good, but obsolete; Hotchkiss's *Codification* was condemned as utterly useless; and the work of Howell Cobb of Houston County was thought to be unsuited to the requirements of either the bench or the bar.[9]

To provide Georgia lawyers, judges, and untrained justices of the peace with a portable, well-organized, easily understood digest, became the purpose of Cobb's undertaking. His plan was to bring together in a single work the statutes of Georgia with a synopsis of the latest judicial interpretation of each act. As he soon discovered, the task was enormous. "The preparation of such a book," he later recalled, "requires that the *same mind* should regulate the *minutiae* as well as the *plan*, and not one hour's labor can be done without the exercise of the judgement in the . . . thousand and one petty questions which arise and which the cursory observer never detects."[10] His decision to supplant rather than supplement Prince's publication necessitated a drastic modification of the deadline set for completion of the project. Instead of finishing in six weeks as originally intended, three and a half years went by before the digest appeared in print.

By the summer of 1849, however, enough work had been expended on the digest to remind Cobb that his efforts deserved a subsidy from the state. As a preliminary step in this direction, he sent letters to prominent lawyers and judges soliciting their support. The response could hardly have been more encouraging. Favorable replies came from all three

---

Montgomery, "The Two Howell Cobbs: A Case of Mistaken Identity," *The Journal of Southern History* 28 (August 1962): 348-55. Among other works, Howell Cobb of Houston County published *A Compilation of Legal Forms, in Use in the State of Georgia* in 1841. A second edition was printed in 1842.

[9]For complaints from lawyers and judges about the inadequacy of the sources of law see "Memorial of Thomas R. R. Cobb to the Georgia General Assembly," pp. 3-16, Emory University Library, Atlanta, Georgia.

[10]Thomas Cobb to Howell Cobb, 29 January [1852], Howell Cobb Collection.

justices of the Georgia Supreme Court, eight superior court judges, and approximately seventy-five practicing attorneys.[11]

In November 1849, Cobb delivered a memorial containing excerpts from many of these letters to Democratic Governor George W. Towns. The memorial requested, not an immediate appropriation, but "a guaranty from the Legislature, *that if the book is worthy*, it shall receive the patronage of the State."[12] To boost the book further, an article appeared in the Milledgeville *Southern Recorder* praising Cobb's endeavor to supply the people with a new and up-to-date digest.[13] Thus, by the time the legislature convened, everything possible had been done to create a climate of opinion sympathetic to the adoption of a revised work of law.

On 6 November, Towns personally approved the proposed digest and urged the legislature to act favorably on Cobb's petition. "The known ability of Mr. Cobb for this undertaking, the advantages he possesses as State Reporter, his industry and his familiarity with the law," stated the governor, "furnish strong guarantees of his success in the contemplated enterprise."[14]

Ten days later the legislature appointed a joint select committee composed of four Whigs and four Democrats to study the memorial. Auspiciously for Cobb, half the committee members had previously expressed sentiments favoring his work, and their endorsement seemed certain.[15]

The report of the committee, submitted to the senate on 20 November, and to the house on 5 December, recommended the passage

---

[11]Among the more famous Georgians who answered were: Robert Toombs, Henry L. Benning, Herschel V. Johnson, Warren Akin, Francis Bartow, Charles J. McDonald, and David Irwin. "Memorial," pp. 3-16.

[12]Ibid., p. 2.

[13]*Southern Recorder*, 30 October 1849. Miller Grieve, the editor of this paper, was an uncle of Cobb's wife. Additional pressure may have been felt by the legislature in December when the members of the Georgia Supreme Court published reports calling for the condensation and simplification of the laws of the state. Ibid., 4, 11 December 1849.

[14]*Georgia House Journal*, 1849-1850, pp. 32-32.

[15]The Committee consisted of three senators—Charles Murphy (Democrat) John D. Stell (Democrat), and Andrew J. Miller (Whig)—and five members of the lower house—Achilles D. Shackelford (Democrat), Thomas C. Howard (Democrat), James A. Nisbet (Whig), Edmund H. Worrill (Whig), and Augustus H. Kenan (Whig). Ibid., p. 65; *Georgia Senate Journal*, 1849-1850, p. 60.

of a resolution instructing the governor "to have the Digest of the memorialist thoroughly examined by competent persons, and if found correct and faithful, that he be authorized to subscribe for a number of copies . . . not to exceed three thousand, at a price not to exceed four dollars per volume.[16]

At this juncture, opposition to the report erupted in both houses of the legislature and forced a motion to table the resolution temporarily.[17] Some opponents of the measure presumably felt, as did one jurist, that it was time to put an end to public expenditures "for the sake of giving encouragement to individual enterprise and talent, or for the purpose of pandering to the *mania of book making.*"[18] Others may have been venting their spite against Howell Cobb whose unionist stance had antagonized the fire-eaters in both parties.[19] For most, however, the question was probably not slavery or the need for a new digest but whether Cobb should again be the recipient of state patronage.

The Cobb family had been incredibly successful in obtaining offices that fall, a fact which was noticed in several newspapers around the state. The Augusta *Daily Chronicle and Sentinel*, for example, censured Howell Cobb and one other politician for grabbing a "Lion's share" of the patronage and providing "most bountifully for their families."[20] Such condemnation apparently had its effect on the legislators, some of whom were muttering that Thomas Cobb ought not to be both reporter and practitioner in a court presided over by his father-in-law.

---

[16]*Georgia Senate Journal*, 1849-1850, p. 82; *Georgia House Journal*, 1849-1850, pp. 179-80.

[17]John B. Cobb to Howell Cobb, 30 November 1849, Howell Cobb Collection; *Georgia Senate Journal*, 1849-1850, pp. 83, 114.

[18]Judge G. E. Thomas had written Cobb on 30 June 1849, that he would disapprove any publication of this sort but went on to say that he was willing to support Cobb's proposed digest because of the great necessity for such a work. "Memorial," p. 7.

[19]Thomas Cobb to Howell Cobb, [January 1850], Howell Cobb Collection. See chapter 5 for a discussion of slavery and politics.

[20]Quoted in Helen Ione Green, "Politics in Georgia, 1830-1854" (Ph.D. diss., University of Chicago, 1945), p. 197. After reading an article in the *Muscogee Democrat*, Howell Cobb's wife exclaimed: "Ah! Mr's Cobb, Jackson, & Lumpkin factions—every attempt will be made to strip them of their honors." Mary Ann Cobb to Howell Cobb, 8 December 1849, Howell Cobb Collection. Excluding the Cobb brothers, who already held office, four of their relatives were elected by the legislature to positions in state government in the fall of 1849. Luther J. Glenn, a brother-in-law, was chosen secretary of the Georgia senate;

Attempting to quiet the criticism, Andrew J. Miller, a Whig friend of Cobb and Judge Lumpkin, amended a senate judiciary bill in such a way as to debar the reporter from acting as an attorney in Supreme Court actions. The bill, as amended, passed the upper house on 8 December.[21]

Concluding that his digest was doomed and that he was now to be deprived of a portion of his law practice, Cobb grew despondent and talked of resigning his post of reporter. Hot indignation soon replaced gloom, however, and galvanized him to action. Smothering the impulse to resign, he mustered votes against the amendment and even prevailed upon the hapless Miller to aid in its defeat. When the legislature recessed for Christmas, Cobb was fairly certain that the house would excise the Miller amendment, but his digest was still in serious difficulty. His brother-in-law believed, erroneously as it turned out, that there was no "chance for him to get any encouragement from the Legislature, in the way of Bookmaking."[22]

Cobb had worked too long and too hard to give up without a final struggle. After attending the Savannah and Talbotton terms of the Georgia Supreme Court in January 1850, he hastened to Milledgeville to stage a last ditch fight for his digest. Persistence had its reward. On 5 February, the report of the joint select committee was accepted unanimously by the senate and forwarded to the house for concurrence. Despite stubborn minority resistance led by two Whigs, Parmedus Reynolds and James N. Ramsey, the house also adopted the report by a vote of seventy-four to twenty-eight.[23]

On the following morning, Reynolds moved to reconsider the previous day's ballot. The defeat of his motion, seventy to forty-one, prompt-

---

James Jackson, a cousin, was elected judge of the Western Circuit; Henry R. Jackson, another cousin, and formerly federal district attorney, was elected judge of the Eastern Circuit; and John H. Lumpkin, a nephew of Judge Lumpkin, was elected judge of the Cherokee Circuit. *Southern Recorder*, November 1849; Howell Cobb to Mary Ann Cobb, 11 November 1849, Cobb-Erwin-Lamar Collection.

[21]*Georgia Senate Journal*, 1849-1850, pp. 171-72; Miller Grieve to Joseph Henry Lumpkin, 14 December 1849, Lumpkin Papers. There was a precedent for the above action. The act creating the Georgia Supreme Court had prohibited the reporter from practicing law during his tenure in office. This provision was repealed in 1847. See *Acts of the General Assembly*, 1845, p. 23, ibid., 1847, p. 82.

[22]L. J. Glenn to Howell Cobb, 15 January 1850, Howell Cobb Collection.

[23]*Georgia Senate Journal*, 1849-1850, p. 494; *Georgia House Journal*, 1849-1850, pp. 676-77.

ed him to remark that the legislature might "as well open the State treasury and give it to the Cobbs for they would get it any how."[24] On 14 February, Governor Towns signed the joint resolution, which directed him to appoint a special committee to study the digest whenever it was completed and, if found satisfactory, to purchase 3,000 copies at four dollars each.[25]

"The legislature subscribed for my Book *at last*," wrote an obviously relieved Cobb upon his return to Athens. "I had hard work for it."[26] And much hard work remained. From February through September 1850, he devoted every spare moment to the digest, causing his mother to worry about his health. "Tom does not look well, he labors too hard," she declared. The "book added to his other business does not give him time to take a long breath."[27] In reality, Cobb thrived on mental exertion. Friends and colleagues never ceased to be amazed at his reservoir of energy and at the massive quantity of work which he could dispatch in short order.

In preparing his digest, Cobb was faithful to his preannounced plan. Indeed, he felt obligated to follow the format of Oliver H. Prince, though he did so "in some instances against his own sense of propriety."[28] Preserving his predecessor's system of alphabetized headings and chronologically arranged statutes, he added a number of subheadings to achieve greater clarity and utility. This modification was essential; otherwise, as Cobb pointed out, the mass of relevant legislation listed under a single title would have become "a Cretan labyrinth to the young lawyer, or the more unskilled officer."[29]

Cobb further improved upon Prince's plan by including notes on the

---

[24]*Georgia House Journal*, 1849-1850, pp. 694-95; Sarah R. Cobb to Sister, 8 February 1850, Howell Cobb Collection.

[25]"Report of the Joint Select Committee," Original Manuscripts File #2, Georgia Department of Archives and History.

[26]Thomas Cobb to Howell Cobb, [January 1850], Howell Cobb Collection.

[27]Sarah R. Cobb to Howell Cobb, 5 April, 6 September 1850, ibid.

[28]Thomas R. R. Cobb, comp. *A Digest of the Statute Laws of the State of Georgia, in Force Prior to the Session of the General Assembly of 1851, With Explanatory Notes and References*; *and also*, *With Notes*, *Giving the Exposition of the Statutes*, *by the Supreme Court of the State*; *Together With an Appendix*. . . . (Athens GA: Christy, Kelsea and Burke, 1851), p. iii. Hereinafter cited as Cobb, *Digest*.

[29]Ibid., pp. iii-iv.

Georgia Supreme Court's construction of the laws and by appending a reference to invalidated acts at the end of each main section, "thus giving at one view *all the legislation* on the subject" whether still in force or not. To determine what was or was not existing law demanded the frequent exercise of discretion. As a rule of thumb, Cobb preferred to avoid sins of omission, even at the risk of "inserting doubtful law . . . , leaving it to the properly constituted tribunal finally to decide the question."[30]

In the fall of 1850, the manuscript was ready for presentation to the special committee selected by Governor Towns. The composition of this committee assured Cobb that his digest would receive the fairest possible treatment. Two of the three members, Francis H. Cone and Edmund H. Worrill, were on record as favoring the work, and the third, Junius Hillyer, was an old family friend. On 15 October, after comparing the manuscript with other compilations of Georgia law, the committee reported to the governor that "The plan and arrangement . . . is simple, plain and intelligible. . . . And the whole execution of the work bears abundant testimony to the accuracy, ability, and carefulness of the Compiler."[31] On the strength of this report, Towns subscribed for the authorized 3,000 copies and advanced $2,000 from the state contingency fund to help Cobb defray expenses, pending an appropriation at the next meeting of the legislature.

During the ensuing eight months, Cobb made final revisions in the digest, employed printers and a binder, and wrote a preface in which he took special pains to point out that "this is the *first* effort to publish such a book *at home*."[32] This reference to home publication was an early mani-

[30]Ibid., p. iv, viii. Prince recognized, in 1821, that the absence of judicial interpretations in his digest was a deficiency. Since no state supreme court existed at the time and since superior court decisions were often contradictory (in most cases not even recorded) he was powerless to remedy the shortcoming. See Oliver H. Prince, comp. *A Digest of the Laws of the State of Georgia* . . . , 2d ed., (Athens GA: Oliver H. Prince, Publisher, 1837), pp. 8-9.

[31]Cobb, *Digest*, p. iv.

[32]Ibid, iii; Thomas Cobb to Howell Cobb, 14 December 1850, Mary Ann Cobb to Howell Cobb, 2 January 1851, John W. Burke to Howell Cobb, 8 July 1851, Howell Cobb Collection. Once again his mother was troubled about his health. "Tom . . . looks thin and pale," she wrote to her eldest son. "Dr. Simms says . . . [he] is over studying . . . & if he does not quit he will be broke down before he is thirty. I want you to give him a good talk when you come home. It keeps me very unhappy, he sits up too much at night writing." Sarah R. Cobb to Howell Cobb, 14 January 1851, ibid.

festation of his incipient southern nationalism, one element of which was a cry for independence from northern publishing firms. Completed in June 1851, his new *Digest of the Laws of Georgia* went on sale at White's University Book Store in Athens on 31 July, and soon thereafter in Philadelphia through the firm of T. and J. W. Johnson.[33]

On 3 November 1851, Governor Towns, whose term in office was expiring, transmitted his farewell message to the legislature. Commending Cobb's *Digest*, he informed the lawmakers that all copies authorized under the joint resolution of 1850 had been ordered at a purchase price of four dollars each and that $2,000 had been paid already to "afford becoming encouragement to this enterprise," which in his opinion, would have "utility with every class of our citizens."[34] And, indeed, the "New *Digest*," as it was frequently called, quickly became the leading authority on Georgia law and proved useful to lawyers and non-lawyers alike both in and out of the state.[35]

Before the legislature could react to the outgoing governor's remarks by appropriating the $10,000 still owed, Cobb began pushing for new guarantees in regard to his *Digest*. To ensure full and efficient distribution of the work and to define the terms of any subsequent sales to the state, he framed a set of resolutions and persuaded a member of the house to introduce the measure. Unable to be in Milledgeville to lobby personally for its passage, he wrote to various legislators and requested his brother, who was elected in October to succeed Towns, to use his influence with friends in the legislative branch. Although Cobb insisted that he wanted only those privileges accorded Prince in 1837, the effect of his proposal was to increase substantially the number of volumes required by the state as well as the cost.[36]

Approved on 15 December 1851, Cobb's resolutions empowered the

---

[33]*Southern Banner*, 31 July 1851; Thomas Cobb to T. & J. W. Johnson, 10 September 1851, Gratz Collection.

[34]*Georgia House Journal*, 1851-1852, pp. 32-33.

[35]Cobb's *Digest* was cited by opponents as well as exponents of slavery. See, for example, George M. Stroud, *A Sketch of the Laws Relating to Slavery* (Philadelphia, 1856; second edition); John C. Hurd, *The Law of Freedom and Bondage* (New York, 1862); Joseph C. Stiles, *Modern Reform Examined* (Philadelphia, 1850). The last named book was an attack on abolitionism.

[36]Thomas Cobb to Howell Cobb, 25 November 1851, Howell Cobb Collection.

governor to furnish his *Digest* to inferior court judges, inferior and superior court clerks, ordinaries, sheriffs, coroners, and justices of the peace. The governor was also required to keep five hundred copies in reserve and to buy extra volumes, if needed, paying not more than five dollars for each. In compliance with these instructions, Howell Cobb immediately ordered a large number of additional volumes at the maximum price and apparently left it up to his brother how many more would be necessary. In January 1852, two sums were appropriated, totaling $13,500. The first $10,000 was to pay the balance due on the original 3,000 digests and the remaining $3,500 was for 700 copies purchased under the authority of Cobb's resolutions.[37]

It was Thomas Cobb's intention, moreover, to provide the state with another 300 copies, but before this number could be delivered he was challenged by a certain Dr. Martin (perhaps Robert E. Martin, state librarian). "I have read today two very vexatious letters from Dr. Martin about my Digest," Cobb wrote to his brother.

> In the first he goes into count to show that instead of needing 1000, under the Resolution of the last legislature, only 500 will be needed. *I have already delivered 738*. Now I am perfectly willing to stop at that if you say so, and perhaps it would be best, as Dr. M. has been officious enough to count noses and try to diminish my sale.[38]

Cobb's estimate of the number of books needed may have been slightly high but was certainly not exorbitant.[39] Nevertheless, the circumstances surrounding the sale and distribution of the *Digest* smacked of favoritism and set the stage for later charges of corruption against the Cobb brothers.

Realizing that his own *Digest*, like that of Prince, would soon be out

---

[37]*Acts of the General Assembly*, 1851-1852, pp. 14-18, 568; Thomas Cobb to Howell Cobb, 6 April 1852, Howell Cobb Collection.

[38]Thomas Cobb to Howell Cobb, 18 April 1852, private possession of Dr. E. Merton Coulter.

[39]A subsequent legislature provided that 5,000 copies of the laws and 4,000 copies of the journals were to be printed to meet the needs of the state. These figures come close to and even exceed, in the case of the laws, the estimate of Cobb. *Acts of the General Assembly*, 1853-1854, pp. 78-79. Furthermore, the ceiling price of five dollars does not seem unreasonable when compared to law books in other states. The price of a volume of court reports in Pennsylvania in 1845, for instance, was four dollars. See Surrency, "Law Reports," p. 59.

of date and believing that the body of Georgia law was "increasing so rapidly as to render any future Digest of the same almost impracticable," Cobb drafted a bill requiring the biennial publication of all subsequent legislative enactments.[40] This measure, signed by Governor Howell Cobb on 12 January 1852, sought to prevent a recurrence of the chaotic conditions existing between 1847 and 1852, when lawyers had complained that Prince's work was so obsolete that laborious, costly, and time consuming research was necessary to determine a given point of law. Used in conjunction with his *Digest*, these annotated compilations would place the latest legal information at the immediate disposal of every attorney and citizen in the state. Through Cobb's foresight, the legal profession was thus to be saved considerable inconvenience, and the people were no longer to be kept in ignorance of the law for extended periods of time. That, at any rate, was the aim of the Act of 1852.

Unfortunately, dilatory publication of the laws not only defeated this laudable purpose but caused Thomas and Howell Cobb to be accused of dishonesty. Shortly after the passage of the Act of 1852 Thomas Cobb reluctantly agreed to become the first compiler under the new law. One condition of acceptance was that the engrossed acts of the current legislature be made ready for him at once. "I do not wish to delay *a day* in commencing this work," he informed his brother.[41]

Fearing the possibility of delay from another quarter, he warned: "There will be some trouble about *proof-reading* arising from the folly of the Legislature in electing a Public Printer out of Milledgeville."[42] To preclude such trouble he suggested that the state printer, Samuel J. Ray of the *Macon Telegraph*, be persuaded to surrender the work to Colonel Miller Grieve of the Milledgeville *Southern Recorder*. His proposal was well-meant but politically naive, and, it is safe to say, not seriously considered.[43]

---

[40]*Acts of the General Assembly*, 1851-1852, p. 253. The bill also stipulated that the format and printing style of these compilations were to be patterned after Cobb's *Digest*. As a consequence, the statute books improved in appearance and utility. Ibid., 1853-1854, p. 78. It might be noted here that Cobb was merely carrying out his original 1847 design of providing a supplement (in this case supplements) to the existing *Digest*.

[41]Thomas Cobb to Howell Cobb, 29 January [1852], Howell Cobb Collection.

[42]Ibid.

[43]Ibid. The state's printing patronage was an extremely lucrative prize which the

Collecting the engrossed acts at the state capital, Cobb returned to Athens where he completed his assignment quickly and forwarded the manuscript to Ray for proofreading and printing. Then, on 6 April 1852, he sent the governor a bid from a man named Day, who offered to bind the laws at the rate of twenty cents per volume. Day had bound Cobb's *Digest* and, in Cobb's estimation, was an excellent craftsman with a solitary flaw—a tendency to "drink a little too much."[44]

Passing through Macon a month later, Cobb learned, quite by accident, that Ray had awarded a contract to some other binder and agreed to pay seven to eight cents more than Day had charged, "a difference to the State," Cobb calculated, "upwards of three Hundred Dollars." Convinced that Ray was guilty of petty graft, Cobb put a stop to it by pointing to the provision in the Act of 1852, granting the governor, not the printer, the power to designate the binder and fix the rate. "It was a *swindling* operation," Cobb reported to his brother. "There is no doubt he shared the profits."[45]

Much more serious was Ray's failure to publish the laws and journals on time. Physical illness and financial embarrassment threw him months behind schedule, and it was pure luck that he finished the work before dying on 6 January 1853.[46] Not everyone was willing to accept Ray's misfortunes as the real reason for the prolonged delay in publishing the laws and journals of 1851-1852. Cobb blamed it on the outmoded Act of 1836, upon which the prevailing system of public printing was based. But a certain William Martin of Dahlonega, Georgia, insisted that the belated publication was caused by the Cobbs, who "jobbed the cash" appropriated by the legislature for printing purposes. Challenged by a friend of the

---

newspapers of Georgia greedily sought at the beginning of every meeting of the legislature. Having won the contract over stiff competition in 1849, Ray naturally would have been in no mood to give up a portion of the printing to one of his rivals. Public printers, it might be added, were elected every two years to print the acts of the succeeding legislature. Hence, Ray was obligated to publish the laws passed during the legislative session of 1851-1852.

[44]Thomas Cobb to Howell Cobb, 6 April 1852, Howell Cobb Collection. Day's bid was ten cents less than the governor was authorized to pay under the Act of 1852. *Acts of the General Assembly*, 1851-1852, p. 253.

[45]Thomas Cobb to Howell Cobb, 11 May 1852, Howell Cobb Collection.

[46]*Southern Banner*, 13 January 1853; *Acts of the General Assembly*, 1853-1854, p. 153.

governor, he emphatically repeated that Thomas and Howell Cobb "did steal the money."[47] This was a gross fabrication. Cobb had foreseen the possibility of a delay as early as January 1852, and had tried to fend against it. Though hardly responsible for Ray's personal plight or for weaknesses in the Act of 1836, he and his brother were vulnerable to criticism, more vulnerable indeed than a dead printer or an old law of which few outside of governmental circles were aware.

Because ugly accusations of dishonesty were circulating and because the laws and journals had not appeared as promptly as the people had a right to expect, some sort of official explanation was necessary. It came, late in 1853, from the pen of Thomas Cobb, who dissected the Act of 1836, pinpointed abuses, and proposed remedies.

The state printer, in his opinion, was overpaid and insufficiently regulated. The "unhappy effect of this," he alleged, "has been to make the public printing an object of so much interest as to carry it away from the Capitol [sic] . . . to remote portions of the State." The upshot, as he predicted a year earlier, was,

> delay in the comparison of proofs with the records at Milledgeville and a corresponding delay in the distribution of the laws. So great was this during the past two years as to present the spectacle of a million of people subject for two entire year[s] to laws, which had never been published and distributed.[48]

Minor correctives would not suffice, Cobb contended. "I would recommend a thorough and radical change in this system," including expansion of gubernatorial powers to cope with irregularities, confinement of the public printing to Milledgeville, and a more realistic formula in determining the proper compensation for printers.[49]

While all but the last of these recommendations were incorporated in the governor's final message to the legislature in November 1853, only the first received legislative approval.[50] The idea of restricting the public

---

[47]Joseph J. Singleton to Howell Cobb, 5 January 1853, Howell Cobb Collection.

[48]Undated, unsigned document written by Thomas R. R. Cobb, ibid.

[49]Ibid.

[50]*Acts of the General Assembly*, 1853-1854, pp. 77-79. Another passage in the governor's message composed by Thomas Cobb called for the creation of an attorney general's office, but this was defeated in the house. *Georgia House Journal*, 1853-1854, pp. 27, 705-706.

printing to the captial was rejected on the ground that "it would be creating a monopoly at the Seat of Government which would alike be dangerous in precedent and unjust to the other presses of the State." [51]

With the expiration of his brother's term, Cobb's involvement in printing reform and also his services as compiler of the laws and journals came to an end. If he wished to remain in office, as some who were close to him seemed to think, he failed to communicate that fact to the new governor, Herschel V. Johnson, who appointed one John Rutherford to the post of compiler. Reputedly Cobb was incensed by what he deemed an intentional slight, and, so Johnson heard, "has made some animadversions susceptible of an interpretation which implicates me in blame." The governor regretted the misunderstanding. "At no time," he explained to Howell Cobb, "did I regard your brother as desiring the appointment, but on the contrary, supposed that he not only acquiesced in, but rather preferred Rutherford to have it. I am sorry that this matter has produced dissatisfaction."[52]

Cobb, it can be conjectured, would probably have refused the appointment had Johnson offered it. He had given up the spring term of court worth about $1,000 in business to compile the acts of 1851-1852 for a mere $800. The rewards of the office, in this instance a loss, hardly offset the worries that accompanied them. In any case Cobb was no longer forced to rely on petty governmental posts to make ends meet. He was now a highly regarded lawyer of solid means. Enormous profits derived from his *Digest*, an annual income from attorney's fees approximating $7,000, and a reporter's salary amounting to $1,000 a year provided a strong measure of financial security and not a few luxuries.

In the winter of 1851-1852 he invested $10,000 in state bonds as a kind of insurance policy for his family and, in the spring, purchased furniture in Charleston, South Carolina, for two octagonal shaped wings

---

[51]*Georgia House Journal*, 1852-1854, pp. 153-54. The merit of Cobb's recommendation was recognized by Governor Herschel V. Johnson. In November 1855, when the laws and journals were again published late, he urged the legislature to require "this work to be performed at the Seat of Government." His advice, like Cobb's, was ignored. Ibid., 1855-1856, pp. 24-25.

[52]Herschel V. Johnson to Howell Cobb, 4 March 1854, Howell Cobb Collection. Cobb, it was reported, was also angered by the removal of his brother-in-law, Williams Rutherford, Jr., as auditor of the state-owned Western and Atlantic Railroad. See also John B. Lamar to Howell Cobb, 16 January 1854, ibid.

which were added to each side of his house during the summer. The new wings coupled with white columns stood forth boldly against a dark colored background and gave the edifice such a striking appearance that John B. Lamar was inspired to remark: "It presents the most imposing front of any residence I know of in the state."[53] Cobb's other assets included seventeen slaves, 230 acres of land in Clarke County, town lots worth at least $9,000, two carriages, and a variety of additional property and investments valued for tax purposes at $21,000.[54]

A readiness to lend financial assistance to numerous relatives and friends was a reflection of his continuing prosperity in later years. In 1855 he assumed one-third of a large debt accumulated by his parents and, in the following year, advanced $500 to his sister to help in the construction of her new home. To his brother-in-law, John C. Whitner, he loaned a like sum, enabling him to buy part ownership in a dry goods firm in West Point, Georgia, and, when James A. Sledge bought the *Southern Banner* from Hopkins Holsey in 1853, Cobb put up a portion of the down payment.[55]

Cobb's affluence testified to his success as a courtroom attorney. "As a lawyer," commented the *Southern Banner*, "Mr. Cobb is second to no man in the South, and we doubt very much if the Union . . . can produce an abler advocate."[56] His reputation was enhanced, no doubt, by the publication of his *Digest* and the many volumes of *Georgia Reports*, but, in the eyes of his clients, it rested squarely on his ability to represent their interests effectively in court. According to the editor of the *Western Law Journal*, constant study, thorough knowledge of the law, "strict attention to business," and careful preparation of cases were the requisites of professional competence.[57] In every respect Cobb was qualified.

---

[53]John B. Lamar to John A. and Lamar Cobb, 15 June 1852, Howell Cobb Collection; Thomas Cobb to Howell Cobb, 18 April 1852, private possession of Dr. E. Merton Coulter; Mary Ann Cobb to Mrs. O. H. Prince, 13 July 1852, Jackson-Prince Papers.

[54]Clarke County, Georgia, "Tax Digest," 1852.

[55]Williams Rutherford, Jr. to Howell Cobb, 25 December 1855, Sarah R. Cobb to Mary Ann Cobb, 27 December 1856, Receipt signed by Williams Rutherford, Jr., March 1856, John B. Lamar to Howell Cobb, 9 May 1853, Thomas Cobb to Howell Cobb, 24 December 1855, John C. Whitner to Howell Cobb, 7 February 1856, James A. Sledge to Howell Cobb, 1 September 1856, Howell Cobb Collection; *Southern Banner*, 12 May 1853.

[56]*Southern Banner*, 11 December 1856.

[57]Charles M. Haar, ed., *The Golden Age of American Law* (New York: G. Braziller, 1965), pp. 51-55.

An aggressive courtroom orator and a clever legal tactician, Cobb combined forensic skill with a devasting style of cross-examination and underpinned all with sound and meticulously researched briefs. His fiery speeches and relentless interrogation of witnesses won praise from some but angered others. Infuriated by his verbal assaults, two men threatened him with violence in 1850, and in 1861 a witness could still vividly remember being savagely cross-examined by Cobb in a case occurring three years earlier.[58] Concerning his summation in defense of an accused murderer in 1855, the *Southern Banner* reported: "we have heard it pronounced by old and young, enthusiasts and dispassionate men, learned and travelled gentlemen, to have been the ablest and most powerful speech they ever listened to."[59] But, according to one local source, his "greatest intellectual effort" came in a hotly contested will case (*Martin v. Mitchell*) that stretched on for four years and was fought successfully all the way to the Georgia Supreme Court.[60] In short, it seems fair to conclude, in the words of Dr. E. Merton Coulter, that Cobb was "at the head of the bar throughout the state."[61]

Cobb's cases ranged in nature from petty theft to patricide and from individual small claims to major corporate causes. In the opening stages of a million dollar damage suit against the Blue Ridge Railroad company, he outmaneuvered two of South Carolina's finest lawyers, C. G. Memminger and J. J. Pettigrew, and, in the same case, skirted dangerously close to an improper suggestion when he advised his brother to work for the appointment of F. G. Moses to a federal judgeship. "If we should find it necessary to go into the Dist. Court of So[.] Ca[.] with our Blue Ridge RR Case," he wrote, "might it not be of service for the Judge *to feel* under some obligation to us?"[62]

---

[58]Thomas R. R. Cobb to Marion Cobb, 8 October 1861, Thomas R. R. Cobb Collection; Sarah Cobb to Howell Cobb, 25 February 1850, Howell Cobb Collection; *Southern Banner*, 21 August 1855, 21 August 1856, 30 September 1858.

[59]*Southern Banner*, 23 August 1855.

[60]*Southern Watchman*, 9 September 1858.

[61]E. Merton Coulter, "William D. Martin and the School He Endowed: Martin Institute," *The Georgia Historical Quarterly* 50 (June 1966): 141-47, contains a description of the *Martin v. Mitchell* will case. Hereinafter cited as, Coulter, "William D. Martin."

[62]Thomas Cobb to Howell Cobb, 9 May 1856, Howell Cobb Collection.

His efforts in the Blue Ridge case did not go unnoticed by his client, Anson Bangs and Company. "A letter from your brother furnished us with the gratifying intelligence that he has obtained an order against the Blue Ridge Rail Road Cos.," a spokesman for the company informed Howell Cobb.

> The Defendants asked further time, but the Court refused to grant it. . . . This under the circumstances cannot be other than a great advantage gained. . . . Through the great tact and energy of your brother . . . the South Carolina Nullifiers will be brought to their senses one of these days.[63]

Such was Cobb's prestige by 1856 that he could and did command large fees for his services, but no sum was too small to capture his attention. When a client offered to pay him twenty-five dollars, he declared: "I think he might be screwed up to $30."[64] On another occasion, after winning a long and difficult appeal, he reminded Alexander H. Stephens, his colleague in the case, that the "matter of fees . . . remains to be settled." Besides a $500 retainer already paid to each lawyer, Cobb suggested that the client "should pay liberally, and . . . that an additional $2,000 a piece is *as little* as we should take."[65] He received an even larger fee for his part in the previously mentioned Martin will case. In this instance legal fees ran to $12,485 of which his share was $3,350 or slightly more than one fourth of the total.[66]

In the long run, Cobb's most significant achievements were not his victories in the courtroom, but the preparation of multiple volumes of *Georgia Reports*, his *Digest*, and above all, a civil code, which encompassed, for the first time in American history, a relatively complete statement of the salient principles of common as well as statutory law.[67]

---

[63]A. Birdsall to Howell Cobb, 30 December 1856, "Bill of Complaints," 1856, ibid.

[64]Thomas Cobb to Linton Stephens, 5 December 1850, Alexander H. Stephens Manuscripts, Perkins Library, Duke University.

[65]Thomas Cobb to Alexander H. Stephens, 4 June 1860, Alexander H. Stephens Papers, Manuscripts Division, Library of Congress.

[66]Coulter, "William D. Martin," p. 147.

[67]Common law doctrines had been incorporated in the early penal codes of Georgia, but the substantive common law had never been included in any civil code in the United States prior to the adoption of the Georgia Code of 1863. Marion Smith, "The First Codification of the Substantive Common Law," *Tulane Law Review* 4 (February 1930): 178-89. Hereinafter cited as Smith, "First Codification." Albert B. Saye, *A Constitutional*

The legal profession, in most if not all of the states, had long debated whether it was either feasible or expedient to reduce the law, especially the common law, to the form of a code. Opponents of codification insisted that comprehensive codes were impossible to perfect, not to say unnecessary, impractical, and destructive of an effective, time-honored system based on "the hoarded wisdom of a thousand years." The "moment that the common law shall become the text of a positive code," they argued, "it will cease to be common law; it will be inflexible in its application, and subject to none of those implied and reasonable exceptions and modifications, which now constitute its peculiar character."[68]

Countering these objections, the proponents of reform asserted that it was "little short of an absurdity to declare, that, because no perfect laws can be made, therefore no laws would be made. Even the common law does not pretend, in the slightest degree, to be a perfect system." Granted that any legal system was bound to contain flaws, it was still possible, they contended, to codify common law doctrines and to do so without depriving them of flexibility. "Now, certainly," reported a Massachusetts code commission, "if a rule or doctrine of the common law exists in a determinate form or with a determinate certainty, it is capable of being expressed in the text of a Code." And once expressed, the report continued, it became a clear and positive guide for lawyers and a beginning point for judicial construction. "It will have a tendency to suppress useless and expensive litigation" and "will greatly abridge the labors of judges, as well as of the profession, . . . instead of imposing the necessity of constant researches through all the past annals of the law."[69]

The fight for codification spanned several decades and enlisted the support of numerous individuals, none of whom fought more vigorously and with more determination than David Dudley Field and Timothy Walker. Field spent a lifetime agitating for legal reform in New York,

---

History of Georgia 1732-1945 (Athens GA: University of Georgia Press, 1948), p. 246. Hereinafter cited as Saye, *Constitutional History.* Richard H. Clark, "The History of the First Georgia Code," *Georgia Bar Association Reports* 7 (May 1890):160. Hereinafter cited as Clark, "First Georgia Code." According to Surrency, "Law Reports," p. 60, greater labor and creativity were required of reporters in the nineteenth than in twentieth centuries.

[68]Haar, ed., *Golden Age of American Law*, p. 253.

[69]Ibid., pp. 251, 254, 256.

with only limited results in that state. Due to his efforts a procedural code was adopted in 1848, but the attempt "to reduce into a written and systematic code the whole body of law of the State" failed.[70]

In the meantime, influenced indirectly by the report of the Massachusetts code commission (headed interestingly enough by conservative Justice Joseph Story) and more immediately by the Massachusetts Practice Act of 1851, three states—Alabama, Maryland, and Tennessee—adopted codes of procedure, while several other states modeled reforms on the New York code. None of the various codes adopted prior to 1863 covered all facets of jurisprudence; therefore, none entirely satisfied the goal set by reformers such as Field and Timothy Walker, who advanced the cause of codification through the columns of the *Western Law Review*. What they wanted, and what Georgia had the distinction of being the first to provide, was a complete codification of the law, both substantive and adjective.

Georgia's accomplisments in legal reform during the "golden age of American law" were largely unappreciated outside the confines of the state. Noting this fact, Judge Joseph H. Lumpkin commented in a report to the legislature in 1849 that "New-York, which is supposed to have gone a whole bar's-length and more beyond any other State in the Union, in the work of progress and reform, is content to end pretty much where Georgia started, half a century ago."[71] Even with allowance for state pride, there was still much truth in what he said. As early as 1816, for example, Georgia had adopted a criminal code "the first of its kind in the country," containing both common and statute law, and this code was substantially revised in 1833 by a commission composed of Lumpkin, William Schley, and John A. Cuthbert.[72]

Nevertheless, as Lumpkin also noted, there was room for improve-

---

[70]Several so-called "Field codes" were completed by the close of the Civil War, but only one—the penal code—was ever adopted in New York, and that belatedly in 1881. Henry M. Field, *The Life of David Dudley Field* (New York: Charles Scribner's Sons, 1898), pp. 74-90; Allen Johnson and Dumas Malone, eds., *Dictionary of American Biography* (New York 1930), 3:359-62. For the movement as a whole see Charles Warren, *A History of the American Bar* (Boston: Little, Brown & Co., 1911), pp. 447-540.

[71]*Southern Recorder*, 4 December 1849.

[72]Erwin C. Surrency, "The First American Criminal Code: The Georgia Code of 1816," *The Georgia Historical Quarterly* 64 (Winter 1979):420-31; Clark, "First Georgia Code," p. 160; *Southern Banner*, 7 December 1833.

ment and hence he proposed mild reforms which involved retention of the existing civil and criminal code "in its fundamental features," but, as he put it, "to lop off only its excrescences, to winnow away the rottenness which the mildew of time has produced, and engraft on the main stock such new provisions as will accommodate the whole to the present state of society."[73] Thomas Cobb's new *Digest* had achieved the lopping, winnowing, and engrafting process that Lumpkin had in mind. "It was not, strictly speaking, a code, but," in the opinion of a former associate justice of the Georgia Supreme Court, "it was a code in embryo," which permitted "the practicing lawyer to find the controlling laws."[74] This conservative reform was considered sufficient by many Georgia judges and lawyers. "Any attempt at Codification will be a failure," Judge E. A. Nisbet had advised Cobb in 1849. "This was the mistake with Mr. Hotchkiss."[75]

Apparently Cobb held a somewhat similar view. In 1852, for instance, he doubted the practicability of future digests and seemed to feel that the biennial publication of the laws would meet the requirements of the people and the profession. There is nothing in the evidence to suggest that he ever envisioned the need for a general code embodying the whole of Georgia law until the idea was brought before the legislature by George Gordon of Chatham County.[76]

Impressed by the Alabama Code of 1852 and perhaps by the prolonged national debate on law reform, Gordon sponsored a bill in the lower house on 29 November 1858, calling for the codification of the laws of the state. The bill passed without opposition on 8 December, and was

---

[73] *Southern Recorder*, 4 December 1849.

[74] Bond Almand, "The Preparation and Adoption of the Code of 1863," *Georgia Bar Journal* 14 (1951-1952):164. Hereinafter cited as Almand, "Code of 1863."

[75] "Memorial," p. 3. See also Clark, "First Georgia Code," p. 150, in which the author, a contemporary of Nisbet, recalls that "Codes were deemed impracticable, to a particular extent impossible."

[76] *Southern Recorder*, 2 December 1858. Something of a minor controversy arose over who deserved credit for originating the idea of codification. William A. Lewis of Cumming, Georgia, claimed the honor in a letter to the *Southern Watchman*, whereupon his contention was immediately challenged. For this tempest in a teapot, see *Southern Watchman*, 30 December 1858, 6, 13 January 1859.

signed by Governor Joseph E. Brown on the following day.[77] It provided for three commissioners whose function would be,

> to prepare . . . a Code, which shall as near as practicable, embrace in a condensed form, the Laws of Georgia, whether derived from the Common Law, the Constitution of the State, the Statutes of the State, the Decisions of the Supreme Court, or the Statutes of England of force in this State; and shall be modeled, if practicable, upon the present Code of Alabama. Said Code shall be completed within twenty months from the passage of this Act; and shall . . . supercede [sic] all other laws and decisions.[78]

The next day, the legislature elected David Irwin, Iverson L. Harris, and Herschel V. Johnson as commissioners to codify the laws.[79] Convinced that the task was impossible within the time allotted, the latter two declined to serve, forcing Governor Brown to find replacements. On 7 January 1859, appointments were tendered to Thomas Cobb and Judge John Nichols. When Nichols also declined, Brown turned to Richard H. Clark, who accepted with alacrity. Cobb, on the other hand, dallied until near the end of the month before finally agreeing to take the post. As an inducement, Brown had indicated that the legislature would probably allow the commissioners extra time in which to complete the work, and in December 1859 it did so.[80] Thus, almost by accident and with no little persuasion was Thomas Cobb given the opportunity to take part in a

---

[77]*Georgia House Journal*, 1858, pp. 196, 218, 301; *Georgia Senate Journal*, 1858, pp. 277, 387-88, 405; *Acts of the General Assembly*, 1858, pp. 95-96.

[78]*Acts of the General Assembly*, 1858, pp. 95-96.

[79]*Georgia Senate Journal*, 1858, p. 443; *Georgia House Journal*, 1858, p. 348; *Southern Recorder*, 14 December 1858. The nominees were selected by party caucuses held the previous evening.

[80]The legislature also substantially increased the compensation of the commissioners, and Cobb promptly applied for his share. *Southern Recorder*, 20 December 1859; Thomas Cobb to Joseph E. Brown, 28 December 1859, Thomas R. R. Cobb Collection, Perkins Library, Duke University; *Georgia House Journal*, 1859, pp. 26, 438; *Georgia Senate Journal*, 1859, pp. 113, 162, 590; *Acts of the General Assembly*, 1859, p. 13; Joseph E. Brown to T. R. R. Cobb, 7 January 1859, Joseph Brown to George A. Gordon, 7 January 1859, Joseph Brown to R. H. Clark, 12 January 1859, Joseph Brown to Thomas Cobb, 14 January 1859, Joseph Brown to James J. Diamond, 31 January 1859, Joseph E. Brown Papers—Felix Hargrett Typescript, University of Georgia Libraries. Sketches of David Irwin and Richard H. Clark appear in Northen, ed., *Men of Mark*, 3:418, 505. For favorable mention of Cobb's appointment see *Southern Watchman*, 4 February 1859.

project of mammoth scope, for which he, more than any other, would receive credit.

In the early months of 1859, the commissioners met in Atlanta to formulate a plan of procedure. They decided at the outset that the intent of the Act of 1858 did not require a detailed statement of every conceivable law applicable to Georgia but rather a summary of "the great fundamental principles of our jurisprudence from whatsoever source derived, together with such Legislative enactments . . . , as [are] necessary and proper."[81] Where the legislature or the judiciary had pronounced unmistakably on a point of law, no change was to be made; otherwise, it was the duty of the commission to supply omissions, to resolve conflicting statutes and decisions, to clarify the laws and arrange them in appropriate chapters, in brief, "to reconcile, harmonize, render consistent the body of the Law, so as to give shape and order, system and efficiency, to the sometimes crude, and often ill expressed, sovereign will of the State."[82]

Agreeing upon a division of labor, the commissioners separated the general code into four component parts. The first part—"Political and Public Organization of the State"—was to be the work of Clark. Cobb was to prepare parts two and four, dealing with the "Civil Code" and "Penal Laws." Part three—"Code of Practice"—was the responsibility of Judge Irwin. It was further agreed that each commissioner would periodically submit portions of his manuscript to the others for suggestions and that a second meeting would be held when the project was completed to iron out differing interpretations.[83]

Cobb's assignment was simple in one respect and complicated in another. Part four, entitled "The Penal Laws," posed no problem whatever. It merely required the readoption of the Penal Code of 1833 with minor revisions. However, long deliberation, much ingenuity, and no little learning were necessary in the preparation of the "Civil Code," for it demanded the careful selection and concise restatement of substantive common law doctrines, the codification of which represented the unique feature of the Georgia Code.

Cobb was chosen by his colleagues to draft the "Civil Code" because of

---

[81]R. H. Clark, T. R. R. Cobb, D. Irwin, codifiers, *The Code of the State of Georgia* (Atlanta: John H. Seals, 1861), p. iii.

[82]Ibid., p. viii.

[83]Ibid., p. iv; Clark, "First Georgia Code," p. 144.

his intimate knowledge of the leading legal source books, and, from these authorities, he drew the basic principles of common law.[84] His task was analogous to the decision making processes of 19th century American jurists. According to Dean Roscoe Pound, "judges simply put the guinea stamp of the state's authority upon propositions which they found worked out for them in advance. Their creative work was often a work of intelligent selection." Thus, Cobb's labors were not so creative as intelligently selective.[85]

Selecting the proper law for inclusion in the Code was by no means an easy matter. Dozens of volumes of legal tomes had to be consulted and many crucial decisions made. Some laws were abolished outright, and, in a number of instances, where common law concepts appeared outmoded or unjust, Cobb substituted civil law doctrines. At least once a new law, making seduction a criminal offense, was introduced.[86]

When the commissioners met again at the Atlanta Hotel in August 1860, the seduction law generated a discussion about the penalty to be imposed. Cobb, the father of several daughters, manifested an inordinate interest in the question and apparently wished to coerce the seducer by law to marry his victim. A prison sentence would allow the seducer to "pose as a hero through the bars of the jail," he argued, "and would become the admiration of other enterprising young men, who would not object to being behind bars themselves, for an exploit that would so much distinguish them."[87] Unswayed by this specious argument, Clark took

---

[84]Richard H. Clark, *Memoirs of Judge Richard H. Clark*, ed. Lollie Belle Wylie (Atlanta: Franklin Printing and Publishing Co., 1898), p. 395. Hereinafter cited as Clark, *Memoirs*.

[85]Roscoe Pound, *The Formative Era of American Law* (Boston: Little, Brown & Co., 1938), p. 138. Referring to Cobb's part of the general code, Pound wrote that it was composed "of extracts from the ordinary text books of the common law in use in the United States at the time." Moreover, "Such a thing could not have been done without the text books. Indeed, there are gaps in that code exactly where there were gaps in the text book legal literature of the time. Courts not infrequently wrote opinions out of the text books exactly as the Georgia code commission made a code out of them." Ibid., pp. 151-53. Hereinafter cited as Pound, *Formative Era*.

[86]For specific examples see Smith, "First Codification," pp. 184-189; Almand, "Code of 1863," p. 167; Clark, "First Georgia Code," pp. 158-59. Almand incorrectly credits Cobb with modifying a common law rule relating to evidence. This change was made by David Irwin.

[87]Clark, "First Georgia Code," p. 158.

exception to the proposed punishment. The issue was finally compromised by giving the seducer a choice between a *bona fide* offer of marriage or a stiff term in prison.[88] This attempt to legislate morality was typical of Cobb, who later tried to push a bill through the Confederate Congress prohibiting the delivery of mail on Sunday.

Working day and night for nearly a week, the commissioners reached agreement on all but three of more than 5,000 code sections. A decision on these three was held in abeyance until October 1860, at which time the entire code was to be presented to a joint legislative committee for review and revision. Elected in the winter of 1859, this committee was to meet with the commissioners at least twenty days prior to the opening of the next legislature.[89]

Cobb arrived in Milledgeville early in October 1860, for a third and final conference with his colleagues before the joint legislative committee convened. "I am up again before breakfast," he wrote to his wife on the eleventh. "All the day yesterday and until a late bed-hour we were hard at work preparing for the committee. They organized yesterday afternoon and we are able to meet them this morning at 8 1/2 o'clock."[90] Only eight of the original fifteen committeemen were present at the first meeting, and never more than nine attended the remaining sessions, which lasted until 17 October. One unnamed member, Cobb complained to his wife, "will give us a vast amount of trouble. He is worse than ever as *I am told* he is drinking again. If you knew what a conceited ass he was sober you might imagine what a troublesome fool he would be drunk, but my duty is plain, I should discharge it and leave the result to God."[91]

For the next two weeks, his duty consisted largely of reading his part of the general code and joining debates on disputed sections. Criticisms were thoroughly aired and all proposed amendments were accepted or rejected by a majority vote. When the last section received the committee's stamp of approval, the commissioners distributed copies of the table of contents to legislators and to various newspapers and presented the manuscript code to Governor Brown for his inspection. Favorably

---

[88]*Code of Georgia*, pp. 549, 827.

[89]Ibid., p. v.

[90]Thomas Cobb to Marion Cobb, 11 October 1860, Thomas R. R. Cobb Collection, University of Georgia Libraries.

[91]Ibid.

impressed, the governor recommended immediate adoption of the code and added that defects, if any, could be corrected by later legislation.[92]

On 12 November 1860, Hines Holt, chairman of the joint committee, submitted a report to the legislature. It lauded the efforts of the codification commission, reiterated Brown's recommendation, and, by implication, singled out Cobb's part of the code for special mention. This code, the report stated,

> so entirely extensive in its aims and purposes as to define in intelligible form . . . out of the body . . . of the common law, . . . , mischiefs and rights, duties and obligations, and to present in intimate and close connection therewith, Constitution and Statutory provisions, . . . , is of rare, if not in the code, now presented, of original occurence.[93]

The report concluded with the suggestion that the commissioners be retained to compile an index and supervise the publication of the project.

On 19 December, an act declaring the *Code of the State of Georgia* "hereby adopted" and "to be of force . . . on the first of January, 1862," was approved; and, the following day, a second act, authorizing the commissioners to index and publish the *Code* likewise passed.[94]

Finding it inconvenient to participate in this stage of the work, Clark requested Irwin and Cobb to assume the full burden. They consented and the latter immediately sketched out his ideas about printing to the Governor.[95] Before anything further could be done Georgia seceded from the Union. In March 1861, the secession convention resolved that the *Code* must conform to the laws and constitution of the Confederacy. Since extensive revision was necessary, the date of publication had to be

---

[92]*Southern Banner*, 1 November 1860; *Georgia House Journal*, 1860, p. 31.

[93]*Georgia Senate Journal*, 1860, p. 65.

[94]*Acts of the General Assembly*, 1860, pp. 24-25. The legislature amended the *Code* slightly in several respects. For instance, all laws enacted during the current session were added to the *Code*, and state laws, "having reference to the city of Savannah, &c., as codified by order of the City Council of Savannah . . . ," were also included. A provision in the Act of 20 December 1860, granting the governor and the commissioners the power to award a contract to publish the *Code*, offended state printers, Boughton, Nisbet, and Barnes, who insisted that official printing of any description was rightfully theirs. Feeling cheated, they tried unsuccessfully to influence Thomas Cobb through his brother. See Boughton, Nisbet, and Barnes to Howell Cobb, 19 December 1860, Howell Cobb Collection.

[95]Thomas Cobb to Joseph E. Brown, 25 December [1860], Telamon Cuyler Collection.

postponed. Caught up in the secession movement, involved in the formation of the Confederate Government, and then engaged in raising a force to fight in the Civil War, Cobb had precious little time to devote to the *Code.* Nonetheless he offered valuable suggestions and assisted Judge Irwin in making necessary changes through April 1861.[96]

In the end, however, Irwin, with the help of his son-in-law, George N. Lester, a member of the 1860 joint committee, completed the assignment. After innumerable delays, the *Georgia Code* was finally published in 1862 to take effect on 1 January 1863, twenty days, coincidentally, after Thomas Cobb was killed at the battle of Fredericksburg.[97]

Cobb's reputation as an outstanding legal mind rests ultimately on his contribution to the *Georgia Code.* His skill in court, of course, brought some fame and considerable fortune; his *Digest* and *Reports* of the decisions of the state Supreme Court were timely and of immense utility to the profession; but his role in the codification of Georgia law was the key to the praise showered upon him by posterity. Eventually, the names of his collaborators were almost forgotten, and the *Georgia Code* was often spoken of as Cobb's *Code.* Resenting this fact, Clark recorded in his *Memoirs*: "It is not necessary to the reputation of General Cobb to give him the entire credit of the code, and it is an injustice to his" fellow commissioners.[98]

The tendency to identify the *Code* with Cobb extended even to its flaws. The work, asserted Linton Stephens, "is pretty full of . . . Tom Cobb's characteristics," especially his "propensity to regulate everything in the world (and in the next too) by rules of his own fabrication. It is a great . . . *forbearance* that the book does not prescribe rules to govern the chamber maids in the manner of carrying out the piss-pots." Despite his criticism that "Excessive legislation is the chief fault of the book," Stephens was forced to admit that the *Code* was "not . . . so bad as I expected" and noted further that Judge Charles J. Jenkins, one of the few

---

[96]David Irwin to Joseph E. Brown, 12 February, 25 April 1861, ibid.

[97]*Code of Georgia*, pp. iv-v, ix-x; Grice, *Bench and Bar*, p. 305. A new state constitution was promulgated shortly after the adoption of the *Code* rendering portions of the latter inapplicable. See Linton Stephens to Alexander H. Stephens 22 January 1863, Stephens Correspondence, University of North Carolina Library.

[98]Clark, *Memoirs*, pp. 396-97.

jurists who had read the work even half way through, "had pronounced it excellent."[99]

The *Georgia Code* was indisputably a cooperative endeavor, with each commissioner contributing a major part and passing on the work of others. If it "stood the test time," as various Georgia jurists have claimed, it was only because the parts of the whole were equally well done. Yet even Clark, at his moodiest, was willing to admit that Cobb deserved first honor among the commissioners, that his share of the work demanded the most learning, and that he succeeded admirably in the novel task of codifying substantive common law principles—a first in American legal history.[100]

Undeniably, Cobb left his imprint on the jurisprudence of Georgia. Throughout his life and for years afterward his legal publications were in general use, and his singular contribution to the *Georgia Code* served, Pound tells us, as "an authoritative text book of the common law at a time when many questions remained unsettled in that jurisdiction and libraries in which to find the materials for passing upon them were not generally at hand."[101]

By the end of the decade Cobb had reached the zenith of his career. His reputation at the bar was fixed and his proficiency as a reporter and codifier of state law was widely recognized. As one might expect, his earning power and property holdings kept pace with his professional growth. The aggregate value of his property had nearly tripled since 1852 and his income was substantial enough to permit five long northern tours in the fifties (1852, 1853, 1856, 1858, 1859) with stops at posh watering places in Virginia and at first class hotels such as the Girard House in Philadelphia and the Astor House in New York. As a man of considerable means he gave large dinner parties, contributed generously to religious

---

[99]Linton Stephens to Alexander H. Stephens, 4 January 1863, Stephens Correspondence, University of North Carolina Library.

[100]Clark, *Memoirs*, pp. 396-97. Writing half a century later, Associate Justice Bond Almand declared: ". . . the present code is nothing more than the code of 1863, with the addition of the enacted laws of force in 1933, with only slight modifications." Almand, "Code of 1863," p. 170. "It is certain," wrote a member of the Atlanta Bar in 1930, "That the Georgia code of 1861 has been carried forward with few changes into every subsequent code." Smith, "First Codification," pp. 188-89. See also Grice, *Bench and Bar*, p. 303.

[101]Pound, *Formative Era*, p. 151. Despite this statement Pound was a critic of 19th century codes, which he deemed premature. The *Georgia Code* was no exception. "It is not

and civic enterprises, collected an impressive personal library, and rode about town in a carriage driven by Jesse, one of his twenty-three slaves.[102]

It would be a gross distortion, however, to portray Cobb as some sort of snobbish aristocrat riding to hounds, holding lavish balls, disdaining those who made money in trade, and taking his leisure at fashionable resorts simply for the fun of it. For all his affluence, Cobb was never a spendthrift; he had little leisure time, displayed a puritanical attitude toward frivolous entertainment such as dancing and cards, traveled for his wife's health rather than for pleasure, and had several relatives, including his younger brother, who depended on the mercantile business for their livelihood. Although Cobb indisputably belonged to the Georgia elite, he managed to maintain constant contact with the common people through the practice of law, through political support for his brother whose constituency was composed primarily of small, nonslaveholding farmers, and through participation in revivals. In truth, Cobb was more a representative of the middle and lower classes than of the planter aristocracy, and his values were those of the average southern evangelical.

---

a code in the modern sense," he asserted. And again, "Georgia adopted a civil code, such as it was, on the eve of the Civil War. California adopted Field's draft codes. In a comparison of abstract systems the common law is at its worst."

[102]Clarke County, "Tax Digests," 1857, 1858, 1859, 1860. The total value of Cobb's property fluctuated in these years, but the average was $104,489, including town property, slaves, household goods, and rural acreage. Cobb was but one of many southerners of his social rank to travel in the North during the antebellum period. See John Hope Franklin, *A Southern Odyssey. Travelers in the Antebellum North* (Baton Rouge: Louisiana State University Press, 1976).

CHAPTER 3

Southern Evangelical

Portraits of Thomas R. R. Cobb's parents,
John Addison Cobb and Sarah Robinson Cobb
(courtesy of Mr. Milton Leathers of Athens GA)

Thomas Cobb had a deep and abiding concern for religion, a religion that was typically southern evangelical in nature and inseparably linked to moral reform and a defense of slavery. In many respects it complemented his study of the law; both relied heavily on textual authority, rules, and form; both dealt with human behavior and purported to offer certain punishment for iniquity; both attempted to impose system and order on society; and both could be slanted by an able sophist, such as Cobb, to suit almost any purpose, sometimes the same purpose—for example, a defense of slavery. But, if religion and the law were compatible, they were also contradictory in some ways. The study and practice of law was essentially an intellectual process, demanding a logical, businesslike approach. Evangelical religion, on the other hand, was rooted in emotion. It derogated reason while stressing faith, and it denied the value of material gain and earthly glory, the end product of Cobb's legal striving.

In common with other southern evangelicals, Cobb suffered through a traumatic religious transformation that permanently colored his outlook on life. The conversion experience, according to Anne C. Loveland,

> always involved a conviction of sinfulness leading to feelings of despair and resignation which then gave way to a lifting of the burden of guilt and a feeling of acceptance by God. In most cases such religious experience was the outgrowth of Christian nurture, of a

> cultural context in which religious values and exercises were accepted and practiced.[1]

Conversion was followed in fairly rapid order by church membership, anxiety about the salvation of family members and others, absorption in religious affairs, endless soul-searching to determine one's fitness to continue God's work, and ultimately, for some, the ministry.[2] Cobb's experience fit the general pattern perfectly. He was nurtured by a devout Baptist mother and was educated under the sway of Dr. Alonzo Church, a Presbyterian clergyman, who taught him moral philosophy and evidences of Christianity, from which courses Cobb may have distilled ideas for one of his subsequent essays on religion.[3] Soon after graduation from Franklin College he fell under the influence of his future wife and father-in-law, both of whom were staunch Old School Presbyterians, and their gentle coaxing was, no doubt, the decisive factor in his ultimate choice of denominations.

Despite his early religious bent and despite regular attendance at the First Presbyterian Church, Cobb failed for several years to experience an inner conviction of sufficient strength to warrant a profession of faith. There had been hope in the fall of 1846, during a revival that engulfed the community, that he might be saved, but, though profoundly affected and reputedly "a changed man," he was not swept within the pale of grace for another two years.[4] When the great event finally happened in 1848, again during a revival, his mother rejoiced:

> My own dear Tom . . . has been in an anxious state of mind for some time. . . . I never saw any one [sic] suffer so except his father. . . . He went up to be prayed for several days and nights without getting relief, till Saturday week at night meeting he found peace. . . . Oh, my dear Sister, never did my poor heart feel so filled up with love and praise to God, when I heard my child burst out in singing and praising God. I shouted aloud. . . .[5]

---

[1]Loveland, *Southern Evangelicals p. 4.*

[2]Ibid., pp. 4-16.

[3]Thomas Cobb to editors of the New York *Observer*, 6 September 1859, Gratz Collection. For an example of Cobb's early religious inclinations, see his impromptu remarks on the subject of God's creativity in "Minutes of the Phi Kappa Society," 11 March 1843.

[4]Sarah R. Cobb to Mary Ann Cobb, 21 September 1846, Howell Cobb Collection; Sarah R. Cobb to Martha Jackson, 22 October, 9 November 1846, Jackson-Prince Papers.

[5]Sarah R. Cobb to Martha Jackson, 4 September 1848, Jackson-Prince Papers. A

Cobb formally joined the Presbyterian Church on 3 September 1848, and immediately set about trying to convert his brothers and sisters. For a short period he even contemplated entering the ministry, but, probably out of deference to the material welfare of his family and because he already had a profession, he dropped the idea of becoming a clergyman and, instead, plunged headlong into a welter of religious, benevolent, and moral reform enterprises.[6]

Southern evangelicals usually espoused some type of temperance reform. In the 1840s they supported the Washingtonian and Sons of Temperance movements but in the 1850s their enthusiasm for secular temperance organizations tended to wane. "Presbyterians were particularly apprehensive," explains Anne Loveland, "because temperance reformers seemed to place too much reliance on temperance societies, pledges, and legal action to promote moral reformation" and too little on the agency of religion. "Thus . . . the chief means of advancing the cause of temperance," at least in the minds of some southern Presbyterian divines, "was the conversion of individuals to religion rather than the formation of voluntary associations for reform."[7]

Cobb's affiliation with the institutional aspects of the temperance movement was fleeting and peripheral. He spoke at a large Washingtonian rally in Athens in 1843, was elected a delegate to the state convention of the Georgia Temperance Society in 1854, and his reputation as a temperance advocate was apparently well enough known in certain circles by 1859 for John H. Seals, editor of the *Georgia Literary and*

---

minister who was visiting Athens at the time later recalled that the young lawyer was profoundly moved. "Such was his ardent nature," stated the clergyman, "that he was made to feel most deeply his sinfulness. . . ." *Southern Banner*, 11 February 1863. Samuel S. Hill, Jr., *The South and North in American Religion* (Athens GA: The University of Georgia Press, 1980), p. 32 argues that southern Presbyterians were exceptions to the "emotional experience of conversion." If Cobb is any example, Hill's conclusion requires qualification.

[6]Sarah R. Cobb to Martha Jackson, 4 September 1848, Jackson-Prince Collection Loveland, *Southern Evangelicals*, p. 6, notes that "Conviction of sin—the feeling which initiated the religious experience—generally occurred between the mid-teens and early twenties," usually before young evangelicals had settled upon an occupation. The ministry, therefore, allowed them to combine religion with a livelihood. Cobb, however, was twenty-five at the time of his conversion and had been practicing law for six years. Although the ministry was appealing, he simply could not afford to abandon his profession.

[7]Loveland, *Southern Evangelicals*, pp. 144, 155.

Temperance Crusader, to include his name as one of the contributing authors for a projected new illustrated version of that journal.[8] Barring these minor activities, however, he appears to have done little or nothing for temperance societies per se. The reason for his lack of involvement can only be guessed at. Perhaps he agreed with fellow southern evangelicals that individual religious conversion was the proper cure for intemperance, or perhaps he felt, as did his father-in-law, that the movement was becoming too ultra in its aims. Judge Lumpkin, himself a believer in legal as well as moral suasion, was alarmed at the proposal to enact in Georgia a coercive law similar to that of Maine. In a public letter declining reelection as president of the state temperance convention in 1854, he advised the delegates to "disclaim, . . . if you would ever secure success at the *South*, any . . . intention to enact the *Maine* Liquor Law, or any other upon this subject, which will authorize the *searching for, or seizure, confiscation and destruction of private property*."[9] Such a law probably smacked of abolitionism to Lumpkin and Cobb, who may have concluded that if one type of property could be confiscated so could another with the inevitable result being the destruction of slavery.[10]

Whatever the reason, after 1854 Cobb took no further official part in the temperance movement; and, even though he continued to condemn strong drink as the curse of mankind, he never embraced an extreme teetotaler position. At Christmas he allowed his slaves a little toddy and, during the Civil War, dispensed a modicum of whiskey to his troops to fortify their health and morale. For his own use a very occasional glass of wine was not altogether unwelcome. A gift of wine from his sister-in-law, for instance, was cordially received but was evidently rationed out slowly.

---

[8]*Southern Banner*, 13 July 1843, 15 June 1854; John H. Seals to Alexander H. Stephens, 17 October 1859, Stephens Papers. It was Seal's belief that the paucity of illustrations was "the only reason why Southern papers are so far behind those of the North in popularity and circulation," and he proposed to rectify the shortcoming. This hint at southern patriotism would have struck a responsive chord in Thomas Cobb, whose southern nationalism was, by 1859, more pronounced than his activity in temperance causes.

[9]*Southern Banner*, 29 June 1854.

[10]H. A. Scomp, *King Alcohol in the Realm of King Cotton. Or a History of the Liquor Traffic and of the Temperance Movement in Georgia from 1733 to 1887* (N.P.: Press of the Blakely Printing Company, 1888), p. 494, suggests that slavery was a factor in Judge Lumpkin's thinking.

"It will last me . . . a long time," he scribbled in a note of thanks. "Though a *strong* Calvinist, I do not need the *strong* drink old Calvin did."[11]

Cobb's interest in reform did not begin and end with temperance. Throughout the latter half of the 1850s he led a vigorous campaign for the improvement of educational opportunities at every level—from common schools and female academies to the Lumpkin Law School and Franklin College—with an eye toward safeguarding the morals of youth and the values of southern society. In addition he spoke out against desecration of the Sabbath, going so far as to sponsor a bill in 1861 to prohibit Sunday mail delivery; participated in the formation of a local chapter of the Young Men's Christian Association, serving as one of the vice presidents; and threw himself wholeheartedly into all matters pertaining to the Presbyterian Church, including its controversies.

One such controversy took place in the spring of 1854 when a year-old conflict between the uptown and downtown members over the proper location for a new house of worship surfaced publicly. The former faction, to which Cobb and Judge Lumpkin belonged, favored construction near the fashionable Cobbham section of Athens, whereas the downtowners preferred to build anew on the old site. In May, when the downtown leaders met, somewhat surreptitiously it seems, and collected $4,400 to forward their design, Cobb promptly held a counter meeting at his home and the following day personally raised $5,000 ($1,000 of which came from his own pocket) to promote the uptown plan.[12] His vigorous response had its reward. The congregation approved the site he desired and in 1856 a new church was completed within easy walking distance of his house.

Recognizing his leadership ability, the Presbyterian hierarchy offered to make him an elder in January 1855.[13]. Apparently surprised by the nomination but highly honored, Cobb was reluctant to accept the

---

[11]Thomas Cobb to Mary Ann Cobb, [June 1855], Howell Cobb Collection. Cobb was here alluding to a newspaper anecdote claiming that John Calvin required nearly two hundred gallons of wine quarterly for himself and family. *Southern Banner*, 14 June 1855.

[12]*Southern Banner*, 19 May 1853, 18 May 1854; Mary Ann Cobb to John B. Lamar, 19 May 1854, Howell Cobb Collection; Sarah R. Cobb to Sarah M. R. Prince, 21 May 1854, Jackson-Prince Papers.

[13]William L. Mitchell to T. R. R. Cobb, 24 January 1855, William Letcher Mitchell Papers, Southern Historical Collection, University of North Carolina, Chapel Hill NC.

position partly because he felt unworthy. "I have often feared," he confessed, "that I brought discredit . . . on my profession of Religion."[14] In the end, of course, he consented to serve and became, more than ever, a force to be reckoned with in the affairs of the church.

Cobb's religious sentiments did not reach their full intensity until the winter of 1857-1858, when a crushing personal tragedy brought out the zealot in him. During a scarlet fever epidemic in the fall of 1857, his daughters contracted the disease. On the morning of 14 October, Lucy, the eldest, died.[15] There had been deaths in the family before. Cobb had buried infant sons in 1851 and 1853, his favorite aunt had died in 1853, and his father had succumbed to cancer in 1855; but none of these grieved him as did the death of his thirteen-year-old daughter. "I never saw any one as much distressed as Uncle Tom is," observed a nephew on the day of the funeral.[16] Nor did Cobb ever fully recover from his grief. Four years later he could still be found privately shedding tears and writing anguished poems to her memory.

To cope with his sorrow, Cobb turned instinctively to religion. He informed his elder brother that "were it not for the hope of a Resurrection through Jesus when I shall again fold in my arms my first born and I fear best loved child, I know not what my poor brain would do." The "death of my precious Lucy has made me nestle closer to my Saviour's feet. . . . My heart had wandered far away. Even the future of my sweet child had made me covet fame, place and wealth. God spoke and how puerile do they all appear."[17]

Remembering his brother's skepticism and wishing to overcome it, he added: "you have confidence in me about many things. You ask my advice and sometimes follow it. Then take my word there is a reality in

---

[14]Thomas Cobb to William Mitchell, 26 May 1855, Thomas R. R. Cobb Collection.

[15]Frank Lumpkin to Howell Cobb, 14 October 1857, Howell Cobb Collection. Lucy Cobb had a premonition of her death and reflected it in a poem to her parents entitled "Death." S. R. Cobb to Mary Ann Cobb, 23 November 1857, ibid.

[16]John A. Cobb to John B. Lamar, 15 October 1857, ibid. The previous day he had written: "It goes very hard with Uncle Tom as he thought more of Cousin Lucy than the rest of his children." John A. Cobb to Mary Ann Cobb, 14 October 1857, ibid.

[17]Thomas Cobb to Howell Cobb, 4 November 1857, ibid. In this passage Cobb was expressing a key southern evangelical characteristic: a sense of alienation from worldly affairs. On this point see Loveland, *Southern Evangelicals*, pp. 93-95.

the religion of the Cross. . . . Believe me, today, I would rather see you an humble follower of Jesus than President of the United States."[18]

This marked the beginning of Cobb's career as a self-appointed apostle. Thereafter he was bent upon regenerating every unconverted individual in the vicinity of Athens. The Prayer Meeting Revival of 1858 afforded him a broad field in which to test his talent for saving souls. The techniques of this nationwide revival differed little from those of previous decades. Lay leadership, avoidance of sectarian doctrines, and union (nondenominational) prayer meetings were among its chief characteristics.

Theologically, the revival was an outgrowth of the Second Great Awakening (1795-1835), which had produced a new divinity in keeping with the democratic tone of the age.[19] Exponents of the new divinity claimed that man was capable of resisting sin by his own volition. Deploring the fatalism inherent in Calvinistic dogma, with its emphasis on the utter depravity of man and his total dependence on God, they insisted that man need not wait passively for a miracle to experience conversion. On the contrary, he might choose of his own free will between sin and salvation. They also held the view that religion was basically quite simple. It should not be complicated by weighty sermons on abstruse theological points. Instead, it ought to be made comprehensible to the average intellect. By ignoring sectarian differences and minimizing the metaphysical aspects of religion, advocates of the new divinity hoped to promote Christian unity and appeal to the emotions of the individual. By 1858 their beliefs had become orthodox and their methods firmly entrenched. Even Old School Presbyterians, who originally condemned the new divinity as heretical, had adopted its terminology and techniques but not the doctrine of free will.[20]

---

[18]Thomas Cobb to Howell Cobb, 4 November 1857, Howell Cobb Collection.

[19]William G. McLoughlin, Jr., *Modern Revivalism: Charles Grandison Finney to Billy Graham* (New York: The Ronald Press, 1959), pp. 10-11, 99-100, 162-63; Timothy L. Smith, *Revivalism and Social Reform in Mid-Nineteenth Century America* (New York: Abingdon Press, 1957), pp. 45-62.

[20]Loveland, *Southern Evangelicals*, p. 162, argues that the "new divinity" was never accepted in the South. The religious conduct of those Baptists, Methodists, and Old School Presbyterians of Cobb's persuasion living in and around Athens, Georgia, would seem to belie her contention. To practice Finney's theology did not mean that one would necessarily adopt the radical reforms urged by some of his disciples. Indeed, as one authority on

In Athens the Revival of 1858 followed the national pattern. Union prayer meetings were held daily in the law office of Cobb's brother-in-law, William W. Lumpkin. The Union Evening Bible Class was founded under a set of rules which stipulated: "That no subject of a denominational or sectarian character, or calculated to offend the prejudices of any, shall be introduced or discussed." And at night, prayer meetings were conducted by lay leaders in the Methodist Church and in the Demosthenian Hall of Franklin College. When the crowds became too large for these places, other churches opened their doors to relieve the pressure.[21]

Cobb was at the center of the revival activity. He led evening prayer meetings, exhorted individuals in private, and was the mainstay of the Presbyterian Sunday School, which he reorganized and rejuvenated. "Tom has been filled with love and zeal," reported his sister, "and has been instrumental in doing much good."[22]

A great deal of Cobb's proselyting was aimed at the youth of Athens, and it began in the bosom of his own family circle where daily prayer and Bible reading were encouraged, where the unregenerated were entreated, and where religion was presented as a thing of love and peace rather than fear and damnation. "Most obvious among the purposes of family religion," writes Donald Mathews, "was its nurturing children so that when they came to adulthood they would be susceptible to conversion."[23] To guide children in the right direction became Cobb's mission in life. "If I had only known thirty years ago what I feel now," he lamented,

---

Finney has recently written: "The new-light theology and moral-reform message articulated by Finney differed only in emphasis from the revival spirit of the South and New England." William G. McLoughlin, *Revivals, Awakenings, and Reform. An Essay on Religion and Social Change in America, 1607-1977* (Chicago: University of Chicago Press, 1978), p. 130. Hereinafter cited as McLoughlin, *Revivals, Awakenings, and Reform.*

[21] *Southern Banner* 6 May, 9 September, 8 April 1858; S. R. Cobb to Howell and Mary Ann Cobb, 6 April 1858, John A. Cobb to John B. Lamar, 14 April 1858, Howell Cobb Collection.

[22] Laura Rutherford to Mary Ann Cobb, 23 April 1858, Howell Cobb Collection; A. L. Hull, "A Historical Sketch of the Sunday-School of the Presbyterian Church, of Athens," records of the First Presbyterian Church, Athens GA. In espousing Christian unity as opposed to narrow sectarianism, Cobb was following in the footsteps of his father-in-law who had urged interdenominationalism many years before. See Joseph H. Lumpkin to Robert J. Breckinridge, 18 November 1839, Robert J. Breckinridge Papers, Manuscript Division, Library of Congress, Washington DC.

[23] Mathews, *Religion in the Old South*, p. 99.

> it seems to me I could have prayed to God to enable me to dedicate myself to his [sic] service like Samuel of old. Now if I could only persuade . . . *all* of the little ones . . . to resolve . . . to be like Samuel . . ., loving and serving God from early youth, I should feel as if I had done a greater work than if I had conquered an army or discovered a new world.[24]

He converted his nephew in April 1858, after the two had prayed together for two hours beside the grave of his daughter.[25] Another nephew, John A. Cobb, proved more obstinate. "Johnny has attended . . . few of the meetings," he told the boy's mother. "I have tried to get him to my house to talk with him, but he will not come."[26] There were others who seemed, at least to an enthusiast like Cobb, to be deaf to the pleas and warnings of their elders.

"How many there are still out of the pale of the blessed communion," he exclaimed in alarm to Elder William Mitchell. "My dear Brother, are we and our Brother Teachers faithful enough? Why is it that so many still remain out of the ark of safety?"[27] Again, in more vivid terms, he expressed anxiety over the spiritual recalcitrance of young Presbyterians:

> Have their hearts received . . . the first coating of iron which the evil one forges out of mercy spurned and convictions disregarded? Are the vaults of Hell resounding with the demoniac laughter of spirits damned, rejoicing . . . at the prospect of welcoming to their own misery spirits who might have dwelt in the region of [God]?[28]

He prayed this would not be the case, but "should one or another be taken away, and no . . . ray of hope brighten the dark tomb, we must not murmur for *God reigns*."[29]

Cobb's adherence to Calvinistic doctrine was unmistakable: mankind was degraded by vice, and God was the sovereign all-powerful ruler of the

---

[24]Thomas Cobb to William L. Mitchell, 11 July 1858, Thomas R. R. Cobb Collection.

[25]S. R. Cobb to Howell and Mary Ann Cobb, 6 April 1858, Howell Cobb Collection.

[26]Thomas Cobb to Mary Ann Cobb, 9 April 1858, ibid.

[27]Thomas Cobb to William L. Mitchell, 20 June 1858, Thomas R. R. Cobb Collection.

[28]Thomas Cobb to William L. Mitchell, [1858], ibid.

[29]Ibid. Besides working with young people, Cobb joined his fellow superintendent William L. Mitchell in organizing a Sunday school class for adult men and prevailed upon Joseph Jones, son of the Reverend Charles C. Jones, Jr., to help coordinate it. See Robert Manson Myers, ed., *The Children of Pride. A True Story of Georgia and the Civil War* (New Haven: Yale University Press, 1972), pp. 392-93.

universe, whose will was so absolute "that not a sparrow falls to the ground without His consent."[30] Yet, within this predestinarian framework, he perceived a function for the revivalist, which was to teach sinners "how to act when they hear the voice of God at the door of their hearts."[31] Employing the language, methods, and emotionalism of the new divinity, he tried to indoctrinate unrepentant relatives and neighbors in the meaning of Christianity to prepare them for the divine call.

The ultimate design of the Christian religion, as Cobb conceived it, was to harmonize the imperfections of man with the perfection of an infinitely good and merciful God. A reconciliation was possible only if man experienced a "new birth," that is, a change of heart. Since man alone was incapable of purifying his own heart, God provided a means to that end. Operating indirectly, perhaps through the agency of a revivalist, God infused the human heart with a love of Christ, whose suffering had atoned for man's sins. In exchange for this benevolence, Cobb continued, God expected man to have faith in Christ as his personal Savior. Real faith, in turn, required a feeling of depravity followed by a realization that divine assistance was needed to surmount it.

Thus, as Cobb explained it, regeneration was a drawn-out process, which began with an admission of sin and a faith in redemption through Christ. The consequence of faith was a love of God. Converted by God's love, the heart was cleansed of corruption, for averred Cobb, "how can pride, envy, hatred[,] malice or any other wicked passion exist in a heart full of love to God and love to our neighbors."[32] The final result of all this was a spiritual transformation, the "new birth," which made man fit for salvation.

Cobb's religious conceptions were emotionally inspired, ambiguous, and decidedly unintellectual. Believing that the means to salvation "must be . . . *comprehended* by every man of *every grade of intellect*," he avoided complex theological questions.[33] Since consistency and clarity of thought

---

[30]Thomas Cobb to Howell Cobb, 4 November 1857, 30 November 1858, Howell Cobb Collection.

[31]Thomas Cobb to William L. Mitchell, 11 July 1858, Thomas R. R. Cobb Collection.

[32]Thomas Cobb to Howell Cobb, 8 September 1858, Howell Cobb Collection. The resemblance between the theology of Cobb and Finney is unmistakable. Compare the foregoing account of Cobb's views with the analysis of Finney's in McLoughlin, *Revivals, Awakenings, and Reform*, pp. 124-29.

[33]Thomas Cobb to Howell Cobb, 30 November 1858, Howell Cobb Collection.

were less important to his purpose than the stimulation of religious feelings, he seldom tried to resolve apparent contradictions. Hence, in one breath he postulated an omnipotent and omniscient deity who determined all things and in the next spoke as though man were free to choose his eternal destiny. Faith, then, not logic, was the key to Cobb's religion. Simply "Believe and be saved."[34]

In Athens, during the spring of 1858, many did profess their faith and were reportedly saved. "The Religious Revival... continues," proclaimed the *Southern Banner*, "and a spirit of deep, earnest interest in spiritual matters, is... increasing in our community. Accessions have been made to the different churches during the past week."[35] In April, as the religious enthusiasm mounted, Cobb departed Athens on the first leg of a long journey which led to New Orleans, then up the Mississippi River to St. Louis, and finally eastward to Washington, Philadelphia, New York, and resorts in Virginia. The trip, lasting three months, was undertaken primarily to restore the health of his wife, but it was made to serve religious purposes whenever and wherever possible. Along the route he visited numerous Sunday schools, noting their size, facilities, rituals, and methods of instruction. He also wrote frequently to the children of the Athens Presbyterian Sunday school and ordered books for their use and instruction. Attending a conference of Sunday school teachers in Philadelphia, he learned that it was customary in many of the churches to hold special Sunday afternoon prayer meetings for the teachers and their pupils. "Could we not do something of this kind in our school?" he inquired in one of his weekly letters to Elder William Mitchell.[36]

Earlier in his travels, Cobb served as an unofficial representative of the Hopewell Presbytery at the annual General Assembly of the Presbyterian Church, which met in New Orleans in May.[37] Encountering a group of delegates on the way to the conference, he was impressed with

---

[34]Thomas Cobb to Howell Cobb, 8 September 1858, ibid.

[35]*Southern Banner*, 8 April 1858.

[36]Thomas Cobb to William L. Mitchell, 20 June 1858, Thomas R. R. Cobb Collection. See also Thomas Cobb to pupils, 4 July 1858, records of the First Presbyterian Church, Athens, Georgia.

[37]*Minutes of the General Assembly of the Presbyterian Church in the United States of America with An Appendix* (Philadelphia: Presbyterian Board of Publication, 1858) 15:260, 267. Hereinafter cited as *Minutes of the General Assembly.*

their piety and delighted to hear their narratives of "the wonderful work God was doing all over the land." On the boat from Montgomery to Marion, Alabama, he related to Mitchell, "the songs of Praise and the earnest prayer of Faith were heard above the noise of the steam and the whistle where they were never heard before."[38]

After this New Orleans seemed unspeakably sinful. Righteously indignant, he again wrote to Mitchell:

> I have never had my religious feeling so shocked as this day, seeing the utter disregard to the Sabbath. . . . The streets are crowded with carriages and omnibuses, the shops are all open, the people busy in traffic, and every now and then, a procession of some society, starting off on a pleasure excursion . . . , pass[es] in front of this Hotel. Great placards were on the streets announcing a grand balloon ascension this afternoon and also a theatre, a circus and an opera besides sundry balls tonight, and a race over the race course this evening. I have heard often of the desecration of the Sabbath in this city, but I had no adequate conception of it.[39]

Having witnessed such sights, Cobb could not resist warning a class of Sunday school children at Dr. Benjamin M. Palmer's Presbyterian Church of the temptations that surrounded them. As he spoke band music blared through the window. Dispensing with propriety, he compared the city to Sodom and Gomorrah, though to do so was admittedly "not perhaps in good taste."[40]

Leaving New Orleans in mid-May, Cobb steeled himself for sordid scenes of rowdiness, gambling, and drunkenness aboard the Mississippi steamer *John Simond*. He was therefore pleasantly surprised to find "not . . . a gaming table, a pack of cards, or a drunken man on this River" after three days of travel.[41] But, two months later at Rock Alum Springs, Virginia, a place recommended by several doctors for the alleged curative effect of the water, his pious sensibilities were once more offended. Although friendly and well-mannered, the guests spent their time play-

---

[38]Thomas Cobb to William L. Mitchell, 2 May 1858, Thomas R. R. Cobb Collection.

[39]Thomas Cobb to William L. Mitchell, 9 May 1858, ibid.

[40]Ibid. At the risk of redundancy it should be stressed that Cobb's disgust with Sabbath desecration was a typical southern evangelical reaction and not simply an eccentric, moralistic priggery of his own.

[41]Thomas Cobb to William L. Mitchell, 20 May 1858, ibid.

ing cards and billiards, bowling, and dancing. These amusements, wrote Cobb, "are very distasteful to us. . . . Hence we join in none of th[e] sports and would not remain except in the hope of health[.]"[42]

Neither Rock Alum nor a brief stay at White Sulphur Springs did much to improve the health of his wife. Ending his sojourn in Virginia on 21 July, he returned to Athens on the twenty-fifth, and quickly resumed his role as the town's leading lay revivalist. During court week in late August and early September, he assisted local ministers in promoting revivals in Walton, Jackson, and other counties in the circuit. His preaching "charmed and delighted everybody," according to William G. Delony, a lawyer and fellow townsman, who expressed the opinion that "the Presbyterians ought to make an exception to their rule and give Cobb a license to preach and he will wake up all this upcountry."[43]

Simultaneously Cobb launched a four month campaign to convert his brother, who was then serving in Buchanan's cabinet. "I have reproached myself," he wrote to the secretary of the treasury on 8 September,

> that for the many days I was with you during the past months I cannot remem[ber] a single pressing personal appeal that I made to you on the subject of your own salvation. The truth is that, as my elder brother, I have always looked up to you and reverenced you and I believe I could approach the Presidency himself with less hesitancy to urge upon him his soul's salvation than I can you.[44]

Notwithstanding this hesitancy, he repeatedly belabored his brother with long religious communications. "You must know," he persisted, "that if I am sincere in my own belief . . . I cannot rest easy while you deny the Savior."[45]

Although religious excitement in Athens abated somewhat from time to time, Cobb's zeal remained constant. In June 1859, during a period of renewed spiritual awakening, his sister-in-law remarked that "Tom is the moving spirit in all. He is deeply engaged in the work of converting

---

[42]Thomas Cobb to Sarah R. Cobb, 12 July 1858, Jackson Scrapbook.

[43]W. G. Delony to Rosa Delony, 19 August 1858, William G. Delony Collection, University of Georgia Libraries.

[44]Thomas Cobb to Howell Cobb, 8 September 1858, Howell Cobb Collection. See also Thomas Cobb to Howell Cobb, 2 September 1858, ibid.

[45]Thomas Cobb to Howell Cobb, 8 October 1858, private possession of Dr. E. Merton Coulter.

souls. One night last week he and Cousin James [Jackson] became so happy they *shouted*, as is reported."[46] Besides lending vitality to the union prayer meetings and to the affairs of the Presbyterian Church and Sunday school, Cobb was often called upon to settle disputes among the members of his denomination. As a peacemaker, his efforts did not always meet with success. Such was the case in the spring and summer of 1859, when a comic opera quarrel developed between Mrs. Elizabeth Craig, the daughter of Dr. Alonzo Church, president of Franklin College, and Dr. E. A. Wurm, organist of the First Presbyterian Church.

Elizabeth Craig had been a widow since 1852. She was a beautiful woman, strong willed and socially prominent. Her circle of acquaintances included some of the foremost politicians of both parties, among them Alexander H. Stephens, Howell Cobb, and President James Buchanan, at whose invitation she lived for a time at the White House. When in Athens, which was seldom, Mrs. Craig attended the Presbyterian Church, where she was looked upon as the prima donna of the choir. A fine vocalist, she had been instrumental in raising the subscription to purchase the church organ, but the responsibility for hiring Wurm as the organist belonged to the board of trustees, of which Cobb was an influential member.

Wurm's playing apparently left a great deal to be desired, and it suffered even more by comparison with the melodious performances of Morris Steinert, who, though Jewish, had been recently employed by the Episcopal Church.[47] After hearing both Wurm and Steinert, Mrs. Craig became openly and rudely critical of the abilities of the former and, without consulting the trustees, offered the latter nearly twice what he was receiving from the Episcopalians to play for the Presbyterians. Deeply chagrined, Wurm resigned.

At this juncture the trustees, led by Thomas Cobb, intervened. Refusing to honor Mrs. Craig's arrangement with Steinert, they pointed out that Wurm had been retained for a year and still had six months left

---

[46]Mary Ann Cobb to Howell Cobb, 15 June 1859, Howell Cobb Collection. See also M. P. Pope to Father, 7 June 1859, Col. David C. Barrow Papers, University of Georgia Libraries.

[47]Steinert also tuned and repaired pianos and gave private lessons on various instruments including the melodeon, guitar, violin, and violoncello. *Southern Banner*, 22 July 1858.

before his contract expired. In retaliation, Mrs. Craig persuaded the choir to strike. Unless Steinert performed, she announced, the choir would sit with the rest of the congregation and be silent. The trustees were equally adamant: either Wurm played or no one would, and the choir could do as it pleased. On the following Sunday, the choir loft was empty, and, since Dr. Wurm would not withdraw his resignation, the organ was closed.[48]

By now the Presbyterian congregation had divided into factions, one supporting Mrs. Craig and the other Thomas Cobb and the trustees. "It is an ugly business all around," wrote the wife of Howell Cobb, "and has excited more bitterness than has existed here for many years."[49] Hoping to avoid the unpleasantness, many members of the church maintained a studied neutrality, and the most non-committal of all was the minister, Dr. Nathan Hoyt, whose only solution to the problem was the admonition to "Pray—Pray all the time." Since the pastor had abdicated leadership, Cobb took it upon himself to approach Mrs. Craig in an effort to restore harmony. A letter to the widow stressing the need for Christian forbearance and three long conversations were totally unavailing. The "organic derangements," reported a visitor to the Presbyterian Church, "are far from being settled."[50]

Word of the local cause célèbre, laughingly styled "The Craig and Cobb War" by those not directly involved, soon reached the ears of President Buchanan, who pronounced himself an ally of Mrs. Craig. "I have never seen him in a higher glee," commented a member of the treasury department.[51] The situation may have seemed humorous to the president, but to Thomas Cobb it was a serious matter which went beyond the immediate issue of organ music. To begin with, Elizabeth Craig subsequently used her influence in an attempt to defeat a plan to reorganize Franklin College, a plan which Cobb favored and which she attributed primarily to him. Her utter hostility to the scheme strongly suggests lingering rancor over the organ episode. Secondly, the organ controversy revealed latent discontent with Cobb's broad and sometimes officious

---

[48]Mary Ann Cobb to Howell Cobb, 20 May 1859, Howell Cobb Collection.

[49]Mary Ann Cobb to Howell Cobb, 2 June 1859, ibid.

[50]R. M. Johnston to Linton Stephens, 14 June 1859, Stephens Papers, Library of Congress.

[51]P. L. Clayton to Howell Cobb, 6 August 1859, Howell Cobb Collection.

management of church affairs. His wife was so upset by the frequency of the complaints that she implored him "to give up . . . everything and let her have some peace and quiet."[52]

For the sake of his wife's health, which was still bad, and because he had no wish to be the cause of further friction and disunity in the church, Cobb resigned his trusteeship and, toward the end of June, left with his family for Montvale, Tennessee. The trip was of short duration. Finding the place hot and dull, the Cobbs traveled to a resort area in Montgomery County, Virginia, where they intended to remain for several weeks. "I have here," wrote Cobb, "what I [s]eldom have at home, leisure."[53] He was not to enjoy it long.

From Washington, D. C., came the distressing news that the youngest son of Joseph T. Lumpkin, his brother-in-law, was critically ill with scarlet fever. "We have received Telegraphic Despatches every day from Howell informing us of his condition," Cobb notified his mother.

> This morning the news is that he is extrem[ely] ill and the result doubtful[.] Marion and her Mother feel that it is their duty to go to poor Joe's relief[.] It is very unfortunate f[or] Marion. I hoped she w[as] improving and I fear th[e] trip to Washington wi[ll] do her no good and ma[y] do her harm. But a[ll] things are directed by ou[r] Heavenly Father.[54]

Leaving Montgomery County, Virginia, the Cobbs arrived in Washington on 19 July. Eight days later Lumpkin's son died. The vacation trip thus ended even more depressingly than it had begun.

On 30 July, Cobb was forced to return to Georgia in order to meet the August term of court. Back in Athens, he was soon absorbed in work—legal, educational, and religious. As his sister-in-law had noted perceptively a month or so before: "He suffers in mind still about Lucy and its his business alone that saves him from despair."[55]

Four months after his return from Washington, D. C., Cobb received an unsolicited assignment from the Presbyterian Synod of Georgia. At its second session in Jacksonville, Florida, on 3 December 1859, the Snyod

---

[52]Mary Ann Cobb to Howell Cobb, 27 June 1859, ibid.

[53]Thomas Cobb to Sarah R. Cobb, 10 July 1859, Jackson Scrapbook.

[54]Thomas Cobb to Sarah R. Cobb, 17 July 1859, ibid.

[55]Mary Ann Cobb to Howell Cobb, 27 June 1859, Howell Cobb Collection.

elected the Reverend Joseph C. Stiles as a synodical evangelist "to labor among our feeble and destitute churches . . . , and, also, as far as opportunity offers, among all our churches, wherever the Providence of God may open the door."[56] A committee was appointed to fix the rate of compensation for these services, and a second committee composed of five representatives from each of the various presbyteries was selected to raise the necessary funds. Cobb was one of the five chosen from the Hopewell Presbytery.[57]

Stiles worked among the "feeble and destitute churches" of the Synod of Georgia for about five months before arriving in Athens. He appeared in late July 1860, and his evangelical activity during August and September revived the religious interest of the whole community. Meetings were held in the Presbyterian and Baptist churches, and, at Cobb's request, the Phi Kappa Hall was opened for worship.[58] "Dr. Stiles is received as an Apostle by all our people and almost all the Christian Brethren," Cobb reported to a ministerial friend. "His labors are blest everywhere. May God sustain him."[59]

Ironically, the Presbyterians benefited less from Stiles' evangelizing than did some of the other denominations. This was especially true in the rural areas outside Athens. "Our own denomination is receiving some accessions," wrote Cobb, but "the great in-gatherings are made by our Baptist and Methodist Brethren." Far from begrudging them these converts, he exclaimed: "Thank God that Souls are being saved!" Then, in a different tone, he added:

> I have almost despaired of ever enlarging *our* borders among our rural population unless there is a radical change in our Church

---

[56]*Minutes of the Synod of Georgia at their Fifteenth Annual Session* (Atlanta: Franklin Painting House, 1859), p. 8. Hereinafter cited as *Synod Minutes*.

[57]Ibid., p. 9. Earlier that year the General Assembly of the Church had selected Cobb, among others, to attend the "third centennial celebration of the Presbyterian reformation in Great Britain, in 1860." *Southern Watchman*, 16 June 1859.

[58]*Southern Watchman*, 6 September 1860; M. A. Lamar to Aunt, 5 September [1860], Howell Cobb Collection; "Minutes of the Phi Kappa Society," 8 September 1860; M. J. Randolph to Cousin, 2 October 1860, Edward Harden Manuscripts, Perkins Library, Duke University.

[59]Thomas Cobb to R. K. Porter, 24 August 1860, Charles Colcock Jones, collector, *Autograph Letters and Portraits of Signers of the Constitution of the Confederate States*, Perkins Library, Duke University. During this period Cobb continued to conduct prayer meetings in towns where his law practice took him.

> Economy. What hope is there of this while our ministers and people are so wedded to the old? I try to comfort myself with the idea that God knows best the mission of our Church and will overrule even our errors to His Glory. But . . . my heart sometimes yearns for a wider field of usefulness for my beloved Church.[60]

The conservatism of which he complained manifested itself at the next synodical meeting, held in Columbus, Georgia, in November 1860. At this session, the delegates voted to terminate Stiles' mission.[61] Anxious to retain the evangelist for another year, Cobb was enraged at the action of the synod and blamed it on the envy of a few self-centered ministers. Church members, elders, deacons, and most clergymen, he declared to Stiles, "appreciated and were willing . . . to continue your services. I am ashamed to own, my dear Sir, that there were even *a few* Ministers who did not."

Since the synod would not continue Stiles' employment, Cobb was determined that the Hopewell Presbytery should do so. This presbytery "needs and wants your services," he wrote. "The salary and double of it can be raised easily. The question is, Will you come and labor with us?"[62] Stiles's response to this invitation is not extant, but it must have been negative. Secession excitement already gripped the South, overshadowing all else and causing revivalism to fade in the vicinity of Clarke County. The cause of disunion also captured the full attention of Thomas Cobb, who imbued it with a religious significance akin to revivals. In fact, the two movements were intimately related in his mind. He deemed both to be holy crusades called forth by God and perpetuated by faithful Christians of all denominations. Nor was he alone in this conviction. Throughout the South secession was justified on moral and religious as well as political and legal grounds.

Powerful and persuasive Old School Presbyterian divines, such as Dr. James H. Thornwell and Dr. Benjamin M. Palmer, were among the earliest and loudest advocates of secession, and many lesser ministers of the same denomination, such as Cobb's close friend R. K. Porter of Waynesboro, Georgia, preached sermons in support of disunion. They

---

[60]Ibid.

[61]*Synod Minutes*, 1860, p. 20.

[62]Thomas Cobb to Joseph C. Stiles, 11 December 1860, Joseph C. Stiles Correspondence, Henry E. Huntington Library, San Marino CA.

were joined by Methodists, Baptists, and Episcopalians.[63] Upon hearing that an overwhelming number of Methodist clergymen in Georgia were for immediate secession, Cobb told his sister-in-law that if he could "get the *women* and preachers to go with him" in the movement, no one else mattered.[64] "This revolution," he later asserted,

> has been accomplished mainly by the Churches. I do not undervalue the . . . politicians, still I am sure that our success is chiefly attributable to the support which they derived from the cooperation of the moral sentiment of the country. Without *that*, embodying as it obviously did the will of God, the enterprise would have been a failure.[65]

Secession, of course, was the end product of several decades of sectional tension. The Reverend James H. Thornwell "expressed the view of most southern evangelicals when," according to Anne Loveland, "he described the conflict between abolitionists and slaveholders as a conflict between 'Atheists, Socialists, Communists, Red Republicans, Jacobins on the one side, and the friends of order and regulated freedom on the other.' "[66] Cobb shared Thornwell's opinion about the nature of the dispute. By 1860 he had come to equate the northern masses with abolitionism, abolitionism with radical, madcap reform, and all three

---

[63]Lewis G. Vander Velde, *The Presbyterian Churches and the Federal Union 1861-1869* (Cambridge: Harvard University Press, 1932), pp. 27-31. Hereinafter cited as Vander Velde, *Presbyterian Churches.* T. Conn Bryan, *Confederate Georgia* (Athens: University of Georgia Press, 1953), pp. 231-33; H. Shelton Smith, *In His Image, But . . . Racism in Southern Religion, 1780-1910* (Durham NC: Duke University Press, 1972), pp. 166-88. Hereinafter cited as Smith, *In His Image.*

[64]Mary Ann Cobb to Howell Cobb, [9] December 1860, Howell Cobb Collection.

[65]*The Southern Presbyterian* (Columbia SC), 20 April 1861. Although unsigned, the authorship of this article has been ascribed to Cobb. See James W. Silver, *Confederate Morale and Church Propaganda* (1957; reprint ed., Gloucester, Mass.: Peter Smith, 1964), p. 93. Since the content and style of the article have all the earmarks of a Cobb written piece, I have accepted Silver's contention. Interestingly enough Cobb's hypothesis about the importance of the church in the secession movement is borne out by Silver, who writes: "The Church was the most powerful organization influencing the lives of men and women in the South in the days before and during the Confederacy. Clergymen led the way to secession. They were quite successful in helping the people to identify God, the right, and the destiny of history with slavery, the Confederacy, and the war. They established the certainty that the Lord was with his chosen people in victory and defeat. They were responsible for the association of religion with politics and war." See also Vander Velde, *Presbyterian Churches,* p. 31.

[66]Loveland, *Southern Evangelicals*, pp. 258-59.

with the Republican party. "Look at its leaders," he exclaimed in a speech to the Georgia legislature,

> the mad preachers, like Cheever and Beecher; the Fourierites, led by Greely [sic]; the Sewards and Summers, and Hales and Fred Douglas [sic]. Look at its cohorts, and see their mottled ranks—free negroes and bootblacks, coachmen and domestics, infidels and free-lovers, spiritual rappers and every other shade of mania and folly.[67]

What Cobb and Thornwell were manifesting in their rhetorical polarizations was an accumulation of years of disillusionment with the abolitionist and perfectionist tendencies of northern secular and evangelical reformers. Cobb and other southern evangelicals, as mentioned earlier, emphasized the reformation of the individual through religious means and conservative moral reform rather than the perfection of society. Their northern counterparts, on the other hand, pushed a whole host of social and economic programs, including the abolition of slavery, which sought basic societal changes. Such changes were perceived by southerners as a direct threat to their entire way of life, a threat not to be tolerated. Thus, while evangelicals in both sections had much in common, they parted company on two fundamentally related issues: slavery and the purpose of reform.[68]

Southern evangelicals reacted with particular indignation to the abolitionist charge that slaveholding was a sin. Finding this accusation utterly insupportable, they penned innumerable scriptural justifications for the peculiar institution. Cobb went beyond most evangelicals by publishing in 1858 a comprehensive treatise that defended slavery socially, economically, legally, historically, and scientifically as well as religiously.[69] One brief, derivative chapter entitled "Negro slavery

---

[67]Candler comp., *Confederate Records*, 1:171-72.

[68]McLoughlin, *Revivals, Awakenings, and Reform*, pp. 136-37; Loveland, *Southern Evangelicals*, pp. 161-62, 174; Drew Gilpin Faust, "Evangelicalism and the Meaning of the Proslavery Argument: The Reverend Thornton Stringfellow of Virginia," *The Virginia Magazine of History and Biography* 85 (January 1977), pp. 3-17. Hereinafter cited as Faust, "Evangelicalism and the Proslavery Argument."

[69]A good summary of the Biblical defense of slavery is in Smith, *In His Image*, pp. 129-37. Loveland, *Southern Evangelicals*, pp. 207-209, argues that a majority of southern evangelicals defended slavery but not as a positive good. If true, Cobb was decidedly in the minority. Cobb's proslavery argument will be considered in full in chapter five.

viewed in the light of Divine Revelation" was devoted to Biblical arguments. Drawing upon the customary passages from the Old and New Testaments (for example Genesis 9:25, Leviticus 25:44, 46; Luke 17:7-10, and 1 Corinthians 7:20-22), he attempted to prove that, far from being a sin, slavery was actually sanctioned by God. To the general assertion "that were the great principles of Christianity perfectly implanted in every heart, . . . the institution of slavery would end," Cobb replied that, on the contrary, neither slavery nor class distinctions would end but rather the need to enforce them.

> Revelation teaches us that God gave different gifts to different men. . . If every man in the community thoroughly appreciated his own gifts, and was therewith content, then each would, unbidden, assume that position in the scale of life to which his talent fitted him. The rulers would be pointed out of God; the subjects would rejoice to obey. The master would recognize a brother in his servant; while the servant would take pleasure in the service of his Lord. Nothing would be constraint. Everything would be free-will. Such is the Apostle's idea of the perfect law of liberty in Christ. . . . Such would be the glorious fruit of the complete triumph of the Gospel of Christ. In the present dispensation, it would seem that we need hardly expect it.[70]

Although the millennium was still a long way off, there was excellent reason, in Cobb's judgment, to be optimistic about the institution of slavery. It was, he argued, a positive good, one proof of which was the superior moral condition of American Negro slaves when compared to that of free blacks found anywhere in the world. In advancing a positive good theory, however, he never insisted that the institution was perfect. There were flaws in the system, he admitted, but these could be ameliorated and to that end he urged a variety of laws to protect slaves from abuse.

Cobb reflected southern evangelical thinking not only in recognizing blemishes in the system but in favoring religious instruction for blacks and in condemning efforts to reopen the African slave trade in the 1850s and 1860s. Practicing what he preached, he permitted his own slaves to read the Bible and to attend Sunday school and church. Clearly he adhered

---

[70]Cobb, *Law of Slavery*, pp. 63-64. For an interesting sidelight which places Cobb in a millennialist tradition see Jack P. Maddex, Jr., "Proslavery Millennialism: Social Eschatology in Antebellum Southern Calvinism," *American Quarterly* 31 (Spring 1979), pp. 46-62.

to what Donald Mathews calls the "evangelical slaveholding ethic."[71] The ethic dictated the creation of a religious and humane environment for slaves, but it could just as easily serve as a method of control. If slaves could be taught that Christianity meant submissiveness to the will of the master ("the Apostle's idea of the perfect law of liberty in Christ"), then the slave owner's lot would be happier and his benevolence rewarded. That a connection existed between the religious bearing of the slave and his obedience to authority was implicit in Cobb's description of the character of the American Negro. "He is superstitious and reverential," wrote Cobb,

> and consequently is very susceptible of religious impressions, exhibiting, in many individual instances, a degree of faith unsurpassed, and a Christian deportment free from blemish. He is passive and obedient, and consequently easily governed.[72]

Whether viewed as an agency of control or as a matter of moral uplift or both, the evangelical slaveholding ethic was not inspired, at least in Cobb's case, by a sense of guilt.[73] There was nothing in Cobb's upbringing or adult experience to convince him that slavery was intrinsically wrong. Indeed, the reverse was true. His parents and their closest kin had been model masters and mistresses. They were kind to their servants and invariably respectful of slave family relationships. "On my father's plantation," Cobb recollected, "an aged negro woman could call together more than one hundred of her lineal descendants. I saw this old negro dance at the wedding of her great granddaughter. She did no labor for my father for more than forty years before her death."[74] His mother, especially, became attached to her servants, and, even in the aftermath of the financial debacle of 1837-1841 when the family fortune was at a low ebb, she still stoutly resisted every suggestion that some of them be sold.

---

[71]Mathews, *Religion in the Old South*, pp. 167-84.

[72]Cobb, *Law of Slavery*, pp. 39-40. For the relationship between moral stewardship, social order, and control of blacks see Faust, "Evangelicalism and the Proslavery Argument," pp. 10-12.

[73]For the thesis that guilt was central to the proslavery stance of southerners see Charles G. Sellers, Jr., "The Travail of Slavery," in Sellers, ed., *The Southerner as American* (Chapel Hill: The University of North Carolina Press, 1960), chapter 3; Ralph E. Morrow, "The Proslavery Argument Revisited," *Mississippi Valley Historical Review* 48 (June 1961), pp. 79-94; Mathews, *Religion in the Old South*, pp. 173, 249.

[74]Cobb, *Law of Slavery*, p. cciii, footnote 1. John Addison Cobb's brother was also a

Following the family tradition, Cobb adopted a paternalistic attitude toward his slaves. He cared for their physical needs, calling in Dr. Crawford Long at the first sign of sickness; clothed them adequately (linsey-woolsey in the winter, lighter garments in the summer); and provided bountiful quantities of tasty food. Chicken, fish, pork, hoecake, light bread, and biscuits supplemented by possum meat, greens, potatoes, and other vegetables were regular fare. At Christmas "great sacks of apples, oranges, candy, and cake" were sent to the slave quarters, where parties, dancing, singing, and banjo picking livened up the night.[75]

Cobb's children developed an affection for some of the servants, referring to them as aunt and uncle, and were thrown in constant contact with slave youngsters living on the premises and next door at Judge Lumpkin's place. The intimate exposure of white children to the slave culture troubled Cobb a great deal. "A social evil of no small magnitude," he asserted,

> is the imbibing by children of the superstitions, fears, and habits, of the negroes, with whom they are necessarily, to some extent, reared. The negro is not yet more than semi-civilized. The marvellous and unearthly ghosts, witches, and charmings, are mingled even with religion. Great caution is necessary, on the part of the Southern mother, to protect the young children from such influences.[76]

For all his paternalism, Cobb never lost sight of the fact that slavery was an economic system, that blacks were held in bondage to make life

---

benevolent master. In his will he emancipated one faithful retainer, provided money and land for another, expressed confidence that his wife, Sarah Cobb's sister, would treat his slaves "with all that kindness with which I used them," and declared that "whenever any of my Negroes become old and unfit for labour that they be liberally supported from my Estate. . . . " Will of Major Howell Cobb, Jefferson County, Georgia, "Court of Ordinary, Wills," Book A.

[75]George P. Rawick, ed., *The American Slave: A Composite Autobiography. Georgia Narratives* (1941; second reprint ed., Westport CT: Greenwood Publishing Company, 1974), 12: 178-81. Hereinafter cited as *Georgia Narratives*. This work contains an interview with Susan Castle, a seventy-eight year old former slave of Thomas Cobb. Many details of her narrative have been corroborated from other sources lending credibility to the accuracy of her memory.

[76]Cobb, *Law of Slavery*, p. ccxx. Other southern evangelicals felt a similar concern. See Mathews, *Religion in the Old South*, p. 141. Cobb did not concoct his impression of black superstition out of the whole cloth. One of his own slaves recalled that adult blacks "used to tell de children dat when old folks died dey turned to witches. I ain't never seed no ghostes, but I sho' has felt 'em. Dey made de rabbitts jump over my grave. . . ." *Georgia*

easier for whites, and that discipline was necessary to maintain control of the institution. As a result he worked his servants from five in the morning until ten at night with little leisure time except after the noon meal on Sunday and at Christmas. He bought, sold, and hired out slaves to suit his needs; "to let a false tenderness for . . . negroes" bring financial ruin was, in his opinion, foolish.[77] Further, he refused to tolerate obstreperous or slothful behavior. Too much noise in the slave quarters was quickly squelched, verbal chastisement was commonplace, and light cuffing for minor breaches was not unknown. More serious offenses, such as wanton disobedience, were met with whipping and sale. When a female slave named Susan rebelled—attempting even to slap Cobb's face—he sold her along with four of her youngest children to a man who was reputed "to be good to his servants."[78]

Although opposed, as a rule, to the separation of families, Cobb felt that, at times, as in the case of Susan, circumstances forced slaveholders to act contrary to conscience. "To regulate properly this relation by legislation, so as to prevent inhumanity on the one hand, and not to bind too much the owner's power of selling an unworthy or unruly slave on the other," he acknowledged, "requires great sagacity and prudence."[79]

Cobb was able to manage his slaves strictly without incurring an excessive amount of overt resistance. He seems not to have been plagued by runaways, and, if the memory of one ex-slave can be trusted, his image among the servants was that of a "good" master. But, when away from home, the slaves took advantage of his absence to make life miserable for Marion. She nagged them, often to no avail, and was less popular than her husband. During the Civil War, the problem of slave contentiousness apparently became a serious problem for her. "Don't let the negroes

---

Narratives, 12:181. For evidence of mutual affection between the Cobb family and some of their slaves see *Southern Banner* 29 October 1857; Leonora Clayton to Mary Ann Cobb, 27 July 1856, Howell Cobb Collection.

[77]Thomas Cobb to Howell Cobb, 25 April 1846, Howell Cobb Collection; E. Merton Coulter, "Slavery and Freedom in Athens, Georgia, 1860-1866," *The Georgia Historical Quarterly*, 49 (September 1965): 268-69; *Georgia Narratives*, 12:180.

[78]Sarah Cobb to Sarah M. Jackson, 6 May 1847, Jackson-Prince Papers. The slave Susan, interestingly enough, was the grandmother of Susan Castle, whose recollections were included in *Georgia Narratives*.

[79]Cobb, *Law of Slavery*, p. ccxxi.

worry you," Cobb instructed her in 1861. "Put Billy out at Jack Ware's. I know he is troubling you. Throw off all petty annoyances." Two weeks later he again wrote: "How are the negroes behaving? Don't let them annoy you. Hire, sell, do anything to have quiet and peace at home."[80]

In the final analyses, Cobb's experience with the institution of slavery was not dissimilar from that of dozens of other slave owners. For instance, John A. Quitman of Mississippi, who owned four plantations and hundreds of slaves, had many of the same difficulties as Cobb and solved them in much the same way; also, like Cobb, he was able to reconcile his idyllic view of slavery with the reality of slave resistance and institutionalized abuses and hence felt no personal remorse over the continued operation of the system.[81]

Cobb was not an expansionist of Quitman's ilk, however, and in the fifties favored sectional compromise. Since he entertained no doubts whatever about the efficacy and essential rightness of slavery, he was perplexed by northern antislavery sentiment but believed that reason could prevail. Toward the close of the decade, he published articles in the northern press and a book, *The Law of Negro Slavery*, in an effort to make people in the North understand that the institution of slavery was not a horrible and un-Christian thing. When he failed to persuade them, he reacted aggressively. Concluding that abolitionist fanatics had captured the Northern mass mind, he cast off a lifetime of unionist devotion and assumed a leading role in the secession crusade. By 1860 he was the very epitome of a southern nationalist, opposed to compromise of any kind and eager for permanent independence.

Southern nationhood meant more to Cobb than political division; it meant separate religious institutions. Methodists and Baptists had long since broken with their northern brethren. Now it was the turn of the Old School Presbyterians to disunite. In June 1861 Cobb supported the move to withdraw the Synod of Georgia from further association with the

---

[80]Thomas Cobb to Marion Cobb, 14, 28 September 1861, Thomas R. R. Cobb Collection; *Georgia Narratives*, 12:179-80. For the difficulties of other southern women in handling slaves see Anne Firor Scott, *The Southern Lady From Pedestal to Politics 1830-1930* (Chicago: The University of Chicago Press, 1970), pp. 46-49. Hereinafter cited as Scott, *Southern Lady*.

[81]Robert E. May, "John A. Quitman and His Slaves: Reconciling Slave Resistance with the Proslavery Defense," *The Journal of Southern History*, 46 (November 1980): 551-70.

General Assembly of the Presbyterian Church because the Assembly had gone on record as upholding the Union. Then, in December 1861, he gave his blessing to the establishment of a separate General Assembly of the Presbyterian Church of the Confederate States of America, which published an "Address to all the Churches of Jesus Christ throughout the Earth," declaring that:

> Two nations, under any circumstances, except those of perfect homogeneousness, cannot be united in one church, without the rigid exclusion of all civil and secular questions from its halls. . . . Much more must this be the case where the nations are not simply rivals, but enemies—when they hate each other with a cruel hatred—when they are engaged in a ferocious and bloody war, and when the worst passions of human nature are stirred to their very depths.[82]

The movement for southern independence obviously necessitated not only new religious organizations but new political and legal structures—new state constitutions, law codes, and a southern national government. A key figure in the nation building process, Cobb saw it all as the handiwork of God and maintained that "every Christian should put his support of the Southern Government on the footing of obedience to God."[83]

With the outbreak of war, his attempt to define the Confederate cause as a religious crusade as well as a political movement became complete. Not only was the South the defender of the faith against the "hellish schemes of. . . . a set of devils . . . out of Hell," but, like some Homeric deity, God actually intervened, Cobb believed, to spare Confederate lives and ensure southern military successes. "God is our refuge a very present help in trouble," he wrote, paraphrasing the 46th psalm. "He has never yet deserted the righteous cause. He never will. . . . I can go to the cannon's mouth with that psalm on my lips."[84] Until the day of his death on the battlefield at Fredericksburg, Cobb clung to this conviction.

---

[82]Quoted in J. Treadwell Davis, "The Presbyterians and the Sectional Conflict," *The Southern Quarterly*, 8 (October 1960): 123-24; *Southern Banner* 19 June 1861.

[83]*Southern Presbyterian*, 20 April 1861.

[84]Thomas Cobb to Marion Cobb, 8 May 25, 27 July 1861, Thomas R. R. Cobb Collection.

CHAPTER 4

Educational Reformer

Top photograph: Lucy Cobb Institute, ca. 1865
Bottom photograph: Front drawing room of Lucy Cobb Institute

Thomas Cobb firmly believed that "Action is the command of God," and, in keeping with this commandment, he participated fully in the civic and religious affairs of the community. "His wife says that no enterprize is started, no quarrel or disturbance created, but Tom must have a finger [in it]," commented a sister-in-law. And, she agreed, "it is true he has *a finger* in everything going on in town. . . . But it is the life of the man, and his wife would be *unhappy* if he was not as *popular* as he is."[1]

Unfortunately, there was an officious quality to Cobb's involvement in local, and larger, matters that often proved irksome. His nephew hinted at this personality trait when he reported to his mother that he would attend a stockholders' meeting as proxy for his father "but of course will have to vote as Uncle Tom wants as he is determined on doing something with it and there is no use apposing [sic] him in this commun-

---

[1]Mary Ann Cobb to Howell Cobb, 27 June 1859, Howell Cobb Collection. Cobb's activities ranged from the sundry religious pursuits mentioned in the previous chapter to service as town warden (1848) and attorney (1849), president of the board of trustees of the Oconee Hill Cemetery, trustee of the Lucy Cobb Institute, and promoter and incorporator of the Equitable Life Insurance Company in Athens. On numerous occasions he was called upon to speak and to settle disputes. See ibid.; *Southern Banner* 13 October 1859, 11 October 1860; Hynds, *Antebellum Athens*, pp. 43, 46, 50, 116, 145, 154, 164.

ity."[2] Alluding to the same quirk, Linton Stephens summed up Cobb's character, or rather this one aspect of it, in a letter to his brother.

> Tom Cobb was very much of a yankee by nature, and the likeness was not stronger in any point than in his *meddlesomeness*—an itching to put his finger into everybody's pie, and an unhappiness when he couldn't get it in. Of all the men I ever knew I don't think of one who has or had a stronger conviction than he did that things went right only when he directed them.[3]

Nevertheless, Cobb got things done and, consequently, was very much in demand as a mover and shaker of events. His boundless energy and complete dedication to any cause he espoused made him a valuable ally. Even so strong a critic as Alexander H. Stephens was constrained to say of Cobb, shortly after the latter's death, that "He . . . did a great deal that will be useful. . . . and with all his characteristic faults I liked him more than I did the average of men of his class and sincerely regret his loss."[4]

During the last ten years of his life, few causes were more important to Cobb than education. By the 1850s southern schools and universities were dominated, Donald Mathews tells us, by evangelicals who "promised parents that their institutions taught and enforced a broad Evangelical morality" and who, "as responsible stewards of public order, social cohesiveness, and civic pride," were eager to educate their daughters as well as their sons.[5] Personal considerations, evangelical inspiration, civic duty, and sectional fear all converged at this point to force Cobb to the forefront of educational reform in Georgia and to intensify his nascent southern nationalism.

The father of three daughters in 1850, Cobb was vitally interested in their intellectual development, and, it was only natural, that his first endeavor in the field of education should have been on behalf of female education. In 1851 there were two girls' schools in Athens—Grove Hill Seminary, located on property owned by Cobb, and the Female Academy.

---

[2]Lamar Cobb to Mary Ann Cobb, 11 January 1860, Howell Cobb Collection.

[3]Linton Stephens to Alexander H. Stephens, 4 January 1863, Stephens Correspondence.

[4]Alexander H. Stephens to Linton Stephens, 16 January 1863, Stephens Correspondence.

[5]Mathews, *Religion in the Old South*, pp. 89, 119.

Neither school received much support from the residents of Athens, many of whom preferred to educate their daughters in larger institutions found elsewhere in the state, abroad, or in the North, where, complained the anonymous author of an article in the *Southern Banner*, "they have their feelings continually wounded with reflections upon their domestic institutions, or return home with minds half prejudiced against their native State."[6]

Cobb's children attended the seminary, and its survival depended primarily upon his patronage. He employed the instructors and personally guaranteed them a minimum income regardless of the amount raised by tuition fees.[7] Despite his generosity, teachers were difficult to retain. Grove Hill Seminary averaged a new instructor about every two years, and the same was true of the Female Academy. Occasionally, teachers left in the middle of a term, forcing both schools to suspend operations from time to time.

In 1852 a public spirited citizen called attention to this deplorable situation and pointedly asked: "Why is it that almost every teacher coming among us . . . becomes discouraged and leaves the place?"[8] A belated answer to his question came two years later. Instructors resigned, it was claimed, because "they were more annoyed by the whims and fancies of parents and children than they cared to put up with."[9] This allegation was true, perhaps, but the rapid turnover in teachers was symptomatic of a deeper problem which lay with the schools themselves.

"A Mother," reputedly the sister of Thomas Cobb, writing in the Athens newspapers, argued cogently that the course of study offered in the local schools was so shallow that young girls were "sent into the world at the age of fifteen or sixteen, with minds undisciplined and uninformed, to buffet with the cares and difficulties of life." Perceiving the inadequacy of the schools at home, many parents sent their daughters away to be educated, while others, she asserted, seemed merely apathetic. "For fifteen or twenty years has the cause of female education in Athens lain dormant," she declared.

---

[6]*Southern Banner*, 24 August 1854.

[7]Ibid., 29 May 1851, 28 May 1857.

[8]Ibid., 8 January 1852.

[9]Ibid., 7 September 1854.

> We . . . call upon . . . Athenians to awake from their lethargy. . . . Let vigorous measures be at once adopted to establish in our midst a school . . . of such reputation that those who came here to educate their sons, may at the same time educate their daughters. There are wealth and talent sufficient for the undertaking. We hope there are some with liberality and gallantry enough to begin the enterprise.[10]

Within a year the enterprise was initiated under the leadership of Thomas R. R. Cobb. On 9 April 1855, a joint stock company was organized for the purpose of "erecting and keeping in operation a Select Female High School in Athens with an appropriate Primary Department."[11] The articles of agreement required the sale of 150 shares of stock (at a par value of one hundred dollars each) before a stockholder's meeting could be called and before subscribers could be legally bound to redeem their pledges. Six days after the agreement was signed, Cobb already had solicited $10,000 in subscriptions and was confident that he could raise the additional $5,000 necessary to start the project officially.[12] Recognizing his preeminence in this endeavor, the stockholders at their first annual meeting elected him chairman of a five man board of trustees, which was "given absolute power over all the details of the Company to carry out its objects."[13]

In accord with this blanket authority, the trustees purchased eight acres of land on the Watkinsville Road (now Milledge Avenue) as a site

---

[10]Ibid., 24 August 1854. A. L. Hull, *Annals of Athens*, pp. 180-81, identifies the author of this article as Laura Rutherford, wife of Williams Rutherford, Jr., and further contends that Cobb responded to the plea for action without knowing that his sister was the "Mother" in question. It is highly improbable, however, that Cobb decided to act on the basis of one anonymous communication to the local newspapers. More likely his decision grew out of a general demand for improvement in female education and a desire to provide the best schooling possible for his daughters.

[11]The articles of agreement forming this company are in Phyllis J. Barrow, "A History of Lucy Cobb Institute" (Master's thesis, University of Georgia, 1951), appendix, p. 4. Hereinafter cited as Barrow, "History of Lucy Cobb."

[12]Sarah R. Cobb to Mary Ann Cobb, 14 April 1855, Howell Cobb Collection.

[13]Henry Hull, Jr., head of the Athens branch of the Bank of the State of Georgia, Stevens Thomas, president of the Bank of Athens, John H. Newton, well-to-do merchant, and Albon Chase, former editor of the *Southern Banner*, were the other trustees. In 1857, Dr. H. R. J. Long replaced Albon Chase on the board, and in 1860 Stevens Thomas surrendered his seat to B. F. Hardeman. Cobb continued to serve as chairman until his resignation in September 1861.

for the new institution. The site was selected, Cobb reported to the stockholders in May 1856, only "after a thorough inquiry and investigation."[14] Following his report, resolutions were adopted approving the action of the board and instructing its members to increase the total subscription to $20,000 by 1 July, on which date the trustees were "to proceed, forthwith, to execute their trust, with whatever subscription they may at that time have upon their books."[15]

Although the board of trustees received bids from contractors in the summer of 1856, actual construction did not begin until the spring of 1857, and yet another year passed before the Athens Female High School was finally completed.[16] The building—three stories high, with a veranda across the front and space inside for fifty female boarders plus teachers' quarters, classrooms, and a library—inspired the admiration of the town. "It is as perfect a thing of the kind as I ever laid eyes on," exclaimed one resident of Athens, "the blocking off and coloring is capital."[17] Very "spacious and handsome," observed the editor of the *Southern Banner*, who added: "With a new . . . Building, new Furniture, new apparatus, new Pianos, Harps, and with teachers of . . . experience and ability, we cannot but safely predict the realization of the hopes of the Patrons."[18]

Besides all else that was new, the Female High School had been given a new name and had taken on new meaning for Cobb. In March 1858, the trustees had proposed to honor his deceased daughter by calling the school Lucy Cobb Institute. "The suggestion . . . surprised me," Cobb responded, "but I must confess gratified me. I feel if thereby some memory of her virtues might be perpetuated in the community, even when my name is forgotten, I must yield."[19] Henceforth, he considered the Institute as a personal possession, a shrine to his dead daughter. "I am

---

[14]*Southern Banner*, 29 May 1856. The trustees also invested $800 in two lots belonging to Franklin College. "Minutes of the proceedings of the Prudential Committee of the Board of Trustees of Franklin College," 6 December 1855, 31 May 1856.

[15]*Southern Banner*, 29 May 1856.

[16]Ibid., 31 July 1856, 2 April 1857, 7 January, 26 August 1858.

[17]William White to T. R. R. Cobb, 5 July 1858, Howell Cobb Collection.

[18]*Southern Banner*, 3 June, 4 November 1858.

[19]Thomas Cobb to Dr. H. R. J. Long, 28 March 1858, Barrow, "History of Lucy Cobb," appendix, p. 3.

busy about my School," he informed his brother, "my pet, my darling's monument."[20]

The main task confronting the trustees between August and the end of October 1858, was the employment of a staff. Cobb had planned originally to teach in the Institute in order to perfect the education of his eldest daughter. Her death blighted this intention, but he was determined that only the most qualified instructors would be hired.[21]

By 14 October, the trustees had appointed a principal, R. M. Wright, formerly head of the Washington Female Seminary in Wilkes County, Georgia, an excellent choice, according to the Athens newspapers. The rest of the staff was selected during the ensuing three weeks, and to preclude possible charges of sectarianism, the appointments were apportioned among several orthodox Christian denominations.[22]

The last person to be employed, and the only one to whom there was any objection, was Dr. E. A. Wurm, whose services, it was reported, were obtained "at considerable trouble and expense."[23] Some of the Episcopalians were disappointed that Wurm was appointed to head the music department instead of their organist, Morris Steinert. Their complaints on this score, characterized as "quite a tempest in a tea pot" by Howell Cobb's wife, were a prelude to the "Craig-Cobb War" mentioned in the previous chapter.[24] At various times Cobb displayed anti-Semitic tendencies, and his extreme religious bias may, in this instance, have operated against Steinert, who, being Jewish, probably was not considered seriously for the position. In choosing Wurm, a Presbyterian, over Steinert, a Jew, the trustees had settled for less than the best talent available.[25]

---

[20]Thomas Cobb to Howell Cobb, [?] December 1858, Howell Cobb Collection.

[21]*Southern Banner*, 26 August 1858; *Southern Watchman*, 14 October 1858; Thomas Cobb to Sarah R. Cobb, 7 October 1858, Jackson Scrapbook.

[22]*Southern Banner*, 14 October 1858; *Southern Watchman*, 14 October 1858.

[23]*Southern Watchman*, 4 November 1858. Wurm's wife was employed at the same time to teach ornamental and needle work. Besides Wright and the Wurms, five other instructors had been hired. For a list of these see ibid., 23 December 1858; *Southern Banner*, 23 December 1858.

[24]Mary Ann Cobb to Howell Cobb, 24 May 1859, Howell Cobb Collection.

[25]The evidence for Steinert's superior abilities is derived from sources friendly to Cobb. Ibid.; Mary Ann Cobb to Howell Cobb, 2 June 1859, ibid.; *Southern Banner*, 30 September 1858.

More laudable was the decision to utilize guest lecturers as a regular part of the school's academic program. This feature was undoubtedly Cobb's idea. Elected to the Franklin College board of trustees on 7 November 1858, his first act was to request that professors be allowed to lecture at the Institute whenever their duties permitted. His motion carried, and a few weeks later the *Southern Banner* announced that, in addition to the college professors, a group of gentlemen had agreed to address the student body semi-monthly.[26]

Thus, by the last week in December, the trustees, having arranged for a series of lectures, hired a staff, planned a curriculum, and equipped a building, were finally ready to open the new school. On 10 January 1859, after three years and nine months of preparation, the Lucy Cobb Institute began operation with an enrollment of about one hundred students, including the daughters of Thomas Cobb and several of his nieces.[27]

From the first, Cobb had been the vital force in founding the female high school in Athens, and his efforts did not relax once it became a reality. Four weeks after the Institute officially opened, he began raising money to expand the facility. To John B. Lamar, a prospective contributor, he wrote:

> You have heard perhaps of a pet school I have started in Athens bearing the name of my loved daughter. While it has commenced under most favorable auspices, it needs to complete it one other Building. We have exhausted the liberality of our towns people. Not being sectarian, we cannot appeal to any Denomination to help us. Our only hope is the liberality of personal friends. We need about $10,000.[28]

Under Cobb's paternalistic supervision the Institute flourished. Involved in every phase of the school's affairs from the most important decisions to the most petty details, he influenced financial policy at stockholders' meetings, formulated rules governing the students, pre-

---

[26]*Southern Banner*, 23 December 1858; "Minutes of the Board of the University of Georgia," 1858-1871, vol. 4, pt. 1, pp. 4-6.

[27]*Southern Banner*, 13 January 1859; Mary Ann Lamar to Mary Ann Cobb, 28 January 1859, Lamar Cobb to Mary Ann Cobb, 3 February 1859, Howell Cobb Collection. The Institute was incorporated on 2 December 1859, by an act of the legislature. *Acts of the General Assembly*, 1859, p. 83.

[28]Thomas Cobb to John B. Lamar, 7 February 1859, Howell Cobb Collection.

vailed upon local citizens to donate silver cups as prizes for the best pupils, chaperoned social events, and escorted the boarders to church on Sunday.[29] "He employs his time in looking after the Lucy Cobb institute," remarked an amused friend, "and is in great trouble because he cant [sic] keep the College boys from looking at his girls." He "will have to adopt veils."[30]

Despite his protectiveness, a scandal rocked the school in May 1859, when a day student, the sixteen-year-old daughter of I. M. Kinney, an Athens merchant and Methodist lay preacher, eloped with a former employee of her father who had been discharged for drunkenness and gambling. That she was not a boarder was a relief to Cobb, but his reaction was nonetheless stern. A scheduled picnic was cancelled, and the rules were revised and tightened to prevent such a thing from ever happening to a boarding student.[31] "We are *as strict* as we can be," Cobb avowed afterwards. "The complaint against us is founded on our strictness."[32]

Neither the elopement of a student nor a fabricated story to the effect that the school was designed to provide wives for the sons of wealthy citizens of Athens harmed the reputation of the Institute to any apprecia-ble degree. In January 1860, enrollment was again over one hundred and donations totaled nearly $7,000.[33] Congressman John H. Lumpkin, who had transferred his daughter from a school in Salem, North Carolina, to the Institute in Athens, informed Howell Cobb that he was "much pleased with the prospect of her improvement at this Institution," and added:

---

[29]These activities are referred to in Lamar Cobb to Mary Ann Cobb, 11 January 1860, Howell Cobb, Jr. to John B. Lamar, 16 January 1860, ibid.; Mary Ann Cobb to [?], [1859], Cobb-Erwin-Lamar Collection; *Southern Banner*, 12 May 1859, 26 January 1860.

[30]William H. Hull to Mary Ann Cobb, 4 February 1859, Howell Cobb Collection.

[31]Mary Ann Cobb to Howell Cobb, Jr., 13 May 1859, ibid.

[32]Thomas Cobb to Mary Ann Cobb, 22 January 1861, ibid. A brochure circulated by the trustees in 1860 and 1861 stipulated that boarders "will be regarded with parental watchfulness, the most careful attention being given to their health, and the cultivation of their manners and morals. The rooms of the Teachers are among those of the pupils. Visitors are not received by the Boarding pupils, except with a suitable introduction to the Principal, from parents or guardians. Pupils are not allowed to leave the premises unattended . . . , nor to spend the night or Sabbath out of the Institute, unless *with parents* or *guardians*." See Barrow, "History of Lucy Cobb," appendix, pp. 11-13.

[33]*Southern Banner*, 26 January, 2 February 1860.

> My visit to Athens has caused me to think much more highly of your Brother Thomas R. R. Cobb than I did before—he has always been a favorite with me, but when I see the effort he is making in behalf of male and female Education in our State, and the deep interest he feels in the morals of the boys and girls that come with in [sic] the circle of his influence, I not only admire but love him.[34]

Cobb's commitment to female education, though manifesting the relatively progressive view that women had minds worthy of cultivation, concealed a thoroughly conservative social intent. The female intellect, it turned out, was to be sharpened not as a means of abetting her escape from the accustomed domestic sphere but as a vehicle through which orthodox southern moral and racial values could be transmitted to future generations.[35] Cobb betrayed this purpose, perhaps unconsciously, in a speech to the alumni society of Franklin College, when he digressed from his main theme long enough to urge southern women to use their leisure hours in writing literature for southern youth. "Let our Southern Mothers be the guides to knowledge of our Southern children," he exclaimed. They "have the heart—the education—the intellect—the piety—the time."[36]

The sort of literature Cobb had in mind, however, was not "the sarcasm of Lady Bulwer, nor the philosophy of Madame de Stäel, nor the infidelity of George Sand, nor the late *Sabellianism* of Miss Beecher," but works emulating the pious sentimentality of Catherine Marie Sedgewick, Hanna More, Lydia Sigourney, and Marie McIntosh, whose novels defined and fostered the nineteenth-century ideal of true womanhood, the ideal of purity, piety, domesticity, and submissiveness.[37]

In his own domestic relations Cobb reflected the dichotomy inherent

---

[34]John H. Lumpkin to Howell Cobb, 23 January 1860, Howell Cobb Collection. John H. Newton, an Athens merchant, preferred, on the other hand, to send his daughters to Wesleyan College in Macon, Georgia, because he thought the advantages were better there. See John H. Newton to Daughters, 29 March 1859, Carlton-Newton-Mell Collection, University of Georgia Libraries.

[35]Mathews, *Religion in the Old South*, p. 120.

[36]Thomas R. R. Cobb, *Educational Wants of Georgia, An Address Delivered Before the Society of the Alumni of Franklin College, At Its Annual Meeting* (Athens GA: Reynolds and Bro., 1857), pp. 15-16. Hereinafter cited as Cobb, *Educational Wants*.

[37]Cobb, *Educational Wants*, pp. 15-16; Herbert Ross Brown, *The Sentimental Novel in America 1789-1860* (New York: Pageant Books, Inc., 1959), pp. 17, 100, 116, 183, 282-332; Barbara Welters, "The Cult of True Womanhood: 1820-1860," *American Quarterly*, 18 (Summer 1966): 151-74. See also Scott, *Southern Lady*, pp. 4-5, 22-34.

in the southern evangelical desire to educate females without really widening their horizons. He loved his wife ardently, admired her many virtues, and respected and accepted her opinions on issues both public and private.[38] But he also assumed, without question, that her proper role was to bear and care for children, manage the household, and salve his battered ego when it was buffeted too strongly in the rude world. His daughters, though provided with an education, would presumably follow her example.

Cobb's connection with Lucy Cobb Institute, and with women's education in general, came to an abrupt end while he was serving in Virginia as commander of the Georgia Legion. In September 1861, he received a letter from his wife explaining that their eldest daughter had quarreled with her teacher, Eliza H. Ferris, and had been withdrawn from the school along with her sister.[39] Already annoyed with Miss Ferris for some obscure reason, he was in no mood to be objective. "I don't know when I have been so enraged," he exclaimed.

> If I could get my hands on Miss Ferris tonight I am sure I would slap her face well—woman as she is—and as to the Trustees of the School I hold them in the utmost contempt. This mail carries the resignation of my Trusteeship. I give no reason for it except my absence. You . . . did right to take my children away from the ungrateful hussies. . . . No whining apologies will pacify me. I charge you do not let them pacify you or cause my children to return. If they have induced you to send them back, I require you, as you love me, to take them away at once. . . . I look upon contact with such pandering hussies, as pollution to my little girls. I have but one request to make of the Trustees and that is that they will change the name of the school. I do not wish my angel child to have her memory blurred by the connection of her name with such people. Don't think that I am writing under excitement. I am perfectly cool. . . .[40]

---

[38]Cobb's marriage was one of those happy relationships described in Scott, *Southern Lady*, pp. 40-42.

[39]The cause of the quarrel is unknown, but a classmate remarked that "Sallie and Callie Cobb have stopped school[.] Sallie had a fuss with Miss Ferris. . . ." Nellie to Howell Cobb, Jr., 29 September 1861, Carlton-Newton-Mell Collection. Evidently there were serious internal problems at the Lucy Cobb Institute as early as 1859. A visitor reported that "the state of affairs there is becoming worse every day. I cannot give you the particulars." John T. Norris to Col. David Barrow, 14 November 1859, Barrow Papers.

[40]Thomas Cobb to Marion Cobb, 23 September 1861, Thomas R. R. Cobb Collection. Cobb's sister-in-law had no qualms about the character or capabilities of Miss Ferris. Enrolling her daughter at the Institute in September 1861, she wrote: "I went yesterday . . .

Discovering that Henry (Hench) Hull, Jr., a friend and member of the board of trustees, had attempted to appease his wife by putting the episode in its proper perspective, Cobb heatedly defended his daughter and adamantly refused to entertain the notion that she might have been even partly at fault. "Tell Hench for me," he instructed, "that rather than my child succumb to that hussy I would place the torch, myself, to the Institute and burn it to the ground."[41] Such obstinacy ruled out a friendly solution to the misunderstanding, and consequently Cobb's association with the Institute ended in an atmosphere of pettiness and ill will.[42]

The Lucy Cobb Institute was only one of several educational projects occupying Cobb's attention during the late 1850s. The establishment of a system of free public schools, the reorganization of Franklin College, and the founding of a law school were the others.

The movement for free common schools in Georgia dated back to 1817, but decades of agitation had produced only one tangible result: the creation of a poor school fund which was apportioned in haphazard fashion under the terms of a law passed in 1843.[43] Designed to educate the children of indigent parents, the act was a failure. A group of educators

---

and entered her as a scholar. I did so more willingly than I anticipated because . . . Mary Ann [the daughter] will be entirely under Miss Ferris' charge." Mary Ann Cobb to Howell Cobb, 18 September 1861, Howell Cobb Collection. Later she wrote her son that "Yr Sister . . . likes Miss Ferris. . . ." Mary Ann Cobb to Son, October 1861, ibid. See also M. J. Randolph to Cousin, 5 January 1863, Edward Harden MSS., in which it was reported that Miss Ferris had been hired to teach in Washington, Georgia, and was "thought to be competent."

[41]Thomas Cobb to Marion Cobb, 26 September 1861, Thomas R. R. Cobb Collection.

[42]"Let the ungrateful people about Athens take sides against me and my children if they will," Cobb grumbled in October. Twelve days later, he again wrote on the subject: "The calm reflection of weeks has only confirmed . . . my first judgment. It was shameless ingratitude in my Co-Trustees to allow my child to be treated thus by a stuck up hussy. Send in my resignation at once, if you have not done it before." In December 1861, he was still very much opposed to the return of his daughters to the Institute. "But," he explained to his wife, "I remember you told me they seemed so lost without the association of the other girls, that I fear I would curtail their happiness." Hence, he relented somewhat and left it to his wife to "judge what is best." Knowing his feelings in the matter, she decided against sending them back, a decision which pleased him. Thomas Cobb to Marion Cobb, 4, 16 October, 30 December 1861, 28 January 1862, ibid.

[43]For repeated efforts to found a system of free schools in Georgia between 1817 and 1852, see Dorothy Orr, *A History of Education in Georgia* (Chapel Hill: The University of North Carolina Press, 1950), pp. 69-103, 158-64. Hereinafter cited as Orr, *Education in Georgia*.

meeting in Marietta in 1851 declared that it was "very defective, unjust in its operation and not at all calculated to accomplish the object in view."[44] Little wonder, then, that twenty percent of the white population of Georgia was illiterate and that an even higher percentage possessed only the rudiments of an education.[45]

Cobb had been involved in none of the early campaigns to promote common schools. In fact, as late as August 1857, in a speech to the alumni society of Franklin College, he maintained that:

> Slave labor and its consequence, a necessarily sparse white population, render it impossible ever to introduce successfully in a slave holding State that system of Common and Free Schools which is the boast and the ornament of some of the Northern States. The wisdom and experience of the wisest and best of Georgia's sons have been taxed for years to devise the surest and most feasible plan for insuring an elementary education to all of our people. The Act . . . , known as our Poor School Law, was the result; and I believe I speak the sentiment of the intelligence of the State, in saying that this Act places the system upon the best footing that the situation of the country will allow. At any rate, I have not the vanity to suppose that I can suggest a better, or the boldness to venture upon such a proposition.[46]

In his treatise on the *Law of Negro Slavery* published the following year, Cobb reiterated his belief that a well-developed common school system could not exist in areas where expansive plantations precluded a large white population. Yet, beginning in August 1858, he not only proposed a plan calling for free schools capable of "educating every child in the State" but wrote newspaper articles, petitioned the legislature, and made speeches in support of it.[47]

This reversal was not as complete as it appears. Although still of the opinion that in the slaveholding, plantation regions of south and south-

---

[44]*Southern Banner*, 6 November 1851.

[45]E. Merton Coulter, *Georgia: A Short History* (Chapel Hill: The University of North Carolina Press, 1947), pp. 285-86; Orr, *Education in Georgia*, pp. 102-103, 163; *Southern Recorder*, 18 December 1855.

[46]Thomas R. C. Cobb, *Educational Wants*, p. 6.

[47]Cobb, *Law of Negro Slavery*, p. ccxv; *Southern Banner*, 19 August 1858. Cobb's change of position did not go unnoticed. He was accused of inconsistency in an article signed "Homespun," which appeared in the *Southern Watchman*, 3 November 1859.

western Georgia a program such as he contemplated was impractical, Cobb saw no reason why the more densely populated parts of the state could not enjoy the advantages of public education, and to this end he devoted a great deal of his time and energy for the next two years.

That he now had the "boldness to venture upon such a proposition" was due, in no small measure, to an intensification of his sectional bias. It was hardly a coincidence that his sudden interest in educational reform came during the climactic phase of the slavery controversy. Reflecting his grave concern over the fact that young Georgians, male and female, attended institutions in the North, where they were allegedly subjected to abolitionist influences, and over the fact that subversive ideas were unobtrusively infiltrating the South via textbooks and imported teachers, he asserted in October 1858:

> As Georgians, should we not be ashamed that our sons are forced to be sent to Northern Colleges in order to receive the highest educational privileges? That even *abolitionized Yale* has at this time *forty-five* young men from the South, whose parents prefer to submit to the degradation of placing their sons under the tuition of our worst enemies, rather than deprive them of the best opportunity of becoming educated?[48]

His address to the alumni society the previous year also underscored his fear of abolitionist subversion. "A great and palpable educational want," he had noted, "is a want of properly qualified teachers—home-born and home-bred." A second need was southern textbooks portraying slavery from the Southern point of view—"books that shall teach truths not to be unlearned." Finally, to check the exodus northward and abroad, advanced schools were needed "where college graduates . . . may prosecute successfully those branches of science or the arts to which their inclination may lead them."[49] Concluding, he declaimed: "let us unite in an earnest effort to redeem our State's fair honor—to promote her glory—to

---

[48]*Southern Watchman*, 28 October 1858.

[49]Cobb, *Educational Wants*, pp. 6-7, 9, 11. For similar views expressed by others see *Southern Recorder*, 28 July, 10 September 1857; *Southern Watchman*, 30 December 1858; John S. Ezell, "A Southern Education for Southrons," *Journal of Southern History*, 17 (August 1951):303-27; John McCardell, *The Idea of a Southern Nation. Southern Nationalists and Southern Nationalism, 1830-1860* (New York: W. W. Norton & Company, 1979), pp. 166, 169. It is clear from these sources that Cobb was mirroring a widespread sentiment.

build up her University—to make Georgia, in her educational privileges, . . . the Empire State of the *World*."[50]

Having summoned the alumni to action in 1857, Cobb opened a vigorous campaign for common schools on 18 August 1858, while attending Clarke County superior court in Watkinsville. Speaking in courthouses throughout the Western Circuit and in Atlanta and Marietta, his activities attracted widespread attention. "Wherever he goes," declared the Athens *Southern Watchman*, "he gains converts by the scores and by hundreds."[51]

It was Cobb's contention that Georgia had the financial means to educate all children between the ages of eight and eighteen free of charge. Free schooling for rich and poor alike, he felt, would remove the stigma of pauperism which had been attached, in the minds of many, to previous schemes of public education. His plan envisioned a permanent educational fund derived from various sources, chiefly the earnings of the state-owned Western and Atlantic Railroad. The fund would be used to build schools, pay teachers, and defray the cost of sending a number of destitute students to college.

In answer to a critic who, misinterpreting his remarks, assumed that a large portion of the fund was to be set aside as a subsidy for colleges, Cobb replied:

> It is true, and lamentably true, that, at present, a *collegiate education is beyond the reach* of the sons of the poor men of our State; and I have said time and again, that our State mocks her poor young men, when she pretends to educate them, by opening the doors of old field schools, but keeps forever barred to them the doors of the High Schools and Colleges. Now my proposition is, to require the Trustees of the State University and also of other Colleges to *board, clothe, and educate, free of expense*, a specified number of poor young men, selected by a suitable tribunal *in each county in the State*.[52]

In exchange for these benefits, the student thus educated was expected to teach in his own county for a period equivalent to the time spent in

---

[50]Cobb, *Educational Wants*, pp. 22-23.

[51]*Southern Watchman*, 2 September 1858; *Southern Banner*, 19, 26 August 1858; *Southern Recorder*, 14 September 1858.

[52]Open letter to the editor of the *North-East Georgian* published in the *Southern Banner*, 28 October 1858.

college. "Thus," explained Cobb, "in a few years, every neighborhood in Georgia will be furnished with *competent, home-taught* Teachers."[53]

Cobb was not alone in the common school movement, nor was his plan particularly unique, for, in one form or another, its basic features had been urged before.[54] Nevertheless, he was generally regarded as one of the foremost champions of the cause, and, as such, his views carried weight with Governor Joseph E. Brown and other advocates of educational reform.[55]

At a meeting of the Southern Central Agricultural Society in Atlanta in October 1858, he was appointed to a committee of five to formulate a memorial for presentation to the legislature at its upcoming session.[56] The memorial, clearly bearing the impress of Cobb's ideas, outlined a system of free public schools to be financed by local taxes and the proceeds of the state railroad. This plan, though admittedly not feasible in thinly populated South Georgia, was practicable elsewhere in the state and, insisted the memorialists, should be implemented forthwith by legislative action.

On 3 November 1858, Governor Brown recommended the passage of a bill containing all the basic proposals advanced in the memorial, and several days later Cobb spoke at length to the legislature urging the adoption of such an educational program.[57] As one disgruntled opponent of common schools later remarked: "all that the most untiring perseverance and industry could accomplish was done, to secure the success of the measure."[58]

---

[53]Ibid.

[54]See for example *Southern Recorder*, 21, 28 July, 10 September 1857; Joseph H. Lumpkin to George R. Gilmer, 8 October 1830, Georgia Department of Archives and History; David W. Lewis, *Report on Public Education with Appendixes Giving Statistics of School Returns, and Other Documents on the Subject* (Milledgeville GA: Boughton, Nisbet & Barnes, state printers, 1860), p. 3. Hereinafter cited as Lewis, *Report on Education*.

[55]*Southern Recorder*, 12 October 1858; *Southern Watchman*, 21 October 1858; *Southern Banner*, 21 October 1858.

[56]*Southern Recorder*, 2 November 1858. Lewis, *Report on Education*, pp. 35-39, contains the memorial.

[57]*Southern Recorder*, 9 November 1858. Judge Lumpkin also spoke on the same subject. See *Southern Watchman*, 18 November 1858.

[58]*Southern Banner*, 1 September 1859.

If such were possible, the movement succeeded almost too well. Williams Rutherford, Cobb's brother-in-law, perceived "a readiness on the part of the Legislature to do *something* for Education in Georgia, but," he concluded rather pessimistically, "the trouble will be found in the fact that every man has a plan of his own, and I suppose nothing will be done."[59] His supposition nearly came true. Besides the governor's proposals and the memorial of Cobb's committee, two senate bills were referred to the committee on public education and free schools, and the house debated still another measure. To add to the confusion, a member of the senate made the unnecessary suggestion that, since Cobb had "devoted much time and attention to the great subject of education . . . ," he should be requested "to lay before this body such a plan as he may think proper and practicable to insure the education of all the youth of the State."[60]

The upshot was an act passed in December 1858, which merged the existing poor school fund with an annual appropriation of $100,000 from the income of the Western and Atlantic Railroad. Money from the combined fund was to be apportioned among the counties according to the number of children between the ages of eight and eighteen living there. Before a county would be eligible for a share of the fund, the ordinary and grand jury had to devise a local school system and report the plan to the governor. Should these officials fail in their assignment, state money would be expended under the old poor school law, or not at all.[61]

In the past, county officers had been notoriously remiss in matters pertaining to education.[62] To encourage them to perform their duties under the Act of 1858 and to provide some semblance of uniformity, Cobb drafted a model plan, which was printed and circulated among the counties by the state department. As applied to Clarke County, it pro-

---

[59]Williams Rutherford to Howell Cobb, 16 November 1858, Howell Cobb Collection. For an equally pessimistic view see *Southern Watchman*, 18 November 1858.

[60]*Southern Watchman*, 9 December 1858; Orr, *Education in Georgia*, p. 173; *Georgia Senate Journal*, 1858, pp. 129, 225.

[61]For a discussion of this law see Orr, *Education in Georgia*, pp. 173-74; Elbert W. G. Boogher, *Secondary Education in Georgia 1732-1858* (Philadelphia: n.p., 1933), p. 69.

[62]The indolence of these officials was a major factor in the failure of previous educational programs. For complaints on this score see *Southern Banner*, 6 November 1851.

posed the creation of approximately twenty school districts containing not less than twenty nor more than one hundred students. Three trustees were to be elected in each district, whose function it would be to employ teachers, build schools, and keep records. During the first year of operation, all funds received from the state, supplemented by an increase in local taxes, were to be utilized in the construction of new buildings and the repair of old ones. In succeeding years, the entire amount was to be devoted to the sole purpose of guaranteeing every child, eight to eighteen, at least three months of free elementary education. Finally, and not surprising in light of Cobb's religious bent:

> The daily reading of the Bible shall be part of the exercises of every district school; the schoolhouses shall be free, should they be wished, during the Sabbath for the use of Sabbath schools, or other religious exercises, and during the week also, for such religious exercises at hours when not occupied by the school. We [the Clarke County Grand Jury] also earnestly request the trustees . . . to enlist the services of some competent person . . . in their district to teach regularly a union Sabbath school in each of said districts.[63]

Six counties eventually adopted Cobb's plan in whole or part, including Clarke County, the grand jury of which had called upon him directly for advice.[64]

In March 1859, Governor Brown sent a circular letter to all county ordinaries calling for statistical information revealing how well the system was working. Eager to know the results, Cobb requested Brown to "Stir up Thweatt [Peterson Thweatt, the Comptroller General] to get all the statistics possible about our Educational progress, especially the number of Counties adopting the new scheme."[65] The number was disappointing. Some reported no program while others, after brief experimentation, fell back on the old poor school system, and in certain counties, Cobb noted with regret, "the Ordinaries . . . utterly neglected to carry out these suggestions, but . . . rather employed their time in seeking

---

[63]Ibid., 24 February 1859.

[64]Ibid., 17 March 1859. The Jackson County Grand Jury modified Cobb's proposals in various ways. For instance, the "daily reading of the Bible . . . was not strictly *required*, but earnestly *recommended*."

[65]Thomas Cobb to Joseph E. Brown, 20 May 1859, Thomas R. R. Cobb Papers, Perkins Library, Duke University; *Southern Watchman*, 7 April 1859.

to convince the citizens of the impracticability or unfitness of the scheme."[66]

By the summer of 1859, opponents of free public education were becoming increasingly vocal. One critic saw in the provision for daily Bible reading a trend toward "sectarianism, and thence to an established church by force of law." He also feared the possibility of compulsory school laws which would deprive "many families of every means of support at their command" and usurp "parental authority and tutelage." Summarizing his objections, he condemned "the whole common school system as based upon robbery, the offspring of tyranny, destructive of the natural rights of parents over their children, and of toilers over their earnings."[67]

More than a little disturbed by these attacks, Cobb wrote two letters in August 1859, defending free public education and published them in several newspapers in September. His efforts, he complained, "to give direction to a demand originating with the people themselves—has excited sneers of some in high places . . . and been received with doubts by many to whose wisdom and experience on other questions I implicitly submit." He was distressed to hear,

> that some, either ignorantly or designedly, are endeavoring to excite the poor with the delusive assertion that the effort now is, to take the fund provided for education of *Poor* children, and divert it to the purpose of educating the Rich. . . .
>
> I can understand why, in the Southern and Southwestern Part of the State, where population is very sparse . . . , good men should doubt the practicability of attaining an end so desirable in every part of the State. But in Cherokee [County], where every mountain top is alive with Free White Voters . . . , and many are oppressed with poverty . . . why such citizens . . . should hesitate a moment in demanding from the State that the People's money should go to educate the people's children, is, I confess, past my comprehension.[68]

---

[66]*Southern Watchman*, 22 September 1859.

[67]*Southern Banner*, 1 September 1859. At least one teacher, for reasons not specified, preferred the old poor school system to the new plan of public education. See B. F. Litton to Brother, 11 November 1861, Weir-Boyd Letters, Perkins Library, Duke University.

[68]*Southern Watchman*, 22 September 1859. See also *Southern Banner* 15 September 1859.

Cobb did not pretend that the Act of 1858 was without fault. The failure to provide for a superintendent to coordinate the activities of the counties was, in his opinion, a major defect, resulting in a total lack of uniformity. An equally grave mistake had been made in allowing the initiative to rest in the hands of "irresponsible county officers" and transitory grand juries. "The last Legislature took a long step in the right direction," he conceded, "when it initiated a plan for furnishing additional funds. But these will be useless—nay, . . . will be *wasted*, unless some efficient scheme is adopted for successful and harmonious action."[69] Indeed, "If we would keep our Rulers pure and uncorrupted, let us not leave a half million of dollars annually [obtained from the state railroad] subject to their discretion. I do not impeach them—I merely aver that *they are men*."[70]

Although warning his readers not to expect perfection, Cobb assured them that shortcomings in the prevailing educational system could be remedied, if only the people would demand it loudly enough. "I do not desire to see this subject mingled with politics," he stated. "Yet, I would say to every voter whose heart is with us in this cause have the *pledges of your candidates before you vote for them*. Up to the first Monday in October, *you are masters*. After that time you are merely *constituents*."[71]

Cobb's appeals were unavailing. In November 1859, Governor Brown urged the legislature to enlarge the educational fund and establish the office of superintendent of schools, but most of his requests were disregarded. Instead, a few inconsequential amendments were enacted which did nothing to correct the fundamental weaknesses in the system.[72] At this point the common school movement collapsed, and any hope of reviving it was shattered with the coming of secession and Civil War. Cobb made no further attempt to foster the development of free schools. By the winter of 1859, a multiplicity of other causes and events already were absorbing his attention, among them the reorganization of Franklin College and the founding of a law school.

Cobb's interest in Franklin College antedated by many years his

---

[69]*Southern Watchman*, 22 September 1859.

[70]*Southern Banner*, 15 September 1859.

[71]*Southern Watchman*, 22 September 1859.

[72]*Georgia House Journal*, 1859, p. 35; Orr, *Education in Georgia*, pp. 174-75.

concern for common schools. He had been a model student, first in his class academically, obedient to regulations, and active in the Phi Kappa Society. After graduation he became a dedicated alumnus and a staunch defender of the board of trustees, to which body he was elected on 7 November 1858.[73]

Long before his elevation to the board, however, Cobb sought to influence its decisions. Such was the case in 1846 when his brother-in-law, Williams Rutherford, Jr., applied for a professorship at Franklin College. Upon learning of Rutherford's candidacy, Cobb went to work to secure his election. "I have never felt a deeper interest in any matter in my life," he announced to his brother near the end of July.[74]

Initially his efforts appeared to be successful. In January and again in June, he reported optimistically on Rutherford's prospects and seemed to think that only the presence of his brother at the August meeting of the board would be needed to guarantee victory. Howell was not so sure. He warned that unless commitments from some of the Whig trustees were obtained the outcome was dubious at best.[75] As if to confirm his doubts, Colonel John Billups, a Whig trustee from Athens, upon whom Thomas Cobb had counted, decided to switch his support to Dr. John LeConte, Rutherford's chief competitor for the post.

LeConte was a scholar destined for renown who, since his graduation from the College of Physicians and Surgeons in New York, had been practicing medicine, writing scientific articles, and enhancing literary society in Savannah, Georgia.[76] Despite his superior credentials, Cobb belittled his writings, characterized him as "a perfect nincompoop,"

---

[73]For his defense of the trustees see Cobb, *Educational Wants*, p. 13; *Southern Banner*, 28 October 1858; Thomas Cobb to Governor Brown, 14 September 1860, Cobb folder, Original Manuscripts file no. 2, Georgia Department of Archives and History.

[74]Thomas Cobb to Howell Cobb, 25 July 1846, Howell Cobb Collection. The idea of running Rutherford originated with Cobb's mother, who warned about her son-in-law's inability to manage the Cowpens Plantation profitably. See Thomas Cobb to Howell Cobb, 29 January 1846, Williams Rutherford, Jr. to Howell Cobb, 7 February 1846, ibid.

[75]Thomas Cobb to Howell Cobb, 29 January, 25 June 1846, Howell Cobb to Mary Ann Cobb, 12, 20 July 1846, ibid.

[76]Richard Arnold to C. R.Gilman, 29 June 1855, Richard H. Shryock, ed., "Letters of Richard D. Arnold, M. D., 1808-1817," *Historical Papers*, series 15, Trinity College Historical Society (Durham: Duke University Press, 1925), pp. 74-75.

lacking in common sense, and even stooped to repeating vile gossip about the doctor's wife.[77] Convinced that his brother-in-law was the best man for the job and unpleasantly surprised by Billups' defection, he wrote angrily to his brother that LeConte's Whig affiliation, not his merits, had won the vote of Judge Charles Dougherty and that Billups, "of late a kind of ass wiper to Dougherty, must go for him too."[78] In brief, Rutherford's chances were now negligible.

In August, LeConte was chosen to fill the position and for the next ten years occupied it with distinction but not without controversy.[79]. In 1856 he quarreled openly and bitterly with President Church over the duties of a professor, and this conflict led to the resignation of almost the entire faculty.[80] In the reorganization that followed, Rutherford was finally employed. "Is not this good?" rejoiced Cobb. "He really deserves it and what is better it is [a] situation he can [r]etain for life if he desires it. A better man could not have gotten it."[81]

Ironically, the loss of John LeConte, the most intellectually talented member of the faculty, coincided with a movement to expand the facilities and curriculum of Franklin College to provide students with greater opportunities for advanced study within the state. At the forefront of this movement was Thomas Cobb.

Addressing the alumni society in the late summer of 1857, Cobb accused both the state and the alumni of being complacent about the progress of Franklin College. If Georgia wished to rid herself of northern domination, he argued, the institution must be transformed into a full-

---

[77]Thomas Cobb to Howell Cobb, 25 July 1846, Howell Cobb Collection.

[78]Ibid.

[79]*Southern Banner*, 11 August 1846. Rutherford and his wife accepted defeat gracefully. Sarah Cobb was livid with rage, however. She censured all those who voted against her son-in-law. Sarah R. Cobb to Mary Ann Cobb, 8 August 1846, Howell Cobb Collection.

[80]E. Merton Coulter, *College Life in the Old South* (Athens GA: The University of Georgia Press, 1951), pp. 160, 193-98; *Southern Banner*, 18 December 1856. The Reverend W. T. Brantly, an ally of Church, and William H. Waddel, a language tutor, were the only faculty members retained.

[81]Thomas Cobb to Sarah Cobb, 11 December 1856, Jackson Scrapbook. Elizabeth Craig, the daughter of Dr. Church, was of the opinion that her father had gained a faculty "possessed of common sense as well as Book learning," an obvious allusion to LeConte's alleged lack of practicality. E. C. Craig to My Dear Friend [Mary Ann Cobb], 15 December 1856, Howell Cobb Collection.

fledged university. To accomplish that goal, larger legislative appropriations and generous private endowments would be absolutely imperative.

The purpose of higher education, in his view, was to cultivate and train the mind for further intellectual growth. Graduates of Franklin College, however, were unable to pursue their studies beyond the level of a bachelor's degree because the state had failed to provide the necessary schools of advanced learning. Denied the opportunity to specialize at home, they were forced to leave the state (if they could afford it) or else enter the overcrowded professions of law and medicine. As a result, declared Cobb, "your Professors, your Authors, your Engineers and your Manufacturers are, in the main, imported like other goods of foreign growth."[82]

From this situation stemmed another consequence which he deemed dangerous in the extreme. Northern writers and publishing firms virtually monopolized the textbook field and thus were able to disseminate antislavery ideas in the schools and colleges of Georgia. Texts on moral philosophy, for instance, began with the premise that slavery was contrary to natural law. Yet, observed Cobb,

> Believing, . . . , as we do, that this Institution is based upon the Law of Nature and the Revelation of God, ought not our youths to be taught the reasons for such belief? Every graduate of every Northern College is sent forth armed and panoplied with the hackneyed arguments of Sentimental Abolitionism. Your graduate cannot explain the Declaration of Independence, unless forsooth your Professor has abandoned the text book, and sought by argument and lecture to refute the false lesson which is placed in the student's hand to learn.[83]

The educational needs of Georgia—competent, native born teachers, Southern textbooks, and postgraduate schools—could all be met, contended Cobb, by expanding Franklin College into a university in fact as well as name. Such an institution, he added, would become "a great balance wheel in our Educational System." It would prepare teachers for public schools, provide new opportunities for promising graduate students, and produce scholars capable of supplanting northern literary influences. To encourage the latter aim, he proposed that scholarships be

---

[82]Cobb, *Educational Wants*, p. 10.

[83]Ibid., p. 9.

awarded to select Georgia graduates, liberal enough to "enable the poorest to prosecute his labors with ease" and requiring "of him no duties save the prosecution of his studies and his labors." In addition, a fund should be established to assist these scholars in the publication of their works. "This or some such plan you must adopt," he insisted, "or you will be tributary forever to Boston and New York."[84]

One thousand copies of Cobb's speech were printed for public consumption lending force to the growing current for educational reform and to the emergence of southern nationalism. By November 1858, a campaign to revamp Franklin College along the lines set forth in the alumni address was in full swing.[85] Appointed to the prudential committee of the board of trustees, Cobb worked in close harmony with two of its members, William L. Mitchell and Henry Hull, Jr., in developing a reorganization plan which was submitted to the full board on 2 August 1859.[86] Referred to a special committee of five composed of Cobb, Mitchell, Robert Toombs, and two others, it was reported back favorably two days later.[87]

The plan called for the abolition of the freshman and sophomore classes, in lieu of which an advanced academy or gymnasium was to be instituted "to secure and promote the morals of its pupils, and advance their education as rapidly and as certainly as their natural endowments and previous training will admit."[88] The assumption behind this facet of the plan was that boys of fourteen and fifteen were led astray during the first two years of their college life, but in a gymnasium relatively remote from the main campus they might be "watched over night and day until fully prepared for the Junior Class."

---

[84]Ibid., p. 14.

[85]Lewis, *Report on Education*, pp. 127-134, 145-149; *Southern Recorder*, 9, 30 November 1858.

[86]The prudential committee supervised college affairs between sessions of the board and was usually composed of trustees who lived in or near Athens. Hull was chosen to sit on this committee on the same day as Cobb, and both were selected on a motion by William L. Mitchell. "Minutes of the Board of Trustees," vol. 4, pt. 1, pp. 4-5, 8. According to Elizabeth Craig, Cobb and Hull sponsored the plan, while Mitchell, because of his long membership on the board, actually introduced it. E. C. Craig to Alexander H. Stephens, 12 August 1859, Stephens Papers, Library of Congress.

[87]"Minutes of the Board of Trustees," vol. 4, pt. 1, p. 11.

[88]For the plan as originally reported see ibid., pp. 11-18. Unless otherwise indicated, all further quotations are from this report.

The college proper was to consist of junior and senior students who were theoretically mature enough "to realize the responsibility of their position" and inspire "hopes of their success in study, and the maintenance of good morals." The curriculum, unchanged except for minor modifications, was to be taught by four professors and the president, whose duties the committee report made clear would include not only classroom teaching and administration of the college proper but the promotion of good public relations as well.

The plan also proposed to incorporate within the university system three independent, self-supporting schools—law, agriculture, and civil engineering—and, if these succeeded, to add others as circumstances warranted. Endowed fellowships granted to outstanding graduates of Georgia colleges for the purpose of advanced study in one of the several university schools and scholarships to aid indigent young men were contemplated as future but very real possibilities.

A final section canvassed ways and means to finance the reorganization. Since the university schools were to be self-sustaining and since fellowships and scholarships were to be based largely on private endowments, the major expense would be the construction of the gymnasium and a fireproof three story building in which to house a library, a museum, and lecture rooms for the university schools. These two structures could be erected without delay, the committee report continued, by utilizing funds, totaling $36,000, which were already available to the trustees. It was now possible, the report concluded,

> [to] put in operation independent of State aid, a scheme far beyond anything yet attempted at the South, a scheme which promises . . . to enlarge the boundaries of knowledge among our people, to develop the vast physical resources of our State and above all to protect that most critical period in the boy's life, lying between his 14th and 18th years.

Though bold in appearance, the plan of reorganization was actually very modest. The only real innovation was the proposal to replace the freshman and sophomore classes with a gymnasium to prepare young men morally and intellectually for the college proper. Far from demanding any radical departures, the plan merely recommended an enlargement of the existing system. As noted, it entailed no great expenditure of public money; the curriculum was to remain essentially the same as it had always been; fellowships and scholarships were certainly not new in 1859; and the groundwork for two of the university schools—agriculture and law—had been laid in previous years, while the third—civil engineering—and any others that might emerge in the future were to be allowed to develop gradually as the need for them arose.[89] In brief, the plan anticipated a rather cautious, yet firm and feasible, expansion of the facilities and scope of Franklin College in order to make it, as Cobb had declared in 1857, "a well endowed, well organized University."[90]

Nevertheless, there was opposition to the plan, especially to that part providing for the elimination of the freshman and sophomore classes. Five trustees supported a motion to postpone further discussion of the report until the board met again in November 1859. It was defeated by a vote of fourteen to five, whereupon another motion was introduced to strike out the clause relating to the gymnasium. When it, too, was defeated, this time by a vote of twelve to five, Judge Lumpkin moved that the "program on reorganization be adopted and referred to the Prudential Committee for all necessary details and that the same shall not go into effect until after the meeting of the Board in November next."[91] This resolution was agreed to and the trustees adjourned.

Between the August and November sessions of the board opposition to reorganization persisted. Professor Richard M. Johnston was dubious about the success of the plan. "If the scheme . . . should not prove to be a good one, the College will need strong men to save it from ruin," he wrote to Alexander H. Stephens. "The only motives for favoring it at all was to save the boys of fourteen and fifteen . . . from immoral influences of college life upon them." At any rate, "I doubt now seriously whether the

---

[89]The curriculum of the college proper, it was suggested, "might be relieved of a few studies that more properly belong to the university schools . . . as, for example, the law of nations might very properly be turned over to the Law School." For attempts by the trustees to initiate a scholarship program see ibid.; *Southern Banner*, 28 October 1858; Cobb, *Educational Wants*, pp. 21-22. In 1854 William Terrell donated $20,000 to promote agricultural instruction at Franklin College. The plan of reorganization simply stipulated that the Terrell professorship should be divorced from the college proper to form the nucleus of a separate school of agriculture. Precedents for a school of law went back even further. As early as 1843, the trustees had authorized a chair of law in connection with the college, and as late as June 1859, a new law department founded under the auspices of Cobb, Judge Lumpkin, and William Hope Hull was sanctioned by the Board. The origin and growth of the latter are treated in greater detail elsewhere in this chapter.

[90]Cobb, *Educational Wants*, p. 16.

[91]"Minutes of the Board of Trustees," vol. 4, pt. 1, p. 18.

whole scheme except the erection of the building will not be abandoned at Milledgeville on account of the hostility there is to it, and especially the notion that it is an Athens scheme."[92]

Elizabeth Craig, who apparently still felt aggrieved at Cobb's stand against her during the organ controversy, was caustic in her criticism of both the plan and its proponents. For two months she tried to enlist the help of Alexander Stephens in combating this "mad scheme," as she called it, this "extreme folly and humbug, set on foot for the benefit of a few, and without any regard to the public good." It was, she insisted, nothing more than "a local arrangement for the benefit of two families [Cobb and Hull]."[93] Coloring the facts to fit her prejudices, she commented sarcastically:

> The folly of the scheme cannot be fully comprehended until it is known that $37,000 . . . is to be expended on two buildings, a Law lecture room, and a Gymnasium high school for the benefit of the rich boys of the town of Athens, whose parents think to make them good boys by placing them in prison.[94]

Three days later she urged Stephens to attend the November meeting of the board and forestall implementation of the prudential committee's proposals. "I hear," she wrote, that "the advocates of the scheme are beginning to have some doubts as to their being able to carry it through, they say the opposition of the minority is too strong for them, . . . but I know the men, and they will not leave a stone unturned."[95]

Henry Hull, Jr. appears to have taken the lead in formulating the final plan of reorganization and in suggesting modifications to make it more palatable to the trustees. Cobb, on the other hand, played a rela-

---

[92]Richard M. Johnston to Alexander H. Stephens, 12 August 1859, Stephens Papers, Library of Congress. More than half of the trustees who voted for the plan were residents of Athens. This was not the first time that the preponderant influence of Athens men in public affairs had excited jealousy and opposition. In 1855, when William Hope Hull sought election to the Georgia Supreme Court, strenuous objections were raised against him on the ground that two of his fellow townsmen, Thomas Cobb and Judge Lumpkin, already held positions in that court. John H. Underwood to Howell Cobb, 18 October 1855, John Lumpkin to Howell Cobb, 3 November 1855, Howell Cobb Collection.

[93]Elizabeth Craig to Alexander H. Stephens, 12 August 1859, Stephens Papers, Library of Congress.

[94]Elizabeth Craig to Alexander H. Stephens, 29 September 1859, ibid.

[95]Elizabeth Craig to Alexander H. Stephens, 2 October 1859, ibid.

tively inconspicuous role at this point. He collaborated with Hull and with the other members of the prudential committee in working out the details of reorganization as directed by the board, but his energies were devoted mainly to the law school, which was scheduled to open on 1 October 1859.[96]

The precedent for such a school had been established in 1843, when the board of trustees created an unsalaried chair of law and elected Joseph H. Lumpkin to fill it.[97] Although permitted to charge fees, use college facilities, and appoint any hours he wished for instruction, Lumpkin was unable to spare much time for teaching. Poor health and his responsibilities as presiding judge of the Georgia Supreme Court interfered with his professorial duties; hence, for all intents and purposes, the chair of law became vacant, and young men seeking to enter the legal profession continued, as in the past, to read law in the office of an attorney who was often too busy with his own practice to give adequate supervision to his students. As a consequence, Georgia lagged behind the more progressive states of the North in the study of jurisprudence, as it did in most branches of learning.

Determined to improve the quality of legal education in his native state, Cobb joined Judge Lumpkin and William Hope Hull, a family friend and former law partner of Howell Cobb, in founding a law school in Athens in conjunction with Franklin College. A prospectus published on 1 June 1859, stated that one of the foremost aims of the founders was,

> to teach law, not as a collection of arbitrary rules, but as a connected logical system, founded on principles which appeal for their sanction to eternal truth. We shall endeavor to train . . . those faculties that make up what we call a "legal mind," and so send out our pupils, prepared to apply to every case as it arises, the test of controlling principles, which power, as we all know, is what makes the true lawyer, as distinguished from the mere legal quibbler.[98]

Practical as well as theoretical knowledge being essential to the complete lawyer, moot courts were to be conducted as an integral part of the

---

[96]Richard M. Johnston to Alexander H. Stephens, 6 September 1859, Elizabeth Craig to Alexander H. Stephens, 29 September 1859, ibid.; John B. Cobb to Howell Cobb, 25 May 1859, Howell Cobb Collection; *Southern Banner*, 8 September 1859.

[97]"Minutes of Board of Trustees," vol. 3, pp. 108-10.

[98]Prospectus entitled "University of Georgia, Law Department," 1 June 1859, p. 1, University of Georgia Libraries. Since plans for a law school were announced publicly a

program, so that "we shall . . . send forth our students, not only *learned*, but *skilled*."[99] The prospectus closed with the explanation that "Judge Lumpkin will give to the School such attention as is in his power, consistently with the duties of his judicial position. The other lecturers [Cobb and Hull] will be regular in their attendance."

The announcement of a new law school was greeted enthusiastically by the editor of the *Southern Banner*. "A good law school has been one of the greatest wants of our community and our State," he proclaimed. "We rejoice to know that there is now a prospect . . . of such a one in our midst."[100] The prospect became a reality in October, when the school began its first session. Fourteen students were present to hear the opening lectures on international, constitutional, and common law delivered by Cobb, Lumpkin, and Hull respectively, and the size of the class soon increased to twenty-five.[101] The academic regimen, consisting of three lectures daily, heavy outside assignments, and moot court on Saturday, appeared to be fairly rigorous, at least for Howell Cobb's son, who complained: "Uncle Tom gives such long lessons that [it] is as much as I am able to do to get over them."[102] The standards set in the first term were not relaxed in subsequent sessions. A protégé of Alexander Stephens wrote to him in December 1860:

> We are getting along pretty well with our studies; we have just commenced Equity, and expect to get through the Statutes by Christ-

---

full month before the board of trustees met, permission to operate the school in connection with the University must have been secured from the prudential committee on which Cobb was an influential member. This committee not only sanctioned the law school but included it in the plan of reorganization, which, as previously explained, was reported to and approved by the board in August 1859.

[99]Ibid. The goals outlined in the prospectus and the curriculum, the textbooks, and methods of instruction adopted in the new law school were almost identical to those of older and better known institutions such as Harvard and New York University. Moot courts, for instance, were an indispensable aspect of every reputable law school, and all attempted to teach law as a science. Chitty, Blackstone, Greenleaf, Story, and various others were standard authorities used in the Georgia law school as they were elsewhere.

[100]*Southern Banner*, 2 June 1859.

[101]"Minutes of the Board of Trustees," vol. 4, pt. 1, pp. 40-41; Mary Ann Cobb to Howell Cobb, 6, 11 October 1859, Lamar Cobb to John B. Lamar, 19 October 1859, Howell Cobb Collection.

[102]Lamar Cobb to Mary Ann Cobb, 3 November 1859, Howell Cobb Collection.

> mas. We will then finish Greenleaf; we are more than half through with it now. Then come Cobb on Slavery and Dean's Medical Jurisprudence; but it will not take us long to get through them, as we get about one hundred pages at a lesson.[103]

By the time the board of trustees convened in Milledgeville to consider the prudential committee's final plan of reorganization, the law school had been operating successfully for a month. Though included within the framework of the proposed university system, the law school was actually an independent entity and would therefore continue to function no matter what the board decided in regard to reorganization.

The plan submitted by the prudential committee in November 1859, was substantially like the one outlined in August, although it contained a few changes in the interest of economy. The freshman and sophomore classes were still to be separated from the college proper and housed in a new building (the gymnasium) "located some convenient distance from . . the college grounds yet . . . near enough for the pupils to attend church."[104] Also provided for were the so-called university schools, which, in reality, amounted to nothing more than postgraduate courses offered on sundry subjects by the regular faculty. The law school was the exception, of course, but only because it could stand alone without financial assistance from the board. Otherwise, the trustees would probably have been content to re-create the old chair of law supported exclusively by student fees.

If anything, the final plan was even more moderate than the original proposals, suggesting that the exponents of reorganization had compromised to placate the minority. After some debate and the addition of various amendments, the plan was approved on 2 November.[105] It did not bring into existence the well-developed system envisioned by Cobb in 1857, but it was an attempt to better higher education in Georgia.

On 4 November, the plan was submitted to the Senatus Academicus for final consideration prior to legislative action. A motion to endorse the

---

[103]James D. Russ to Alexander H. Stephens, 9 December 1860, Stephens Papers, Library of Congress. See also James Russ to Alexander H. Stephens, 18 June 1860, Stephens MSS, Perkins Library, Duke University; T. R. R. Cobb to T. & J. W. Johnson, 24 September 1859, Gratz Collection.

[104]"Minutes of the Board of Trustees," vol. 4, pt. 1, pp. 22-23.

[105]Ibid., p. 22.

work of the board was immediately opposed by one senator who claimed that he did not comprehend the details of the reorganization and was loathe to commit himself at this juncture. In response to this objection, Cobb succinctly explained the plan, stressing again the fact that under the old system young students were often led astray and ruined permanently. "Let Senators answer," he challenged, "how difficult it is to keep themselves free from moral taint here at the Capitol when they have been removed from the influence of wife and home. They then may know how inadequate the system heretofore pursued in colleges is to afford sufficient moral restraint over boys."[106] A number of senators remained unconvinced by this argument, but after additional debate the motion to adopt the new plan of reorganization was passed by a vote of seventy-six to forty-eight.[107]

In February 1860, Cobb and his colleagues on the building and prudential committees chose the site for the gymnasium. Five months later the cornerstone was laid, and in April 1862, the new University High School, as it was called, was dedicated.[108] By this time, however, the Civil War was in progress. Students were dropping out of college to join military units, and enrollment, particularly among the upper classmen, declined so drastically that division of the student body in accordance with the plan of reorganization was out of the question. Thus, the plan was abandoned, and in October 1863, Franklin College closed for the duration of the war.

The Civil War also had a disastrous impact on the Lumpkin Law School, so named by an act of incorporation passed on 19 December 1859.[109] Until the outbreak of hostilities, the institution had grown steadily in size and prestige. The number of students more than doubled between October 1859 and November 1860, and by early January 1861,

---

[106]*Southern Recorder*, 8 November 1859.

[107]Ibid. Cobb's defense of the new plan was attacked in an article signed "J." This antagonist ventured the hope that the trustees would "retrace their steps before they . . . ruined the venerable institution over which they have been constituted guardians." Ibid., 31 January 1860.

[108]The cornerstone bore the inscription: "This spot was selected by the prudential committee of the board of trustees of the University of Georgia." E. S. Sell, *History of the State Normal School* (Athens GA: 1923), p. 15. *Southern Watchman*, 5 February, 7 May 1862.

[109]*Acts of the General Assembly*, 1859, pp. 84-85. "A bill to organize a Law School in

two classes, totaling forty-nine graduates, had been awarded diplomas which entitled them to practice law in any court in Georgia.[110] Satisfied that their training had been of the best, the students praised both the program and the professors. "I have yet to hear of the first student who has not been highly pleased with the School," asserted one would-be lawyer, and members of the first graduating class unanimously adopted a set of resolutions "recommending the Lumpkin Law School to every one who had chosen the legal profession."[111]

The success of the school was due, in no small way, to the industry of Thomas Cobb, whose dedication to the institution was illustrated by his remark to Alexander Stephens that "*No office* can draw me away from the 'Lumpkin Law School' until it becomes a 'fixed fact'."[112] Unfortunately, his dedication to the cause of disunion was stronger than that, and it conflicted constantly with his academic responsibilities. After missing a number of classes in December 1860, to campaign for secession, he shortened the school term by twenty days in order to serve as a delegate to

---

connection with the University of Georgia" was introduced in the lower house by William G. Delony, Democratic representative from Clarke County, on 3 November. On the twenty-fifth the house judiciary committee reported a substitute, entitled "A Bill to incorporate the Law School of Joseph H. Lumpkin, Thomas R. R. Cobb, and Wm. H. Hull, in the town of Athens," which passed. By excluding all reference to a connection with the University, the substitute measure confirmed the independent status of the Lumpkin Law School. Nevertheless, a close relationship continued to exist between the two institutions. For instance, the law school held its commencement exercises in the college chapel and advertised in the Franklin College catalogue. As specified in the plan of reorganization, the board of trustees conferred Bachelor of Law degrees on law graduates, even though the professors of the law school were empowered under the act of incorporation to grant diplomas to their students. *Georgia House Journal*, 1859, pp. 41, 46, 75, 176; "Minutes of the Faculty," 2 April 1860; *Catalogue of Franklin College*, 1860-1861; "Minutes of the Board of Trustees," vol. 4, pt. 1, pp. 40-41; *Southern Watchman*, 9 August 1860.

[110]"Minutes of the Board of Trustees," vol. 4, pt. 1, pp. 40-41; Lamar Cobb to Johnnie, 6 April 1860, Pope Barrow to John A. Cobb, 12 April 1860, Howell Cobb Collection; James D. Russ to Alexander H. Stephens, 13 November 1860, Stephens Papers, Library of Congress; *Southern Banner*, 16 January 1861.

[111]*Southern Banner*, 2 August, 29 November 1860. See also G. W. S. Twiggs to Alexander H. Stephens, 20 March 1860, Stephens MSS, Perkins Library, Duke University; George Smith to Aunt, 27 March 1861, Baber-Blackshear Collection, University of Georgia Libraries.

[112]Thomas Cobb to Alexander H. Stephens, 23 June 1860, Stephens Papers, Library of Congress.

the Georgia secession convention held in Milledgeville in January 1861.[113] Then, in April, at the beginning of a new term, he again absented himself from the classroom. This time he was gone for several weeks to attend the second session of the Confederate Congress in Montgomery, Alabama, and upon his return to Athens in late May, he became engrossed in raising a military command. Following the lead of their elders, the law students, like the students at Franklin College, left school to enlist in the army. Finally, on 26 June 1861, the *Southern Banner* laconically reported the demise of the Lumpkin Law School. "The exercises of this school are closed," read the notice, "not to be resumed until the termination of the war."[114]

In promoting secession, Cobb temporarily undermined the tangible results of his educational activities. Ironically, the motivation was the same in each instance. Fearful that Georgia was being inundated by ideas inimical to the southern way of life, he vigorously espoused a variety of reforms designed to better education at all levels. Hopefully, in his view, such improvements would counteract antislavery threats to the status quo. When the danger to southern institutions appeared to be too great to combat in this manner, he advocated immediate, complete, and permanent separation from the Union. Disunion, however, led to war, and the war, in turn, closed the law school and the college, defeated plans for a university system, deterred the common school movement, and even divorced him from the Lucy Cobb Institute. Nevertheless, Cobb left an educational legacy that bore fruit in the post-Civil War years with the continuation of the Lucy Cobb Institute, the resurrection of the Lumpkin Law School, the establishment of a public school system, and the expansion of Franklin College into a true university.

---

[113]James D. Russ to Alexander H. Stephens, 9 December 1860, ibid. Normally the first term ended on 1 February, but on this occasion graduation ceremonies were conducted on 11 January. *Southern Banner*, 9 January 1861.

[114]*Southern Banner*, 26 June 1861. Enrollment began dropping as early as March 1861. See George Smith to Aunt, 27 March 1861, Baber-Blackshear Collection.

CHAPTER 5

Defender of Slavery

Portrait of
Thomas R. R. Cobb's
eldest daughter,
Lucy Cobb,
at about age 3

Later portrait of
Lucy Cobb,
who died at age 13

During the Mexican War (1846-1848) and for twelve years afterward, Thomas Cobb was both a sectionalist and a unionist, that is, he defended southern interests within a national context and supported sectional compromise in the hope that differences would not become irreconcilable. He censured fire-eaters of the South as well as free-soilers and abolitionists of the North—the one for refusing to accept reasonable compromises, the other for their constant attacks on slavery, and both for endangering the union and his brother's chances for political advancement.

By the end of the 1850s, however, Cobb's unionist sentiments, badly eroded by years of slave controversy, gave way to a full-fledged ideology of southern nationalism. Elements of an inchoate southern nationalism had been evident in his thinking earlier in the decade, including a distinctively southern evangelicalism that feared radical social reform; an ardent belief in the necessity for southern schools, textbooks, teachers, literature, and publishing houses; and, most significantly, a positive good theory of slavery.[1] The secession crisis of 1860 acted as a catalyst to merge these

---

[1]John McCardell, *Idea of a Southern Nation*, chapter 2, identifies the proslavery argument as "The Great Distinguishing Characteristic" of southern nationalism. Concerning religion and education, he writes that the main aim of both was "to define,

nationalistic elements in Cobb's mind and to produce a well-defined and clearly articulated idea of southern nationhood.

One facet of southern nationalism never endorsed by Cobb was the forcible expansion of slavery and territory. This issue was nourished by the Mexican War. Like most Georgians, Thomas Cobb responded emotionally to the outbreak of hostilities in 1846. "Our government has permitted itself to be insulted long enough," he exclaimed. "The blood of her citizens has been spilt on her own soil. It appeals to us for vengeance."[2] At the same time, as noted in the opening chapter, he was opposed to the seizure of Mexican territory as part of the retribution. "Let us whip her decently," he argued, "and give her a good government such as the *people* wish. If they *afterwards wish* to be annexed we can do it. I am for extending the area of freedom but not by war."[3]

There were those, however, who saw the war as a plot to expand the institution of slavery, not freedom, and who sought to prevent the spread of this institution by voting for the Wilmot Proviso, which stipulated that slavery would be banned in territory taken from Mexico as a result of war. Northern conservatives as well as southerners were disturbed by the implications of this measure. "Its [sic] agitation," declared Pennsylvania Democrat James Buchanan in August 1847,

> can produce no effect but to alienate the people of different portions of the Union from each other; to excite sectional divisions and jealousies; and to distract and possible destroy the Democratic party, on the ascendancy of whose principles and measures depends, as I firmly believe, the success of our grand experiment of Self Government.[4]

Cobb could not have agreed more and undoubtedly shared the opinion of his father-in-law, who observed to Howell Cobb that "For the bold and

---

inculcate, and enforce orthodoxy, thus helping to prepare the Southern mind for separate nationhood." Ibid., p. 226. For similar views stressing the distinctiveness of southern religion see Hill, *South and North in American Religion*, pp. 49-51; Loveland, *Southern Evangelicals*, p. 265. See also Carl Degler, *Place Over Time*, pp. 60-68, 93, for the "limited distinctiveness of the Old South" based primarily on the institution of slavery.

[2]Thomas Cobb to Howell Cobb, 12 May 1846, Howell Cobb Collection.

[3]Thomas Cobb to Howell Cobb, 25 June [1846], ibid.

[4]Quoted in Philip S. Klein, *President James Buchanan: A Biography* (University Park PA: The Pennsylvania State University Press, 1962), p. 201. Hereinafter cited as Klein, *Buchanan*.

decided stand taken by Mr. Buchanan and other distinguished Democrats at the North, the South owes them a deep debt of gratitude."[5] Consequently Thomas Cobb endorsed Buchanan for the Democratic nomination in 1848. To balance the ticket, he preferred someone from the lower South and mentioned David E. Twiggs of Georgia, John A. Quitman of Mississippi, and William R. King of Alabama as acceptable possibilities.[6] Instead, the Democrats nominated Lewis Cass of Michigan and William O. Butler of Kentucky. "We have the nominations," Cobb advised his brother.

> I am "reconciled" not very much "delighted." I am not [a] great admirer of Cass, although I think it a generous act on the part of Northern Democrats to nominate both anti Wilmot Proviso men. I think a more *judicious* ticket could have been selected. *Michigan* and Kentucky are too close together to have *both* candidates. I don't see what strength Butler carried to Cass. . . . And on the score of military glory, Scott or Taylor . . . will overshadow that of either.[7]

Cobb's lukewarm reaction to the Democratic candidates revealed an absence of partisan loyalty (a reappearance of antipartyism). Whatever support he grudgingly gave to the national party, then or later, was predicated entirely upon the assumption that cooperation between moderate northern and southern Democrats would promote sectional harmony, further the presidential aspirations of his brother, and simultaneously safeguard slavery and the union. Since none of these vital concerns seemed to be jeopardized by either the Democratic contenders or Zachary Taylor, the Whig candidate, Cobb manifested little interest in the campaign. "I can give you no political news," he explained to his brother in July 1848, "for honestly, I have not informed myself enough to give a judgement. There is no doubt Taylor is the *strongest* man the Whigs could run in Georgia." But, he repeated, "My opinion is not entitled to any weight for I have not taken the pains to inform myself. I should suppose however the race in Georgia would be close. *The chances being in favor of Taylor.* I speak more from abstract reasoning than facts."[8]

---

[5]Joseph H. Lumpkin to Howell Cobb, 21 Janaury 1848, Phillips, ed., *Correspondence*, p. 94.

[6]Thomas Cobb to Howell Cobb, 27 January 1848, Howell Cobb Collection.

[7]Thomas Cobb to Howell Cobb, 31 May 1848, ibid.

[8]Thomas Cobb to Howell Cobb, 18 July 1848, ibid.

His lack of knowledge and indifference also stemmed from the fact that he was too busy practicing law, preparing his *Digest*, and assisting James M. Kelly in the publication of the fourth volume of *Georgia Reports* to be much aroused by a contest in which the crucial issue of whether the Mexican cession would eventually become free or slave territory was, in the words of one scholar, "beclouded by the major-party candidates, who understood that their main aim was to win the election and hence felt they had to appeal in the same breath to both northern and southern voters."[9] In any case, he was neither perturbed nor particularly surprised when Zachary Taylor carried Georgia and fourteen other states to win the November election.

If the slavery question had been glossed over during the campaign of 1848, it was not ignored for long. In January 1849, John C. Calhoun focused attention on the issue, much as David Wilmot had done in 1846, by publishing the so-called "Southern Address" signed by forty-eight southern congressmen. Reciting numerous instances of alleged northern aggression, including failure to enforce the Fugitive Slave Law and provocative attacks on slavery and the slave trade in the District of Columbia, he urged southern unity as a means to protect southern rights and institutions.[10]

Arraying himself against the senator from South Carolina, as he had done in 1846, Congressman Howell Cobb refused to endorse the "Southern Address," partly because it "*designedly* failed to make any discrimination between Northern Democrats, Whigs and abolitionists." Calhoun's primary purpose, he averred to Buchanan, was to create "a *Southern sectional party*. . . . Unless I am sustained, the result must be the disruption of the democratic party as a *national* party, which would be the accomplishment of Calhoun's schemes ever since I have been in public life."[11]

Seldom at odds with his brother on questions of political moment,

---

[9]Holman Hamilton, *Prologue to Conflict: The Crisis and Compromise of 1850* (New York: W. W. Norton & Company, 1966), p. 9. Cobb had just been appointed assistant reporter of the Georgia Supreme Court. See Chapter 2.

[10]Ibid., pp. 10-11; Charles M. Wiltse, *John C. Calhoun: Sectionalist*, 1840-1850 (New York: The Bobbs-Merrill Company, 1951), pp. 378-88.

[11]Howell Cobb to James Buchanan, 17 June 1849, Phillips, ed., *Correspondence*, p. 164.

especially those affecting the congressman's career, Thomas Cobb accepted the conclusion that Calhoun and his followers were aggravating the slavery issue merely to gain a political advantage. In his estimation, they were little better than the abolitionists, for both were guilty of actions detrimental to his brother, the union, and the Democratic Party. Writing to Howell Cobb in December 1849, he commented pessimistically: "From appearances I suppose you are beat [for the House speakership] by *Calhounism* and *Abolitionism*. I dont [sic] know which is worse. If you are beaten, write me at length explaining the reasons."[12]

Contrary to Thomas Cobb's expectations, his brother was not defeated, but the balloting had been so prolonged and feelings so bitter that the congressman experienced no elation over his victory. Noting this, Cobb tried to bolster the new speaker's spirits. "I was sorry to see the sad tone of your letter," he wrote sympathetically.

> You are not easily depress[ed], and hence my greater regret. In your office as Speaker you have laid down the right rule. Do *right. Do your duty*, come what may. Trust the result to God and your Country. You will be abused. That is inevitable. Let it always be *unjust* and *unfounded* and it will elevate instead of injuring you.[13]

The abuse, when it came (and much of it was already in evidence), flowed mainly from the pens of pro-Calhoun newspaper editors and from the mouths of Georgia Democrats who had espoused the "Southern Address" and were currently talking of a southern rights convention to be held in Nashville, Tennessee, in June 1850. Only a few Whigs, fire-eaters like State Senator William W. Clayton of Athens, were openly critical of Howell Cobb's opposition to the movement sponsored by Calhoun. The rest of the Whig Party followed the lead of Robert Toombs and Alexander H. Stephens, both of whom joined Cobb and a relatively small number of Democrats in the fight for moderation.

By the winter of 1849-1850, the "Southern Address," the probable admission of California as a free state, and the publicity given to the

---

[12]Thomas Cobb to Howell Cobb, 1 December 1849, Howell Cobb Collection.

[13]Thomas Cobb to Howell Cobb, 9 January 1850, Ibid. Sixty-three ballots were required to elect a speaker. According to Howell Cobb, the Calhoun men had opposed his nomination in the Democratic caucus but voted for him on the floor rather than support his chief opponent, Massachusetts Whig Robert C. Winthrop. Howell Cobb to Mary Ann Cobb, 27 November, 4, 22 December 1849, Phillips, ed., *Correspondence*, pp. 176-79.

forthcoming Nashville convention had generated sufficient excitement to force the Georgia legislature to take two important steps. First, it empowered Governor George Towns to convoke a state convention in the event that California was allowed to enter the Union under a free-soil constitution and, second, it authorized him to set a date for the election of delegates to the meeting in Nashville.

During most of this session, Thomas Cobb was in Milledgeville lobbying to have his *Digest* adopted. Returning to Athens in January 1850, he notified his brother that public opinion was less aroused over the slavery issue than were the politicians and that its agitation was "intended as *a lick at you.* The scoundrels descend to the meanest tricks to undermine you. It is all in vain."[14] Three months later he was still convinced that the agitation over slavery and southern rights was largely a contrivance of demagogues and not a true reflection of the people's will. "As to public sentiment here about the Nashville Convention," he reported:

> The slaveholders are all agog and making a miserable noise. . . . While the mass[,] [know]ing nothing and caring nothing about it, are normally attached to the Union, *much more so* than I had supposed. The misery is that they have no mouthpiece, while the other brawlers are manufacturing a spurious public sentiment into which *all* will eventually fall.[15]

While the people might ultimately succumb to extremist propaganda, he saw no immediate cause for alarm. "There will be *no vote, comparatively* in this District," he assured his brother. "I think when the vote comes to be counted the Nashville Convention people will be ashamed of it. For myself, I avow myself a Union man."[16]

His election prediction was quite accurate. The turnout was very light, and in some counties the polls were not even opened.[17] A similar

---

[14]Thomas Cobb to Howell Cobb, [January 1850], Howell Cobb Collection.

[15]Thomas Cobb to Howell Cobb, [3 April 1850], ibid.

[16]Ibid. He said essentially the same thing to an acquaintance from Cassville, Georgia, in March. John Burke to Howell Cobb, 27 March 1850, ibid.

[17]According to a resident, only two persons voted in Athens, one of whom was W. W. Clayton. Howell C. Flournoy to Howell Cobb, 7 April 1850, ibid. In several instances, delegates-elect refused to attend the convention. See Horace Montgomery, *Cracker Parties* (Baton Rouge: Louisiana State University Press, 1950), pp. 22-23.

lack of enthusiasm was manifest in other southern states. Though unrepresentative, the Nashville convention assembled, as planned, in June 1850. After adopting a series of resolutions enumerating southern rights the delegates adjourned to stir up popular support for their cause and to await the outcome of the compromise proposals then being debated in congress.

When the famous Compromise of 1850 was enacted in September, Governor Towns, in accordance with the authority granted by the legislature, called a state convention for December to determine Georgia's response to the compromise measures. Delegates to this convention were elected on 25 November and the result was an overwhelming victory for the Union candidates, which tended to bear out Thomas Cobb's contention that the "people are for the Union and will sustain . . . any honest effort to compromise honorably."[18]

Viewing the settlement as an honorable adjustment of sectional differences, Cobb personally acceded to it and lauded both Buchanan and New York Democrat Daniel S. Dickinson for urging their constituents to abide by the new Fugitive Slave Law. "Dickinson's speech . . . is a *jewel*," he exclaimed, and "Buchanan's letter entitles him to the Presidency for two Terms."[19]

If the compromise was to become a finalty, the South as well as the North would have to accept its provisions, and, on this score, Cobb was apprehensive that the act prohibiting slave traffic in Washington, D. C., might prove a stumbling block. "*My own* feeling," he informed his brother as early as May 1850,

> is that the abolition of the Slave Trade in the District is not only *allowable* but *desirable*. The only fear is to make the people understand the question when these demagogues cry out "Abolition." The good hearted and *honest* will be with you. Unfortunately their voice is *seldom raised* and *never* heard.[20]

Nonetheless, the proponents of compromise (the "good hearted and honest") were given an opportunity to express their sentiments at the December convention, which they dominated to such a degree that Cobb

---

[18]Thomas Cobb to Howell Cobb, 7 May 1850, Howell Cobb Collection.

[19]Thomas Cobb to Howell Cobb, 14 December 1850, ibid.

[20]Thomas Cobb to Howell Cobb, 7 May 1850, ibid.

worried they might "get to quarrelling among themselves."[21] In reply to his brother-in-law, who had been elected to the convention and who had written for advice on the proper policy to pursue, Cobb suggested that the delegates should issue a formal statement urging the slave states to refrain from extreme measures and appealing to the free states to act in compliance with the national compact, meaning apparently no interference with slavery in the District of Columbia and enforcement of the Fugitive Slave Law. Aside from this, he warned his brother-in-law to resist any attempt by the Southern Rights Democrats to reestablish old ties with Union Democrats, because "the *left-siders* were too bitter ever to be sincere in a reunion."[22] These broad guidelines, termed the "Cobbham Platform" by his father-in-law, were acted upon in Milledgeville near the end of the year.

On 10 December, the state convention adopted the Georgia Platform proclaiming Georgia's devotion to the Union and her acceptance of the Compromise of 1850 as a permanent solution to the sectional conflict provided that all parties adhered faithfully to the bargain. Two days later the Constitutional Union Party headed by Howell Cobb, Robert Toombs, and Alexander H. Stephens was formed as a counterforce to the Southern Rights Party, which had been organized the previous August and which objected to the compromise on the ground that it required the South to make too many concessions.[23]

In the fall elections of 1851 the Constitutional Unionists gained control of the legislature and elected Howell Cobb governor of Georgia; but these successes by no means ensured the permanence of the Union coalition. As the presidential election of 1852 approached, Georgia politicians began once again to identify with the national Whig and Democratic organizations, and in the process the local Union and Southern Rights parties fell apart. "The *fire-eaters*, now Democrats," noted Thomas Cobb in January 1852, "are very willing to make *common cause* with

[21]Thomas Cobb to Howell Cobb, 14 December 1850, ibid.

[22]Joseph H. Lumpkin to "My Dear Sir," 9 December 1850, ibid., gives the substance of Cobb's suggestions.

[23]The Southern Rights Party was composed mainly of Democrats, while the Constitutional Union Party drew its strength primarily from the Whigs, who were allied with a pro-compromise Democratic minority led by Howell Cobb. Montgomery, *Cracker Parties*, pp. 25-36; U. B. Phillips, *Georgia and State Rights* (Washington: Government Printing Office, 1902), pp. 163-66.

the Union men" for the purpose of sending a united delegation to the Democratic convention in Baltimore.[24]

Though opposed to such a merger in 1850, he now favored it and thought also that it might be desirable to arrange a state meeting which would bring together "all those who are willing to go into the Baltimore Convention and desire the Compromise to be adopted as a final adjustment of the Slavery question." If the call contained no reference to party labels, he continued, then "in my judgment *all* the Democrats and most of the *Union Whigs* and *all* the Southern Rights Whigs would come in and our State be nearer a Unit than ever."[25]

His judgment was faulty, and it was naive of him to think that all factions would coalesce under the Democratic banner. The Whigs, generally speaking, manifested little interest in such an alliance,[26] and even the Democrats found it difficult to forget past animosities. Far from any wish "to make common cause with the Union men," as Cobb supposed, Southern Rights Democrats sought recognition as the "regular" Democratic Party of Georgia in an effort to isolate Howell Cobb and his Union supporters. The upshot was that two delegations were sent to Baltimore, one representing the so-called Regulars and the other the Union Democrats.

At Baltimore in June 1852, both factions were seated and managed to compose their differences long enough to cast a combined vote for James Buchanan. A convention deadlock developed, however, which was not broken until the forty-ninth ballot, when dark horse candidate Franklin Pierce was finally nominated on a platform promising to maintain the Compromise of 1850. The split between Union and Southern Rights Democrats continued in Georgia and in other southern states throughout

---

[24]Thomas Cobb to Howell Cobb, 29 January [1852], Howell Cobb Collection.

[25]Ibid.

[26]There were exceptions, of course. A number of old-line Whigs, like Judge Lumpkin and Asbury Hull, endorsed the Democratic ticket in 1852. See *Southern Banner*, 8 July 1852. But the Whig majority preferred to back the nominee of their own party. A few steadfast Unionists, Whig and Democrat, led by Alexander H. Stephens, tried in vain to keep the Constitutional Union Party alive by campaigning for Daniel Webster, while the most extreme advocates of southern rights registered a protest against all compromise candidates by voting for George M. Troup, a former governor of Georgia. Phillips, *Georgia and State Rights*, pp. 167-68.

the ensuing campaign. In spite of it, Pierce carried the South, except for Tennessee and Kentucky, and won the election of 1852.[27]

Since Union Democrats had helped to deliver Georgia's electoral vote to Pierce, Thomas Cobb entertained the hope that his brother, whose term as governor was coming to a close, would receive a cabinet post. His enthusiasm in this regard was dampened, however, by the news that John A. Dix, a New York free-soiler, might be named secretary of state. Airing his objections, he wrote:

> If you are offered a seat in a piebald Cabinet—especially with *John A. Dix*—my voice is against an acceptance. Your skirts are clear of contamination of free-soilers. Keep them so. You may think I am troubling myself unnecessarily, but I should not be at all surprised were you offered a seat, as unlikely as it now appears. If Pierce has any sense (of which I am beginning to be doubtful) he must see that there is not a man in this Country so *indispensable* to him as *yourself*, or whose appointment would give more confidence to his administration.[28]

Although Dix was subsequently omitted from the cabinet, Cobb remained dissatisfied with Pierce's patronage policies. The failure to include his brother in the official family was an obvious reason for his discontent; another was the exclusion of Union men from positions of importance. He was particularly critical of the president's chief advisors, William L. Marcy and Jefferson Davis. The former was too friendly with New York free-soilers to suit him, and the latter, a Southern Rights Democrat, was reputed to have secessionist sentiments. The selection of these two politicians to head, respectively, the departments of state and war was intended by the president to symbolize party and sectional unity.[29] Yet, it seemed to Cobb that the reverse was true and that Pierce, out of weakness, had betrayed a tacit pledge made in his inaugural address to reward Union Democrats for their dedication to the Compromise of 1850.

---

[27]Phillips, *Georgia and State Rights*, pp. 167-68; Eugene H. Roseboom, *A History of Presidential Elections* (New York: The MacMillan Company, 1957), pp. 145-48. For the intricacies of Georgia politics in 1852 see Montgomery, *Cracker Parties*, pp. 45-91.

[28]Thomas Cobb to Howell Cobb, 25 January 1853, Howell Cobb Collection.

[29]Cobb was not alone in his complaints. See, for example, John B. Lamar to Howell Cobb, 11 June 1853, ibid.; Roy Nichols, *Franklin Pierce: Young Hickory of the Granite Hills* (Philadelphia: University of Pennsylvania Press, 1958), pp. 229, 276-79. Hereinafter cited as Nichols, *Pierce*.

Criticism of the administration's appointments was widespread and long lasting, and it was accompanied by a new crisis in national affairs. In 1854 congress enacted the Kansas-Nebraska Bill, which divided the Whigs and fostered the growth of the Republican and Know-Nothing parties. Alienated by the antislavery attitudes of their northern allies, the southern Whigs either drifted into the Democratic camp or joined the Know-Nothing movement. In Georgia, Alexander H. Stephens, Robert Toombs, and many of their Whig followers aligned with the Democratic Party in support of the Kansas-Nebraska Act and worked to defeat Know-Nothing candidates in the state elections of 1855. The Democrats not only gained control of the state government but elected six of Georgia's eight congressmen, among whom were Stephens and Howell Cobb, the latter returning to the House after an absence of four years.[30]

The Thirty-fourth Congress convened in December 1855, and like the Thirty-first Congress, over which Howell Cobb had presided, it failed to organize promptly. None of the parties—Republican, Democratic, or American (Know-Nothing)—could muster sufficient votes to elect a speaker. As a consequence, Pierce was forced to hold his annual message in abeyance pending a decision by the House.[31]

Thomas Cobb had watched the progress of the speakership contest with some interest and thought he saw a way to resolve the deadlock. "If you have adjourned for the holidays without a Speaker," he wrote to his brother on Christmas eve, "Let me make a suggestion. Off in the distance we see the outlines of the mountain better than those who are on it." The Democrats, he advised, should strike a bargain with the Americans by offering to elect a Know-Nothing Speaker in exchange for a major share of the committee assignments. "The result of this," he claimed, "will be to bring all of the National KNs into the Democratic Ranks."[32]

He was aware that the Democrats preferred to elect a presiding officer from their own ranks and admitted that, from a purely partisan point of view, "the independent stand taken by the Democracy is *wise* and *best* for the party. But," he added,

---

[30]*Southern Banner*, 3 January 1856; Montgomery, *Cracker Parties*, pp. 135-53; Phillips, *Georgia and State Rights*, p. 178.

[31]Nichols, *Pierce*, p. 435.

[32]Thomas Cobb to Howell Cobb, 24 December 1855, Howell Cobb Collection.

> *the Country* is in danger. Party should be secondary[.] The success of [Nathaniel P.] Banks [the Republican candidate] will shake this Confederacy, I fear[,] to pieces. Any combination then to save the Country from such a calamity.[33]

There was a certain similarity between this proposal and his advocacy of state unity in 1852. In each instance, his objective was to retain political power in the hands of moderate men who were committed to a permanent settlement of the slavery question. The Compromise of 1850 and the Kansas-Nebraska Act were the basic ingredients of such a settlement, the touchstones of sectional peace, and, in Cobb's opinion, the Union could not be perpetuated unless the letter and the spirit of these two measures were enforced. The Republicans were hostile to both; therefore, if politicians wished to avoid a national disaster, they must, he firmly believed, put aside party interests and form a common front against antislavery agitators. The fire-eaters also posed a threat, but at the moment they were less dangerous than the Republicans, or so it appeared to him.

Cobb's scheme for unity was no more feasible in 1855 than in 1852. Know-Nothing congressmen were too jealous of their party autonomy to risk absorption by the Democrats, and primarily for this reason all attempts at fusion failed. Thus, the balloting for a speaker went on for weeks, ending at last on 1 February 1856, with the election of Banks.[34]

Pierce, meanwhile, had become most anxious to forward his annual address to the Congress. Spurred on by Howell Cobb and Alexander Stephens, he broke precedent and submitted it in January before the House had organized. Despite reports of fraud and violence in Kansas, the president, in his message, denied that the situation was serious enough to warrant direct executive interference. He then rebuked the Republicans for opposing the Kansas-Nebraska Act, which embodied a "complete recognition of the principle that no portion of the United States shall undertake through assumption of the powers of the General Government to dictate the social institutions of any other portion." Further, he blamed them for keeping alive the slavery controversy out of a "fanatical devotion to the supposed interests of the relatively few

---

[33]Ibid.

[34]Nichols, *Pierce*, pp. 436, 441, 443.

Africans in the United States" and in utter "disregard [of] the interests of 25,000,000 Americans."[35]

Cobb's reaction to the message perhaps typified the feeling of many Union Democrats in the South. "Pierce's message is a noble document," he remarked, "but will he act up to it? He sacrificed the true men before with his word pledged by his inaugural. He means well, but he is surrounded by scoundrels. I want to vote for him again. But I do not wish to continue Marcy [and] Davis in office."[36]

As a matter of fact, Cobb was prepared to vote for any Democratic nominee who promised to safeguard southern rights and to advance his brother's political career. Since Pierce, Buchanan, and other leading aspirants for the nomination expressed views compatible with the moderate southern position on slavery, his final choice depended entirely upon which of the various candidates would do the most for his brother.[37] By the late spring of 1856, it appeared that Buchanan was the man to back.

In the meantime, Cobb worked in conjunction with John E. Ward of Savannah to develop sentiment favorable to his brother among the Georgia delegates to the Democratic convention in Cincinnati.[38] One of the delegates with whom he talked at length was Thomas W. Thomas, an Elberton politician, who was intimate with Stephens and Toombs. Thomas, once a close friend of Howell Cobb, recently had censured him for allegedly thwarting his chance for election to the Georgia Supreme Court.[39] From Wilkes County in March, Thomas Cobb reported the substance of the conversation to his brother:

---

[35]Ibid., pp. 432-34.

[36]Thomas Cobb to Howell Cobb, 16 January 1856, Howell Cobb Collection.

[37]Commenting on Howell Cobb's ambitions, Robert Toombs declared: "He is now playing between Pierce and Buchanan, and I know one of them knows it and think it very probable that the other does too." Robert Toombs to Thomas W. Thomas, 9 February 1856, Phillips, ed., *Correspondence*, p. 360.

[38]Thomas Cobb to Howell Cobb, 24 March 1856, John E. Ward to Thomas R. R. Cobb, 15 May 1856, Howell Cobb Collection.

[39]For the details of this dispute see John H. Underwood to Howell Cobb, 18 October 1855, Thomas W. Thomas to Howell Cobb, [1855], Howell Cobb to Mary Ann Cobb, 7 November 1855, ibid.

> He [Thomas] says that he did have feeling on this matter, but that it is all past. . . . He speaks kindly of and about you and you need have no fear about his action . . . unless *Toombs and Stephens* are adverse to you. If they are Thomas will act on their line of policy. He has determined to go to Cincinnati. T. and S. are very warm for Pierce. This is the universal feeling in Georgia. Next to him they want [Stephen A.] Douglas. I cant [sic] get either of them to come to the contingency of a Southern candidate. My own opinion is, from their studied silence, that they are averse to anything that we contemplate[.] I intend before leaving this Court to have a still plaine[r] talk with Thomas.[40]

Cobb's efforts to create a delegation friendly to his brother and to promote, not incidentally, a southern candidate were apparently unsuccessful. According to John E. Ward, who was elected to preside at the Cincinnati convention, the Georgia delegates, with few exceptions, were hostile to the congressman's ambitions and would have openly repudiated him "if the opportunity had occurred."[41] They were prevented from doing so only by the fact that Howell Cobb had cast his lot with the winning candidate, James Buchanan, whose popularity strongly manifested itself in Georgia a month before the Cincinnati convention convened in June. "Buchanan stock is rising," announced Thomas Cobb after a trip to Upson County in May. "I find the leading Democrats generally believe old Buck is the man for us. My own notion is that it would be right for the Ga[.] Del[.] to compliment Pierce with their united vote on the first Ballot and then put in for the Buckeye."[42]

To the great chagrin of Convention Chairman Ward, the Georgia delegation voted for Pierce on the first six ballots.[43] On the seventh, it shifted to Buchanan, who was nominated ten ballots later. Notwithstanding the recalcitrance of Georgia's representatives, the result was beneficial to Howell Cobb. "The feeling for you at the North, at the East, and at

---

[40]Thomas Cobb to Howell Cobb, 24 March 1856, ibid.

[41]John E. Ward to Howell Cobb, 5 July 1856, Phillips, ed,. *Correspondence*, p. 372.

[42]Thomas Cobb to Howell Cobb, 9 May 1856, Howell Cobb Collection.

[43]"I am grieved and mortified about our own delegation," Ward complained on the second day of the convention. "The indications are so strong in favor of Buchanan that it is difficult to see how men can resist. Yet they do resist, and the intrigues to defeat him are disgusting." John E. Ward to Howell Cobb, 3 June 1856, Phillips, ed., *Correspondence*, p. 367.

the West was overwhelming," Ward informed the congressman a month after the convention adjourned. "I think all of your friends will tell you that if the South is not opposed to you at the next convention you will most assuredly receive the nomination." It was essential, however, to counteract the opposition of southern fireeaters. They "will strike you," Ward continued, "unless their fangs are drawn, and this can only be done by a distinct recognition by the next Administration."[44] The fulfillment of Cobb's ambition to become president was thus linked to the election of Buchanan in 1856 and to his ability to obtain southern support without losing his northern allies.

Returning from Savannah in June, Thomas Cobb notified his brother that "news of the Dem. Nominations was spreading through the State as I travelled and I can truly say was received with *general approbation*. The Fire *Eating* Dems. *do not heartily* approve, but," he explained,

> [they] are afraid to say much. The genuine Democracy are rejoiced, and the Americans are so cowed (a portion of them) that I think they will make a virtue of necessity and *run no opposition* in Georgia. This is the policy avowed of the old line Whigs, such as Judge Lumpkin and Mr. Asbury Hull. In fact these two have announced their intention to support the ticket. Buchanan will carry the State by 20,000 against any ticket.[45]

Cobb was less certain about Buchanan's chances in the nation at large. His phobia over the growing power of antislavery forces, aggravated earlier by the election of Banks to the House speakership, was exacerbated by the Republican candidacy of John C. Frémont on a platform of free soil, free speech, free men. Accepting Democratic campaign propaganda at face value, he assumed, as did many others, that the election of Frémont would mean the disruption of the Union.[46] He was relieved, therefore, when Buchanan won in November. "I believe now," he wrote,

---

[44]John E. Ward to Howell Cobb, 5 July 1856, ibid., p. 372.

[45]Thomas Cobb to Howell Cobb, 16 June 1856, Howell Cobb Collection.

[46]At a family dinner in October, Cobb's sister-in-law reported to her husband that "Tom said very seriously that he thought if the Democrats carry . . . Pennsylvania by your efforts, and the Union is saved in Buchanan's election, you ought to have a monument . . . *right* by the side of the Washington Monument equally as large and tall." Mary Ann Cobb to Howell Cobb, 7 October 1856, ibid. For Democratic attempts to make the preservation of the Union the central theme of the campaign see Klein, *Buchanan*, pp. 257-59.

"that no other man but Mr. Buchanan could have been elected with the opposition we have encountered at the North. He was . . . the most suitable man for the times."[47]

The Union had been saved, but to make the victory complete his brother would have to receive "distinct recognition" in the form of a cabinet appointment. Cobb thought the latter should accept nothing less than the state department; and, for a time, the congressman insisted on that position. Eventually, however, he consented to step aside for Lewis Cass in order to defeat the designs of Stephen Douglas and Jefferson Davis.[48] Learning of this, Cobb wrote disapprovingly: "Is General Cass to be Premier?" He hoped not, he explained to his brother, "simply because I want you to be. If he is, let me give my advice and don't you take any other of the Cabinet offices. There is no reputation to be made there that you need aspire to."[49]

Howell Cobb had no intention of following such advice. There was a great deal to be gained by serving in some capacity, and when Buchanan officially offered him the post of treasury secretary, he accepted. Subsequent events confirmed his judgment, for he became the undisputed leader of the cabinet and a personal favorite of the president.

The new administration had been installed less than three months when the actions of territorial Governor Robert J. Walker magnified the Kansas controversy. Walker, a Buchanan appointee, was the fourth governor to undertake the thankless task of attempting to restore order in the violence-torn territory. Beginning his term in May 1857, at the proslavery capital of Lecompton, he proclaimed that climatic conditions in the territory were not conducive to the institution of slavery and that the slave issue would ultimately be resolved not by politics but by a thermometrically determined isothermal line. He further declared that under no circumstances would "Congress admit Kansas as a slave or free state, unless a majority of the people shall first have . . . decided this question for themselves by a direct vote on the adoption of the Constitu-

---

[47]Thomas Cobb to Howell Cobb, 15 November 1856, Howell Cobb Collection.

[48]Douglas and Davis were behind the appointment of Cass for personal reasons. But, according to Buchanan's biographer, by endorsing their candidate, Cobb had "knocked all their calculations into 'pi'." See Klein, *Buchanan*, pp. 266-67.

[49]Thomas Cobb to Howell Cobb, 17 January 1857, Howell Cobb Collection.

tion."[50] Later, at the free-soil town of Topeka, he declared that delegates to the forthcoming constitutional convention must abide by this dictate. If they refused, he was ready to join the free-soil element in demanding a popular referendum.

Walker's speeches aroused a storm of protest in the South. The so-called "Ultras"—those who would be content only if Kansas became a slave state—were positive that Walker's remarks revealed a desire on the part of the administration to promote the aims of the free-soilers. "*We are betrayed*!" exclaimed Thomas W. Thomas. "Our victory is turned to ashes on our lips, and before God I will never say well done to the traitor [Walker] or to his master who lives in the White House."[51]

At the height of the furor, Thomas Cobb was relaxing with his family at Madison Springs near Athens. He had been there only a few days when Thomas W. Thomas arrived. "Judge Tom Thomas has been here for the last 24 hours," he related to his brother, "and has talked about nothing except Walker and Kansas. He professes the greatest friendship for you and says that Toombs and Stephens have the same, but he says that they will undoubtedly denounce the Administration on this Walker business."[52] Cobb tried to placate the Elberton politician and pointed out that condemnation of the administration would destroy Democratic unity and pave the way for an alliance between the "Ultras" and the American Party. He also explained that it was virtually impossible for Buchanan to remove Walker on the basis of two speeches. This was a realistic appraisal. The president had to consider northern Democrats who approved Walker's addresses as well as southern Democrats who objected to them. Walker's dismissal might have won support in the South, but it would have alienated party members in the North. Hence, Buchanan's only alternative was to sustain the territorial governor.

Cobb argued with Thomas to no avail and afterwards stated: "A split in Georgia is inevitable[.] I believe the people, if properly enlightened

---

[50]Roy F. Nichols, *The Disruption of American Democracy* (New York: The MacMillan Company, 1948), pp. 102-12.

[51]Quoted in Klein, *Buchanan*, p. 293. See also *Southern Banner*, 20 August 1857; Robert Toombs to W. W. Burwell, 15 July 1857, Phillips, ed., *Correspondence*, pp. 403-404.

[52]Thomas Cobb to Howell Cobb, 15 July 1857, Howell Cobb Collection.

will sustain the administration, although I sincerely believe *Walker* to be *its foe.* He is playing for the succession. . . . There is trouble ahead."[53]

Contrary to the assertions of Thomas, Stephens and Toombs did not denounce the administration. After a long conversation with Toombs in October, Cobb "found him . . . *as hot an administration man* as I have met in Georgia" and very complimentary of Buchanan's "Silliman letter," which branded the free-soil Topeka government as "illegal and dangerous." Toombs "is evidently now strongly on your line," he reiterated to his brother. "He says Stephens is with him."[54]

By this time, Cobb had ceased to be overly concerned about a division in the Georgia Democratic Party as a result of the Walker affair. Toombs and Stephens appeared to be safely behind the president, and the state election returns indicated that "Ultra" candidates were being defeated. "The result," he wrote, "is very gratifying."[55] What worried him now was the situation in Kansas itself.

A proslavery constitutional convention had been elected in June 1857. It met in September, adjourned temporarily, and was scheduled to reconvene on 19 October. Of vital importance was the question of whether to submit the constitution, with optional clauses on slavery, to the people for ratification. Buchanan wanted the delegates to agree to a plebiscite and told Walker that he was "willing to stand or fall" on that issue. As usual Howell Cobb supported the president's position; nonetheless, he was fearful that the convention might not conform to this policy, in which case "it will produce the most dangerous crisis we have yet had on the Kansas question."[56] Reaching the same conclusion, Thomas Cobb warned: "If Kansas is rejected with a pro-slavery constitution because of

---

[53]Ibid. Howell Cobb accepted his brother's belief that Walker was politically motivated and repeated the idea to Stephens. Howell Cobb to Alexander H. Stephens, 23 July 1857, Stephens Papers, Emory University Library, Atlanta, Georgia.

[54]Thomas Cobb to Howell Cobb, 1 October 1857, Howell Cobb Collection. Stephens had written to Thomas W. Thomas that he could not "afford to quarrel with Buchanan now . . . the admission of Kansas as a slave state is at stake." Thomas W. Thomas to Alexander H. Stephens, 12 January 1858, Phillips, ed., *Correspondence*, p. 428.

[55]Thomas Cobb to Howell Cobb, 8 October 1857, Howell Cobb Collection.

[56]Klein, *Buchanan*, p. 295; Howell Cobb to Alexander H. Stephens, 19 September 1857, Phillips, ed., *Correspondence*, p. 423.

the failure to refer for ratification the most doubtful battle ever fought for the Union will be ahead of us. I tremble for the result."[57]

Buchanan's agents barely succeeded in convincing the convention to adopt the president's program. The people were given the choice of a constitution "with slavery" or a constitution "without slavery." If they ratified the latter, a provision was to be inserted which would guarantee that "property in slaves now in the territory shall in no manner be interfered with."

The decision of the Lecompton Convention infuriated free-soilers and fire-eaters alike. The Republicans charged that the people were deprived of the right to vote on the constitution per se and that regardless of how they voted slavery would continue to exist in Kansas. Southern extremists, on the other hand, were alarmed over the possibility that Kansas might become a free state and therefore opposed submission of the constitution to a popular vote.

Senator Stephen A. Douglas also criticized the action of the Lecompton Convention. On this issue he broke with Buchanan, who was determined to uphold it. In his annual message of 8 December the president recommended congressional approval of the Kansas constitution no matter which option the people chose in respect to slavery. Believing that the only way to end the controversy was to admit Kansas to statehood without delay, he refused to heed the urgings of both Douglas and Walker to disavow the work of the Lecompton delegates and call a new convention.

On the morning of 11 December 1857, Thomas Cobb read a telegraphic abstract of Buchanan's message. He agreed wholeheartedly with the president's position and commended his stand against Douglas and Walker. "The truth is," he declared, "*Walker* and *Douglas* are both throwing *high die* for the Northern Democracy" as a means of securing the party nomination in 1860.[58] In some quarters, the Illinois senator was

---

[57]Thomas Cobb to Howell Cobb, 8 October 1857, Howell Cobb Collection.

[58]Thomas Cobb to Howell Cobb, 11 December 1857, ibid. Five months earlier, Cobb had accused Walker of currying favor with the free-soilers to improve his chances to succeed Buchanan. Thomas Cobb to Howell Cobb, 15 July 1857, ibid. Interestingly enough, Thomas W. Thomas now alleged that Howell Cobb was pursuing the identical tactic. "Douglas has as much right to be President as Cobb," he declared. "Cobb has been openly playing for the free-soil support of the North in the next nomination. . . . I say Cobb has

looked upon as the only man standing between Howell Cobb and the presidency, and there was evidence of a movement on his behalf in Georgia. Warning his brother of this fact, Cobb wrote:

> I did not get to Milledgeville, but I am *sure* from all I heard that *Stephens* is pushing the *Douglas line* against you. More than half of his speech there was praise of Douglas I learn. I can never hear of *one word* said in *your praise*. Now I do not distrust Toombs. I have confidence in him, *if Stephens will let him alone*. I do not think Stephens dislikes you *personally* but he cannot bear your elevation above him. Toombs is of a nobler cast. I felt it as a duty to give you this *repeated* warning.[59]

The Stephens-Douglas coalition thus became the bête noire of Thomas Cobb and his brother.

On 21 December, ten days after Cobb dispatched his letter of warning to his brother, the Lecompton Constitution "with slavery" was ratified by a fragment of the Kansas population, and in February 1858, Buchanan transmitted it to the Congress with his endorsement. The president was confident that the Senate would vote to admit Kansas under the Lecompton Constitution, but in the House, where anti-Lecompton forces were strong, he anticipated serious opposition. Persuading himself that the Union was in jeopardy, he wrote: "if the Lecompton Constitution should be defeated in the House, . . . I apprehend it will be the beginning of the end."[60] Secretary Cobb presumably shared the president's apprehensions, for he consulted by mail with his brother on what should be done in case Kansas was rejected with a proslavery constitution. Specifically, should Georgia invoke the fourth plank in her Platform of 1850, which stipulated: "That the State . . . will and ought to resist, even (as a last resort) to a disruption of . . . the Union . . . any refusal to admit as a State any Territory applying because of the existence of Slavery therein"?

In his reply, Thomas Cobb argued against a step so drastic. Union sentiment in Georgia was still very viable, he contended. Indeed, the American Party was apparently planning "to be the *nucleus* for the formation of a great Union Party at the South, should resistance be made

---

been doing this because he is the President as much as if he were sworn in." Thomas W. Thomas to Alexander H. Stephens, 12 January 1858, Phillips, ed., *Correspondence*, p. 427.

[59]Thomas Cobb to Howell Cobb, 11 December 1857, Howell Cobb Collection.

[60]Quoted in Klein, *Buchanan*, p. 311.

by the Democrats to the rejection of Kansas." To insist that such rejection was in violation of the Georgia Platform would merely provide the Americans with a pretext for action. "Now," he acknowledged,

> if Lecompton came untainted by any suspicion that it does not speak the will of the majority, and was rejected purely because of its slavery clause[,] the people of the South would be an unit, but the undoubted fact that[,] it is *not* the *will* of a majority gives a coloring of excuse to its opponents that will oppress those who advocate the extreme measures on account of its rejection. Moreover, there are certainly evidences of paltry tricks in the framers of that instrument to thwart the will of a majority . . . and also in saddling a slave population, small as it is, upon the State which would prove powerful handles in a party at the South whose watchword was "the Union."[61]

Kansas would never become a permanent slave region, he was convinced, even if Congress accepted the Lecompton Constitution. "*Again*," he emphasized, "Kansas is and must be a free State. To make her rejection a casus belli is to make war upon an abstraction," and he doubted the expediency of fighting for this particular principle. Nevertheless, the "issue has been forced upon us by the unwise and foolish course of Southern men in Kansas and the still more unjustifiable conduct of the Free State men in that Territory," and some sort of response from Georgia would seem to be necessary in the contingency that Congress turned down the Lecompton Constitution.

Beyond suggesting that a state convention be held to "let the wisdom of her best sons mark out the future course," Cobb had nothing concrete to propose. In fact, he questioned whether any solution would suffice to save the Union.

> To human vision the continuance of this Union is an impossibility. So many shocks will loosen the base of the most settled mountain. It is useless to argue the question of Slavery with the North. Her demagogues have sown to the wind and they cannot control the whirlwind.

But, he continued,

> my faith is strong in a Providence which overrules the destiny of nations[.] I believe that just so long as this Union will promote the great ends which He has in view . . . so long will it continue and . . . when it falls *it will be for good purposes* that he permits it.[62]

---

[61]Thomas Cobb to Howell Cobb, 26 March 1858, Howell Cobb Collection.

[62]Ibid.

In brief, Cobb advised his brother to avoid a direct sectional confrontation on the Kansas question because of the Union tradition in Georgia and because the Lecompton Constitution made a mockery of the popular sovereignty concept, as Douglas and the Republicans had contended all along. Unable to offer any workable solution to the problem, he gloomily predicted the eventual collapse of the Union, placed his trust in Providence, and concluded by urging the secretary to "spend one hour each day in solemn private communion with God . . . to guide you in your public duties."[63]

The controversy over the Lecompton Constitution, as had been true of past disputes involving slavery, was abated by compromise. Realizing that the anti-Lecompton men in the House could not be overridden, Buchanan supported the English bill authorizing a new referendum in Kansas. The bill passed on 30 April 1858, and on 2 August, the voters of Kansas soundly defeated the Lecompton Constitution.

Cobb's faith in compromise answers to the slavery question had been shaken severely by the Kansas difficulties. Every compromise since 1850 had been preceded by a crisis, and every crisis had undermined the foundation of national unity to a dangerous degree. The Union, he believed, could be held together, if at all, only by averting further conflicts; but to avert them, antislavery advocates must halt their aggressive activities, and he perceived no real possibility of this. "To believe us humane and just would grate not only on their prejudices but on their pride," he theorized. "The Union is profitable *to them* and they have hitherto yielded their feeling for their *purse*. But pride and fanaticism are more powerful than interest and hence, I have but little faith in the continuance of this Union."[64]

Yet, for all his dire prognostications, Cobb refused to abandon at least a faint hope that the agitation might be terminated, somehow, perhaps by some miracle, before it was too late. His earnest desire for sectional harmony (on the basis of the Compromise of 1850, Supreme Court decisions favorable to the South, and rigid adherence to the legal doctrines of interstate comity) was reflected in his book entitled *An Inquiry into the Law of Negro Slavery in the United States to which is prefixed,*

---

[63]Ibid.

[64]Ibid.

An Historical Sketch of Slavery (Philadelphia, 1858). Referring to the recurrent crises that had so frequently disturbed the tranquility of the nation, he wrote:

> It is not my purpose to extend this sketch, by giving the history of the conflicts. . . . They have threatened, seriously, the existence of the government. Suffice it to say, that the right of each State to regulate for itself its domestic relations . . . seems now to be acknowledged by the Statesmen of the country; and that, hence, the existence of slavery in a State is no ground for rejecting its admission into the Union. The slave-trade in the District of Columbia has been properly abolished; and slavery therein . . . is left . . . to abide the fate of the institution in the adjacent States. . . . The right to prohibit slavery in the territories . . . has been denied by the Supreme Court in a late and most elaborate decision [*Dred Scott v. Sandford*]. And the same Court long since decided, that an attempt to regulate the domestic slave-trade between the States, would give virtually to Congress the right to abolish or establish slavery in every State of the Union [*Groves v. Slaughter*]. That these questions may be allowed here to rest, and be no longer used as hobbies by interested demagogues to excite sectional strifes for personal advancement, should be the sincere wish of every true American citizen.[65]

Cobb's study of the legal and historical aspects of slavery was the product of nearly eight years of labor. From the outset two obstacles hampered his progress: the inadequacy of source materials in his native state and, secondly, a lack of time.

To compensate for the shortage of information, he enlarged his personal library, which was later made available to students of the Lumpkin Law School; utilized libraries in Washington, Philadelphia, and New York during periodic visits to those cities; and solicited the assistance of Simon Greenleaf, a distinguished lawyer, former Dane Professor of Law at Harvard, and the author of a major treatise on evidence. Responding to Cobb's request, Greenleaf consulted and copied lengthy excerpts from a variety of authorities located in the university library at Cambridge. In the preface to his work, Cobb expressed gratitude for this service. "The MSS, sent me are in his own handwriting, and I prize them as relics of a great and good man."[66] Once completed, his research was

---

[65]Cobb, *Law of Slavery*, pp. ccx-ccxi.

[66]Ibid., x. Greenleaf died on 6 October 1853. For a biographical sketch see Allen Johnson and Dumas Malone, eds., *Dictionary of American Biography*, 20 vols. (New York: Charles Scribner's Sons, 1943), 7:583-84.

laudably extensive, ranging through a mass of newspapers, periodicals, law codes and digests, court decisions, histories, literary works, travel accounts, scientific treatises, political essays, legal commentaries, legislative journals, the Bible, and other books by European and American authors.

The time factor was harder to overcome. Because of an arduous law practice, his research and writing had to be accomplished in spare moments stretched over a period of several years. As late as October 1857, he complained: "*I cannot get time* to prepare my MS for the press. I do not believe I ever shall till I run away from home."[67] By March 1858, however, the work was in the hands of a Philadelphia publisher, T. and J. W. Johnson, and in October it went on sale at White's University Book Store in Athens.

"I have submitted it to the public," Cobb told his brother, "without the advice or counsel of a single friend. My confidence is solely in the honesty of every conviction which I have announced as truth."[68] Complimentary copies of the book were distributed to various state governors, cabinet officers, and Supreme Court justices, and additional volumes were sent to newspapers and periodicals for review. "My object," he declared, "is *circulation* and notice. Then if the Book fails, it has no intrinsic merit."[69]

In the final analysis, Cobb's *Law of Negro Slavery* was an encyclopedia of proslavery argumentation. He did more than cite legal precedents to buttress the theory that slavery was a positive good. Going behind the law, he drew on science, sociology, economics, moral philosophy, history and Scripture to prove that Negro slavery was not a peculiar institution established by specific legal enactments and decisions, but rather a natural state which was regulated, not created, by existing laws.

In denying that municipal law was essential to the establishment of slavery, Cobb was challenging a substantial body of legal precedent dating

---

[67]Thomas Cobb to Howell Cobb, 8 October 1857, Howell Cobb Collection.

[68]Thomas Cobb to Howell Cobb, 26 March 1858, Howell Cobb Collection. Judge Lumpkin was too busy to read the manuscript, and Cobb decided not to impose upon his brother because "I thought the Book might prove unacceptable & I did not wish to involve you in any manner in its fate."

[69]Thomas Cobb to Howell Cobb, 13 November 1858, ibid.

back to the famous British case of *Somerset v. Stewart* (1772) in which Lord Mansfield, the Chief Justice of the Court of King's Bench, declared that slavery could be introduced only by the exercise of positive law. Cobb was not alone in his challenge. As Paul Finkelman has recently noted: "Somerset had been much criticized on this point, since . . . in fact positive law had rarely been used to establish slavery."[70]

To substantiate his case for the naturalness of Negro slavery and thus refute Mansfield and other jurists, Cobb devoted the first two-fifths of his study to a general history of the institution from the ancient Hebrews and Egyptians to the *Dred Scott* decision in 1857 and spent the last three hundred pages investigating the legal status and treatment of the slave "as a person." A second volume covering the slave "as property," though contemplated, was never completed.[71] His work, it seems fairly certain, was intended for a national audience. Since he hoped to counteract abolitionist propaganda in the North while reenforcing existing proslavery sentiment in the South, common sense dictated a moderate tone. Avoiding polemics on so emotional a subject was not easy for a man of Cobb's temperament but, on the whole, he succeeded, and it was not mere cant when he wrote in his preface: "My book has no political, no sectional purpose. I doubt not I am biassed by my birth and education in a slaveholding State. As far as possible, I have diligently sought Truth, and have written nothing which I did not recognize as bearing her image. So

---

[70]Paul Finkelman, *An Imperfect Union. Slavery, Federalism, and Comity* (Chapel Hill: The University of North Carolina Press, 1981), p. 208. Hereinafter cited as Finkelman, *Imperfect Union.* Many state courts based decisions on the Mansfield doctrine but two in particular, both of which Cobb cited in his book, reflected the *Somerset* positive law principle: *Commonwealth v. Ames* (1836) in Massachusetts and *Lunsford v. Coquillon* (1824) in Louisiana. For the historical import of these cases see ibid., 103-11, 208-209. Legal historians have recently pointed out that the Mansfield decision was frequently misinterpreted, misquoted, and misapplied by American courts. Cobb, however, understood the case correctly. He accurately perceived the limitations of the decision, demonstrated the errors of various American jurists on the subject, and characterized Mansfield's summary, not unfairly, as "a vacillating, doubting, irregular, disjointed effusion." His analysis, in brief, coincides with that of modern historians. Cobb, *Law of Slavery*, pp. 163-180; Finkelman, *Imperfect Union*, 16-17, 38-40, 185-86; Jerome Nadelhaft, "The Somerset Case and Slavery: Myth, Reality, and Repercussions," *Journal of Negro History* 51 (July 1966): 193-208.

[71]In fact, Cobb had already begun collecting material for this new volume. Thomas Cobb to J. D. B. DeBow, 18 November 1858, J. D. B. DeBow Manuscripts, Perkins Library, Duke University.

believing, I neither court nor fear criticism."[72] Having reiterated for public consumption what he had said privately to his brother a few months earlier, Cobb proceeded to set forth his version of the "truth."

"To understand aright . . . the Law of Slavery," he began, "we must not be ignorant of its history." Involuntary servitude "has been more universal than marriage, and more permanent than liberty," and "Its beginning dates back at least to the deluge." It had flourished among the early Hebrews, Egyptians, Assyrians, Greeks, and Romans; it had taken root in Persia, India, China, and Japan; in short, no nation "has been so barbarous," he insisted, "as not to introduce it amongst its customs."[73]

The evidence Cobb adduced from history implied that slavery was the natural condition of the Negro, and he was certain that the law of nature affirmed it. A study of Grotius, Blackstone, Puffendorf, Vattel, Montesquieu, Hobbes, and others persuaded him that no universally acceptable definition of natural law had yet been formulated but that any definition must take cognizance of human nature. As Cobb defined it, the law of nature, "when applied to man in his intercourse with his fellowman," was an "obligation which reason and conscience impose, so to shape his course as to attain the greatest happiness, and arrive at the greatest perfection of which his nature is susceptible." It therefore followed that "whatever interferes with the attainment of this happiness and perfection does violence to the law of his nature, and whatever promotes or is

---

[72]Cobb, *Law of Slavery*, p. x. Several able scholars have argued that proslavery treatises, such as Cobb's, were not written for northern consumption but were aimed inward at southerners. Charles Sellers and Ralph Morrow, cited in chapter three, insist, in the words of David Donald, that "the deepest purpose of the proslavery argument was to purge the southerner . . . of his guilt over owning slaves." Donald rejects this hypothesis and suggests alternatively that the "deepest purpose . . . was not so much to convince the North, to persuade the nonslaveholder, or to remove guilt. . . . It was to celebrate a bygone age in which southern life had had—or was supposed to have had—cohesion, unity, and grace." Donald, "The Proslavery Argument Reconsidered," *Journal of Southern History*, 37 (February 1971):3-18. While an extended debate is not possible here, it should be mentioned that there is evidence demonstrating that some southern defenders of slavery, including Cobb, were attempting to appeal, at least in part, to northern readers. Concerning The Reverend Thornton Stringfellow, for instance, Drew Gilpin Faust writes: "He never abandoned faith in the possibility of converting the North to the Southern cause." Faust, "Evangelicalism and the Proslavery Argument," p. 14. See also H. Shelton Smith, *In His Image*, p. 136; *Southern Banner* 4 November 1858.

[73]Cobb, *Law of Slavery,* introduction and chapters 1-8 of the historical sketch.

consistent therewith is sanctioned by the law of his nature." Furthermore, "*natural rights* depend entirely upon the nature of the possessor. . . . Hence to speak of the natural right to personal liberty is unphilosophical, until the previous question is settled, that such liberty will conduce to the happiness and perfection of the possessor."[74]

The enslavement of persons intrinsically the equal of the master class would obviously pervert the law of nature, "because it promotes not their happiness, and tends not to their perfection." If, however, an inferior people were uplifted through a system of slavery, "then their enslavement is consistent with the law of nature, and violative of none of its provisions."[75]

Relying heavily on the findings of George R. Gliddon, an archeologist, and Dr. Josiah C. Nott, a noted ethnologist, he concluded that the Negro was innately inferior to the Caucasian, that he was physically fitted by nature for a life of labor, and that the institution of slavery was absolutely essential to his progress.[76] The Negro inevitably retrogressed when allowed his freedom, Cobb argued, because of a weak intellect and low morality. In Haiti and the British West Indies, where slavery had been abolished, the Negro had declined to a state of barbarism, and the effects of emancipation in the United States had been nearly as ruinous. Compared to the slave, the free Negro in America was practically a degenerate. The cause, he claimed, was not "prejudice of color"; rather it "lies deeper: in the nature and constitution of the negro race."[77]

---

[74]Ibid., pp. 16-17.

[75]Ibid., pp. 17, 21-22.

[76]Ibid., pp. 23-40. Nott and Gliddon collaborated in writing two books entitled: *Types of Mankind* (1854) and *Indigenous Races of the Earth* (1857). Cobb drew upon the works of many other naturalists, Egyptologists, ethnologists, and theologians who presented historical and biological arguments for the innate inferiority of blacks. Among those cited were: James K. Paulding, *Slavery in the United States* (1836), J. H. Guenebault, *Natural History of the Negro* (1837), Samuel George Morton, *Crania Americana* (1839), Josiah Priest, *Slavery, As It Relates to the Negro or African Race* (1843), and various essays by Louis Agassiz. For a discussion of these and other sources see George M. Frederickson, *The Black Image in the White Mind. The Debate on Afro-American Character and Destiny, 1817-1914* (New York: Harper & Row Publishers, 1971), pp. 50, 71-96, 137. Hereinafter cited as Frederickson, *Black Image.*

[77]Cobb, *Law of Slavery*, pp. cciv—ccv.

Cobb thus reached the conclusion that Negro slavery and natural law were not only compatible but complementary. The facts proved, he declared,

> that a state of bondage, so far from doing violence to the law of his [the Negro's] nature, develops and perfects it; and that, in that state, he enjoys the greatest amount of happiness, and arrives at the greatest degree of perfection of which his nature is capable. And, consequently, . . . negro slavery, as it exists in the United States, is not contrary to the law of nature.[78]

Although greatly influenced by the racial theories of Nott and Gliddon, Cobb stopped short of accepting their hypothesis that the Negro was a distinct species, an hypothesis that encountered hostility from a number of southern clergymen who adhered to a concept of race unity based on a literal construction of the Scriptures. Despite the fundamentalism of his own convictions, Cobb refused to be drawn into the debate. His line of inquiry did not require an opinion on the validity of race diversity, and he refrained from giving one. His equivocation suggests that he found the data gathered by Nott and Gliddon more useful in sustaining his proslavery position than disturbing to his religious beliefs, and this was probably true of other southern evangelicals as well.[79] In brief, without relegating blacks to a subhuman level, Cobb continued to view them as biologically and therefore unalterably inferior to whites and capable of only limited mental and moral improvement. Nevertheless, Christian duty and civilized behavior demanded that these lesser beings be treated humanely.

Unlike an absolute or pure form of slavery in which the "slave loses all *personality*, and is viewed merely as property," the system prevailing in the United States was relatively mild and limited in scope, according to Cobb. Absolute slavery, he wrote, "exists at this day in none of the

---

[78]Ibid., p. 51. Since slavery was reputedly sanctioned by natural law, Cobb assumed that it must be approved by God, for, in his opinion, the law of nature was synonymous with divine will. "To be content, in searching for that will, without opening the book of His Revelation, would be unbecoming the Christian philosopher," he announced at the beginning of a chapter entitled: "Slavery viewed in the light of Revelation." At the close of the chapter, he repeated his previous conclusion that "until the nature of the African . . . becomes by some means radically changed, there is nothing in his enslavement contrary to the law of nature." Ibid., pp. 53-64.

[79]Ibid., pp. 27-28; Frederickson, *Black Image*, pp. 76, 82-85; McCardell, *The Idea of a Southern Nation*, pp. 76-84.

civilized nations of the world," whereas "the latter has, at some time, been incorporated into the social system of every nation whose history has been deemed worthy of record." The institution, he stated further, "in its . . . limited signification, is applied to all involuntary servitude, which is not inflicted as a punishment for crime." Moreover, in this type of system, the slave, though included "under the general class of *things*," possessed some "rights as a person, and is treated as such by the law."[80] The institution of slavery in the United States had been so modified, he asserted,

> partly by natural law, partly by express enactment, and more effectively by the influence of civilization and Christian enlightment, that it is difficult frequently to trace to any purely legal sources many of those protecting barriers, the denial of whose existence would shock an enlightened public sense.[81]

In other words, slavery as practiced in the South was humane and beneficial to the Negro, whose rights were protected and whose person was regulated by municipal law and local custom.

Among the rights theoretically enjoyed by the Negro slave was the right of personal security. Homicide and inhumane treatment of slaves were crimes forbidden by specific constitutional provisions or statute laws in all states, explained Cobb. "The personal security of the slave being thus protected by express law, becomes *quasi* a right belonging to the slave as a person."[82] To defend that right, however, the slave had to rely on the justice of the courts or the mercy of his master. Only under the most extreme circumstances might he use force to protect himself from death or maiming. Even so, the slave, for all practical purposes, was

---

[80]Cobb, *Law of Slavery*, pp. 3-4.

[81]Ibid., p. 84. After defending the institution of Negro slavery on the basis of natural law, history, and the Bible, Cobb justified its introduction into the United States in narrow legalistic terms. The origin of slavery in the United States, he stated, "is found . . . in purchase, of persons already in a state of slavery in their own land. The law does not go back of that fact, to inquire into the foundation of that slavery there, but recognizing the right of the master there to sell, sustains the title of the purchaser from him." Ibid., p. 65. Because "all the negroes introduced into America were brought as slaves, the black color of the race raises the presumption of slavery, contrary to the principles of the common law, which would presume freedom until the contrary is shown. This presumption is extended, in most of the States, to mulattoes or persons of mixed blood, casting upon them the onus of proving a free *maternal* ancestor. In others, it is confined to the negroes." Ibid., p. 67.

[82]Ibid., p. 93.

utterly defenseless against the brutality of his owner. Recognizing this as "one of the most vulnerable points in the system of negro slavery," Cobb thought that additional safeguards should be enacted. He proposed the imposition of stringent penalties on slaveholders found guilty of cruelty and large rewards for information leading to their conviction. He also advocated divesting such individuals of slave property forever.[83]

Rape was another offense which ought to be indictable, he believed. The owner might sue for trespass, but the slave had no legal recourse, especially if the master committed the act in question. Alleging that transgressions of this sort seldom happened, because "the known lasciviousness of the negro, renders the possibility of its occurrence very remote," Cobb nonetheless favored some kind of punishment "for the honor of the statute-book."[84]

Besides personal security, the common law guaranteed every citizen the right to personal liberty and private property. Not being a citizen, the slave was not entitled to either. "The right of personal liberty . . . is utterly inconsistent with the idea of slavery," commented Cobb, "and whenever the slave acquires this right, his condition is *ipso facto* changed."[85] Until his status was so altered by law, it was the master's prerogative to restrain him; but the same privilege did not necessarily extend to third parties. Indeed, Cobb argued that, in the absence of statutory provision to the contrary, a slave might disobey anyone "who has no right to control him" and that such disobedience "would be no justification . . . for a battery or other injury committed on the slave." On the other hand, public policy demanded, or so it appeared to Cobb, "that so long as two races of men live together, the one as masters and the other as . . . slaves, to a certain extent, all of the superior race shall exercise a controlling power over the inferior."[86] Hence, slave patrols and laws permitting third parties to

---

[83]Ibid., pp. 94, 97-98. His definition of cruelty did not include corrective punishment, which he himself indulged in.

[84]Ibid., pp. 99-100. In an earlier chapter, Cobb characterized the Negro as inherently licentious. "Lust is his strongest passion," he wrote, "and hence, rape is an offense of too frequent occurrence. Fidelity to the marriage relation they do not understand. . . ." Ibid., p. 40. Elsewhere he denied that miscegenation was the result of slavery. "The prevalence of the evil is attributable to other causes. The most prominent of these is the natural lewdness of the negro." Ibid., p. ccxix.

[85]Ibid., p. 105.

[86]Ibid., p. 106.

apprehend fugitive slaves were deemed essential to the welfare of the community. Privately he even condoned vigilantism as a means of control. Upon learning in 1861 that an obstreperous black had been lynched, he declared: "The mob did right. I would have helped them had I been there, and I hope every unruly negro about Athens will be treated in the same way."[87]

The ownership of private property was another common law right denied the slave. "His person and his time being entirely the property of his master, whatever he may accumulate by his own labor, or is otherwise acquired by him," wrote Cobb, "becomes immediately the property of his master."[88]

The slave suffered numerous other disabilities, some of which affected his personal security, the one right, it would seem, which differentiated the American institution from a pure or absolute system of slavery. For example, he could not testify against whites, make contracts, or initiate court actions. Unable to bear witness against a member of the master class or bring suit against a brutal master, the Negro slave was deprived of a means to protect himself from cruel and inhuman treatment. "That this . . . exclusion of a negro from testifying may, in many supposable cases, operate harshly and to the defeat of justice, especially in reference to the cruel treatment of slaves, is an undeniable fact," Cobb conceded. Yet, he immediately qualified this statement by saying that "the indiscriminate admission and giving credit to negro testimony would not only, in many cases, defeat justice, but would be productive of innumerable evils in the relation of master and slave."[89]

What he favored was moderate reform which would allow the Negro to be a witness in cases involving vicious abuse by persons other than his master, provided no white man was available to testify for him. With this exception, the law was prudent, he believed, to restrict the testimony of slaves to actions in which Negroes were the sole parties; otherwise, their reputed propensity for lying would make a farce of justice. "That the negro, as a general rule, is mendacious," Cobb averred, "is a fact too well

---

[87]Thomas Cobb to Marion Cobb, 24 July 1862, Thomas R. R. Cobb Collection.

[88]Cobb, *Law of Slavery*, p. 235.

[89]Ibid., pp. 232-33.

established to require . . . proof, either from history, travels, or craniology."[90]

Disqualified as a witness against whites, the slave's security was undermined further by an inability to make contracts. Consequently, his marital arrangements had no standing in law, and he was constantly confronted with the possibility of being separated from his family. Cobb acknowledged this as an evil but, as usual, found mitigating circumstances. The marriage relationship, though unrecognized by law, was sanctioned by public sentiment, he claimed, and "rarely, if ever," was it disturbed by an arbitrary act of the master. Still, some sort of statute should be passed, he felt, to prevent the "unnecessary and wanton separation" of man and wife on those few occasions when it seemed likely to occur.[91]

It is obvious that Cobb saw nothing basically wrong with the institution of Negro slavery in the United States; and if abuses were detected, more often than not, he excused them. Throughout his treatise, he developed the theme that slavery was a product of the ages, justified by natural law, history, science, and the Scriptures, and that it was governed by enlightened positive law, which sought to balance the rights of both slave and master. While the institution admittedly had shortcomings, the flaws were neither serious nor beyond remedy. Summarizing this view, he asserted:

> Whenever the laws regulating their [the slave's] condition and relations . . . allow a rigor, or withdraw a privilege without a corresponding necessity, so far they violate the natural law, and to removal of such evils should be directed the efforts of justice and philanthropy. Beyond this, philanthropy becomes fanaticism, and justice withdraws her shield.

---

[90]Ibid., p. 233. In an earlier chapter, Cobb had made substantially the same remark. "The negro is naturally mendacious," he stated without proof, "and as a concomitant thievish." Ibid., p. 40.

[91]Ibid., pp. 242-45. Having suggested this reform, Cobb at once proceeded to explain why in some instances it would not be feasible. To "fasten upon a master of a female slave, a vicious, corrupting negro, sowing discord, and dissatisfaction among all his slaves . . . and to provide no relief against such a nuisance, would be to make the holding of slaves a curse to the master." Ibid., p. 246. In a later chapter, he defended, as necessary, laws which imposed more severe penalties on slaves than on whites for the same offense. Ibid., pp. 266-67.

> That the system places the negro where his natural rights may be abused, is true; yet this is no reason why the system is in itself wrong.[92]

The need, then, as he perceived it, was not the abolition of slavery (the destruction of which, in his opinion, would bring ruin to master and slave alike), but laws to "correct the excess, punish the abuse, and ameliorate the system."[93]

If state law could regulate and protect the slave, it could also emancipate him, as even proslavery theorists were forced to admit. This fact led Cobb to investigate the question of whether a slave might lawfully gain his freedom by escape into, transit through, or sojourn in a free state. In answering this legal riddle, he resorted to a principle of international law which he had espoused as early as 1852. The "personal *status* of every man is determined by the law of his domicil[e]," he declared, "and whether he be bond or free . . . he remains so everywhere until a new domicil[e] is acquired."[94] It was therefore reasonable to assume that a slaveholder who took up permanent residence in a free state must surrender his slaves in accord with the laws of his domicile. But, by the same token,

> if a citizen of a slaveholding State . . . should be compelled by necessity or misfortune to pass through the territory of a non-slaveholding State with his slaves, it is equally clear, upon the principles before stated, that the *status* of the slave is not changed; and the declaration, by the courts of such a State, that this transit contravened the policy of their laws, or was prejudicial to the interest of their government, would be viewed by all candid minds as a mere pretence and evasion.[95]

This interpretation of international law was applicable to the domestic scene, he insisted, because the "spirit of this compact of Union imposes a weighty obligation upon every State composing it, with scrupulous nicety to extend to the citizens of every other State, the full measure of their rights under the Comity of Nations."[96]

---

[92]Ibid., pp. 51-52.

[93]Ibid., p. 52.

[94]Undated, unsigned document written by Thomas Cobb, Howell Cobb Collection.

[95]Cobb, *Law of Slavery*, p. 128.

[96]Ibid., 188.

Cobb had originally applied the principles of comity in the case of *Lemmon v. The People* as part of a public protest against the decision of Judge Elijah Paine of the Superior Court of New York. In 1852 Jonathan and Juliet Lemmon, citizens of Virginia, stopped for a few days in New York with eight slaves en route to Texas. The slaves were seized by the authorities and liberated by Judge Paine on the ground that slavery was illegal in New York and the law allowing slaveholders the privilege of nine months sojourn in the state had been repealed in 1841. The decision became a minor cause célèbre attracting attention in northern and southern newspapers and legislatures. At the request of his brother, who was then serving as governor of Georgia, Cobb drafted an opinion of the case, the substance of which was inserted in Howell's annual message of November 1853. It read:

> If it be true that the citizens of the slaveholding States, who by force of circumstances, or for convenience, seek a passage through the territory of a non-slaveholding State with their slaves, are thereby deprived of their property in them, and the slaves *ipso facto* become emancipated, it is time that we know the law as it is. No court in America has ever announced this to be law. It would be exceedingly strange if it should be. By the comity of nations the personal status of every man is determined by the law of his domicile. . . . This is but the courtesy of nation to nation founded not upon the statute, but absolutely necessary for the peace and harmony of States and for the enforcement of private justice. A denial of this comity is unheard of among civilized nations, and if deliberately and wantonly persisted in, would be just cause of war.[97]

The *Lemmon* case symbolized a complete breakdown in interstate comity. As northern courts increasingly denied comity to slaveholders in transit with their servants, southern courts retaliated by refusing "to recognize or uphold freedom based on free-state residence or sojourn, or even direct emancipation in a free-state." The rapidly escalating judicial and legislative clash of the 1850s demonstrated, as Paul Finkelman has shown, that the United States "was well on its way to dissolving its judicial and legal bonds when secession completed the process."[98]

Cobb obviously understood that continued northern violations of

---

[97] *Georgia House Journal*, 1853-1854, pp. 32-33. For the details of the *Lemmon* case and the reaction to it see Finkelman, *Imperfect Union*, pp. 296-312; *Southern Banner*, 2 December 1852.

[98] Finkelman, *Imperfect Union*, p. 11.

interstate comity would lead inevitably to the destruction of the Union; but, unlike many southern jurists, who placed "fidelity to the institution of slavery" above "fidelity to abstract concepts of law," he also comprehended that southern courts no less than northern judiciaries must pay mutual respect to one another's laws if the nation was to endure. Thus, at a time when southern judges belligerently contributed to national division, Cobb underscored his unionist political views by urging reciprocal application of the principles of comity. Citing an early Kentucky case, *Rankin v. Lydia* (1820), in which freedom was granted to a slave because of her long domicile in Indiana, he declared approvingly:

> In Kentucky . . . this doctrine underwent investigation, and the distinction contended for, drawn clearly by the Court, viz.: that a "fixed residence," or being domiciled in a non-slaveholding State, would operate to release the slave from the power of the master; but that the transient passing or sojourning therein, had no such effect.[99]

Consistent with *Rankin v. Lydia,* and equally revealing, was his conclusion about the related case of *Strader v. Graham* (1850). In this instance, three slaves had been allowed by their master to travel and work in Ohio without supervision. They subsequently escaped to Canada and a suit for the value of the slaves and the cost of their recapture was appealed to the United States Supreme Court. Chief Justice Roger B. Taney ruled that the laws of Kentucky governed the status of the fugitive slaves; whether or not, upon return to Kentucky, they were entitled to freedom would depend entirely "upon the laws of that State, and could not be influenced by the laws of Ohio." Although usually in sympathy with the judgments of the Taney court, Cobb took issue with one facet of this decision. "I am not prepared to sanction, fully, this statement," he explained, "for, if the residence in Ohio has effected the emancipation of the slave, that *status* would not be changed by a return to the slaveholding State."[100] Clearly Cobb was adhering steadfastly to the ideal of legal accommodation among the states even where the rights of blacks were involved.

Just how important Cobb considered the question of interstate comity is indicated by the fact that of six chapters, all purporting to deal with the

---

[99]Cobb, *Law of Slavery*, p. 216; Finkelman, *Imperfect Union*, pp. 182, 192-96.

[100]Cobb, *Law of Slavery*, p. 205. For the case in full see Finkelman, *Imperfect Union*, pp. 196-201, 271-74.

same topic ("Slaves Escaping or Carried into Other States"), five actually related to comity and only one, five pages in length, bore directly on the fugitive slave problem per se. Indeed, his opinion on the latter issue was summed in one sentence:

> Having thus shown, upon principle and authority, that the voluntary removal of a slave, by the master, into a non-slaveholding State, does not necessarily, but only in specified cases, emancipate the slave, it follows, *a fortiori*, that the escape of the slave into a non-slaveholding State would not impair the masters rights.[101]

In his defense of slavery, Cobb left few arguments untouched. Painting an idealistic picture of southern society, he contended that slavery fostered republicanism, elevated the poor white, eliminated the conflict between capital and labor, and promoted statesmanship. "Politically, slavery is a *conservative* institution," he contended, which gave every white man, regardless of wealth or education, a special stake in society and a sense of superiority. "Hence, there is no war of classes. There is truthfully republican equality in the ruling class."[102]

Since the labor force in the South consisted almost exclusively of Negro slaves, labor disputes were non-existent; in fact, said Cobb, "there is perhaps no solution of the great problem of reconciling the interests of labor and capital . . . so simple and effective as negro slavery."[103]

Further, slave labor provided the master with leisure time to keep abreast of current political issues and allegedly made him a natural leader of men. "Born to command, and habituated to rule," slaveholders "frequently commend themselves to the nation," Cobb maintained, "by their firmness, their independence, and their fearlessness. These are important elements in the character of a statesman."[104] Elaborating on this thesis, he noted that the "young man of the South *is accustomed to rule*, and even the son of a poor man, without a slave, to a certain extent,

---

[101]Cobb, *Law of Slavery*, p. 221. Cobb's emphasis on comity parallels the modern assessment of its significance by Paul Finkelman cited above.

[102]Cobb, *Law of Slavery*, p. ccxiii. In his historical sketch, Cobb noted that the Greeks valued liberty yet practiced slavery and suggested that "true philosophy confirms the conclusions of Aristotle and Plato, that this [slavery] is an element essential in a true republic, for the preservation of perfect equality among citizens, and the growth and encouragement of the spirit of liberty." Ibid., p. lix.

[103]Ibid., pp. ccxiii-ccxiv.

[104]Ibid., p. ccxiv.

commands obedience from the negro population. The result is a spirit of independence, which brooks not opposition." And still another result was "a more perfect equality in social life, among the rich and poor, than can be had where the menial servants are of the same color."[105]

Finally, observed Cobb, the interests of slaveholders and non-slaveholders in the South were identical, and both were devotees of the *status quo*. Thus,

> the Southern politician addresses always a body of men having a common sentiment, and not to be influenced to so great an extent by the "humbugs" of demagogues. This is an influential element in forming public opinion, and acts thus conservatively upon the public men of the South.[106]

When Thomas Cobb's racial defense of slavery and claims for the equalizing tendency of the system are superimposed upon his affinity for the upcountry farmer and small planter class—an affinity reflected in his fight for common schools (beneficial to the poor), his revivalist belief in salvation for all regardless of intellect or station in life, and his derogatory characterization of fire-eating slaveholders as "brawlers"—one is tempted to place him at the forefront of what George M. Frederickson calls the "Herrenvolk Democracy." Spokesmen for this element of society were racial theorists who "implicitly or explicitly projected a democratic and egalitarian society for whites, denying that blacks were, in any real sense at all, part of the human community."[107] At the same time, avers Frederickson, they were at odds with the aristocratic pretentions of such men as George Fitzhugh of Virginia and Chancellor William Harper of South Carolina, who posited a stratified "social order in which slavery was part of a large hierarchy maintained by a sense of mutual obligation between superiors and inferiors," who "envisioned a seigneurial society based on the image of a patriarchal plantation," and who justified slavery in the abstract as a paternalistic institution simultaneously capable of controlling racially inferior blacks and providing social security for white workers.[108]

---

[105]Ibid., p. ccxix.

[106]Ibid., p. ccxiii.

[107]Frederickson, *Black Image*, p. 61. Fredrickson quotes Cobb in support of his thesis. Ibid., pp. 58, 62.

[108]Ibid., pp. 58-61.

Nowhere in Cobb's book, public speeches, or private correspondence was George Fitzhugh so much as mentioned, and Chancellor Harper was alluded to only once, but some of the ideas they espoused cropped up in his *Law of Negro Slavery*. For example, his historical sketch skirted close to an abstract justification of slavery (as opposed to a justification on the basis of race alone) and hinted that the patriarchal southern system of slavery was preferable to the wage slavery of white laborers in the North. Elsewhere in his work he postulated, as already noted, an ideal social structure, realizable only with the second coming of Christ, in which all people would know their niche in society and keep to it. Still, Cobb could never bring himself to accept any theory that rationalized the enslavement of racial groups other than the Negro. Indians, "though morally heathen, and intellectually the inferior race," were "not by nature qualified and capacitated for bondage."[109] Blacks, on the other hand, were, he asserted:

> peculiarly fitted for a laborious class. Their physical frame is capable of great and long-continued exertion. Their mental capacity renders them incapable of successful self-development, and yet adapts them for the direction of a wiser race. Their moral character renders them happy, peaceful, contented, and cheerful in a status that would break the spirit and destroy the energies of the Caucasisn or the native American.[110]

In this passage and throughout his book Cobb leaned heavily toward the Herrenvolk Democratic ideology, albeit without going to the extreme of adopting a race plurality doctrine. In the last analysis, however, both strains of proslavery thought (patriarchal and racial) were evident in his work and were propounded for the express purpose of convincing the public that slavery was a positive good for all concerned.[111]

Aside from the advantages supposedly accruing to both Negro and white as a direct result of the slavery system, Cobb's work purported to

---

[109]Cobb, *Law of Slavery*, p. ccxx*iii*.

[110]Ibid., pp. 46-47.

[111]McCardell, *Idea of a Southern Nation*, p. 50; Drew Gilpin Faust, ed., *The Ideology of Slavery. Proslavery Thought in the Antebellum South, 1830-1860* (Baton Rouge: Louisiana State University Press, 1981), p. 17, note 39, both support the notion that racial and patriarchal views were not mutually exclusive but were merged in the minds of most proslavery writers.

show that, for the present, the system was politically, socially, and economically necessary to the South. Concerning the future of the institution, he entertained some doubt. "It would require a prophetic vision to foretell the future of the American negro slaves," he noted.

> Emancipation, in their present location, can never be peacefully effected. Until the white race of the South is exterminated or driven off, it can never be forcibly effected. Amalgamation, to any great extent, is a moral impossibility. Colonization on the coast of Africa would be effected only at immense cost, and . . . sacrifice of . . . lives. . . . So long as climate and disease, and the profitable planting of cotton, rice, tobacco, and cane, make the negro the only laborer inhabiting safely our southern savannas and prairies, just so long will he remain a slave to the white man. Whenever the white laborer can successfully compete with him in these productions and occupy this soil, the negro will either be driven slowly through the Isthmus, to become amalgamated with the races of South America, or he will fall a victim to disease and neglect, begging bread at the white man's door.[112]

According to William S. Jenkins' *Pro-Slavery Thought in the Old South*, Southern theorists were in disagreement over the permanency of slavery. One group, of which Cobb was apparently an example, viewed the institution as transitory, while the other saw it as perpetual. Individuals belonging to the latter category tended to be expansionists, favored the extension of slavery into the territories, and advocated reopening the African slave trade.[113] If Cobb's position on these issues is any indication, the former group would not have been sympathetic to such aggressive designs.

---

[112]Cobb, *Law of Slavery*, p. ccxxi. In a chapter on "African Colonization," Cobb ventured the opinion that the movement to colonize free Negroes in Liberia was a noble but naive experiment, which was doomed to failure. "The danger is," he wrote, "that as the generation of emigrants becomes extinct, their descendants will relapse gradually into . . . heathenism and barbarism. . . ." In order "to prove the capacity of the negro for a self-evolving civilization, he must be left to himself for a few generations. Good men and wise men differ as to the final result. I must confess my own incredulity." Ibid., p. ccxiii. On the relative merits of free versus slave labor, Cobb agreed that the former was the cheaper. But, after pointing out that climate and disease would kill a white worker, that labor strife in the form of a strike would wreck the cultivation of staple crops, and that free Negro labor was impossible, because the Negro "abhors work" and "prefers theft and beggary to industry and thrift," he concluded that, although "the general proposition, that free labor is cheaper than slave, may be true, it would seem that slave labor is the only effectual, and therefore cheapest, labor which the Southern States can use in the production of their staples." Ibid., pp. cci-ccii.

[113]William D. Jenkins, *Pro-Slavery Thought in the Old South* (1935; reprint ed., Gloucester, MA: Peter Smith, 1960), pp. 146-48.

During the Mexican War, Cobb had expressed an aversion for the aims of the ultra-expansionists, and he had always opposed the African slave trade. "It seems there was, and ever has been something in the prosecution of this traffic," he wrote, "which either repels the good man, or else deadens his sensibility, and soon destroys his virtue."[114] The extension of slavery into a territory against the will of the inhabitants was no more warranted, he thought, than abolitionist attacks on the institution itself. He did not object, therefore, to the admission of California as a free state, nor was he among those who insisted that Kansas *must* become a slave state. On the contrary, he had emphatically stated, as previously mentioned, that "Kansas is and must be a free State. To make her rejection a casus belli is to make war upon an abstraction."[115] Thus, from the outset of the political controversy over slavery in the territories, Cobb's voice had been on the side of moderation and compromise. As long as existing laws and Supreme Court decisions on the subject were honestly enforced and as long as political power rested in the hands of men who were willing to resist the extremists of both sections, he was content to let the ultimate fate of slavery remain with the future.

If Cobb's massively documented compendium of proslavery thought was marred in spots by superficiality and ambiguity and if it often dismissed antislavery arguments too cavalierly, at least it was not intended as a vehicle to propagate the views of the fire-eaters. Precisely for this reason and because he had carefully refrained from overly harsh strictures when referring to abolitionists and free-soilers, Cobb undoubtedly hoped that his treatise would be reviewed impartially, like any other serious legal work, and that it would persuade fair-minded men in the North that slavery was not a heinous institution after all but rather a positive good. With no apparent misgiving, the *Southern Banner* predicted that "it is destined to work a great change in the public mind on the subject of slavery in that region, and bring about a more conservative feeling."[116]

Though not quite so laudatory and uncritical as the newspapers in Athens, the *American Law Register* (a Philadelphia publication) gave the

---

[114]Cobb, *Law of Slavery*, p. lxxxi.

[115]Thomas Cobb to Howell Cobb, 26 March 1858, Howell Cobb Collection.

[116]*Southern Banner*, 4 November 1858. See also *Southern Watchman*, 4 November 1858.

book a very favorable reception. "Looking at Mr. Cobb's Treatise . . ., we take pleasure in saying that it is written with great learning and ability," announced the editor. And, he added:

> To those who are of unbiased minds, and are anxious to examine fairly a subject of such national importance, we can honestly recommend Mr. Cobb's Treatise as an able, liberal, and intelligent exposition of the views now held by the leading statesmen and lawyers of the South. If it cannot succeed in shaking the conscientious judgment of the Northern reader on the abstract rightfulness of slavery, it will at least dispel some of his prejudices, and enable him to understand the possibility of a conscientious judgment in another direction.[117]

Few other reviews published outside of the South were so objective or as pleasantly worded as this one. *The Law of Negro Slavery* "has . . . been attacked by some of the free-soil press in the North in the bitterest invective," noticed the *Southern Banner*;[118] and so sharp was the criticism in Horace Greeley's *New York Tribune* that it drew a hot retort from the *Macon Telegraph*. "We need not say that the critic of the Tribune makes no impression on its impregnable logic," exclaimed the Georgia editor. "The fluttering of the Tribune philosophers show that they are scared and hurt."[119]

It might have been more appropriate to suggest that Cobb was "scared and hurt." His fears for the safety of the Union were growing greater, and he was undoubtedly distressed by the negative reaction to his

---

[117]*American Law Register*, 9, (Philadelphia, 1858-1859): p. 447. The work, he continued, "is prepared . . . with the thoroughness and accuracy which belong to an accomplished lawyer. Many vexed questions are examined, but always in a temperate spirit, and with reference solely to legal principles and established precedents." Ibid., p. 448. The editor took exception, however, to Cobb's description of George M. Stroud's *Sketch of the Law of Slavery* as a mere "Abolition pamphlet" and questioned whether Cobb had actually read the most recent edition of that work.

[118]*Southern Banner*, 4 November 1858.

[119]Ibid., 25 November 1858, quoting the reply of the *Macon Telegraph* to a "Broadside at Mr. Cobb's Book." For the broadside see *New York Tribune*, 5 November 1858. See also *New York Times* 8 November 1858; *The New York Herald*, 5 November 1858; *Georgia Journal and Messenger*, 17 November 1858. Cobb's book was also read by John C. Hurd, a legal scholar of independent means, who paused in his own much more detailed analysis of the law of Negro slavery specifically to refute Cobb on various points. John C. Hurd, *The Law of Freedom and Bondage in the United States*, 2 vols. (1862; reprint ed., New York: Negro Universities Press, 1968), 2: 262-263, 408.

book in the North. Even the rather satisfying review in the *American Law Register* indicated that there was little likelihood of a fundamental change in the attitude of northerners toward the institution of slavery. In all probability, this tended to reenforce his earlier conviction that it was "useless to argue the question of Slavery with the North," because demagogues and fanatics in that section had "produced a rancorous hatred of the South in the breast of vast numbers," who "believe us to be Tyrants and oppressors and they are happy in so believing[.]"[120]

Cobb's transition from an exponent of national unity to an uncompromising secessionist and southern nationalist had clearly begun; two years later it was complete. In the interval, he continued to censure southern extremists for their attacks on Buchanan, but his denunciation of the abolitionists was becoming much stronger. In the end, he joined the former and blamed the latter for causing the downfall of the Union. The election of Abraham Lincoln in 1860 proved to his satisfaction that the northern electorate had been won over by abolition propaganda and that the power of government would now be exercised to destroy slavery and with it the South.

---

[120]Thomas Cobb to Howell Cobb, 26 March 1858, Howell Cobb Collection.

CHAPTER 6

Secessionist

Engraving of Thomas R. R. Cobb's brother,
Howell Cobb—congressman, governor, and cabinet member

Shortly after the Democratic national nominating convention adjourned in 1856, Convention Chairman John E. Ward had remarked that only one man stood between Howell Cobb and the next presidential nomination.[1] The man he had in mind was Senator Stephen A. Douglas of Illinois. Since breaking with Buchanan over the Lecompton question, Douglas had been an outspoken critic of the administration. "*Publically* he attacks the administration and the Democratic party as having attempted to perpetrate a fraud," complained Howell Cobb. "*Privately* he indulges in the coarsest abuse of the President and on all occasions is peculiarly abusive of myself. . . . The Democratic party and the South have nothing to hope for from his success."[2]

In mid-November 1858, Thomas Cobb advised his brother that, despite efforts by Alexander H. Stephens to keep it alive, "the Douglas movement in Georgia *is a failure*."[3] Subsequent events belied his judgment. Not only was the Douglas movement very much alive, but in 1859 it gained momentum. Furthermore, many fire-eating Democrats were

---

[1]John E. Ward to Howell Cobb, 5 July 1856, Phillips, ed., *Correspondence*, p. 372.

[2]Howell Cobb to Alexander H. Stephens, 8 September 1858, ibid.

[3]Thomas Cobb to Howell Cobb, 13 November 1858, Howell Cobb Collection.

still aggrieved at the president's Kansas policy, and swelling the chorus of criticism against him were the curses of a group of slave traders, who denounced both Buchanan and Howell Cobb for blocking their efforts to reopen this traffic.

Angered by these assaults on the administration, particularly those emanating from the South, Thomas Cobb inveighed against the Democratic Party and wondered whether attempts by his brother to end the split in its ranks were worth the trouble. It was a party, he exclaimed,

> that rewards Traitors and turns its back on true friends[,] whose presses laud Douglas and . . . abuse *even at the South* Mr. Buchanan and his administration! Standing aloof as I do I confess I look with loathing upon such conduct. Say what we will of Southern honor and chivalry it is undeniably true that the South has been faithless to every Northern man who ever sacrificed himself at home to his principles in protection of Southern Rights.

But, he added,

> I believe God overrules the wrath and lies and bitterness of Demagogues. . . . So long as our United Country can promote his ends and His glory, He will guide, and when it ceases to do this it ceases to be worth preserving. In His justice I incline to think He will yet place in Mr. Buchanan's hands the control of the Democracy.[4]

If the party could be united under the leadership of the president, Howell Cobb's chances for the Democratic nomination in 1860 theoretically would improve. Even with the party divided, he could count presumably on Buchanan's allies in Pennsylvania and New York to back him, and his residence in the South would seem sufficient guarantee of votes from that section. However, as John E. Ward had warned some years earlier, the South might very well prove his undoing. Only "if Southern opposition can be overcome," he had written, was the nomination secure. "You must solve for yourself the question how to do this and yet maintain your power at the North."[5] To gain southern support, it was first necessary to

---

[4]Thomas Cobb to Howell Cobb, 10 July 1859, ibid. Cobb had an exalted opinion of James Buchanan. "I cannot compliment M*r* B. more highly," he wrote later, "than when I say *truly*, everything from him savors more of the style & sentiments of the great first President, than anything I ever read from his predecessors. I am afraid that order of men is but thinly represented among the public men of this day." Thomas Cobb to Howell Cobb, 4 March 1860, ibid.

[5]John E. Ward to Howell Cobb, 5 July 1856, Phillips, ed., *Correspondence*, p. 373.

ensure the loyalty of Georgia, for unless the secretary's native state endorsed him, it appeared unlikely that others would do so.

The importance of political developments in Georgia was not lost on Thomas Cobb. During a session of court at Crawfordville, he probed Robert Toombs on various matters, including Stephens' attitude toward the Democratic nomination. "I took pains to impress on him that you were *no candidate*," he reported to his brother,

> but that your friends did feel anxious in the event your name was suggested at Charleston . . . that no objection or obstacle should arise in the Delegation from your own State. . . . He . . . assured me that . . . Mr S. would be in your favor. I have given you the substance of his remarks. I confess I am incredulous as to Stephens, but I am satisfied Toombs was candid and sincere.[6]

Cobb wanted nothing so much as the nomination of his brother. "I *honestly believe your nomination only will save this Union*," he wrote six months later. "My desire to serve you is secondary to this consideration."[7] Between August and mid-November 1859, he served chiefly by consulting with local politicians and forwarding their views to his brother. "The indications as far as I can learn," he noted optimistically, "are very decided all over the State against a Douglas movement and the Administration is daily gaining power and popularity."[8]

In the meantime, arrangements were being made to hold a Democratic state convention in Milledgeville. Expecting the convention to be announced in early November, Cobb became apprehensive when no call was issued. "*Why is it not?*" he inquired of Colonel David Barrow, a member of the legislature. "I have looked daily for a call and cannot understand the delay[.]"[9] The opponents of Howell Cobb claimed that public notice of the meeting had been deliberately postponed to prevent them from sending an adequate representation. If true, Thomas Cobb was obviously not a party to the plot.[10]

---

[6]Thomas Cobb to Howell Cobb, 24 August 1859, Howell Cobb Collection.

[7]Thomas Cobb to Howell Cobb, 4 March 1860, ibid.

[8]Thomas Cobb to Howell Cobb, 6 September 1859, ibid.

[9]Thomas Cobb to David Barrow, 17 November 1859, Barrow Papers.

[10]Even a few of the politicians who professed not to be anti-Cobb thought the convention notice was too short. See, for example, Herschel V. Johnson to A. E. Cochran and J. M. Spullock, 3 December 1859, Herschel V. Johnson Papers, Perkins Library, Duke

On 8 December 1859, less than three weeks after the call was finally published, a distinctly pro-Cobb convention convened in Milledgeville, designated the treasury secretary as a favorite son candidate, and selected delegates sympathetic to his interests to represent Georgia at the national convention in Charleston, South Carolina, in April 1860. Objections immediately arose from anti-Cobb quarters alleging that the December convention was highly irregular. The state executive committee also manifested its disapproval by authorizing a second convention to assemble in Milledgeville on 14 March 1860.

Although his brother was greatly disturbed by this development, Thomas Cobb saw no real cause for alarm. The only "thing to fear in the March convention," he wrote, "*is the over-confidence of your friends*, and their consequent absence. I am trying to do all I can imprisoned as I am to get a full attendance."[11]

A few days later he was dismayed to learn that his cousin, Henry R. Jackson, a leading Savannah Democrat, could not attend the Milledgeville meeting. "This is terrible," he exclaimed to Colonel Barrow, "and renders it the more necessary that influential men from this part of the State should go." At his urging William G. Delony, an Athens Democrat, agreed to attend the March convention, and Cobb now requested Barrow to be present as well. "I think it *very important*. Howell is much disturbed by Henry's failure. Let me know or come and see me."[12]

Despite this belated activity, Jackson's absence apparently proved decisive. Poorly organized and incompetently led, the Cobb forces were outmaneuvered by a determined, efficient opposition which successfully blocked a motion to reaffirm Howell Cobb's candidacy for the Democratic nomination.[13]

University; Joseph E. Brown to A. H. Stephens, 27 December 1859, Stephens Papers, Emory University Library.

[11]Thomas Cobb to Howell Cobb, 4 March 1860, Howell Cobb Collection. Cobb's wife had given birth to a daughter on 31 January 1860, and was still extremely ill in March. Until she recovered Cobb refused to leave the house except for very short periods of time.

[12]Thomas Cobb to David Barrow, [12 March 1860], Barrow Papers.

[13]*Southern Banner*, 22 March 1860; *Southern Watchman*, 22 March 1860; Milledgeville *Southern Recorder*, 20 March 1860. "If Col. Jackson had come," declared John B. Lamar, "he could have turned the tide of battle. All we wanted was an *earnest* man of ability to rally on & to lead[.]" John B. Lamar to Howell Cobb, 16 March 1860, Howell Cobb Collection. See also John B. Lamar to Howell Cobb, 17 March 1860, ibid.

Thoroughly convinced that the convention had acted contrary to the wishes of a majority of Georgia Democrats, Thomas Cobb refused to concede his brother's defeat. After pondering the situation, he reached the conclusion that the latter's presidential aspirations had not been adversely affected. His reasoning was based on the fact that several Georgia newspapers were condemning the March proceedings "as a triumph of *Douglas Trickery* over the will of the Democracy." The "charge is operating powerfully *in your favor*," he informed his brother. "It is on the mouth of every one" and was reportedly gaining credence in Alabama.[14]

On the strength of this evidence, much of it conjectural, Cobb advised his brother to remain in the background until the Charleston convention was in progress. In case of a stalemate, Alabama could be persuaded, he was sure, to present the secretary as a compromise candidate. Other southern states plus New York and Pennsylvania might back the move. "Then," he concluded, "let your friends from Georgia put on all steam... and you can be nominated." Stephens, he insisted, "has been and is trying to play the very game I map out for you. He was very willing for you to be placed forward to bear the brunt of the fight while he covered himself with a pretended indifference. *The tables are turned.* Let us use it."[15]

Cobb's proposals were the product of wishful thinking. The March convention had canceled the possibility of his brother's nomination, and to interpret it as a victory instead of a defeat was unrealistic to say the least. The success of his scheme was contingent, moreover, upon a deadlock among the major candidates, and such a contingency never

---

[14]Thomas Cobb to Howell Cobb, 18 March 1860, Howell Cobb Collection. At the end of the month, Cobb was still of the opinion "that a tremendous reaction or rather indignation is getting up in the State against the action of the March Convention" and that the feeling was entirely favorable to his brother. See Thomas Cobb to Howell Cobb, 31 March 1860, ibid.

[15]Thomas Cobb to Howell Cobb, 18 March 1860, ibid. Stephens categorically denied playing any such game as Cobb suggested. "I have been a good deal annoyed," he wrote, "by the use . . . of my name in connection with the Charleston nomination, particularly in our own State. . . . I have felt truly mortified at hearing . . . that Mr. Cobb's friends thought I was at the head of the opposition to him. This is utterly groundless. . . ." Alexander H. Stephens to J. Henly Smith, 18 March 1860, Phillips, ed., *Correspondence*, p. 466. See also Stephens to Henry Cleveland, 8 April 1860, Stephens MSS, Perkins Library, Duke University. The *Southern Banner*, a Cobb organ, accepted Stephens' protestations of innocence as true. See *Southern Banner*, 22 March 1860.

occurred.[16] When the Charleston convention met in April, a dispute over the slavery plank in the party platform precipitated a southern walk-out, including two-thirds of the Georgia delegation. Unable to nominate a candidate, the remaining Democrats voted to adjourn and meet again in June at Baltimore.

Georgians were somewhat divided on the necessity of the Charleston bolt, as indicated by the fact that one-third of the state's delegates refused to leave the floor of the convention. Howell Cobb defended the walk-out on the ground that the platform was designed to promote the candidacy of Douglas, whose views, he argued, were inimical to southern interests. He was willing, however, to send representatives to Baltimore to work for some sort of compromise, but, failing in that, they were to go to Richmond, where a rival convention had been planned by a group of the seceding delegates. Stephens, on the other hand, considered the bolt unwise and altogether unwarranted, and even some of Cobb's closest friends seemed to regard it as simply another instance of his continuing vendetta against Douglas.[17]

What the Georgia Democratic Party would finally do in this emergency was to be decided at a state convention in Milledgeville on 4 June. In the meantime, to build sentiment for Howell Cobb's position, a meeting of Clarke County Democrats was held in the Athens town hall on 26 May. Before and during this local rally, Thomas Cobb used his powers of persuasion to win over the doubters and, as chairman of the committee on resolutions, submitted a report which reflected his brother's viewpoint on the current crisis in party affairs. The resolutions were adopted unanimously, and a delegation, entirely pro-Cobb in composition, was chosen to represent Clarke County at the June convention.[18]

---

[16]According to one source, the Pennsylvania delegation would support Cobb only as a last resort. J. Henly Smith to Alexander H. Stephens, 14 March 1860, Stephens Papers, Emory University Library.

[17]H. Hull, Jr. to Alexander H. Stephens, 16 May 1860, Stephens Papers, Emory University Library; R. M. Johnston to Alexander H. Stephens, 16 May 1860, Stephens Papers, Library of Congress; John B. Cobb to Howell Cobb, 18 May 1860, Howell Cobb Collection. Had Douglas not been in such a strong position to win the nomination, it is conceivable that Cobb might not have been so favorably disposed toward the walk-out in Charleston. The fact that intimate friends questioned his motives lends substance to this point. It should be remembered, too, that in the past Cobb had always been a vigorous advocate of party unity.

[18]Pope Barrow to Howell Cobb, 27 May 1860, Thomas Cobb to Howell Cobb, 28 May

"I have waited the result of the meeting here to write to you," Cobb related to his brother two days later. "I found that a *large* majority . . . were anxious to endorse strongly the action of the Seceders. . . . All were willing to endorse *your suggestions* . . . about Baltimore and Richmond." Concerning the state convention in Milledgeville, he assured him that it would be "overwhelming on your line, as against Douglas. *The difficulty will be to control the ultra Fire-eaters*," who presumably would oppose sending a delegation to Baltimore or any other move that remotely resembled an attempt at reconciliation. "You will stand as a middle man," he explained in closing, "and can thus direct."[19]

As Cobb predicted, the June convention followed the proposals outlined by his brother. The walk-out in Charleston received an official blessing from the state party, and a delegation was sent to Baltimore with authority to secede again if the platform failed to meet its approval.

In Baltimore a bitter contest over the seating of delegates brought about the final disruption of the national Democratic Party. Southerners staged a second withdrawal, whereupon the convention nominated Stephen A. Douglas for the presidency and Herschel V. Johnson as his running mate. Gathering at the Maryland Institute, the seceding delegates nominated John C. Breckinridge and Joseph Lane for president and vice president respectively, a ticket which was subsequently ratified by the convention in Richmond.

Now that his brother had ceased to be a presidential prospect, Cobb lost interest in the internal bickering of the Democratic Party. What mattered to him during the campaign of 1860 was not the success of any one candidate, but the defeat of Abraham Lincoln, the Republican nominee, and whether it came at the hands of Breckinridge, Douglas, or John Bell, the Constitutional Union contender, was immaterial.

Thus, while the friends and allies of his brother campaigned for Breckinridge, Thomas Cobb assumed a nonpartisan pose and wrote articles for publication in the northern press, appealing to citizens of that section not to elect Lincoln and thereby "force upon the South the terrible issue of *Disunion*, or *Dishonor*."[20] This was to be his last plea for

---

1860, Howell Cobb Collection. Howell Cobb, himself, and his cousin, James Jackson, were among the delegates elected.

[19]Thomas Cobb to Howell Cobb, 28 May 1860, ibid.

[20]Candler, comp., *Confederate Records*, 1:158.

sectional reconciliation; or, more aptly, it might be termed political blackmail, for in making Lincoln's defeat the quid pro quo of southern adherence to the Union, he was threatening consequences unless his demand was met.

Cobb was in Milledgeville early in October working on the final revision of the *Georgia Code* when word arrived that the Republicans had elected a governor in Pennsylvania. If it is possible to pinpoint the precise moment when Cobb threw off his allegiance to the Union and cast his lot with the extremists, that moment probably came with the receipt of this intelligence. To his wife he wrote:

> The news of the success of the Black Republicans . . . sounded to me as the death-knell of the Republic. I can see no earthly hope of defeating them in November and their success then, whether we will it or not, is *inevitable disunion*. And calmly and coolly, my dear wife, is it not best? These people hate us, annoy us, and would have us assassinated by our slaves if they dared. I know there are good people among them, but I speak of the masses. They are a *different* people from us . . . and *there is no love* between us. Why then continue together? No outside pressure demands it, no internal policy or public interest requires it. *Separation is desirable*, peaceably if we can, forcibly if we must.[21]

In spite of his belief that secession was inevitable and desirable, Cobb awaited the outcome of the presidential campaign with some trepidation. The "Union or the South one or the other is irretrievably gone, if Lincoln is elected," he reiterated. "I confess I feel *very sad*. The forebodings of my mind are of the most depressing character."[22] What really perturbed him, however, was the attitude of the moderates, who counseled restraint at least until Lincoln had taken office and had committed an unmistakable act of aggression. "Already I hear on every side the bold assertion that 'Lincoln will make a good President,' " he declared in disgust, "and all the timid are saying 'Let us wait for an *overt* act.' I confess my confidence in Southern men and Southern principles is daily losing strength. *Money is the moth*."[23]

These comments mirrored clearly the totality of Cobb's transition from unionism to southern nationalism. A moderate during the 1850s, he

---

[21]Thomas Cobb to Marion Cobb, 11 October 1860, Thomas R. R. Cobb Collection.

[22]Thomas Cobb to Howell Cobb, 5 November 1860, Howell Cobb Collection.

[23]Ibid.

had berated the fire-eaters for undermining the integrity of the Union and accused them of demagoguery. Now apparently, it was the moderate element which lacked moral scruples, while exponents of extreme measures, like himself, were the real patriots. Cobb was not consciously hypocritical, merely obsessed with the idea that all Republicans were malign fanatics who would stop at nothing to destroy slavery, which meant, in turn, the destruction of southern society. To temporize in the face of such a menace was to invite disaster, and those who favored a policy of this sort simply could not be sincere, in his opinion. His transformation from a unionist and sectionalist in 1850 to a secessionist and southern nationalist in 1860 exemplified a general trend among southern evangelicals and various other spokesmen for the South.[24]

Worried and uncertain about the future, Cobb sought solace in religion. "I would that I had the faith to trust like David and say to my soul 'Hope thou in God!' It is our only trust. He may save us. Human effort is vain."[25] On election night, 6 November, Cobb prayed at the family altar, as he later put it with pious extravagance, for "God to stay the wrath of our oppressors, and preserve the Union of our Fathers."[26] The following morning he was greeted with a telegraphic dispatch announcing Lincoln's election. Convinced that this was God's way of letting him know that disunion was the proper course, he embarked upon a crusade for immediate and unconditional secession. "We feel," he explained to the Reverend Joseph C. Stiles, "that utter ruin politically, socially and spiritually is our fate in the Union. Hence our firm resolve to separate at once. God grant it may be in Peace!"[27]

His campaign to save the South from disaster began on the night of 10 November 1860. Fearful that Lincoln's election might stimulate slave

---

[24]Loveland, *Southern Evangelicals*, pp. 257-59. The changes reflected in the *Southern Literary Messenger* parallel exactly the transition of Cobb. See McCardell, *Idea of a Southern Nation*, pp. 172-73.

[25]Thomas Cobb to Howell Cobb, 5 November 1860, Howell Cobb Collection.

[26]Candler, Comp., *Confederate Records*, 1:175.

[27]Thomas Cobb to Joseph C. Stiles, 11 December 1860, Stiles Correspondence. To another religious acquaintance Cobb wrote that the secession movement "is not the result of ultraism, but the decided conviction that we are *not safe* in life, liberty or property in the union. We may be mistaken, but *it is too late* to argue the question with us. Good men ought now to turn their attention to the great point of *avoiding war* as the consequence of secession." Thomas Cobb to Dr. S. I. Prine, 25 November 1860, Simon Gratz Collection.

insurrections, the Athens town council summoned a public meeting. Cobb, who dreaded the possibility of slave revolts as much as anyone, delayed a trip to Milledgeville to attend the gathering. Appointed to the resolutions committee, he helped draft a report recommending the organization of auxiliary police patrols in every ward and the creation of a vigilance committee, composed of twenty prominent citizens, empowered to investigate and try persons accused of encouraging slave insurrections and punish those found guilty. The report was adopted without dissent, and the designated number of vigilantes was chosen, Cobb being one of those selected. That the vigilance committee was purportedly set up to protect the innocent as well as to deal with the guilty was hardly an excuse for disregarding established legal processes, and Cobb's willingness to condone, even further, extralegal procedures of this kind illustrated how completely he conformed to the intemperate mood of the times.[28]

During the course of the meeting, several speeches were made advocating resistance to Republican rule, but the highlight of the evening was Cobb's impassioned plea for disunion. An excited law student proclaimed it "the greatest speech *I ever heard* . . ." and urged his father to "Get Mr. Cobb to make the same speech in Milledgeville that he made here. If he does that dilapidated little village will dissolve the Union forthwith[.]"[29]

By the time this letter was written, Cobb had reached Milledgeville and had consulted with Robert Toombs, Henry L. Benning, and other active secessionists. All agreed that Howell Cobb's assistance was required. A telegram, reflecting intense excitement, was dispatched to Washington, D. C. on 12 November, over the signatures of Toombs, Benning, William G. Delony, James Jackson, and Thomas Cobb. It read:

---

[28]In fairness, however, it should be noted that Cobb did intervene that same day to help save a man who was being tried by a mob at the town hall for allegedly expressing free-soil sentiments. The accused was released on a motion by Cobb "with the understanding that the next offense should be punished by hanging." *Southern Watchman*, 15 November 1860; *Southern Banner*, 15 November 1860.

[29]Pope Barrow to David C. Barrow, 13 November 1860, Barrow Papers. See also James D. Russ to Alexander H. Stephens, 13 November 1860, Stephens Papers, Library of Congress.

"Your friends and the friends of Resistance wishes [sic] your presence here. Men are confounded. We need your council. Come at once."[30]

The secretary of the treasury was not prepared to leave Washington on such short notice and was slightly irritated at being pressured in this fashion. He favored secession but hesitated to abandon Buchanan in the midst of a crisis. The correct approach, he contended, "is to withdraw from the union on the 4th of March," after the Republicans had taken office. "To secede whilst the government is in the hands of our friends would be wrong and unjustifiable."[31]

Thomas Cobb was not pleased with his brother's decision. It impaired the secretary's reputation among the secessionists, he told his sister-in-law, and hampered the cause of disunion in Georgia by depriving the movement of an important leader.[32] In December Howell Cobb finally succumbed to the desires of the fire-eaters, resigned from the cabinet, and returned to Georgia in time to participate in the last stages of the secession campaign.

Thomas Cobb, meanwhile, had been devoting all of his energy to the movement. On the night of 12 November, he delivered the most celebrated address of his career before the Georgia legislature. At the outset he disclaimed any partisan purpose, reminding his audience that he had not made a political speech in seventeen years and had "never in the slightest degree interfered in past political contests."[33] In brief, he begged all Georgians to lay aside their differences and reason together calmly and dispassionately to solve the crisis before them. What followed, however, can only be described as a diatribe against the Republican Party and against a decade of abolitionist assaults. It was a kind of catharsis ridding his mind of the last vestiges of union sentiment.[34]

---

[30]Telegram to Howell Cobb, 12 November 1860, Howell Cobb Collection.

[31]Howell Cobb to John B. Lamar, 31 October 1860, ibid.

[32]Mary Ann Cobb to Howell Cobb, [9] December 1860, ibid.

[33]Political activity on behalf of his brother and his own early office seeking, as we have seen, were considered family rather than party matters. Candler, comp., *Confederate Records*, 1: 157.

[34]Ibid., pp. 158, 171-72. A contemporary critic commented that a "close scrutiny of his address, will show that . . . it consists almost wholly of glowing appeals to the passions, ignoring the judgement; and that what argument it contains, is utterly fallacious." *Daily Chronicle & Sentinel* (Augusta GA), 27 December 1860.

Posing the question: "*Is the election of Lincoln a sufficient ground for the dissolution of the Union?*" Cobb advanced a number of legal and political arguments to support an affirmative answer. First, he averred, no less than nine northern states, in effect, had nullified the Fugitive Slave Act by passing personal liberty laws and, consequently, had violated the national compact. "As a lawyer," he lectured, "I am prepared to say that parties to such a contract, who have thus violated its provisions when onerous to them, are not entitled to its privileges." Hence, he concluded, it was the sovereign right of Georgia to declare the electoral votes of the offending states "illegal, and this *election unconstitutional*."[35]

Lincoln's election was also illegal, he maintained, because the framers of the Constitution intended the suffrage for citizens only, and under the *Dred Scott* decision Negroes were not citizens of the United States. Yet, he continued, in spite of an implied prohibition against it, some of the northern states had permitted free Negroes to vote in the national election. "Our slaves," he declaimed, "are first stolen from our midst on underground railroads, and then voted at Northern ballot-boxes to select rulers for you and me. The memory of our fathers is slandered when this is declared to be according to the Constitution."[36]

His third reason for denying the validity of Lincoln's election amounted to this: a sectionally based party had succeeded at the polls with only forty percent of the popular vote and might perpetuate itself in power. That there had been minority presidents before, Cobb granted, but, he insisted, no executive had ever been chosen by such a small percentage of votes, and never had the concept of majority rule been thwarted so blatantly. This development disclosed, in his opinion, a major flaw in the Constitution, namely, the absence of safeguards against the tyranny of the few.

Cobb's defense of majority will at a time when southern politicians were registering their deep concern for minority rights was peculiar, and

---

[35]Candler, comp., *Confederate Records*, 1: 159-60. To argue that one sovereign entity might negate the electoral votes of another sovereign entity because a given state statute was allegedly unconstitutional was absurd and certainly inconsistent with the spirit of a recent statement he had made lionizing Daniel Webster "as the defender and Expounder of the Constitution." For this reference to Webster see Thomas Cobb to Howell Cobb, 4 November 1860, Howell Cobb Collection.

[36]Candler, comp., *Confederate Records*, 1: 161.

it was somewhat clouded by a discursive, but, from the point of view of southern nationalism, very important, commentary on the supposed incompatibility of the northern and southern cultures. Each section, he said, was composed of "a distinct people, having different social organizations, different pursuits, different memories, different hopes, different destinies," all of which proved to his satisfaction that each must go its separate way.[37]

All these differences, of course, implied the existence of a distinctive, perhaps homogeneous, South in which, as he had stated two years earlier in his *Law of Negro Slavery*, the interests of slaveholders and non-slaveholders alike were very similar, if not identical; in other words, a shared set of values was the stuff of southern nationhood.[38]

Cobb found a fourth legal argument for secession in the preamble to the Constitution. The election of Lincoln, he stated, infringed upon the spirit of the Constitution by endangering the "domestic tranquility," which the preamble guaranteed. Crediting every wild rumor, he warned of the imminence of slave insurrections engendered by the Republican triumph. "Recur with me to the parting moment when you left your firesides," he exhorted.

> Remember the trembling hand of a loved wife, as she whispered her fears from the incendiary and the assassin. Recall the look of indefinable dread with which the little daughter inquired when your returning footsteps should be heard. And if there be manhood in you, tell me if this is the domestic tranquility which this "glorious Union" has achieved.[39]

After this lurid outburst came an amazing about face. "I have no fear of any servile insurrection which shall threaten our political existence," he reassured his listeners. "Our slaves are the most happy and contented, best fed and best clothed and best paid laboring population in the world,

---

[37]Ibid., p. 162. It will be recalled that Cobb had expressed the same idea to his wife several weeks earlier.

[38]Cobb, *Law of Slavery*, pp. ccxiii-ccxiv. Leaders on both sides of the secession question made frequent reference to the idea of a homogeneous southern society. For examples see Michael P. Johnson, *Toward a Patriarchal Republic. The Secession of Georgia* (Baton Rouge: Louisiana State University Press, 1977), pp. 41-42. Hereinafter cited as Johnson, *Patriarchal Republic*.

[39]Candler, comp., *Confederate Records*, 1: 163.

and the *most faithful* and least feared."[40] Then, as if to reconcile this contradiction, he went on to explain that, while the Negro majority was trustworthy, a malicious handful, "instigated by the unscrupulous emissaries of Northern Abolitionists," might commit arson and murder. Already a few malcontents had resisted their overseer not seven miles from Milledgeville, he reported, and similar stories of widespread discontent among the slaves filled the newspapers. "What has given impulse to these fears, and aid and comfort to those outbreaks now," Cobb conjectured, "but the success of the Black Republicans—the election of Abraham Lincoln."[41]

In short, because the Republicans had won the presidential election, Cobb charged them with subverting the Constitution, plotting crimes against the South, and disturbing the slaveholder's peace of mind. In reality, his own vivid imagination and his repeated circulation of hysterical rumors did quite as much, probably more, to stimulate the apprehensions of the master class as any specific word or deed on Lincoln's part.

The last half of Cobb's polemic concentrated on the political justification for secession which he deemed of greater significance than the legal aspects of the question. "I must confess," he stated, "that the mere election of a candidate to the Presidency, in a manner legally unconstitutional, does not in my judgment justify necessarily a dissolution of the Union."[42]

This damaging admission, which negated most of his previous argument, was quickly qualified. "As much as I would dislike the triumph of a purely sectional candidate upon a purely sectional platform, I am free to

---

[40]Ibid., p. 164. In his *Law of Negro Slavery*, Cobb had written that "Nine-tenths of the Southern masters would be defended by their slaves, at the peril of their own lives." See ibid., p. cc*iii*.

[41]Candler, comp., *Confederate Records*, 1: 164. Frederickson, *Black Image*, p. 54, again citing Cobb in support of his view, argues that proslavery theorists were able to reconcile the contradiction between slave docility and resistance by seeing the Negro as unstable and "semi-civilized." "Hence docility was not so much his natural character as an artificial creation of slavery. As long as control of the master was firm and assured, the slave would be happy, loyal, and affectionate, but remove or weaken the authority of the master, and he would revert to type as a blood-thirsty savage."

[42]Candler, comp., *Confederate Records*, 1: 168. To speak of an election as being "legally unconstitutional" was a contradiction in terms. What Cobb meant, of course, was that the election was technically legal, but violated the spirit of the Constitution.

say I should hesitate even then to risk the consequences of a dissolution, provided that sectional platform *was upon issues not vital in themselves, or were temporary in their nature.*"[43] To sustain his thesis that Lincoln's election was a sufficient cause for secession, it was essential to prove that the election result was, in itself, a vital matter and that the Republican Party, once in power, would never relinquish control. Cobb did neither, but he tried. Substituting invective for reason, he recounted the growth of abolitionist sentiment in the North and the recurrence of national crises in order to demonstrate that southern willingness to compromise had been for naught; that northern agitators had repeatedly spurned compromise and taken advantage of southern moderation to advance their antislavery designs; and that the election of Lincoln was the last and most serious incident in a long series of events leading to the decline of southern security within the Union and to the eventual destruction of southern institutions.

The issue was obviously vital, he argued, and it was also permanent for the simple reason that Republicanism and fanaticism were synonymous. History and philosophy made it abundantly clear, to him at least, that fanatics never halted of their own volition short of unconditional victory. "Tell me," he demanded,

> when and where the craving appetite of fanaticism was ever gorged with victims. . . . When you have done this, you may then convince me that this is a temporary triumph. . . . Till you do this, I must believe that Lincoln and Seward spoke the truth when they said, this contest is never ended until all these States are either free or slave.[44]

Since the slavery issue was both crucial and enduring, the only solution Cobb could conceive was prompt and permanent disunion. Focusing on the opponents of immediate secession, he endeavored to refute their arguments, which favored delay and circumspection pending an overt act of aggression by the Republican administration. Though never so kind in private, he was clever enough to recognize the honesty of their motives in public. To have done otherwise at this point might have alienated some who were still wavering between delay and instant action. Nonetheless, Cobb left no doubt that he thought a policy of patient waiting was short-sighted and submissive.

---

[43]Ibid.

[44]Ibid., p. 174.

Closing his case for immediate secession with a burst of impassioned oratory, Cobb declared that decisiveness alone could avert civil war and ensure southern liberty and property. "Come then, legislators," he harangued, "wait not till the grog-shops and cross-roads shall send up a discordant voice from a divided people, but act as leaders, in guiding and forming public opinion. Speak no uncertain words, but let your united voice go forth . . . for 'Liberty or Death!' "[45]

Combining the tactics of a courtroom lawyer with the distortions of a demagogue and the zeal of a revivalist, Cobb had presented an emotional plea for secession. He sincerely hoped that it could be accomplished peacefully, but peaceable or not, the dissolution of the Union had to be permanent, he believed. The idea of exploiting temporary disunion to extract concessions and guarantees from the North never entered his mind. Years later Alexander H. Stephens erroneously attributed this stratagem to Cobb and quoted him as saying: "We can make better terms out of the Union than in it."[46]

A restored Union on any terms was completely foreign to Cobb's concept of secession. Without exception, his public remarks and personal correspondence bear this out. His speech to the legislature was important, therefore, not because it placated the moderates or offered the

---

[45]Ibid., p. 182.

[46]Alexander H. Stephens, *A Constitutional History of the Late War Between the States*, 2 vols. (Philadelphia: The National Publishing Company, 1870), 2: 321. Stephens' statement was reiterated by Ulrich B. Phillips in his *Georgia and States Rights*, pp. 204, 208. Phillips subsequently discovered, however, that Cobb's speech of 12 November, "contained nothing of the nature asserted by Stephens" and surmised incorrectly that "Cobb may possibly have used the reformation argument at some other time in the secession campaign." See Phillips, *The Life of Robert Toombs* (New York: The Macmillan Company, 1913), p. 199. Later writers have fallen into the same error. For example, see E. Merton Coulter, *The Confederate States of America, 1861-1865* (Baton Rouge: Louisiana State University Press, 1950), p. 17; T. Conn Bryan, *Confederate Georgia*, p. 5; Avery O. Craven, *The Growth of Southern Nationalism, 1848-1861* (Baton Rouge: Louisiana State University Press, 1953), p. 372; Michael P. Johnson, "A New Look at the Popular Vote for Delegates to the Georgia Secession Convention," *The Georgia Historical Quarterly*, 56 (Summer 1972): 273. Hereinafter cited as Johnson, "Popular Vote for Delegates to the Georgia Secession Convention." Horace Montgomery, *Cracker Parties*, p. 248; J. G. Randall and David Donald, *The Civil War and Reconstruction* (Boston: D. C. Heath and Company, 1961), p. 140; Wilfred B. Yearns, *The Confederate Congress* (Athens, GA: The University of Georgia Press, 1960), p. 3. For a succinct summary of this point see William B. McCash, "Thomas R. R. Cobb and the 'Better Terms' Argument," *The Georgia Historical Quarterly*, 60 (Spring 1976):49-53.

promise of ultimate reunion, but because it demonstrated his unyielding commitment to the cause of immediate, unconditional, and permanent secession and helped set the tone of the disunion movement in Georgia.

Loud applause greeted the conclusion of Cobb's address. John B. Lamar, the brother-in-law of Howell Cobb and an avid secessionist, shouted himself hoarse. Later, barely able to talk above a whisper, he told his nephew that "it was the finest speech he ever heard in his life."[47] Printed in pamphlet form, the address was circulated widely in Georgia. One thousand copies were sent to Macon for distribution at the Cotton Planter's Fair, and John H. Seals, the publisher, was kept busy filling a backlog of orders.[48]

Invitations to speak poured in from various parts of the state, more than Cobb could possibly accept. When not orating, he wrote newspaper articles, attended rallies, and corresponded with secession leaders in and out of Georgia. His days and nights were devoted single-mindedly to the goal of dissolving the Union. "Tom is enthused," wrote his sister-in-law. "He reminds me of the Methodist Circuit riders I used to know in my childhood—so thoroughly infused with the Spirit and the righteousness of the cause—that no physical discomfort dampens his zeal."[49] Her analogy was perceptive. Secession was certainly much more than a political movement to Cobb; it was a crusade to save the South from moral, social, and economic collapse.

In the meantime, the opponents of immediate secession had been given the opportunity to express their views to the Georgia legislature. On 14 November, Alexander Stephens, chief spokesman for the so-called

---

[47]Lamar Cobb to Mary Ann Cobb, 14 November 1860, Howell Cobb Collection.

[48]John H. Seals to John B. Lamar, 1, 15 December 1860, ibid. See also C. H. Hopkins to A. H. Stephens, 4 December 1860, Stephens Papers, Library of Congress. Opponents of secession either ignored or denounced Cobb's speech. The *Rome Tri-Weekly Courier*, 20 November 1860, for example, barely mentioned Cobb's address, but printed an anti-disunion speech by Alexander H. Stephens in full. For typical criticisms of Cobb's speech, see *Southern Enterprise* (Thomasville GA), 21 November 1860; *Daily Chronicle & Sentinel*, 27 December 1860.

[49]Mary Ann Cobb to Howell Cobb, [9] December 1860, Howell Cobb Collection. Cobb corresponded with Maxcy Gregg of South Carolina and may have been in contact with Robert Newman Gourdin of the same state. Gourdin was chairman of the so-called "Association of 1860," a kind of committee of correspondence designed to foment secession in the South. Mary Spencer Ringold, "Robert Newman Gourdin and the '1860 Association,' " *The Georgia Historical Quarterly*, 55 (Spring 1971):501-507.

cooperationists (dubbed submissionists by their adversaries), recommended a southern conference to explore every avenue of a compromise before resorting to extreme measures.[50]

In contrast to Cobb's fiery effort, Stephens' exposition was a masterpiece of prudence and sound judgment. The following evening Benjamin H. Hill, another cooperation leader, argued in much the same vein. Cobb's reaction to both speeches was typically negative. "Their position is *weak*," he scoffed, "very *weak*. They plead for *delay*. They are trying to deceive the people and I am sure the people can and will see it."[51]

It was easy for Cobb to suspect Stephens of duplicity. He had always mistrusted the man and had recently described him as a "wily[,] shrewd politician."[52] His prejudice was fortified late in November when the publication of Stephens' speech gave rise to a widely circulated story to the effect that Cobb had urged the legislators to secede before the masses could make their wishes known. Actually he had advised the legislature to shape public sentiment, not ignore it, but his plea to "wait not till the grog-shops and cross-roads shall send up a discordant voice" was susceptible to misrepresentation.

On 1 December, he penned a denial, which was published in both the *Southern Banner* and the *Southern Watchman* on the sixth. "I take pains to correct this report," he explained, "Because it may hurt the cause of freedom and independence, by exciting a jealousy commendable when justly aroused."[53] His attempt to erase the error was in vain. Antisecessionists repeatedly capitalized on his verbal blunder, citing it as a perfect example of how little regard the disunionists had for the will of the people.[54]

---

[50]As pointed out by Dwight L. Dumond, *The Secession Movement 1860-1861* (New York: The Macmillan Company, 1931), pp. 121-34, the cooperationists were men who opposed separate state action, who favored a southern convention to promote sectional unity, and who differed among themselves "only in the point of time and the conditions on which they would be willing to resort to arms in defense of Southern rights." In no sense were they submissionists. If circumstances warranted and if no other recourse presented itself, they were prepared to accept southern secession from the Union.

[51]Thomas Cobb to John B. Lamar, 17 November [1860], Howell Cobb Collection.

[52]Thomas Cobb to Howell Cobb, 18 March 1860, ibid.

[53]*Southern Banner*, 6 December 1860.

[54]*Southern Watchman*, 19, 25 December 1860; *Daily Chronicle & Sentinel*, 16 November 1860, 23, 27 December 1860; *Southern Enterprise*, 21 November 1860, 13

Cobb clearly comprehended the importance of public opinion and his concern that it be properly influenced was heightened by Governor Joseph E. Brown's call for a state convention to meet in Milledgeville on 16 January 1861. Delegates from each county were to be elected on 2 January. How long Georgia remained in the union would presumably hinge on the outcome of this election. The law authorizing the governor to call such a convention was based on a recommendation by a committee of prominent citizens appointed by the legislature. The committee, a mixture of secessionists, including Thomas Cobb, Francis Bartow, Henry Benning, and Robert Toombs, and cooperationists, like Alexander H. Stephens, Benjamin H. Hill, and Herschel V. Johnson, met on the morning of 15 November 1860, and resolved that since "the present crisis . . . demands resistance," a convention, as noted, should be held "to determine upon the mode, measure, and time of such resistance."[55] One member of the legislature arbitrarily interpreted "resistance" to mean immediate secession and predicted that "the contest before the people will be warm, and the cry of *union* will be used with all the effect that demagogues and party leaders can produce. But my hopes are strong that the magical influence of that word in Georgia has been lost, never more to return."[56]

Sharing this sentiment, Cobb embarked upon a speaking tour of middle and northern Georgia beginning in Athens on 17 November. The thrust of his address in his home town was identical to his speech before the legislature and was well received by a large audience drawn from five surrounding counties.[57]

From Athens Cobb went on to Lexington where the citizens listened politely for three hours and adopted a resolution thanking him for an "able and eloquent address."[58] In Jefferson the response was more enthu-

---

February 1861; W. Strickland to Alexander H. Stephens, 4 February 1861, Stephens Papers, Library of Congress.

[55]Among the other members of the committee were: Governor Brown, Linton Stephens, Joseph H. Lumpkin, and James Jackson. *Federal Union* (Milledgeville GA), 20 November 1860; *Rome Tri-Weekly Courier*, 20 November 1860; *Southern Enterprise*, 21 November 1860; *Southern Watchman*, 22 November 1860.

[56]A. R. Lawton to Robert N. Gourdin, 20 November 1860, Keith Read Collection.

[57]*Southern Watchman*, 22 November 1860.

[58]Candler, comp., *Confederate Records*, 1: 83; T. H. Barrow to [?], 19 [November] [1860], Barrow Papers.

siastic. Here the impact of his speech disquieted the moderates to such an extent that they invited Alexander H. Stephens to counteract its effect.[59] On 7 December, Cobb delivered an inspired oration in Macon, "and such a speech," claimed John B. Lamar, "I never heard before. It was four hours long and nobody was tired, and at the close the audience was enthusiastic. It had a great effect on opinions of everybody."[60] The following night Cobb spoke in Milledgeville and soon thereafter visited Greensboro, where, it was reported, his speech was interrupted by a riot.[61] "I tell you," exclaimed an overwrought newspaper correspondent, "that since Patrick Henry closed his eyes upon earth no such orator has appeared in this country."[62]

On 10 December, Cobb was back in Athens, showing signs of physical fatigue. Apparently his efforts had been worth the strain, for he had written from Milledgeville on the eighth that "Everything is cheering for Secession. Georgia is certain to go out."[63] While confident about the state as a whole, he was not so sure about a number of northern counties in which the success of the immediate secessionists was far from a certainty. In these, he notified his brother, the "Subs [submissionists] are now playing the card of 'Co-operation[.]' They hope to do great things with it."[64]

Perhaps to offset their appeal, but primarily to influence the South Carolina secession convention (due to convene on 17 December) Cobb drafted a cooperation plan of his own which appeared in several southern newspapers.[65] The proposal was simple. South Carolina, holding the first

---

[59]*Southern Watchman*, 12 December 1860; William L. Mitchell to Col. W. L. Mitchell, 3 December 1860, William L. Mitchell Papers, Southern Historical Collection, University of North Carolina Library; G. B. L. Davis to Alexander H. Stephens, 3 December 1860, Stephens Papers, Library of Congress.

[60]John B. Lamar to Howell Cobb, 11 December 1860, Howell Cobb Collection.

[61]James D. Russ to Alexander H. Stephens, 9 December 1860, Stephens Papers, Library of Congress; Mary Ann Cobb to Howell Cobb, [9] December 1860, Thomas Cobb to Howell Cobb, 8 December 1860, Howell Cobb Collection.

[62]*Southern Banner*, 20 December 1860.

[63]Thomas Cobb to Howell Cobb, 8 December 1860, Howell Cobb Collection.

[64]Ibid.

[65]Thomas Cobb to Howell Cobb, 15 December 1860, ibid. His cooperation scheme was published in the *Southern Banner*, the Milledgeville *Federal Union*, the Macon

convention, was to postdate its ordinance of secession. Other state conventions were then to adopt ordinances to take effect on the same day. In the interim, commissioners from all the seceding states would meet to discuss the possibility of creating a new government based on the old Constitution. Without abandoning the secessionist demand for separate and immediate state action, Cobb had thus provided a framework for cooperation. "Such cooperation," he opined, would lend "dignity and moral weight" to the movement. "And while I am free to admit that each State must act for herself and resume . . . her delegated sovereignty, yet I conceive that it is possible and highly desirable that all of them should assign some common day for . . . such resumption."[66]

Although the proposal in no way altered Cobb's basic stance, cooperationist newspapers cited it as proof that he had deviated from his previous commitment to immediate secession.[67] Hastening to correct this misconception, Cobb inserted a letter in the press emphatically denying that he favored delay in order to gain the cooperation of those southern states still clinging to the Union. "On the contrary," he declared, "I favor co-operation with the States which are determined to secede before the 4th of March, 1861."[68]

Without manifesting the slightest apparent interest in his scheme for concerted action, South Carolina seceded on 20 December. Far from registering disappointment over the fact that his plan had been ignored, Cobb celebrated the occasion by participating in a torchlight parade, illuminating his house, and displaying a large transparency emblazoned with the words: "Resistance to Abolition is Obedience to God."[69]

Georgia Journal and Messenger, *The Savannah Republican*, and *The New Orleans Bee*, and a copy of the plan was sent to Colonel Maxcy Gregg, a delegate to the South Carolina convention.

[66]*Southern Banner*, 22 December 1860.

[67]Dwight L. Dumond, ed., *Southern Editorials on Secession* (1931; reprint ed., Gloucester MA: Peter Smith, 1964), p. 368; *Daily Chronicle & Sentinel*, 18, 23 December 1860; *Southern Enterprise*, 2 January 1861; *Montgomery Weekly Advertiser*, 26 December 1860.

[68]*Montgomery Weekly Advertiser*, 26 December 1860. Not all newspapers misconstrued Cobb's plan. The *Southern Watchman*, 25 December 1860, and the *Southern Recorder*, 25 December 1860, both recognized that he had not moderated his views. See also James Mercer Green to Robert Gourdin, 21 December 1860, Keith Read Collection.

[69]*Southern Banner*, 27 December 1860; Thomas Cobb to Howell Cobb, 19 December

Five days before the secession of South Carolina, citizens of Clarke County assembled in the Athens town hall to nominate three candidates for election to the January state convention called earlier by Governor Brown. Thomas Cobb, Jefferson Jennings, and Asbury Hull, a prominent old-line Whig, were chosen to run on a platform advocating immediate disunion and cooperation among the states in substantial conformity to Cobb's plan.[70]

Placing Hull on the ticket was sound strategy. His conservatism was well known and would attract votes from county precincts where the Whigs had been dominant for years. Converted reluctantly to secession, Hull considered it a necessary evil and probably agreed with his son, who belatedly joined the movement with the comment that "Tom Cobb, Toombs and Yancey would carry him and all to the Devil."[71] Hull's ambivalence on the subject of secession was further indicated by the presence of his name on a rival slate of delegates elected by a group of Clarke County cooperationists meeting in Watkinsville on 22 December.[72]

Piqued as usual by any display of opposition, Cobb remarked that "Mr. Asbury Hull has acted in very bad faith towards us and I fear that the dissatisfaction with him will lose us one man. I am trying to head that."[73] He was also trying to head off his own defeat. "A *bitter personal* fight is being made on me in this County," he noted on 15 December, the day of his nomination. "I shall have to work hard to whip it."[74]

1860, Howell Cobb Collection. That part of his plan which proposed an exchange of commissioners to facilitate the formation of a confederate government corresponded to a resolution adopted by the South Carolina convention to send agents to various states with instructions to recommend the organization of a confederacy on the basis of the Constitution of the United States. Since the idea of appointing commissioners had been adopted previously in Alabama and Mississippi and since agents from those states were present at the South Carolina convention, it seems improbable that Cobb's plan had more than an indirect bearing on South Carolina's decision.

[70]*Southern Banner*, 20 December 1860.

[71]Mary Ann Cobb to Howell Cobb, [9] December 1860, Howell Cobb Collection. See also R. M. Johnston to Alexander H. Stephens, 10 January 1861, Stephens Papers, Library of Congress.

[72]*Southern Banner*, 27 December 1860. Dr. M. S. Durham and Captain Isaac C. Vincent were the other candidates.

[73]Thomas Cobb to Howell Cobb, 26 December 1860, Howell Cobb Collection.

[74]Thomas Cobb to John B. Lamar, 15 December 1860, ibid.

Continuing his campaign outside as well as inside Clarke County, Cobb attended rallies in Danielsville on 17 December, and Atlanta on the twenty-first, and spoke at different places every day during the final week of the canvass.[75] His efforts were crowned with success. On 2 January 1861, the Clarke County secessionists won a sweeping victory. Cobb received 654 votes, seventy-five percent of which came from Athens. In Watkinsville, the center of cooperationist strength, he ran behind both Hull and Dr. M. S. Durham, a cooperation candidate, and barely outpolled Jennings. Elsewhere he managed to hold his own with all candidates except Hull, who consistently gained ten to thirteen more votes than Cobb at each of the three remaining precincts.[76]

In the state-wide election the secessionists claimed a substantial victory, despite the fact that a full set of official returns was never published. An incomplete and unofficial set of election statistics submitted by Governor Brown appeared in the *Southern Federal Union* on 30 April 1861. These returns gave the secessionists 50,243 popular votes to 37,123 for their opponents, a majority of 13,120. However Michael P. Johnson contends that the majority for disunion was, at best, 2,520, and, more than likely, the secessionists lost by a small percentage.[77] Although some of the cooperationists conceded defeat, many refused to believe that the people had willingly endorsed immediate secession and predicted that when the convention met on 16 January the division between unionists and disunionists would be very close or even slightly in favor of the

---

[75]Thomas Cobb to Howell Cobb, 18, 26 December 1860, ibid.; W. H. Guffette to Alexander H. Stephens, 5 December 1860, Stephens Papers, Perkins Library, Duke University; Thos. S. Powell to Alexander H. Stephens, 21 December 1860, Stephens Papers, Library of Congress.

[76]*Southern Banner*, 9 January 1861. The official vote in Clarke County was as follows:

Delegates	Athens	Watkinsville	All other precincts	Total
Cobb	490	94	70	654
Hull	391	131	105	627
Jennings	467	73	66	606
Durham	61	124	58	243
Vincent	48	45	27	120

[77]Michael P. Johnson, "Popular Vote For Delegates to the Georgia Secession Convention." Ellen Louise Sumner, "Unionism in Georgia, 1860-1861" (M.A. thesis, University of Georgia, 1960), pp. 180-81, also questioned the validity of these returns.

former side.[78] Not a few cooperationists were of the opinion that the size of the secessionist vote was due to duplicity and demagoguery. Even in Clarke County where the disunionists won easily, the margin of victory (rather than the victory itself) was said to be the result of "trickery and deception."[79] For instance, on election day Thomas Cobb had published a rumor that federal troops from Ft. Sumter were at that moment firing on Charleston, South Carolina. The rumor was false, of course, but it appeared in the newspapers of three counties and, according to one cooperationist editor, was "manufactured out of the whole cloth . . . expressly for the occasion."[80] While denying that he had perpetrated a deliberate fraud, Cobb admitted giving currency to the report and, with no apology, asserted: "I . . . would have sent it to every voter in Georgia if the means had been in my power."[81]

On Monday, 14 January, Thomas Cobb, wearing locally made apparel from head to toe to signify independence from northern manufacturers, left for Macon, where he met John B. Lamar, a delegate to the state convention from Bibb County, and together they traveled to Milledgeville determined to vote Georgia out of the Union forever.

If the reactions of friend and foe alike are any indication, then Thomas Cobb's great secession crusade had a powerful impact on the public mind in Georgia; and therefore he deserves the lofty reputation he

---

[78]For these opinions, which tend to bear out the thesis of Johnson's article, see Alexander H. Stephens to Linton Stephens, 2, 5 January 1861, Stephens Correspondence, microfilm, University of North Carolina Library; Linton Stephens to Alexander H. Stephens, 9 January 1861, ibid.; James P. Hambleton to A. H. Stephens, 7 January 1861, Stephens Papers, Library of Congress; Rich Peters to Alexander H. Stephens, 9 January 1861, ibid.; H. Fielder to Alexander H. Stephens, 7 January 1861, ibid.; A. Hood to Joseph E. Brown, 8 January 1861, Telamon Cuyler Collection; *Southern Watchman*, 16 January 1861.

[79]*Daily Chronicle & Sentinel*, 9 January 1861. Throughout the campaign and after the cooperationists bitterly complained that their opponents were stooping to scare tactics and other unscrupulous activities. See Herschel V. Johnson to Alexander H. Stephens, 30 November 1860, H. V. Johnson Papers, Perkins Library, Duke University; Herschel V. Johnson to Alexander H. Stephens, 9 January 1861, ibid.; C. R. Hanleiter to A. H. Stephens, 1 December 1860, Stephens Papers, Library of Congress; A. H. Wyche to Alexander H. Stephens, 25 December 1860, ibid.; D. G. Cotting to Alexander H. Stephens, 2 February 1861, ibid.; *Southern Watchman*, 16 January 1861.

[80]*Daily Chronicle & Sentinel*, 9 January 1861.

[81]Ibid., 12 January 1861.

now holds among historians as one of the foremost disunion leaders in the state. Only Robert Toombs and Howell Cobb were, perhaps, more influential.[82] What made him effective was the ability to arouse an emotional response from his audience. His inspirational efforts in this regard were not unlike his successful entreaties to revival groups and courtroom juries. Thus, as he moved from town to town preaching disunion, he created a bandwagon psychology. The impression gained hold that the secession movement was righteous and unstoppable and would carry the day in Georgia, even though, as we have seen, it barely won and may very well have lost.

Ironically, Cobb would be remembered as the man who appealed to moderates by urging temporary secession in order to restore the Union on better terms, when, in reality, his position was just the reverse. In his eyes secession was an act of revolution and the next step was the establishment of a new southern nation.

---

[82]It is impossible to measure precisely the relative popular influence of the leading secessionists and to rank them in order of importance. One can only make reasonable guesses and the best guess seems to be that the triumvirate composed of Toombs and the two Cobb brothers was most significant. Emory M. Thomas, *The Confederate Nation 1861-1865* (New York: Harper & Row, Publishers, 1979), pp. 52-53; Johnson, *Patriarchal Republic*, pp. 20-23. However, Governor Joseph E. Brown must be included somewhere among the top secessionists. Joseph H. Parks, *Joseph E. Brown of Georgia* (Baton Rouge: Louisiana State University Press, 1977), pp. 110-28. James Jackson, Francis Bartow, Henry L. Benning, and James Mercer Green were in the second echelon.

CHAPTER 7

Confederate Congressman

Top photograph: Thomas R. R. Cobb's home on Prince Avenue—Athens, Georgia, ca. 1902 (copied from *American Monthly Review of Reviews*—1902)

Bottom photograph: Recent photograph of Thomas R. R. Cobb's home, at the time being occupied by a University of Georgia fraternity

On 16 January 1861, three hundred and one delegates, representing 132 Georgia counties, convened in Milledgeville to culminate the secession movement. After two days of preliminaries, the real business of the convention began. On the eighteenth, Judge Eugenius A. Nisbet resolved that it was the "right and duty of Georgia to secede from the . . . Union, and to co-operate with such of the other States as have or shall do the same, for the purpose of forming a Southern Confederacy upon the basis of the Constitution of the United States." He also proposed that a committee of seventeen be created to draft an ordinance of secession.[1] When the cooperationists countered with a substitute resolution offered by Herschel V. Johnson, it touched off a lively debate in which Thomas Cobb, among others, argued the secessionist side of the question against cooperation spokesmen. The exchange continued until the previous question was moved; the Nisbet resolutions were then brought to a vote and adopted 166 to 130.[2] Appointed to the committee of seventeen, Cobb assisted in framing the requisite ordinance of secession. It was reported

---

[1]Candler, comp., *Confederate Records*, 1: 229-30, 240.

[2]Ibid., pp. 230-36.

on 19 January, and decisively approved by a vote of 208 to 89.[3] Georgia thus became the fifth state to secede from the Union.

The work of the secession convention was far from finished, however. Now that Georgia was an independent entity, the laws and constitution of the state had to be modified to conform to her new status, and such matters as postal arrangements, military preparations, and the validity of law suits still pending in the federal courts had to be considered. To deal with these pressing problems, five standing committees were established under a resolution introduced by Francis Bartow. Cobb was named chairman of the "Committee on the Constitution of the State, and the Constitution and Laws of the United States," which initiated approximately one-half of the ordinances enacted by the convention.[4] It also took under advisement various proposed amendments to the state constitution but made no constitutional recommendations until the second session of the convention in March.

Although diligent and energetic in the dispatch of committee assignments, Cobb found the work rather tedious and soon complained that he was "heartily tired" of it. "Georgia has seceded," he informed his sister-in-law, "and I am satisfied. I want to go home now and nothing but a sense of duty keeps me here."[5]

On 24 January he was called upon to accept a new duty, one that necessitated a prolonged absence from his home and family. Acting on a resolution passed the previous day, the convention elected ten delegates—two at large and one from each of eight congressional districts—to represent Georgia at a convention of seceding states sched-

---

[3]Ibid., pp. 250-52, 256. Before the vote on the ordinance of secession, Benjamin Hill reintroduced the Johnson resolution, which was again defeated.

[4]Ibid., pp. 244, 261-62, 272-74. Among other things, it was the duty of Cobb's committee to determine which federal laws were still applicable in Georgia. Thirteen men served on this committee, including Cobb's brother-in-law, Luther J. Glenn, and Richard H. Clark, his colleague on the commission to codify the laws of Georgia. Linton Stephens, half-brother of Alexander Stephens, Benjamin Hill, and A. H. Kenan were other prominent members.

[5]Thomas Cobb to Mary Ann Cobb, 22 January 1861, Howell Cobb Collection. Three days later, he wrote to his wife: "Another midnight finds me winding up a day of hard labor and turning to love and you. I begin to count the days till I shall see you and am almost ready to count the hours. I shall leave the convention before it adjourns . . . unless extraordinary necessity or Providence interferes." Thomas Cobb to Marion Cobb, 25 January 1861, Thomas R. R. Cobb Collection.

uled to meet in Montgomery, Alabama, on 4 February. Cobb was chosen by acclamation from the Sixth District to serve on the delegation, which consisted of Robert Toombs, Francis Bartow, E. A. Nisbet, Benjamin Hill, Alexander Stephens, A. H. Kenan, Howell Cobb, Augustus R. Wright, and Martin J. Crawford.[6] Except for the latter three, all were members of the convention that elected them, a fact which angered Henry R. Jackson. This "parcelling out offices of distinction among themselves," he snarled, "fills me not simply with disgust, but with dismay." He was particularly appalled that Thomas Cobb and Francis Bartow were parties to the deed. "They have involved themselves, I fear, in an amount of personal explanation which will be destruction to thier [sic] future peace."[7]

Cobb seldom felt the need to justify his actions. He saw himself as a self-sacrificing patriot who had forsaken the company of his family and unselfishly neglected his law practice in order to serve the state. The inference that he was an office seeker would have outraged him had he known of it; but, at the same time, he was probably not entirely pleased himself with the composition of the delegation and undoubtedly distrusted the motives of several of the cooperationist members. In fact, discontent over the choice of these delegates was expressed by a number of individuals. Denouncing A. R. Wright as "obnoxious and objectionable," a Floyd County secessionist declared that "His election by the Convention has been received with universal indignation by the secession party." And similar protests were heard against the selection of Hill and Kenan.[8]

Even before the delegates had been elected, James Mercer Green, a Macon secessionist, suspected that Stephens and Hill wanted to reunite the North and South. They "have already commenced their rotten game of a reconstruction party," he warned, and "we shall have to fight to the bitter end and you [John B. Lamar] ought to study out the elements of the

---

[6]Candler, comp., *Confederate Records*, 1: 294-95; *Daily Chronicle & Sentinel*, 27 January 1861. Toombs and Howell Cobb were the delegates-at-large.

[7]Henry Jackson to Howell Cobb, 28 January 1861, Howell Cobb Collection. See also *Southern Enterprise*, 6 March 1861. For a specific objection to Cobb see W. Strickland to Alexander H. Stephens, 4 February 1861, Stephens Papers, Library of Congress.

[8]Thomas J. Ward to Howell Cobb, 2 February 1861, Howell Cobb Collection. See also William H. Underwood to Howell Cobb, 1 February 1861, L. Fouché to Howell Cobb, [?] February 1861, ibid.; H. R. Jackson to Sir, 26 January 1861, Telamon Cuyler Collection.

contest with Tom Cobb, and others."[9] Opposition to the election of Kenan, Wright, Stephens, and Hill was thus predicated on the fact that they had fought against immediate secession and (at least in the case of Stephens and Hill) on the false assumption that they were plotting to restore the Union. At times Cobb's bitterness toward the so-called reconstructionists appeared to exceed his hatred for the Republicans. The former, in his view, were nothing less than a reincarnation of the old Tory traitors of 1776-1783.

On the day of his election, Cobb sent a note to his wife requesting her to accompany him to Alabama. The following night, he repeated his request. "My dear wife," he wrote, "let me urge, entreat, *pray* you to be ready to go with me to Montgomery."[10] Her reply, that inclement weather made it inadvisable to travel with their year-old daughter, depressed him greatly. His first impulse was to resign as a delegate, but, after thinking the matter over, he decided,

> that it was better to spend two weeks there [Montgomery] than to go either as a commissioner to some other state or to subject myself to be called to military service. I cannot honorably refuse at this juncture to work for the State in some capacity. Is not this the best? And does it not trespass least on my duty to you and my little ones?[11]

Impatient to get home, Cobb hastened to complete his business at the state convention. On 28 January, he introduced a lengthy "Bill of Rights" and moved that it be tabled until the next session of the convention.[12] Then, without waiting for the official adjournment, he left for Athens, where admiring townsmen and a band greeted his return. Responding with an impromptu speech, he praised the secession convention and optimistically predicted a future of peace and prosperity. In conclusion, he thanked the crowd for the reception and invited everyone in for supper. "After doing . . . justice to the good things as comes of appetites sharpened by the keen night air," reported the *Southern Banner*, "the crowd dispersed with renewed cheers for their hospitable entertainer and representative."[13]

---

[9]James Mercer Green to John B. Lamar, 21 January 1861, Howell Cobb Collection.

[10]Thomas Cobb to Marion Cobb, 25 January 1861, Thomas R. R. Cobb Collection.

[11]Thomas Cobb to Marion Cobb, 28 January 1861, ibid.

[12]Candler, comp., *Confederate Records*, 1: 338.

[13]*Southern Banner*, 6 February 1861.

On Saturday, 2 February, Cobb departed by train for Montgomery to implement a resolution of the state convention, which instructed the Georgia delegation to create a temporary political system "modeled . . . on the . . . late Government of the United States" and "to agree upon a plan of permanent Government."[14] Along the way he was joined by other delegates including Bartow, Stephens, and Senator James Chesnut of South Carolina who was accompanied by his wife, the subsequently famous diarist, Mary Boykin Chesnut. On Sunday, three miles outside of Montgomery, the train jumped the track causing minor damage and a delay of two hours. "This comes from Sunday travelling," Mrs. Chesnut remarked to Cobb, who agreed with her wholeheartedly.

Cobb rode the rest of the way in the baggage car, smoking his pipe and chatting congenially with Alexander H. Stephens, whose views he despised and motives he distrusted.[15] Upon reaching the city, he went directly to the Exchange Hotel, where he met his brother and conversed with a number of the other delegates. That night he wrote:

> The universal feeling seems to be to make Howell President of the convention. As to the provisional president of the Confederacy, the strongest current is for Jeff Davis. Howell and Mr. Toombs are both spoken of and there seems to be a good deal of difficulty in settling down on any person. It is generally supposed we will get through in two weeks.[16]

To his disappointment, it required more than a month for the convention to perform its labors. When the proceedings went too slowly to suit him, Cobb became annoyed and, at one point, threatened to leave Montgomery unless the convention got busy.[17]

Actually, the convention worked at a rapid pace. It organized on Monday, 4 February, adopted rules of procedure, and elected Howell Cobb to preside. The next day a committee, headed by Christopher G. Memminger of South Carolina, was appointed to frame a provisional constitution. Concerning the chairman, Cobb commented: "While I do not rate

---

[14]Candler, comp., *Confederate Records*, 1: 331.

[15]Thomas Cobb to Marion Cobb, 3 February 1861, Thomas R. R. Cobb Collection; Alexander H. Stephens to Linton Stephens, 4 February 1861, Stephens Correspondence, microfilm, Southern Historical Collection, University of North Carolina Library.

[16]Thomas Cobb to Marion Cobb, 3 February 1861, Thomas R. R. Cobb Collection.

[17]Thomas Cobb to Marion Cobb, 8 February 1861, ibid.

his talents very high, Memminger is as shrewd as a Yankee."[18] Eventually, he and Memminger developed a fast friendship and, more than once, Cobb counted on him for personal favors.

During the second day of debate, 5 February, Cobb took the lead in suggesting that the convention assume the functions of a legislature as well as a constituent assembly. He felt, however, that the legislative duties of the convention should be limited to a duration of twelve months.[19] The substance of his proposal was eventually incorporated in the Provisional Constitution, under the authority of which the Montgomery convention operated both as a lawmaking body and as a constituent assembly to provide a permanent form of government for the Confederacy.

On 7 February, after only two days of deliberation, Memminger's committee reported a draft of the Provisional Constitution and debate on its provisions began. At the close of a nine hour session, lasting late into the night of the eighth, the Provisional Constitution was adopted and the election of a provisional president and vice president was set for noon of the following day.[20]

Despite personal and political antagonism between Stephens and the Cobb brothers, harmony had existed in the Georgia delegation since the beginning of the convention.[21] But, at a caucus held on the morning of 9 February, unity gave way to factionalism. Stephens opened the meeting by proposing a complimentary ballot for Robert Toombs as provisional president of the new Confederacy. Thomas Cobb objected, arguing that most of the "states were for Davis and that it would place Mr. T. in a false

---

[18]Thomas Cobb to Marion Cobb, 12 February 1861, Thomas R. R. Cobb Collection; *Journal of the Congress of the Confederate States of America* (Washington, D. C.: Government Printing Office, 1904-1905), 1: 18-22. Hereinafter cited as *Confederate Journal.*

[19]*Confederate Journal*, 1: 20, 33, 899. This was in keeping with a resolution passed by the Georgia secession convention, which specified that the "Provisional Government [was] not to extend beyond the period of twelve months from the time it goes into operation." Candler, comp., *Confederate Revords*, 1: 331.

[20]*Confederate Journal*, 1: 31-39.

[21]Hostility also existed between Stephens and Hill, but this, too, was kept under control and later smoothed over by an exchange of notes. See A. H. Kenan and Robert Toombs to Alexander H. Stephens and Benjamin Hill, 14 February 1861, Stephens Papers, Emory University Library.

position."[22] Toombs returned the compliment by nominating Stephens for the vice presidency and was seconded by Kenan and Nisbet. Finding themselves in the minority, the two Cobbs and Bartow walked out of the caucus.[23] Two hours later Jefferson Davis and Alexander H. Stephens were unanimously elected president and vice president of the Provisional Government of the Confederate States of America.[24]

For days thereafter the mere thought of Stephens' success blackened Cobb's mood. "So is the world," he commented bitterly,

> the man who has fought against our rights and liberty is selected to wear the laurels of our victory. The result comes from a maudlin disposition to conciliate the union men by giving the 2nd place in the Confederacy to a Co-operationist. It may help us in the border states in giving them confidence in our conservatism, but it will enervate . . . our own friends at home.[25]

Many delegates did indeed hope that a judicious choice of executive officers would reconcile internal differences and attract the border states. Howell Cobb was one who recognized the logic of this argument, but his implacable brother refused to acknowledge the expediency of any kind of accommodation with the cooperationists and even doubted the wisdom of inviting the border states to join the Confederacy, fearing it might lead to a restoration of the Union. His anxiety on this score was heightened by vague, unfounded rumors to the effect that Davis was sympathetic to the idea of reconstruction. "*If he does not come out boldly in his inaugural* against this suicidal policy," Cobb asserted, "we shall have an explosion here, the end of which I cannot foretell. He *will be denounced* by a large majority of this Congress who are almost unanimous against such a proposition."[26]

---

[22]Thomas Cobb to Marion Cobb, 11 February 1861, Thomas R. R. Cobb Collection.

[23]Ibid.

[24]*Confederate Journal*, 1: 60.

[25]Thomas Cobb to Marion Cobb, 9 February 1861, Thomas R. R. Cobb Collection.

[26]Thomas Cobb to Marion Cobb, 15 February 1861, ibid. The rumors were apparently widespread. A resident of South Carolina read them in a Charleston newspaper and pronounced them "bosh." William Henry Trescot to William Porcher Miles, 6 February 1861, William Porcher Miles Papers, Southern Historical Collection, University of North Carolina Library. Echoing Cobb's sentiments on this subject, a Mississippi delegate declared: "There will be . . . no attempt at re-construction. . . . Those who are not for us are against us. We are out of the Union *and intend to stay out*." James T. Harrison to wife, 17

By the time the president-elect arrived in Montgomery, Cobb was somewhat less apprehensive, having discovered (again by hearsay) that Davis was definitely not a proponent of reconstruction. With his mind momentarily at ease, he signed the enrolled Provisional Constitution and attended the inauguration ceremonies on 18 February. Afterwards, at his desk in the senate chamber of the Alabama Capitol, he wrote: "The inaugural pleased everybody and the manner in which Davis took the oath of office was most impressive. The scene was one worth seeing and remembering."[27]

As yet, Cobb had made no attempt to call upon Davis and had even avoided the president's levee by remaining in his hotel room working on legislation. Justifying his behavior, he remarked: "I hate toadyism so much and especially as . . . my name is connected with the Cabinet."[28] Since he had no intention of accepting a post, he was displaying undue concern for mere appearance, a concern which presumably grew out of a conviction that his fellow congressmen would impute to him the same crass political desires which he constantly ascribed to them.

The number of potential cabinet officers, whatever their motives may have been, was certainly large, and, as the list of hopefuls lengthened, Cobb exclaimed in self-righteous disgust: "I had the folly to believe that there was great patriotism in this movement. God help us, it looks now as if it was nothing but office seeking."[29] He was particularly irritated that Davis had consulted no one in the Georgia delegation, except Stephens, on the matter of appointments. The vice president, whom he regarded as the evil genius of the administration, was suspected of urging Herschel V. Johnson for a place in the cabinet. Johnson's past political differences with Howell Cobb and his more recent opposition to immediate secession, made his appointment offensive to Thomas Cobb. "The best claim to distinction under the existing regime," he grumbled, "seems to be

---

February 1861, James T. Harrison Papers, Southern Historical Collection, University of North Carolina Library. Strong opposition to reconstruction was also expressed in the *Montgomery Weekly Post*, 6 February 1861.

[27]Thomas Cobb to Marion Cobb, 18 February 1861, ibid.

[28]Ibid. Cobb was mentioned in the press as a possible candidate for the position of attorney general.

[29]Thomas Cobb to Marion Cobb, 20 February 1861, ibid.

either to have opposed secession or have done nothing for it."[30] Supported by his brother, he protested to the president, who agreed not to appoint Johnson.

As the official family gradually took shape, Cobb had to admit, in spite of his chronic faultfinding, that the cabinet was strong and satisfactory. Seldom again would he be so magnanimous, and soon his opinion of some of the president's advisors would become inexcusably malicious.

Long before the last cabinet officer had been confirmed, the Provisional Government had gone into operation and a committee of twelve had been constituted to begin work on the Permanent Constitution. Cobb was selected to serve on this committee on 9 February.[31] "This is considered the post of honor in this Congress," he noted with obvious relish. "I prefer it to all others, [but] for . . . ordinary legislation I care little . . . as I do not intend to continue this 'line of business.' "[32]

Nonetheless, as a member of two other committees—judiciary and printing—legislation necessarily occupied a great deal of his time. On 22 February, for example, the judiciary committee reported a bill framed by Cobb to implement Article I, Section 7 of the Provisional Constitution, which prohibited the importation of African slaves from foreign countries.[33] Brought up for debate the next day, Cobb was "forced to defend it from attacks on every side."[34] Further discussion was postponed until 25 February, at which time the Mississippi delegation made a concerted, though unsuccessful, effort to strike out a part of Section 6 requiring the president, under certain circumstances, to dispose of illegally imported

---

[30]Thomas Cobb to Marion Cobb, 25 February 1861, ibid.

[31]Robert B. Rhett of South Carolina was chairman. The rest of the committee was composed of Robert Toombs, James Chesnut of South Carolina, Alexander M. Clayton and Wiley P. Harris of Mississippi, Jackson Morton and James B. Owens of Florida, Richard W. Walker and Robert H. Smith of Alabama, and Alexander DeClouet and Edward Sparrow of Louisiana. *Confederate Journal*, 1: 42.

[32]Thomas Cobb to Marion Cobb, 11 February 1861, Thomas R. R. Cobb Collection.

[33]*Confederate Journal*, 1: 74. Cobb had consistently opposed the African slave trade on moral grounds and had introduced a resolution in the Georgia secession convention to abolish it. Cobb, *Law of Negro Slavery*, p. lxxxi; Ross H. McLean, ed., *Dairy of 1861* by Alexander Means, Emory University Publications Sources and Reprints, series 6, no. 1 (Atlanta, 1949), p. 15.

[34]*Confederate Journal*, 1: 78-79; Thomas Cobb to Marion Cobb, 23 February 1861, Thomas R. R. Cobb Collection.

slaves at public auction. After several minor amendments, the measure passed with only Mississippi opposing.[35]

Cobb had been instrumental in guiding the bill through the Confederate Congress, or at least he claimed full credit for it in a letter to his wife. He was incensed, therefore, when Davis vetoed the measure on 28 February with a brief explanation that Section 6 violated the Provisional Constitution and was "in derogation of its mandate to legislate" effectually against the foreign slave trade.[36] "This," declared Cobb,

> was a fool notion of Mr. [Wiley P.] Harris of Miss. and it seems he has had influence enough with the President to make him adopt it. I shall strive hard to pass it over his head, it will do my soul good to *rebuke* him at the outset of his vetoing.[37]

Cobb's determination to test the president's strength on this issue and "to rebuke him" while the Confederate Government was still in the provisional stage was ill-advised and unnecessary. The issue was not of vital importance to the Confederacy at this point in its development; certainly it was not worth the risk of internal dissension. Moreover, Davis had not objected to the bill as a whole, but had simply questioned the constitutionality of one of its provisions. Conceivably the difficulty could have been resolved by some sort of compromise. Cobb, however, was more interested in avenging the rejection of *his* bill than in settling the matter amicably.

Consequently, when the slave trade bill came up for reconsideration, Cobb was prepared to air his views. On 2 March, he delivered a strongly worded speech criticizing the president's veto message. "I can say to you my wife," he wrote later in the day, "that in my comments on this paper I think I convinced the Presdt's friends that I did not look to that quarter

---

[35]*Confederate Journal*, 1: 82-85. "The weakest delegation here is from Mississippi," Cobb subsequently contended. "Wiley P. Harris is the only man of talent [from that state] and he is bad-tempered and very conceited." Thomas Cobb to Marion Cobb, 5 March 1861, Thomas R. R. Cobb Collection. One can hardly escape the conclusion that Cobb's low opinion of the Mississippians was largely the result of their opposition to the African slave trade bill.

[36]Thomas Cobb to Marion Cobb, 25 February 1861, Thomas R. R. Cobb Collection; *Confederate Journal*, 1: 95.

[37]Thomas Cobb to Marion Cobb, 28 February 1861, Thomas R. R. Cobb Collection.

for office or favor. I was *hot* in my heart and suppressed it as much as I could, but it broke out occasionally."[38]

The chiding had no apparent effect on Davis, and Cobb had neither the influence nor the eloquence to persuade the Congress to override the veto.[39] In subsequent sessions, amendments to the bill were debated, but final action was always postponed. Cobb doggedly refused to give up on the measure. "One or two more questions (the slave trade among them) I should like to settle before I lay aside forever my senatorial robe," he confided to his wife in January 1862.[40] By then, however, it was too late. His term in office was about to expire, and the attention of Congress was drawn to problems of a more crucial nature.

Besides the African slave trade bill, Cobb sponsored legislation relating to international copyright, southern cotton, and Sunday mail delivery. This combination of laws, he envisioned, would gain the support of literary, laboring, and religious groups the world over. "With these three on our side," he stated, "we can bid defiance to potentates and powers."[41] In reality, his proposals had not the slightest chance of accomplishing so grandiose a purpose. Nevertheless, he sought to translate his three-fold aim into law.

To coax, as he put it, "the literary world, especially of Great Britain, to sympathize with us against the Yankee Literary Pirates," Cobb introduced a resolution authorizing the president to negotiate treaties extending copyright privileges to Great Britain, France, and other European states granting reciprocal privileges. It was passed without opposition and signed by Davis on 7 March.[42]

In the past British authors had been aggrieved by the absence of United States copyright statutes to protect their works from unauthorized reprinting, but this was no guarantee that, as a group, they would

---

[38]Thomas Cobb to Marion Cobb, 2 March 1861, ibid.

[39]*Confederate Journal*, 1: 97-98. To pass the bill over the president's veto required a vote of two-thirds of the states. Only three—Georgia, Florida, and South Carolina—voted to override the president, while four states—Alabama, Louisiana, Mississippi, and Texas—voted to sustain him.

[40]Thomas Cobb to Marion Cobb, 29 January 1862, Thomas R. R. Cobb Collection.

[41]Thomas Cobb to Marion Cobb, 7 March 1861, ibid.

[42]Ibid.; *Confederate Journal*, 1: 113-114. For a minor objection to this innocuous measure see *Southern Confederacy*, 18 March 1861.

now show sympathy for the South merely on the strength of one resolution, the effectiveness of which was contingent upon treaty agreements. Literary opinion in England, both favorable and unfavorable to the Confederacy, was shaped by considerations having little or nothing to do with copyright laws; hence, even if a treaty containing copyright provisions had been concluded, it probably would not have altered the views of foreign literary figures to any significant degree. In any event, no treaty was possible until the Confederacy had first been recognized.

Like many of his colleagues in the Confederate Congress, Cobb was certain that recognition would come soon. Never once did he doubt the efficacy of "King Cotton" as an instrument of diplomacy. European dependence on southern cotton, he believed, would secure for the Confederacy not only quick recognition but also the sentiment of the "working world."

In February, he broached a "cotton scheme" suggested by his father-in-law, Judge Joseph H. Lumpkin, a scheme which involved export restrictions on the chief staple crop of the lower South. Congressmen with whom Cobb talked felt that the plan was premature. To curtail the supply of cotton immediately, they argued, might alienate foreign governments needlessly. Disregarding their judgment, he seized every opportunity to explain his father-in-law's position. On 21 February, he presented the plan in outline and submitted a resolution requesting the finance committee to investigate "the expediency of . . . an export duty on all raw cotton . . . exported from the Confederate States to any foreign country by any other channel than through the seaports of this Confederacy."[43]

Since the bulk of southern cotton was shipped to ports in the North for reexportation abroad, the aim of this resolution was to stop the northward flow of cotton and encourage direct trade between Europe and the southern seaboard. Nothing was done to carry the idea into effect until May 1861, when the finance committee reported a bill to prohibit the exportation of raw cotton and cotton yarn except through Confederate ports or overland to Mexico.[44]

---

[43]*Confederate Journal*, 1: 71. Cobb's remarks in support of this resolution were reported in the *Montgomery Weekly Mail*, 1 March 1861.

[44]*Confederate Journal*, 1: 250-51.

Signed on 21 May, the act proved to have numerous flaws. Private trade with the North continued, and the war department often ignored the law in order to exchange cotton for military supplies.[45] In the end, Cobb's recommendations concerning cotton were of no use in winning either recognition or the sympathy of the "working world." Both as a tool of diplomacy and as a means of financing the war, the "King Cotton" concept was a dismal failure. Cobb did not live to see the refutation of this illusory policy, and so his faith in the power of cotton to achieve grand results remained unimpaired.

His espousal of "King Cotton" rounded out an ideal of southern nationalism that had been years in the making. All the elements were now mentally in place: a self-sufficient economy based primarily on the production of cotton, an independent political system, a proslavery ideology, educational institutions staffed by loyal teachers using southern textbooks, a homogeneous social order, southern literature published by southern firms, separate religious organizations, which in conjunction with education, would instill orthodox ideas and moral rectitude in the new nation's youth, and, overarching the whole nationalistic matrix, a conviction that the Confederate cause was just and blessed by God.

Cobb's deep-seated evangelicalism was at the root of this latter conviction and also at the heart of the third and last of his proposals to win outside support for the Confederate government, a proposal having to do with postal services. Twice he tried to insert a clause in the Permanent Constitution to preclude the delivery of mail on Sunday. "My Sunday amendment if I can pass it will bring the religious world" to the side of the Confederacy, he concluded. "May God help me if I am doing his will!"[46] When his amendment was blocked, he introduced a bill to accomplish the same aim, and again there was opposition. Judge T. J. Withers of South Carolina (whom Cobb despised and called an "infidel" for no other reason than he had refused to kiss the Bible upon taking the oath to uphold the Provisional Constitution) moved to refer the bill to the postal affairs committee. His motion was narrowly defeated; whereupon D. F. Kenner of Louisiana attempted to emasculate the measure by exempting his state and Texas from its provisions. The tone of the

---

[45]Ibid., p. 264; Wilfred B. Yearns, *The Confederate Congress*, pp. 135-36.

[46]Thomas Cobb to Marion Cobb, 7 March 1861, Thomas R. R. Cobb Collection.

Kenner amendment indicated that the author considered Cobb's bill a dangerous precedent, if not a violation of the constitutional clause forbidding Congress to enact laws "respecting an establishment of religion or prohibiting the free exercise thereof."[47] Aware that his bill had little chance of passing, much less attracting the sentiment of the "religious world," Cobb moved that both it and the Kenner amendment be referred to the postal affairs committee. The motion was approved, and nothing more was heard about stopping the mail on Sunday.[48]

If Cobb's legislative program lacked an air of reality, at least his work on the Permanent Constitution was constructive and pertinent. Since 9 February, the committee of twelve had been systematically remodeling the Constitution of the United States to suit the needs and attitudes of the Confederate States. By 15 February, the members had gone over the document once and had begun a section-by-section revision. Cobb, who had been assigned the task of polishing the committee draft, sent one-third of the finished product to the printer on 22 February, and expected to complete the rest by the night of the twenty-third.[49] Three days later, Chairman Robert B. Rhett, described by Cobb as "a generous hearted and honest man with a vast quantity of cranks and a small proportion of common sense," reported the committee draft to the convention, and on the afternoon of the twenty-eighth debate began. It lasted until the Permanent Constitution was adopted on 11 March.

The new Constitution, as Cobb later pointed out to his Georgia constituents, was "really the old Constitution with the states rights construction incorporated as a part." The framers, he explained, purposely embodied in the Constitution "the protection of positive provi-

---

[47]*Confederate Journal,* 1: 122. The Kenner amendment read in part: "The people of . . . Louisiana and Texas recognize perfect freedom . . . to worship their Maker at such times and on such days as they think proper."

[48]Ibid. A previous motion to table was barely lost on a tie vote.

[49]Thomas Cobb to Marion Cobb, 22 February 1861, Thomas R. R. Cobb Collection. Although Cobb wrote most of the original manuscript, three of the twenty-seven pages were drafted by either Edward Sparrow of Louisiana or Robert H. Smith of Alabama. A. L. Hull, "The Making of the Confederate Constitution," *Publications of the Southern History Association* 9 (September 1905): 286, suggests the former. Hereinafter cited as Hull, "Confederate Constitution." However, Charles R. Lee, Jr., *The Confederate Constitutions* (Chapel Hill NC: The University of North Carolina Press, 1963), p. 88, states that more likely it was Smith.

sions against the inroads of latitudinous constructions, fanatical perversions, and lobbying corruption."[50] In short, the power of the Confederate government had been circumscribed to protect the rights of the states and to ensure greater fiscal responsibility.

Some of the particularist features in the Permanent Constitution were directly attributable to Cobb. For instance, he persuaded the committee of twelve to include in Article III, Section 2, which defined the judicial powers of the Confederate courts, the statement that "no state shall be sued by a citizen or subject of any foreign state."[51] This change was approved by the convention along with an amendment offered by Alexander Stephens which deprived the Confederate courts of jurisdiction in cases "between citizens of different States."[52] Cobb voted with the majority in favor of Stephens' revision as well as his own.

On still another occasion, he sought to limit the power of the central government by proposing that "Congress shall never deny the rights of citizenship to any free white citizens of the several States, nor grant the rights of citizenship to other persons to whom the same are denied by the several States."[53] Had his amendment passed, the validity of the naturalization laws would have rested entirely upon the caprice of the states.

Cobb's interest in naturalization was more than a reflection of his adherence to the doctrine of states rights. It manifested a conviction, which had been central to his thinking since the outset of the secession movement, that only by excluding all northern influences could the southern way of life be perpetuated. Unless southern homogeneity was safeguarded from such influences, restoration of the Union, he felt, was almost inevitable. Thus, to keep southern institutions inviolate and to preserve the "purity" of the Confederate population, he had urged, in

---

[50]*Southern Banner*, 10 April 1861. See also E. A. Nisbet to Judge [Linton Stephens], 19 February 1861, Stephens Papers, Emory University Library.

[51]Hull, "Confederate Constitution," p. 289. This was merely a rewording of the Eleventh Amendment to the United States Constitution.

[52]*Confederate Journal*, 1: 878.

[53]Ibid., p. 967. Cobb also secured the adoption of an amendment forbidding Congress to alter the times set by the states for the election of Confederate senators. But Lee, *Confederate Constitutions*, p. 91, incorrectly credits him with an amendment giving state legislatures the power, under certain conditions, to impeach Confederate officials. This resolution was introduced by John Gregg of Texas. See *Confederate Journal*, 1: 862.

committee, that restrictions on naturalized citizens be incorporated in the original draft of the Permanent Constitution. His advice was rejected by the committee of twelve, but he subsequently fought to repeal the naturalization laws and succeeded. On 29 January 1862, he wrote:

> The result of this day's work repays me, for on motion Congress has repealed all the Naturalization Laws, and as far as we have the power, have left the record of our condemnation of all efforts hereafter to admit to citizenship either the scum of Europe or the refugees of Yankeedom.[54]

Evidently, President Davis did not share Cobb's xenophobic outlook. He vetoed the bill, declaring it a rank injustice to aliens who had commenced naturalization proceedings and who had been aiding the Confederate cause. "That there is no present necessity for such legislation," he added, "is obvious." And, as to the future, it was very questionable "whether legislation intended to effect the entire exclusion from citizenship of all who are not born on the soil will be deemed in accordance with the civilization of the age."[55]

Cobb's stand on naturalization was by no means his only or most important effort to maintain the status quo. His fear of change and ultimate reunion extended even to the admission of the border states, whose failure to support the Confederacy excited his suspicions. "In fact, if they come," he reasoned, "a bare majority will drag with them a large unwilling minority," a minority either devoted to the Union or, at best, lukewarm in its feeling toward the Confederacy. "Why," he asked,

> should we wish to introduce this discordant element into our harmonious Confederacy? Now our people are perfectly homogeneous. Their interests are identical. There can be no conflicts from partial or unjust legislation. This will not be true when the border states come in.[56]

Considering the location and resources of the border region, a little discord would have been a small price to pay for its active support, but

---

[54]Thomas Cobb to Marion Cobb, 29 January 1862, Thomas R. R. Cobb Collection. A further example of Cobb's determination to erect barriers against northern intrusions was a bill offered by him on 28 February 1861, denying northern plaintiffs access to Confederate courts. Thomas Cobb to Marion Cobb, 28 February 1861, ibid.; *Confederate Journal*, 1: 93, 113.

[55]*Confederate Journal*, 1: 758-60.

[56]*Southern Banner*, 10 April 1861.

Cobb feared a greater menace than mere disharmony if the border states were allowed to join the Confederacy. Economic factors, he perceived, might induce the border states to advocate the piecemeal admission of the Old Northwest. "The dead carcass of the . . . Union," he warned,

> may be gradually resuscitated under the specious guise of *reorganization* and *assimilation*. One after another of the Northwestern states may be admitted into our League until we shall find ourselves with the same faithless confederates, again breaking their bonds, and again violating their oaths.[57]

To prevent such an occurrence, Cobb had urged the committee of twelve to adopt a constitutional clause barring all but slave states from Confederacy.[58] Instead, the committee included a clause in Section 3, Article IV granting admission to any new state upon a two-thirds vote of each house of the Confederate Congress. While it was technically possible for free states to be admitted under this provision, the committee of twelve had taken care not to jeopardize the institution of slavery by such admissions. Article IV, Section 2, clause 1, for example, gave slave owners "the right of transit and sojourn in any State of this Confederacy, with their slaves," and clause 3 provided for the return of fugitive slaves. Furthermore, Section 3, clause 3 of the same article required the Congress to recognize and protect slavery in territory acquired by the Confederacy. It appeared unlikely, therefore, that the institution of slavery would be endangered by the admission of a few free states.

Cobb was not convinced. In his opinion, "this suicidal policy" would lead to the addition of a large block of non-slaveholding Northwestern states, whose motives he doubted and whose presence, he presumed, would destroy the common identity of the Confederate States. His fears were aggravated by the arrival in Montgomery of George N. Sanders, reputedly an agent of Stephen A. Douglas. "I found out yesterday, why George Sanders was here," he wrote on 6 March.

---

[57]Ibid. Cobb was responding here to a speech by Alexander H. Stephens. Cobb was by no means alone in his opposition to the admission of nonslaveholding states. See, for example, *Southern Confederacy*, 30 March 1861; *Montgomery Weekly Post*, 6 February, 10, 16 April 1861; *Montgomery Weekly Mail*, 20 March 1861.

[58]Hull, "Confederate Constitution," p. 289.

> He . . . is working to keep out of the Constitution any clause which will exclude "Free States." The game, now, is to reconstruct *under our Constitution.* There will be a hard fight on this question when we reach it. Stephens and Toombs are both for leaving the door open. Wright goes with them and Hill also we fear.[59]

Despite these defections, Cobb was positive that a majority of the Georgia delegation would back him in a floor fight to keep the free states out of the Confederacy. He was less certain, however, about the final outcome of such a contest. To his wife he explained:

> Confidentially and to be kept a secret *from the public*, Mr. Davis is opposed to us on this point and wants to keep the door open. The Mississippi Delegation are wax in his hands, Harris and [Alexander P.] Clayton leading them and both obsequio[u]sly anxious to please. I am much afraid of the results.[60]

Article IV, Section 3, pertaining to the admission of new states, came up for debate on 7 March. The next day Cobb introduced the following amendment: "But no State shall be admitted which, by its constitution or laws, denies the right of property in negro slaves, or the right of the master to recapture his slave." His amendment passed, but R. W. Walker of Alabama, the member of the committee of twelve who had framed the original section, immediately moved to reconsider the vote. His motion carried and upon reconsideration Cobb's amendment was defeated.[61]

That Cobb was disturbed by this setback was indicated by his subsequent criticism of only this one feature of the Permanent Constitution. Unlike Alexander H. Stephens and R. H. Smith of Alabama, both of whom welcomed the possibility of uniting the Northwest and the Confed-

---

[59]Thomas Cobb to Marion Cobb, 6 March 1861, Thomas R. R. Cobb Collection. Lee, *Confederate Constitutions*, pp. 114-15, believes that Sanders was in fact an agent of Douglas and had come to Montgomery for the express purpose of "lobbying for a constitutional provision allowing the admission of free states into the Confederacy." See also Gerald M. Capers, *Stephen A. Douglas Defender of the Union* (Boston: Little, Brown and Co., 1959), p. 217; *Montgomery Weekly Post*, 10 April 1861, p. 2.

[60]Thomas Cobb to Marion Cobb, 6 March 1861, Thomas R. R. Cobb Collection.

[61]*Confederate Journal*, 1: 885-86. As Cobb predicted, Toombs, Stephens, Hill, Wright, and the entire Mississippi delegation opposed his proposal. On the final vote the Georgia delegation was divided four to four due to the absence of A. H. Kenan, upon whom Cobb depended for support. The division was not decisive, however, because only two states favored exclusion, while four were against it. Hence, the vote of Georgia could not have altered the result.

eracy,[62] Cobb gloomily anticipated dire consequences from a renewed association with any portion of the North. Believing that southern independence was assured already, that unity of purpose and conformity of opinion prevailed, and that the Confederacy was economically, militarily, and psychologically capable of resisting all hostile acts initiated by the Lincoln administration, he saw no need to embrace the Northwest or to become overly worried about the failure of the border states to enter the Confederacy. His assumptions were obviously unrealistic. He not only exaggerated the power, patriotism, and economic self-sufficiency of the South, but seriously underestimated the strength and determination of an industrialized North.

Besides the unsuccessful attempt to exclude non-slaveholding states from the Confederacy, Cobb sponsored a variety of constitutional revisions, both in committee and on the floor of the convention, of which approximately one-half were embodied in the completed document. Most of these dealt with procedural matters and states' rights. A few, such as the defeated amendment to prevent Sunday mail delivery, were trivial when viewed in terms of constitutional development, and none was particularly unique in the sense of adding a new dimension to governmental theory. In truth, all of the important innovations contained in the Permanent Constitution—the item veto, executive budget, single six-year term for the Confederate President, and the "Cabinet in Congress" concept—were introduced by Rhett, Robert H. Smith, Toombs, Stephens, and others. Cobb may have endorsed these ideas, but he did not advance them originally. Doubting his usefulness, he declared early in the proceedings: "I over-estimated the *importance of my presence* in this Congress. They would have gotten along just as well without me."[63] In reality, his indefatigability and vigorously expressed opinions made him a force to be reckoned with. Indeed, a leading authority on the subject credits him with being one of the "principal architects" of the Permanent Constitution of the Confederacy.[64] He had worked tirelessly on the

---

[62]Lee, *Confederate Constitutions*, p. 116; Richard M. Johnston and William H. Browne, *Life of Alexander H. Stephens* (Philadelphia: J. B. Lippincott & Company, 1878), p. 392. Hereinafter cited as Johnston and Browne, *Life of Stephens*. *Southern Watchman*, 10 April 1861.

[63]Thomas Cobb to Marion Cobb, 14 February 1861, Thomas R. R. Cobb Collection.

[64]Lee, *Confederate Constitutions*, p. 147.

committee draft and, in the main, was responsible for the style and form of the final copy. In addition, he participated often in the floor debates and managed to solve an internal improvements controversy which had deadlocked the convention for several days.[65]

This "interminable argument on a single clause in the Constitution referring to internal improvements," he complained, "is yet unfinished and the Lord knows when we shall get through."[66] The dispute centered on Robert Toombs' motion to amend the commerce clause of the committee draft to preclude appropriations for "any internal improvements intended to facilitate commerce."[67] Opponents of this amendment insisted upon a broad interpretation of the commerce clause permitting Congress to appropriate funds for the promotion of navigation, while Alexander H. Stephens thought that money might be appropriated for such projects, provided that the locality which benefited from the improvements paid for them.

Toombs was prepared to accede to the latter proposition, and on 9 March, Cobb offered a compromise amendment based partly on Stephens' position and partly on the views of the internal improvements advocates. Under the terms of his amendment Congress was denied the power to vote appropriations for internal improvements, "except for the purpose of furnishing lights, beacons . . . and other aid to navigation upon the coasts, and the improvement of harbors and the removing of obstructions in river navigation. . . ." Duties were to be levied, however, "on the navigation facilitated thereby . . . to pay the costs and expenses there."[68] All sides were satisfied, and the commerce clause as amended by Cobb was approved.

Weeks before the debate on internal improvements had been concluded, Cobb had become exasperated with the dilatory pace of the proceedings and repeatedly vowed to leave the convention as soon as the Permanent Constitution was adopted. To hasten the day of departure, he prodded the committee of twelve to work faster, coaxed the convention

---

[65]To one outside observer Cobb appeared to be the foremost leader in debate. See Samuel Ward to Hon. William H. Seward, [?] March 1861, William H. Seward Papers, Perkins Library, Duke University.

[66]Thomas Cobb to Marion Cobb, 5 March 1861, Thomas R. R. Cobb Collection.

[67]*Confederate Journal*, 1: 865.

[68]Ibid., p. 891.

into night sessions, and drove himself to the point of physical exhaustion. "I am working too hard and am determined to hold off a little," he confessed to his wife,

> but the fact is my anxiety is so great to despatch my business and get away from here that I trench too much on my rest at night. I can say truthfully that for more than a week past (except Sunday) I have not spent an idle half hour when away from my meals.[69]

His impatience to adopt the Constitution and hurry home was prompted by several considerations. First, he was disgusted by the conduct of his colleagues, many of whom failed to measure up to the high standard of patriotism which he expected of everyone. "I used to think the Court House presented human nature in its most repulsive features," he declared indignantly, "but this political arena gives the darkest picture of frail humanity that I ever witnessed."[70] As if to confirm his judgment, Congress rejected his recommendation that the members, to "set an example of patriotism," should accept no remuneration for their services, but voted themselves a compensation of eight dollars a day plus ten cents a mile travel allowance. "This will pay me the enormous sum of *three hundred dollars*," he noted sarcastically, "for which I have lost, I doubt not in my private business, *three thousand*."[71]

Cobb's compulsion to return to Athens as quickly as possible was reenforced by a painful awareness that his presence at the convention was not indispensable to the Confederate cause. Resenting his secondary role, he remarked: "I wish I had not come here. . . . I magnified myself and have unnecessarily turned aside from my usual life."[72] Yet, whenever his name was mentioned for a position in the government, he went out of his way to announce that "*no office* . . . could be created in this Southern Confederacy which I could be induced to accept."[73]

Special assignments, especially those demanding long separations from his family, he invariably declined. In early March, he twice refused to go as a commissioner to Arkansas, despite the urgent requests of both

---

[69]Thomas Cobb to Marion Cobb, 21 February 1861, Thomas R. R. Cobb Collection.

[70]Thomas Cobb to Marion Cobb, 16 February 1861, ibid.

[71]Thomas Cobb to Marion Cobb, 4 March 1861, ibid.

[72]Thomas Cobb to Marion Cobb, 15 February 1861, ibid.

[73]Thomas Cobb to Marion Cobb, 7 February 1861, ibid.

President Davis and Robert Toombs. Justifying his decision, Cobb pointed out that the Confederate Constitution—"the *chief* object of my coming"—had not been completed; that he had a prior commitment to attend the Georgia convention scheduled to reconvene on 7 March; and that family obligations would prevent him from going. "Well," commented Toombs upon hearing the last excuse, "I told Mrs. Davis that I knew you would go to your wife, that you had been married *seventeen* years to my knowledge and that you were as bad in love . . . as ever."[74]

Later in the month Cobb refused to serve on a committee to revise and digest the body of Federal law which had been continued in force by the Confederacy. "I am perfectly willing to labor for the Confederate States," he informed his brother, who urged him to accept the appointment, "but I cannot abandon my family now to spend two months more in Montgomery. If this is necessary I decline. If I can work *at home* and report to my associates at Montgomery when I return there *in May* then I will accept."[75] Such an arrangement was impractical; and so to others fell the task of revising the laws, a task never completed. In light of his experience and capacity for this type of work, it is not altogether improbable that Cobb's assistance might have made the difference between failure and success.

In the meantime, his desire to conclude the debate on the Permanent Constitution and leave the convention had become overwhelming. "We sat last night until past eleven o'clock and did not pass over *twelve lines*, and today we have commenced again on the same section," he wrote to his wife.

> I don't know what to do, I am worn out and so anxious to see you and yet each day I hope and hope and hope that another day will discharge my duty here and let me fly from this cage to my home. It will take *three days* to enroll the Constitution on parchment for the signature of the members. I have been asked "Won't you stay to sign your name to the Constitution?" Not I, it would be pleasant hereafter for my children to see my name there but I will not stay *one train* to put it there.[76]

---

[74]Thomas Cobb to Marion Cobb, 3, 5 March 1861, ibid.

[75]Thomas Cobb to Howell Cobb, 19 March 1861, Phillips, ed., *Correspondence*, p. 551.

[76]Thomas Cobb to Marion Cobb, 6 March 1861, Thomas R. R. Cobb Collection.

Cobb remained in Montgomery only long enough to propose a final section to the Constitution. It stipulated that whenever five states had ratified the document the Provisional Congress was to set dates for the election of Confederate officials and for the assembling of the permanent Confederate Congress. He then departed for Athens, having authorized the convention to record his name in the affirmative when it voted on the Constitution as a whole.[77]

Cobb's stay in Athens was brief. After spending a few days with his family, he traveled to Savannah, where the state convention had been in session for nine days. He arrived on 16 March, in time to vote for ratification of the Permanent Constitution of the Confederate States of America, which had been adopted in Montgomery on 11 March, shortly after his departure and which was now approved by the Georgia convention 276 to 0.[78]

Prior to Cobb's arrival in Savannah, the delegates had been debating, practically to the exclusion of all else, the merits of reducing the size of the state legislature. This subject had come up on 21 January, during the previous session at Milledgeville. At that time a committee of sixteen had been appointed to determine whether the convention had the power to deal with reduction, a matter which would necessitate a revision of the Georgia Constitution of 1789.[79]

On 26 January, the committee had reported in favor of reduction to make possible a more "economical administration of Government" and also submitted a plan reducing the number of legislators. A minority report challenged the legality of such action and raised objections to the plan of the majority. When it became apparent that the difference would not be settled quickly, Cobb had moved to table both reports until the Savannah meeting.[80]

Thus, from the opening day of the second session of the state convention, reduction had been the prime topic of discussion. Cobb was interested in the question "not simply," he said, "on the picayune grounds

---

[77]*Confederate Journal*, 1: 895-96.

[78]Ibid.; Candler, comp., *Confederate Records*, 1: 458.

[79]Candler, comp., *Confederate Records*, 1: 270, 276, 282-83. The need for reduction had been discussed frequently in previous years by the Georgia legislature.

[80]Ibid., pp. 270, 315-19, 318-19.

of saving a few dollars in annual expenses, but on the higher basis of political necessity." Parroting the philosophy underlying the United States Constitution, he argued that a republican form of government must include a legislature of two houses, one representing the people and the other territory and property. The one checked the other, but if "both represent the same thing they cease to be checks." Under the existing state constitution neither property nor population was clearly represented in either house of the legislature. This was due, he continued, to the periodic creation of small, sparsely populated counties, with the result being that a minority of the people and the smallest amount of wealth and territory had gained a predominant voice in the legislature. "As at present organized," he contended, "the legislature of our state, as an attempt at Republican Government is a *failure*."[81]

In Cobb's view, legislative reorganization was only part of a much broader problem demanding immediate attention. In his opinion, the whole constitution needed a thorough revamping. Concerning the constitution, as originally framed, he asserted:

> no credit was reflected on our state. . . . Its construction was awkward; its taste horrible; its very grammar disgraceful. And upon this original very poor ground-work successive legislatures, swayed by temporary popular prejudices, had inlaid a patchwork of amendments which in their "parti-colors" put to shame even Joseph's coat.[82]

To remedy this deplorable condition, Cobb proposed that the Committee on the Constitution and Laws of Georgia be allowed to revise the state constitution. His resolution passed, with the proviso that the reduction issue, "being now before the Convention," was not to be referred to the Committee until the delegates had agreed upon a final plan.[83]

While the rest of the convention canvassed various schemes to reduce the size of the legislature, the members of Cobb's Committee spent the next several days rewriting the state constitution. Their labors were greatly facilitated by the fact that Cobb had already prepared a draft constitution which served as a basis for the Committee discussions. In

---

[81]*Southern Banner*, 10 April 1861.

[82]Ibid.

[83]Candler, comp., *Confederate Records*, 1: 457-58.

addition, the Committee had at its disposal the "Bill of Rights" introduced by Cobb at Milledgeville on 28 January, and an "Enunciation of Fundamental Principles" drawn up by Simpson Fouché, a convention delegate from Floyd County. From this assortment of documents, the Georgia Constitution of 1861 was fashioned.[84]

The first article in the new constitution was a detailed twenty-eight point "Declaration of Fundamental Principles" derived primarily from Cobb's "Bill of Rights." State bills of rights usually began by identifying sovereignty with the people, from which proposition the concept of delegated powers and the right of revolution were deduced. Cobb's "Bill of Rights" was no exception to the general rule. Paragraphs one, two, and twenty-five reiterated the substance of these traditional doctrines. Scattered elsewhere were numerous corollary rights, most of which could be found in the first ten amendments to the Federal Constitution. In case some fundamental liberty had been overlooked, the last paragraph stated that the foregoing "enumeration . . . shall not be construed to deny to the people any inherent rights which they have hitherto enjoyed."[85]

Interspersed among the philosophical abstractions and specific rights were a variety of governmental principles designed to protect the people from unlawful disturbances, unjust or corrupt legislation, and judicial tyranny. One such principle specified that "A faithful . . . execution of the laws is essential to good order; and good order in society is essential to true liberty."[86] Another sought to prohibit special interest legislation. And still another empowered the judiciary to rule legislative acts contrary to the constitution null and void. The legislature, in turn, was authorized to restrict the power of the court to punish for contempt.

Although the Committee adopted most of Cobb's "Bill of Rights" verbatim, it incorporated a few basic changes, some of which improved upon the original, while others did not. Belonging to the latter category was Section 2 of the "Declaration." In his version, Cobb had written: "All

---

[84]Ibid., pp. 338, 468; Walter McElreath, *A Treatise on the Constitution of Georgia Giving the Origin, History and Development of the Fundamental Law of the State, with all Constitutional Documents Containing such Law* (Atlanta: n.p., 1912), p. 130. Although the authorship of the "Bill of Rights" cannot be proved, it appears to have been largely, if not entirely, the work of Cobb.

[85]Candler, comp., *Confederate Records*, 1: 342.

[86]Ibid., p. 340.

government derives its authority from the consent of the governed, who may . . . annul the same whenever their safety or happiness requires it."[87] With his sanction and possibly at his behest, this was changed in the Committee draft to read: "God has ordained that men shall live under government; but as the forms and administration of civil government are in human, and therefore, fallible hands, they may be altered, or modified."[88]

Perhaps neither statement was really necessary, but at least the former provided a precedented philosophical assumption justifying subsequent rights and principles, whereas the latter sounded like a Calvinistic proclamation with a revolutionary amendment attached (evangelicalism triumphant). Both documents agreed, however, that "No government should be changed for light or transient causes," and that it was the duty of government to protect persons and property.[89]

A second difference concerned the power to tax. Paragraph eighteen of Cobb's "Bill of Rights" defined taxation as a delegated power which "should be exercised . . . only for legitimate purposes of Government."[90] The Committee, on the other hand, preferred a section in Fouché's "Enumeration of Fundamental Principles," imposing more explicit limitations on the taxing power of the state. In its final form the "Declaration" stipulated that "The right of taxation can be granted only by the people; and shall be exercised only to raise revenue . . . , to pay the public debt, to provide for the common defense, and for such other purposes as are specified in the grant of powers."[91]

A third difference was the inclusion in the "Declaration" of a section, similar to one in the Constitution of 1798, prohibiting imprisonment for debt. Cobb's "Bill of Rights" was silent on this subject. Finally, the Committee omitted various portions of Cobb's document which seemed unessential. From the section on religious freedom, to cite but one example, it expunged a redundant introductory phrase pronouncing

---

[87]Ibid., p. 338.

[88]Ibid., p. 519.

[89]Ibid., pp. 338, 519.

[90]Ibid., p. 341.

[91]Ibid., p. 522.

Georgia a Christian state committed to Christian principles, which principles were "independent of all political organizations."[92]

As finally adopted by the Committee, the "Declaration of Fundamental Principles" enumerated (with no discernible regard for system or order) a multiplicity of citizenship rights and placed a number of restrictions on the power of the state legislature, which restrictions might have been incorporated, more appropriately and conveniently, under Article II setting forth the composition, qualifications, and powers of the house and senate.[93] Previous Georgia constitutions, including the Constitution of 1789, had embodied guarantees of personal liberty—such as freedom of the press, freedom of religion, and trial by jury—but none had contained a separate and comprehensive enumeration of the basic rights of the citizen. The "Declaration" was therefore something of an innovation. It filled a void and, according to Cobb, met a long felt need of the legal profession.

Yet, it should be noted that the "Declaration" gave the people no new rights nor provided them with any greater guarantee of personal liberty than had been assured under the Federal Bill of Rights and the Georgia Constitution of 1798. One may even doubt whether the legal profession was seriously handicapped, as Cobb contended, by the absence of such a "Declaration." However, since the Federal Constitution was no longer applicable in Georgia and since neither the Confederate Constitution nor the existing state constitution contained a bill of rights, it was understandable that Cobb and his fellow delegates should have felt that a statement of fundamental principles was not only proper but imperative.

Article II of the Committee draft of the new constitution, defining the functions and organization of the state legislature, corresponded generally to Article I of the old Constitution of 1798. The most controversial sections were those relating to the question of reduction. On 13 March,

---

[92]Ibid., p. 339.

[93]Ibid., pp. 519-23. Special interest legislation, ex post facto laws, and suspension of the writ of haebeas corpus except in cases of extreme emergency were prohibited as were religious tests for holding office, double jeopardy, excessive bail, fines, and cruel or unusual punishment, "laws impairing the obligation of contracts, and retroactive legislation injuriously affecting the right of the citizen." The "Declaration" further stated that a citizen might not be deprived of life, liberty, or property without due process of law and that each was entitled to freedom of thought, opinion, speech, press, religion, petition, and peaceful assembly.

the convention agreed that the senate should be composed of forty-four members selected from as many senatorial districts, but it failed to agree on a plan to reduce the size of the house.[94]

After several days of fruitless debate, Cobb suggested that the lower house of the legislature be increased to 200 representatives, one from each county (132) with the remaining number apportioned among the largest counties. His suggestion, which was based on the belief that, since the senate represented territory, the house must reflect population, clearly conflicted with the demand for reduction and therefore encountered opposition. On a motion by A. H. Kenan, Cobb's proposal and all other plans for apportioning the house were tabled on 18 March. The following day Cobb moved that Kenan's motion be reconsidered and argued strongly for the motion, but he was defeated 131 to 117.[95] As a result, the Committee was forced to leave a blank in the draft constitution pending a final decision by the convention on the issue of reducing representation in the lower house.

Though satisfied with the plan for senatorial reduction which was incorporated in Section 2 of the Committee draft, Cobb was disappointed that the convention did not consent to his idea for enlarging the house. The "*House of Representatives ought to be organized as to speak the voice of the popular majority of the State*," he explained later,

> and for this purpose I earnestly strove. The Convention declined to do it; many who believed with me, being unduly alarmed, in my judgment, lest the popular cry for Reduction would be taken up by the "Tuppenny" newspapers, to bring condemnation upon our action. For myself, I was willing to do right and leave the people to discharge their duty afterwards. I am not afraid of the popular judgment on a righteous act.[96]

His disappointment was lessened somewhat by the inclusion of a clause in Section 5 of Article II requiring a two-thirds vote of each house to

---

[94]Ibid., pp. 415-21. A committee of twenty-four was appointed on 15 March to arrange the senatorial districts. On 20 March, this committee submitted a report to the convention which was adopted. Ibid., pp. 448, 490-93.

[95]Ibid., pp. 475-80; *Daily Chronicle & Sentinel*, 17 March 1861; *Southern Confederacy*, 18, 20, 21 March 1861.

[96]*Southern Banner*, 10 April 1861.

create new counties. This, he believed, would mitigate against a further inequality of representation.[97]

The rest of the Committee draft (Articles III-V) differed from the old constitution in only two important respects. First, the governor was given the power to veto specific items in appropriations bills, a feature adopted undoubtedly from the Confederate Constitution; and, secondly, judges of the Supreme and superior courts were to be "appointed by the Governor with the advice and consent of 2/3rds of the Senate."[98] Justices of the Supreme Court had been elected previously by the state legislature. Hence, their appointment by the executive, with senate concurrence, was a less drastic modification than the appointment of superior court judges, who had been chosen heretofore by the people. This change in the method of selecting judges was the one objection to the new constitution that Cobb thought "plausible enough to demand notice." In response to it, he argued that the popular election of judges might tempt the courts to cater to public opinion in deciding cases, whereas the new method of selection would promote judicial independence from both popular and party pressures. Two-thirds of the senate, he averred, "will seldom, if ever, belong to one political party"; therefore, "*politics can never control the election of judges*." It must be remembered, he concluded, that "in establishing fundamental law, we are providing for many changing years, which should guard against every possible evil."[99]

On 20 March, the work of the Committee was completed, and the next day, in secret session, the convention took up the draft constitution. It was debated for three days, during which time the delegates insisted upon but few amendments.[100] When Article II, Section 3, involving the question of reduction, came up for discussion on 22 March, Cobb moved that the existing means of determining representation in the lower house

---

[97]Ibid.; Candler, comp., *Confederate Records*, 1: 529.

[98]Ibid., pp. 535-37.

[99]*Southern Banner*, 10 April 1861. For some of the objections see *Southern Watchman*, 27 March, 19 June 1861.

[100]Candler, comp., *Confederate Records*, 1: 490-575. Article I, the "Declaration of Fundamental Principles," was amended in one particular. On the second day of debate, a motion was adopted to strike out Section 27, which declared that "All powers not delegated expressly, or by necessary implication are reserved to the people of the state; and in all doubtful cases the denial of the grant is the ground safest for the liberty of the

be retained.[101] Unable to arrive at a new apportionment formula in the earlier debates, in fact, having tabled all such proposals, the convention readily approved his motion. Reduction, then, was effected only in the senate, a reform which afforded, in Cobb's judgment, "a partial and but partial remedy" to the problem of legislative inequality.[102]

A final amendment to the Committee draft, offered by Cobb, was adopted on 22 March. It stipulated:

> This Constitution shall not take effect until the same is ratified by the people. And to this end there shall be an election held . . . on the first Tuesday in July, 1861, when all the citizens of this State entitled to vote for Governor shall cast their ballot either for "Ratification" or "No Ratification."[103]

Thus, for the first time in the history of Georgia a constitution was to be submitted directly to the people for approval. The state convention, having completed its business, adopted the revised constitution on 23 March, then adjourned to await the outcome of the July referendum.[104]

Cobb had a special interest in the fate of the new constitution, for it was largely the product of his labors. He had framed the original draft, chaired the Committee discussions, dominated the convention debates,

---

people." Ibid., pp. 523, 547-48. The reason for rejecting this section was not reported, but one might conjecture that it was simply too vague for practical application. For example, what powers were granted "by necessary implication," and who would decide in cases of doubtful interpretation? Presumably, the Georgia Supreme Court might assume the role of final arbiter, for Section 17 of the "Declaration" empowered the court to declare legislative acts void if they violated the constitution. But, such an inference might itself have been challenged as leaving room for doubt.

[101]Ibid., p. 549. Under the constitutional provision then in force, the house was composed of 169 members apportioned as follows: "The 37 counties having the largest representative population shall have two Representatives each. Every other county shall have one Representative." Representative population was defined in the same section as "all free white persons and three-fifths of the people of color." Unaccountably, the Constitution of 1861 failed to include this or any other definition of representative population. Noting this fact, Bryan, *Confederate Georgia*, p. 14, suggests that this omission "may have caused the large opposition vote" to the new constitution. More likely the cause lies elsewhere.

[102]Candler, comp., *Confederate Records*, 1: 549, 596-97; *Southern Banner*, 10 April 1861.

[103]Candler, comp., *Confederate Records*, 1: 567-68, 612-13.

[104]Ibid., pp. 573, 615.

and served on the committee to revise and collate the amendments adopted on the floor of the convention. He believed, and rightly so, that this constitution was an improvement on the old. It did not alter the basic structure of the government, but it did embody a number of praiseworthy new features, including a bill of rights, the item veto, senatorial reduction, and checks on legislative irresponsibility.

The latter feature was in part a reflection of Cobb's pessimistic view of human nature, a view which his law practice and long and close observation of state politics had done nothing to dispel and much to buttress. While willing to concede that the legislature should have authority to levy taxes for certain types of internal improvements, to encourage education, and "to make all laws . . . necessary and proper for the welfare of the State," Cobb felt, even more strongly, that its power must be carefully circumscribed. Consequently, his defense of the Constitution of 1861 emphasized those sections which prevented, or at least curtailed, unfair, wasteful, and corrupt legislation.

In brief, he had done his best to safeguard the rights of the people and to shield them from the acts of unconscionable politicians, who often spoke for corporate instead of public interests. He was offended, therefore, when critics of the convention accused him of betraying his trust. "In the discharge of that trust," he complained in a speech to an Athens audience,

> along with other noble and patriotic Georgians, I have been charged with usurpation, and a few have tried and are now trying the extent of their feeble powers to bring the odium of our constituents upon our convention. I have no words of recrimination to utter against them; I have no quarter to ask at their hands.[105]

The charge of usurpation stemmed from the fact that the delegates to the state convention had not been expressly empowered to write a new constitution. Replying to this criticism, Cobb admitted frankly, that "This was not the object for which the convention was chosen." However he contended that, since the constitution had to be submitted to the people before it became effective, the delegates should not be censured as "usurpers." Cobb further argued that membership in the Confederacy and the demand for reduction emanating from the people had necessitated some modification in the state constitution. "The Reduction feature," he

---

[105]*Southern Banner*, 10 April 1861.

acknowledged, was not entirely to his liking, but "so far as it goes, deserves your approbation."[106] Objections to the new method of selecting superior court judges he explained away, as previously noted, by asserting that it would promote judicial independence. Otherwise, he stressed the positive aspects of the Constitution of 1861, the ratification of which he heartily recommended.

Speaking in Atlanta as well as in Athens, he reminded his listeners that the state convention had accomplished a great deal in two short sessions. Besides framing a new and better constitution, it had voted to secede, had joined the Confederacy, and had placed the state on a war footing. "While our opponents and enemies have engaged themselves in bitter abuse and hard threats," he asserted, "our people without even a word of recrimination or reproach have kept steadily on the path of independence."[107]

Despite Cobb's efforts to group his opponents in the same category with enemies of the Confederacy, opposition to ratification persisted. "Jim Jackson told me all the Counties above Athens were opposed to the new State Constitution," he wrote early in May. "It would do good to circulate my speech in those counties."[108] A month later the Georgia Constitution of 1861 was adopted by the narrow margin of 795 votes, 11,499 for ratification and 10,704 against it. Compared with voter participation in the election of delegates to the state convention, the turnout was very light. By this time the Civil War had begun, and, as Governor Brown explained, "the thoughts of our people were so much engrossed with the war that little attention was given to any other subject."[109]

In his incisive study of the secession crisis in Georgia, Michael P. Johnson argues that the state underwent a dual revolution in 1860-1861: first, a disunion movement in reaction to the northern antislavery threat

---

[106]Ibid.

[107]Ibid.; J. Henly Smith to Sir, 4 April 1861, Stephens Papers, Library of Congress; *Montgomery Weekly Post*, 10 April 1861.

[108]Thomas Cobb to Marion Cobb, 5 May 1861, Thomas R. R. Cobb Collection; *Southern Watchman*, 19, 26 June 1861; *Southern Enterprise*, 19 June 1861.

[109]Quoted in Saye, *Constitutional History of Georgia*, p. 244. The Savannah *Daily Morning News* declared, however, that "Those who were induced to believe the Constitution was a fraud, were at the polls to defeat it, while the majority of our citizens, believing the opposition would be small, did not take the trouble to vote." Quoted in Bryan, *Confederate Georgia*, p. 14.

and, second, the adoption of a new constitution to prevent the slavocracy from being subverted from within. Thomas Cobb, he claims, "was probably more responsible for the form the second revolution took . . . than any of the" other convention delegates. "Under his leadership, the Committee on the Constitution became the primary vehicle of the second revolution in Georgia."[110] This revolution, he further contends, represented a conscious attempt by conservative slaveholders, some of them former cooperationists, to ensure that Georgia would remain a patriarchal republic, that is, a republic in which slave property would be secure and the "better sort" would continue to rule. In short, in their revision of the state constitution, conservatives sought to curb the power of the people (without seeming to do so) and thus "preserve the status quo by reconciling the tension between the slaveholding minority and the enfranchised slaveless majority."[111] The primary motive behind this conservative revolution was a fear that the Republican Party might appeal successfully to the non-slaveholding masses and undermine the political and social hegemony of the slaveowning elite. In sum, "Secession was driven by political conflict not only between the South and the North but also between the black belt and the upcountry, slaveholders and nonslaveholders, and those who feared democracy and those who valued it."[112]

It is certainly true that Thomas Cobb belonged to the slaveholding upper class and that he defended the system upon which that class rested, but in justifying the latter, he was not necessarily representing the former. To portray him as an ally of the black belt, slaveowning, aristocratic elite against the upcountry, non-slaveholding democracy, requires one to ignore or discount explicit evidence to the contrary and, what is more, to perceive him as a great dissembler concealing his real intentions beneath a torrent of rhetoric and crafty constitutional devices. Any such interpretation defies the facts.

To begin with Cobb was not a member of the tidewater gentry; rather, he was an upcountry lawyer-revivalist, who had consistently battled for common schools and university reform to help the rural poor and who had once characterized slaveholding fire-eaters as "brawlers"

---

[110]Johnson, *Patriarchal Republic*, pp. 124-25.

[111]Ibid., p. xxi.

[112]Ibid.

and "demagogues." Nor had he suddenly softened his view of this class in 1861. In early May, two months before ratification of the new constitution, Cobb indicated that if the Confederacy was "compelled to resort to direct taxation during the war," he would favor "striking at *capitalists* and *slave-owners*."[113] And, a few days later, writing in the same vein, he announced: "I am busily employed trying to get our [the upcountry] Companies away from Savannah. *If left there*, they will be kept all the summer on the coast protecting those rice-planters and their slaves. *I will never consent to this*." Let "them form Companies on the Coast *of their own people*."[114]

These statements underscore his actions at the Savannah session of the state convention, the session at which the so-called second revolution was carried out. What Cobb proposed there seems, in retrospect, to be more democratic than elitist in nature. He advocated, it will be remembered, a larger lower house to allow more adequate representation for the people and also ratification of the constitution by popular vote. Moreover, he extolled every feature of the new constitution which aimed at safeguarding the public from lobbyists, partisan politics, and special interest legislation. In conclusion, what he championed in word and deed was not a patriarchal but a democratic republic (a herrenvolk democracy if you will) reflecting his firm belief in the reality of a social consensus among Georgia whites on the race question, a consensus which no amount of abolitionist propaganda could subvert.

Long before the Georgia Constitution of 1861 was finally ratified on 2 July, Cobb had returned to Montgomery, Alabama, to resume his seat in the Confederate Congress, and, like the rest of the people, his thoughts were drawn to military matters.

---

[113]Thomas Cobb to Marion Cobb, 4 May 1861, Thomas R. R. Cobb Collection. Italics mine.

[114]Thomas Cobb to Marion Cobb, 12 May 1861, ibid.

CHAPTER 8

Cobb's Georgia Legion

Engraving of
Thomas R. R. Cobb's father-in-law,
Judge Joseph Henry Lumpkin

Home of Thomas R. R. Cobb's father-in-law, Judge Joseph Henry Lumpkin, on Prince Avenue, Athens, Georgia

From the election of Abraham Lincoln in the fall of 1860 to the formation of the Confederacy, Cobb had consistently maintained that immediate secession and rapid organization of a new government would ensure peace, ensure it because the North would not dare strike a united South. Reiterating this thesis in February 1861, he asserted that the "chances are decidedly *against war*, there may be a little collision and much confusion, but no bloody or extensive war. The action of Virginia decides the question[.] Peace is certain on her secession."[1]

The Confederate attack on Fort Sumter in April demonstrated the utter fallacy of his prediction. "War is begun," he commented upon hearing news of the bombardment. "The foolish fellows at the North will not believe us in earnest. They will soon learn."[2]

The outbreak of hostilities generated excitement throughout the South. In Georgia, volunteer companies were raised to meet the emergency, and existing military units hastily tendered their services to the state. On 24 April, the Troup Artillery of Athens, commanded by Captain Marcellus Stanley and containing many friends and relatives of the Cobb

---

[1]Thomas Cobb to Marion Cobb, 7 February 1861, Thomas R. R. Cobb Collection.

[2]Thomas Cobb to Col. [David Barrow], 13 April [1861], Cobb-Erwin-Lamar Collection.

family, departed for coastal defense duty in Savannah. Cobb might have been elected captain of this company had he not discouraged it.

Two days after the departure of the Troup Artillery, the Banks County Guards passed through Athens, where they were treated to a free breakfast at the Lumpkin House and a rousing speech by Thomas Cobb, who left town the following day, 27 April, to resume his seat in the Confederate Congress.[3] From Athens to Montgomery, crowds of people and volunteer companies congregated at nearly every station to hear speeches from the dignitaries riding on the train. Cobb spoke twice, but on Sunday afternoon, during a stop at West Point, Georgia, he refused to cater to the assembled throng. "The crowd called on me," he reported,

> but I declined on the ground that it was Sunday and took occasion to give them a lecture of five minutes length on Sabbath-breaking. It was the only speech that was not cheered. From that place to Montgomery crowds at every depot called for the others . . . , but there were no more calls for me.[4]

Cobb reached Montgomery on the evening of the twenty-eighth in an unpleasant frame of mind which was not improved by the inadequacy of his hotel accommodations or by the presence of a large number of office seekers, who seemed to have easy access to important officials in the government. "I am here in the crowd and feeling more saddened than I have since the secession cause was accomplished," he wrote shortly after his arrival.

> Outside of this place, everywhere, pure patriotism seems to be the great controlling principle. Their fights and their liberty the people are striving for. The atmosphere of this place is absolutely tainted with selfish, ambitious schemes for personal aggrandizement. I see it, hear it, and am disgusted with it. God help the country when such things are rising in high places, so far above the great interests of the country.[5]

His mood at the end of the second session of the Confederate Congress was not much better than at the beginning.

---

[3]*Southern Banner*, 24 April, 1 May 1861; Thomas Cobb to Marion Cobb, 22 February 1861, Thomas R. R. Cobb Collection. Congress had been summoned into early session by President Jefferson Davis.

[4]Thomas Cobb to Marion Cobb, 29 April 1861, Thomas R. R. Cobb Collection.

[5]Ibid.

When the Congress convened on 29 April, those members who had not done so before were permitted to sign the Permanent Constitution. Cobb affixed his signature and informed his wife that "I . . . have thus perfected my 'rebellion.' I trust that my children hereafter may recur with pride to it whether by others I am canonized as a saint or hung as a traitor."[6] For the remainder of the session, his thoughts were concentrated mainly on matters pertaining to military defense. "My mind is racked day and night," he related,

> trying to look over the whole field of action to see our weak points to suggest to cabinet officers, and members of Congress and the President himself, for their immediate attention. I doubt not many of them think me very officious, but I cannot help it. The crisis is upon us, and no one seems to me to be sufficiently alive to it. Would to God, I could impress a little of my restless energy into the Executive Departments. They move too slowly for me.[7]

Failing to instill in them his own sense of urgency, Cobb vented his frustration in bitter denunciations of Confederate officials. A great deal of his criticism was aimed at Secretary of War Leroy P. Walker (and later at Judah P. Benjamin). To his wife he complained that "favoritism and nepotism are controlling all public appointments. Some men are holding *three* offices and with others whole families are provided for. . . . The truth is between us, the Secty. of War is utterly unfit for his post."[8] Broadening his attack, Cobb questioned the competence of Secretary of the Navy Stephen R. Mallory; made snide remarks about Vice President Stephens; charged Virginia Governor John Letcher with drunkenness; censured Georgia Governor Joseph E. Brown for obstructing Confederate efforts to raise and arm troops; expressed a suspicion that the Virginia delegation harbored reconstruction sentiments; characterized the leadership of Kentucky, Tennessee, and Virginia as "vacillating and noncommittal," "milk and water," and "submissionist"; condemned all the border states for "their mad devotion to the union"; and declared that Louis T.

---

[6]Thomas Cobb to Marion Cobb, 30 April 1861, ibid.

[7]Thomas Cobb to Marion Cobb, 19 May 1861, ibid.

[8]Thomas Cobb to Marion Cobb, 30 April 1861, ibid. "I was so impressed with the inefficiency of the War Dept. here," he complained again a few days later, "that I feared we could find ourselves in the midst of war without arms and without munitions." Thomas Cobb to Marion Cobb, 3 May 1861, ibid.

Wigfall of Texas "is half drunk all the time and bullies and blusters about everywhere."[9] Even lowly clerks did not escape his vitriolic pen.[10] In short, he envisioned himself as "surrounded by selfishness and intrigue," by indolence and disloyalty, and by "*imbecility* in high places." "If the Lord be not for us," he concluded, "the folly and feebleness of our rulers will ruin us."[11]

Cobb's judgments, in the final analysis, were indiscriminate and overly severe. To be sure, many shared his opinion of Walker, but, like the others, he failed to appreciate the magnitude of the problems besetting the secretary of war or to recognize the importance of his achievements.[12] Furthermore, his suggestion that Walker's appointments were governed by "favoritism and nepotism" was not only unjust but hypocritical. During his brief career as a Confederate congressman, Cobb never scrupled at soliciting military commissions and civil positions for almost every member of his family and for any number of friends.[13] On one occasion he secured a commission for his brother-in-law, Charles M. Lumpkin, who had been serving as a private in the Troup Artillery. Lumpkin was young, inexperienced, and often so intoxicated as to be unfit for duty. Yet Cobb had the temerity to criticize Secretary Walker for allegedly "filling the army roll with the most inefficient unexperienced

---

[9]Thomas Cobb to Marion Cobb, 29, 30 April, 1, 2, 3, 4, 5, 6 May 1861, ibid.

[10]He described one clerk as "a notorious N. Y. rascal" and became obsessed with the idea that a local postal official was a spy. "I still have my suspicions that my letters to you are opened and read," he wrote to his wife. "Notice carefully the envelopes and see if there is any sign of their being tampered with. I should hang this P.M. in quick time, if I had enough to satisfy my own mind of his espionage." Thomas Cobb to Marion Cobb, 8 May 1861, ibid.

[11]Thomas Cobb to Marion Cobb, 1, 2, 4 May 1861, ibid.

[12]For the accomplishments as well as the shortcomings of Walker and Mallory see Rembert W. Patrick, *Jefferson Davis and His Cabinet* (Baton Rouge: Louisiana State University Press, 1944), pp. 104-20.

[13]By the end of the second session of the Confederate Congress, Cobb had attempted, with varying degrees of success, to obtain appointments for no fewer than fourteen friends and relations, including his father-in-law, three brothers-in-law, and his wife's cousin. Howell Cobb to Williams Rutherford, Jr., 11 May 1861, Howell Cobb Collection; Thomas Cobb to Marion Cobb, 20, 28 February, 1, 7 March, 2, 3, 4, 6, 9, 10, 11 April 1861, Thomas R. R. Cobb Collection. In ensuing months, Cobb sought posts for numerous other relatives and close acquaintances.

boys."[14] Nor did he hesitate to use his influence to have the Troup Artillery transferred out of Savannah before the hot, malarial months of July and August arrived. "Howell will help me in this for his Son's sake and Frank Bartow has promised to join me in the request," he explained to his wife.[15] "*If left there*," he wrote subsequently, "they will be kept all the summer on the coast protecting those rice-planters and their slaves." And, he vowed,

> *I will never consent to this.* . . . I will tell the Prest. [President] and his officers to make them form Companies on the Coast *of their own people*. I will bring the matter before Congress if it is persisted in.
>
> Frank Bartow is helping me all he can. He is now at the President's to talk about this matter along with others. It is some consolation to me to know that if I am not in the Camp with the boys I can use my position here to protect them from such a miserable service.[16]

Pressured by Bartow and the Cobb brothers, Secretary Walker agreed to order the Troup Artillery to Virginia, where it was soon to have need of Thomas Cobb's influence again.[17]

Not being a member of the financial, military, or foreign affairs committees, which drafted most of the significant legislation during the second session of the Congress, nor a confidant of President Davis, Cobb was forced to assume a secondary role in the decision-making processes of the Confederate Government. It was not the sort of role that a man of his impatient temperament could accept supinely, and to make his will felt, he flooded the executive departments with various requests and recommendations and launched a personal inquiry into the state of military preparedness in the Confederacy. Although the result of his investigation revealed that Secretaries Walker and Mallory and Governors Letcher and Brown had not been remiss in their duties, he still found fault with their conduct. His hypercritical attitude toward these officials was thus neither

---

[14]Thomas Cobb to Marion Cobb, 30 April 1861, 24 July, 14, 19 August 1861, ibid.

[15]Thomas Cobb to Marion Cobb, 1 May 1861, ibid. Howell Cobb, Jr. was a member of the Troup Artillery. It should be mentioned, however, that Cobb was also trying to effect the removal of other upcountry companies which he felt were unfairly stationed on the coast.

[16]Thomas Cobb to Marion Cobb, 12 May 1861, ibid.

[17]Thomas Cobb to Marion Cobb, 16 May 1861, ibid.; Howell Cobb, Jr. to Mary Ann Cobb, 1 June 1861, Howell Cobb Collection.

a manifestation of superior patriotism, nor the product of an objective evaluation of conditions within the Confederacy, but rather an unflattering reflection of his own highly volatile, sanctimonious, and often vindictive disposition.[18] Seldom consulted by cabinet officials or even apprised of official policy until after it was formulated, Cobb's pride was wounded, and he experienced, as in the first session of the Congress, a feeling of futility. "I am tempted to drop everything and leave at once for home," he exclaimed. "Am I really doing any good here? Is a question I ask myself every day. It troubles me to answer it."[19]

Realizing eventually that the carping, pessimistic tone of his letters was distressing his wife, Cobb began retracting and qualifying many of his former complaints. "*I have never doubted our success for one moment,*" he explained.

> I have been annoyed with the want of that energy which I desired to infuse into these Departments [War and Navy] and I have feared it would result in disasters to our arms at the outset, but I felt it must be temporary and have never feared the final issue. Moreover the Virginia Delegates who were regularly sworn in today, have given me more confidence in that State. She is in earnest and I am relieved much as to my fears. . . . In addition to this the good news of the secession of both Arkansas and Tennessee have kept the cannon booming all day and we are all decidedly in better spirits. If we could only get rid of Secty. Walker and Secty. Mallory and the Lord would kill that drunken Gov. Letcher . . . , I should feel like shouting tonight.[20]

For all his professed patriotism and dedication to duty, Cobb seemed strangely reluctant to make himself available for positions of responsibility. "I told Mr. Toombs," he advised his wife, that "I would not have any office the Govt. could give me" and that "I was not peculiarly fitted for

---

[18]Extremely sensitive to criticism, Cobb could be incredibly petty at times. "I learned yesterday," he reported to his wife, "that the scamp who abused me so in the Atlanta 'Confederacy' came on the cars. I suspected he came to get a surgeon's place in the Army through Stephens. . . . I sent Frank Bartow to the War Office this morning to head off the operation. Fortunately he found Mr. Stephens in the very act of urging the dog's appointment. Frank soon settled the question and the little giant has been showing off his offended dignity all the day. It has gratified me, I must confess." Thomas Cobb to Marion Cobb, 4 May 1861, Thomas R. R. Cobb Collection.

[19]Thomas Cobb to Marion Cobb, 6 May 1861, ibid.

[20]Thomas Cobb to Marion Cobb, 7 May 1861, ibid.

military affairs." But, he added ambiguously, "I was ready gratuitously to give my services to the Government in any matter, which I had peculiar qualifications for it."[21] For a time, he considered the possibility of accepting a diplomatic post, then decided against it. "I have resolved not to go across the water at this juncture," he wrote.

> I prefer being closer to the scene of conflict. Duty does not yet point out to me any change in my present position. I wait patiently. Toombs, Benning, Bartow and Howell are all resolved to try to raise regiments for the war as soon as this Congress adjourns. I shall not attempt any thing of the sort myself. My own conviction is, that my efficiency is more in counsel than on the field.[22]

Despite repeated assertions that he had no intention of entering the military service, Cobb finally yielded to the temptation. Indeed, by the end of May he had definitely made up his mind to follow the example of his brother, Bartow, and others. Weeks before this decision was reached, however, he had begun clamoring for an immediate declaration of war and the capture of Washington, D. C.[23] "I find that most of those with whom I converse here agree with my views about taking Washington City," he alleged. "So soon as Maryland secedes and resumes jurisdiction of the District of Co. and either joins us or asks our co-operation, we shall attack the city. Before that time we shall keep our troops on our own soil."[24]

Formalizing his preference for an aggressive policy, Cobb introduced a resolution on 9 May, authorizing the Confederacy, in effect, to support militarily Maryland's claims to the District of Columbia. His resolution was referred to the committee on foreign affairs, and the next day the report of that committee was tabled.[25] By then, Cobb had already ceased to advocate an assault on Washington. Conceding that Maryland was lost to

---

[21]Thomas Cobb to Marion Cobb, 12 May 1861, ibid.

[22]Thomas Cobb to Marion Cobb, 8 May 1861, ibid.

[23]The Confederate Congress officially declared war on 4 May 1861. Cobb had wished to act sooner. "We have delayed declaring war for two days," he stated. "I wanted to act yesterday." Thomas Cobb to Marion Cobb, 3 May 1861, ibid.

[24]Thomas Cobb to Marion Cobb, 1 May 1861, ibid.

[25]*Confederate Journal*, 1: 200, 207.

the Confederacy, he now stressed the importance of concentrating an army in Virginia to ward off the threat of an invasion.

As part of this new approach, he consented to the transfer of the Confederate Government from Montgomery to Richmond. Although previously opposed to such a move, he was now prepared to defer to the wishes of his colleagues because, as he put it, "Letcher is an imbecile drunkard with but half a heart in this cause. This Government must be where it can overshadow him."[26] It was ultimately agreed that the third session of the Confederate Congress would convene in Richmond in July 1861.

Shortly after the adjournment of the second session of Congress in May, Cobb visited the Troup Artillery, which was still encamped at Savannah, and then returned to Athens to raise a regiment for active duty in Virginia. From the outset, he was determined to organize either a light infantry force supported by dragoons or a legion consisting of cavalry, infantry, and artillery. "My idea *now* is for a *Legion*," he informed his brother on 15 June. "I hope to get arms *for all* from Brown. Is not Georgia entitled to 'a legion'? I propose to call it the 'Georgia Legion.' "[27]

Between early June and mid-July, Cobb recruited most of the infantry and cavalry companies that were to serve under his command and persuaded President Davis to accept the Legion into the Confederate Army. He also secured a pledge from Secretary Walker to attach Captain Stanley's Troup Artillery to the Legion whenever the latter was ready for the field, and from Governor Brown he received a promise of arms and equipment. "Don't be annoyed at my earnestness," he apologized to the Georgia governor upon making a second request for weapons and accoutrements. "When I go into anything it is with my whole soul."[28] Confirm-

---

[26]Thomas Cobb to Marion Cobb, 10 May 1861, Thomas R. R. Cobb Collection. Cobb's views on the probability of a Union attack on Richmond changed from day to day. See Thomas Cobb to Marion Cobb, 6, 7, 10, 11 May 1861, ibid.

[27]Thomas Cobb to Howell Cobb, 15 June 1861, Howell Cobb Collection.

[28]Thomas Cobb to Joseph E. Brown, 8 June 1861, Telamon Cuyler Collection. After this the governor's office was inundated by requests from Cobb and his subordinates. For a few examples see Lt. J. Jefferson Thomas to Governor Brown, 28 October 1861, Capt. W. S. C. Morris to Col. Foster, 23 July 1861, ibid.; Governor Brown to Thomas Cobb, 11 June, 9 August 1861, Brown Papers-Felix-Hargrett Typescript.

ing the vigor of his activities, the *Southern Banner* noted that "Mr. Cobb has taken hold of this matter with his usual energy and success. We had scarcely heard of his determination to form the Legion, before we learned that it was complete."[29] Actually, the *Banner*'s announcement was somewhat premature. The Legion was not yet complete, and many weeks were to pass before it was fully organized and prepared for combat.

In the meantime, Cobb had departed for Virginia to take his place in the Confederate Congress. His arrival in Richmond on 21 July coincided with the battle of First Manassas. Rumors in the city and conflicting reports from the front made it impossible for him to gain a clear picture of what had happened beyond the fact that the Federals had been defeated. "The Telegraph has informed you of our victory and our loss," he wrote to his wife on the twenty-second. "For myself, at present, the former is swallowed up in the latter. Poor Bartow is gone. The last interview I had with him he seemed deeply impressed with the conviction that he should fall. . . . I tried to remove it from his mind, but he reiterated it to the last."[30]

Because of his long and intimate acquaintance with Bartow, Cobb was designated to deliver the eulogy in Congress. Shrinking from the responsibility, he confessed that "Nothing but my friendship for him and the memory of the sincere love that I know he felt for me reconciles me to the task. I am sure I shall do myself no credit for I cannot collect my thoughts and I am very sad."[31] Nevertheless, his performance was apparently all that it should have been, for his brother described the speech as "beautiful and most affecting," and Congressman Warren Akin of Georgia agreed.[32]

Having paid a final tribute to his deceased friend, Cobb quickly recovered from his depression. "I feel bright and well today," he remarked cheerily on the morning of 25 July.

---

[29]*Southern Banner*, 26 June 1861.

[30]Thomas Cobb to Marion Cobb, 22 July 1861, Thomas R. R. Cobb Collection.

[31]Thomas Cobb to Marion Cobb, [23 or 24] July 1861, ibid.

[32]*Confederate Journal*, 1: 279; Howell Cobb to Mary Ann Cobb, 24 July 1861, Howell Cobb Collection; Bell I Wiley, ed., *Letters of Warren Akin Confederate Congressman* (Athens GA: University of Georgia Press, 1959), p. 20.

> As the smoke arises from the battlefield of Manassas, the consequences of the victory become more manifest. *It is one of the decisive battles of the world* and will be estimated in History. Mark my words! . . . If they prepare for another trial at Manassas we shall defeat them again and more easily than we did before. . . . The battle of Manassas, therefore, *has secured our Independence* and hence my classification of it as one of the decisive battles of the world.[33]

A few days earlier, Cobb had been much less confident, but, in the aftermath of victory, he shared with many others a heady feeling of invincibility which caused him to underestimate the resilience of the Union army.

Since his arrival in Richmond, Cobb had been staying at a crowded, uncomfortable hotel, where he was frequently disturbed by visitors, who remained in his room until a late hour. On 25 July, however, he moved from "the noisy hotel, with its uncourteous waiters and clerks" to the home of Assistant Secretary of State William M. Browne.[34] While his new quarters were considerably more pleasant than the old, his daily routine was no less arduous. Each day, after breakfasting with Browne and Secretary Memminger, who was a guest in the same household, he called at various governmental offices, particularly the war department, seeking appointments for friends and relatives, equipping the Legion, and dealing with requests from constituents. The rest of the day and part of the evening were devoted to congressional duties and to visits among the sick and wounded. At night he answered correspondence and studied military manuals. "I never was worked so hard in my life," he wrote. "When I get to bed about midnight I am almost instantly asleep, and seldom wake again till the sun is far risen."[35]

Among the activities absorbing his attention was the establishment of a hospital for Georgia soldiers in Richmond and the formation of a flying hospital for his Legion. The latter consisted of two large tents and substantial quantities of medical supplies, all under the control of Dr. Samuel G. White of Milledgeville. White had a good reputation as a

---

[33]Thomas Cobb to Marion Cobb, 25 July 1861, Thomas R. R. Cobb Collection.

[34]Ibid.

[35]Thomas Cobb to Marion Cobb, 30 July 1861, ibid.

surgeon and Cobb was glad to have him even though he turned out to be a heavy drinker and often curt with the men.[36]

On 1 August, the first and one of the best of Cobb's infantry companies, the Panola Guards, commanded by Captain Gazaway B. Knight, reached Richmond. Notified of their appearance, Cobb hastened to the fairgrounds, where he selected an old race course as the site for "Camp Cobb," so named by his men. "The only objection to my camp," he noted, "is that it is a mile to the Spring. I start them this morning to dig a well."[37]

During the next several days, three more of his infantry companies arrived at the fairgrounds—the Stephens' Rifles (a name which incensed the Cobbs), the Bowden Volunteers, and the Lamar Infantry, respectively led by Luther Judson Glenn, C. A. McDaniel, and Jefferson M. Lamar.[38] Once these troops had been mustered into the Confederate service and settled in camp, Cobb left for Athens. His visit there was brief. "I have [be]en home only three [da]ys," he lamented to his mother.

[36]*Southern Banner*, 11, 25 September 1861; *Southern Watchman*, 25 September 1861; *Southern Federal Union* (Milledgeville), 5 February 1861; Samuel A. Burney to wife, 21 September 1861, Samuel A. Burney Letters, Georgia Department of Archives and History; Thomas Cobb to Marion Cobb, 19, 25, 26, 28 August, 11 September 1861, Thomas R. R. Cobb Collection.

[37]Thomas Cobb to Marion Cobb, 1 August 1861, Thomas R. R. Cobb Collection; Joel C. Barnett to wife, 1 August 1861, Letters of Joel Crawford Barnett, microfilm copy, Georgia Department of Archives and History.

[38]Thomas Cobb to Marion Cobb, 4, 5 August 1861, Thomas R. R. Cobb Collection; Joel C. Barnett to wife, 5 August 1861, Barnett Letters. Captain Glenn, Cobb's brother-in-law, had organized the Stephens' Rifles in April 1861. For some reason the company disbanded in May, but was reorganized in June and accepted into the Legion in July. "This fact," declared one member of the Rifles, "was sufficient for me. I instantly withdrew from the company—and gave as my reason that I would never be commanded by a Cobb." James P. Hambleton to Alexander H. Stephens, 10 July 1861, Stephens Papers, Library of Congress. The name of Glenn's company had created something of a furor within the Cobb family circle. "Mr. Glenn is *unworthy* the honor of being your brother in law. . . . ," fumed Howell Cobb's wife. "I always gave him the credit of having a good heart—tho' he was thriftless and intemperate—but I am forced to believe he is corrupt." Mary Ann Cobb to Howell Cobb, 4 May 1861, Howell Cobb Collection. Thomas Cobb was inclined to agree with his sister-in-law. "It was a very shabby act," he declared. Thomas Cobb to Marion Cobb, 29 April 1861, Thomas R. R. Cobb Collection.

> They seem hard[l]y [thr]ee hours so swiftly [ha]s the hour of parting [ap]proached. My good my best of wives has forgotten herself in her anxious care for me. My little girls smile through their tears to cheer me up. My own heart aches almost to breaking. Dear Moth[er] this is a cruel war that our enemies are waging against us whi[ch] compels me & mine to suffer thus. I try hard not to hate the[m] but God knows how bitterly my feelings are turning against them.[39]

Returning to Richmond in mid-August, Cobb promptly resumed his exhausting routine, involving both congressional and military obligations. The latter occupied most of his time, but not until Congress adjourned on the thirty-first was he free to give his undivided attention to the Georgia Legion.

By the twenty-fifth, all of the cavalry had reported for duty, along with two additional infantry companies—the Poythress Volunteers commanded by Captain W. S. C. Morris and the Tom Cobb Invincibles under Captain F. S. Powell. The mounted wing of the Legion was composed of four companies: Thomas P. Stovall's Richmond Hussars, Benjamin C. Yancey's Fulton Dragoons, William G. Delony's Georgia Troopers, and W. J. Lawton's Dougherty Hussars. On the first day in camp, Lawton's men refused en masse to obey their officers. Apprised of the crisis, Cobb acted quickly and decisively to quell the mutiny. "The officers were disposed to compromise matters," he related,

> but I went over and told the men to go to duty or quit the camp. They are not yet mustered in, or I would have had them put under guard. I saw in a moment that my firm manner put a different phase on the affair. I shall hear no more of it.[40]

Though never a martinet, Cobb justifiably insisted upon discipline in the ranks. He also demanded gentlemanly conduct from officers and men alike and established specific rules against drinking, swearing, and violation of the Sabbath. As might have been expected, the camp regulations caused some grumbling. "Men accustomed to so much liberty as the Geo[.] democracy cannot, it seems, submit with grace to the restrictions

---

[39]Thomas Cobb to Sarah R. Cobb, 12 August 1861, Jackson Scrapbook.

[40]Thomas Cobb to Marion Cobb, 19 August 1861, Thomas R. R. Cobb Collection.

which are necessarily imposed in a camp life," commented Lieutenant Joel Barnett of the Panola Guards.[41] Rumors, having absolutely no foundation in fact, eventually circulated in Athens to the effect that Cobb was a hard taskmaster and an overly strict disciplinarian. "I try to be very kind," he explained in his own defense, "and very rigid on all questions of duty and morality. I laughed at the village rumors. Yet I am sorry that my own town is the only place where people take pleasure in . . . telling lies on me."[42] Toward his men, he was consistently paternal and tried always to protect them from hardship and abuse. "I fear more trouble from the rudeness of army officers to the private soldiers, than any other cause," he declared.

> I am determined to protect my men from such treatment if it makes every army man resign and leave my Legion. These are gentlemen at home and their patriotism has brought them into the field as private soldiers. They shall be treated *as Gentlemen*, except so far as discipline requires.[43]

---

[41]Joel C. Barnett to wife, 21 August 1861, Barnett Letters.

[42]Thomas Cobb to Cally Cobb, 27 September 1861, Thomas R. R. Cobb Collection. "Do not magnify the little beetles which buz around Athens," he instructed his wife. "I am far enough off to see . . . their insignificance and am more troubled by mosquitoes and sandflies. . . . I am trying to do my duty. You know that is my coveted epitaph." Thomas Cobb to Marion Cobb, 26 September 1861, ibid.

[43]Thomas Cobb to Marion Cobb, 28 August 1861, ibid. The curtness of his surgeon, Samuel G. White, also concerned him. "I have lectured Dr. White twice already about having a kind manner towards the sick," he informed his wife. "He is a little *short* though he means no harm. I am determined to see to it, that the sick of my Legion *shall receive kindness* as well as attention." Thomas Cobb to Marion Cobb, 26 August 1861, ibid. On the other hand, when the men drew up a petition to have White removed, Cobb put a stop to it. "I called up the Captains and gave them a few words which crushed the insubordination very soon." Thomas Cobb to Marion Cobb, 29 August 1861, ibid. Within two weeks of the episode, he was happy to report that "Dr. White is becoming much more popular and I think is making [a] reputation with the Legion." Thomas Cobb to Marion Cobb, 10 September 1861, ibid. For further evidence of Cobb's kindness and popularity see William J. Rheny to father, 2 October 1861, William J. Rheney Letters, Georgia Department of Archives; B. E. Yerby to father, 12 January 1862, Confederate War Letters of B. E. Yerby, typescript, Georgia Department of Archives and History. Hereinafter cited as Yerby Letters.

On the whole, Cobb was liked and respected by his troops, who reciprocated his kindness by generally, though not invariably, obeying his rules. Thus he was able to boast: "We have . . . established the character of being the quietest and most orderly camp that was ever pitched near Richmond. I have not had cause to Court Martial a single man."[44] Nevertheless, drinking, swearing, and gambling were evident in the Legion despite everything Cobb could do and a reported case of gonorrhea in November indicated the presence of still another iniquity.[45]

On 28 August, Cobb's commission as a colonel in the Confederate Army was approved, and, upon the adjournment of Congress, he assumed fully the duties of his rank. "I am now regularly installed in command of my legion," he announced on 1 September. "My Congressional labors closed last night near midnight. This morning I put on my uniform and took entire command of my camp."[46] Fittingly enough, he cut his hair short and began growing a beard to give himself a more martial air. "You would laugh at my shorn head and red whiskers in embryo," he noted good-naturedly to his wife.[47]

Eight days after Cobb took permanent command of the Legion, Captain Thomas U. Camak's Mell Volunteers from Athens, Georgia, marched into camp, making the seventh and last of the infantry companies to arrive. Ably led and wearing bright new uniforms the Mell Volunteers quickly took a place beside the Panola Guards as one of the most efficient companies in the command.[48] Except for the Troup Artillery, which had been sent to West Virginia late in July, all elements of the

---

[44]Thomas Cobb to Marion Cobb, 25 August 1861, Thomas R. R. Cobb Collection.

[45]B. E. Yerby to sister, 25 December 1861, 31 January 1862, B. E. Yerby to father, 17 December 1861, Yerby Letters; Joel C. Barnett to Annie, 3 November 1861, Barnett Letters.

[46]Thomas Cobb to Marion Cobb, 1 September 1861, Thomas R. R. Cobb Collection; *Confederate Journal*, 1: 437, 440.

[47]Thomas Cobb to Marion Cobb, 26 August 1861, Thomas R. R. Cobb Collection.

[48]The Mell Volunteers were organized in June 1861, by Reverend Patrick H. Mell, a professor at Franklin College. Mell's wife died in July, and, as a consequence, he was forced to resign in order to care for his children. He was succeeded as captain by Thomas U. Camak, who, until then, had been serving as drill instructor. Although designated as part

Georgia Legion were finally together.[49] By this time the appointment of staff and field officers had also been completed but not without difficulty.

Taking the advice of President Davis, Cobb had selected men with previous military training. His initial choice for second-in-command of the Legion, a post which carried the rank of lieutenant colonel, was Captain Thomas K. Jackson of South Carolina, a graduate of West Point with fourteen years of army service to his credit. His name was submitted to the military affairs committee on 28 August, but when Cobb learned that Jackson had been seen in a drunken condition on the streets of Richmond, he withdrew the nomination and awarded the position to Captain Richard B. Garnett, a cousin of Secretary of State Robert M. T.

---

of the Georgia Legion as early as 3 July, a lack of arms had prevented the company from immediately joining Cobb's command and almost kept it from active service altogether. Authorized originally to enlist six infantry companies, Cobb had filled that quota before the Mell Volunteers could secure arms. But, in August, President Davis permitted him to increase the size of the Legion by two companies, provided they were armed. Cobb wrote at once to his younger brother, John Boswell Cobb, a lieutenant in the Mell Volunteers, and to Captain Isaac S. Vincent of the Clarke County Rifles, urging both to bring their companies if the necessary weapons could be procured. Shortly thereafter, he received a telegram from the former indicating that the Mell Volunteers had obtained arms, apparently from Governor Brown, and were on their way. Nothing, however, was heard from Vincent. Irritated by his silence, Cobb exclaimed that "Vincent's conduct to me is disgraceful, such as convinces me that he is no gentleman. I am glad his company do not come. I fear now that I shall fail to get another company, as Brown cannot be expected to arm any more." At that moment, the captain of the Clarke County Rifles was near death, as Cobb soon discovered. "Vincent (poor fellow) is very ill. . . . I forgive him, and leave him to his fate. His company is at Portsmouth, with no arms but brickbats. . . ." As Cobb anticipated, he was unable to recruit another company. For these events see Thomas Cobb to Marion Cobb, 5, 22, 27, 29 August, 3, 5, 9, [10] September 1861, ibid.; *Southern Banner*, 3, 24 July, 28 August, 11 September 1861; Sarah R. Cobb to John A. Cobb, 21 July 1861, Sarah R. Cobb to Howell Cobb, 25 August 1861, Howell Cobb Collection.

[49]*Southern Banner*, 31 July 1861. This movement by the Troup Artillery, as Cobb understood it, was temporary. The artillerists "are ordered off today," he commented, "but Secretary Walker has positively promised me to attach them to my Legion just as soon as I get into the field." Thomas Cobb to Marion Cobb, 22 July 1861, Thomas R. R. Cobb Collection.

Hunter.[50] Garnett was a capable and popular leader, "a perfect gentleman," in Cobb's estimation, and "an excellent officer."[51] Unfortunately, he remained with the Legion less than three months, being promoted to brigadier general in November 1861.

Because the Georgia Legion was composed both of infantry and cavalry, Cobb was authorized to appoint two battalion majors.[52] For the post of infantry major he selected Edward F. Bagley of Alabama, formerly a lieutenant in the Fourth United States Artillery and a veteran of the Mexican War. Recommended to Secretary Walker as an "intelligent, energetic, and estimable young gentleman," he had been commissioned a lieutenant in the Confederate Army and detailed for ordnance duty at Fort Pulaski.[53] There he had met Captain Marcellus Stanley and other members of the Troup Artillery, who seemed to hold him in high esteem. Acting on their advice, Cobb offered him a place in the Legion. After observing this officer for two months Cobb concluded that "I made a great mistake in making Bagley Major. He is a coarse, ignorant, lazy[,] stingy[,] good[-]for[-]nothing fellow, a perfect drone and tax on me. I would give five hundred dollars to get rid of him," a view apparently shared by many of the men.[54]

Cobb's cavalry major, Pierce Manning Butler Young, was a better officer than Bagley. A graduate of the Georgia Military Institute, he

---

[50]Thomas Cobb to Marion Cobb, 22, 31 August, 1 September 1861, Thomas R. R. Cobb Collection; *Confederate Journal*, 1: 437, 440. Hunter superseded Toombs as head of the state department in July 1861.

[51]Joel C. Barnett to wife, 23 October 1861, Barnett Letters; Thomas Cobb to Marion Cobb, 3, [10], 29 September 1861, Thomas R. R. Cobb Collection; B. E. Yerby to sister, 27 September 1861, Yerby Letters.

[52]Authorization for a cavalry major was not granted, however, until late August. See Thomas Cobb to Marion Cobb, 1 September 1861, Thomas R. R. Cobb Collection.

[53]See George D. Shortridge to L. P. Walker, 9 March 1861, and other enclosures in Bagley's service record. "Completed Service Records of Confederate Soldiers Who Served in Organizations from the State of Georgia," Roll 580, Cobb's Legion, A-Bl, microfilm copies, Georgia Department of Archives and History. Hereinafter cited as "Service Records."

[54]Thomas Cobb to Marion Cobb, 29 September 1861, Thomas R. R. Cobb Collection; B. E. Yerby to sister, 27 September 1861, Yerby Letters.

attended West Point from 1857 to 1861, but resigned in his senior year when Georgia seceded. Commissioned a lieutenant in the Confederate Army in March 1861, he was appointed adjutant of the Legion in August and was promoted to the rank of cavalry major in September to prevent his transfer to another regiment.[55] Cobb had been pleased with Young's work as adjutant and, for a time, was equally pleased with his performance as cavalry major. "He is a very fine young officer, and commands the admiration of all the men," he asserted.[56] However, there was one aspect of the major's personality that irritated Cobb. "Young is efficient but too self-conceited," he complained. "I have to reprove him frequently."[57] Although courageous in battle, Young often conducted himself immaturely and was apparently something of a dandy. Consequently, as the months passed, Cobb's opinion of him sank steadily.[58]

To fill the post of adjutant, which Young's promotion left vacant, Cobb chose Samuel C. Williams, an officer who had previous military training but who was thoroughly disliked by the men. Williams resigned near the end of November, however, to become Garnett's aide, thereby making still another selection necessary.[59] Cobb professed to recognize

---

[55]Thomas Cobb to Marion Cobb, 4 August 1861, Thomas R. R. Cobb Collection; Ezra J. Warner, *Generals in Gray. Lives of the Confederate Commanders* (Baton Rouge: Louisiana State University Press, 1959), p. 348; Lynwood M. Holland, *Pierce M. B. Young. The Warwick of the South* (Athens: University of Georgia Press, 1964), pp. 54-55. Young had been elected lieutenant colonel of Henry Benning's Seventeenth Georgia Regiment but agreed to accept the lesser rank of major in Cobb's cavalry battalion. Dudley M. Dubose, son-in-law of Robert Toombs, had been Cobb's original choice for adjutant. However, when Dubose declined the position to enter his father-in-law's regiment, Cobb remarked that "I do not regret it . . . as I was beginning to feel a little afraid that his want of military knowledge would be a source of trouble to me. I shall select a successor from the army." Thomas Cobb to Marion Cobb, 25 July 1861, Thomas R. R. Cobb Collection.

[56]Thomas Cobb to Marion Cobb, 3 September 1861, Thomas R. R. Cobb Collection.

[57]Thomas Cobb to Marion Cobb, 29 September 1861, ibid.

[58]*The War of the Rebellion: A Compilation of the Official Records of the Union and Confederate Armies* (Washington DC: Government Printing Office, 1880-1901), series 1, vol. 11, pt. 3, p. 660. Hereinafter cited as *Official Records*. Holland, *Young*, pp. 68, 70, 128, inaccurately portrays Young as a friend of Cobb and fails to take note of the colonel's growing dislike for the young man.

[59]R. H. L. Clark to James J. Clack, 1 December 1861, R. H. L. Clack Letters, microfilm copy, Georgia Department of Archives and History. Hereinafter cited as Clack Letters. Benjamin Mell to father, 28 November 1861, Carlton-Newton-Mell Collection, University of Georgia Libraries; B. E. Yerby to sister, 27 September 1861, Yerby Letters.

the importance of an adjutant versed in the ways of the army, yet the replacement he chose was his nineteen-year-old nephew, John C. Rutherford, a sergeant in Delony's Georgia Troopers with no prior experience.[60] To make matters worse, he was reluctant to delegate responsibility to his subordinates and seemed to delight in the fact that some of them were dependent upon him. He personally instructed sentries, conducted all inspections and battalion drills, drafted his own dispatches, and dealt with a variety of other petty details, most of which might have been handled by his officers. As a result he trenched too much on his sleep, was constantly harassed by all manner of trivial problems, and deprived himself of an early opportunity to test the reliability of his subalterns. Compounding his difficulties, he stubbornly refused to learn from the professionals in his command. Indeed, he deliberately set out to demonstrate his superiority over them. To his wife he wrote:

> I am determined to show my men that I know more about every thing connected with military life than any of my officers (army men though they are) and hence I command myself at every exercise and make them obey me. So soon as I feel that I have satisfied my camp on that point I will turn over the onerous duties of drill to them.[61]

In spite of his failure to make effective use of his staff and his total lack of military experience, Cobb gradually instilled discipline in the Georgia Legion and drilled it to a point of proficiency. "My Cavalry companies are the admiration of the city," he bragged. "They do make a very fine appearance. My companies are all doing very well and I think I shall be proud of them."[62] Captain Powell's Tom Cobb Invincibles proved to be an exception. After almost a month of constant drill, they were still unable to master the simplest maneuvers. "They are very stupid," com-

---

[60]John A. Cobb to Mary Ann Cobb, 1 December 1861, Howell Cobb Collection. Like the Mell Volunteers and the Troup Artillery, Delony's company had been recruited in the neighborhood of Clarke County and contained many friends and relatives of the Cobb family. See *Southern Banner*, 10 July, 7, 14 August 1861.

[61]Thomas Cobb to Marion Cobb, 7 September 1861, Thomas R. R. Cobb Collection.

[62]Thomas Cobb to Marion Cobb, 26 August 1861, ibid. "My cavalry," he repeated in September, "are given up to be the finest body of men and horses that has been seen in this city. My infantry are becoming well drilled." Thomas Cobb to Marion Cobb, 14 September 1861, ibid.

mented Cobb.[63] "They are untaught and seem unteachable."[64] Otherwise, the infantry battalion lived up to his expectations and, at least initially, so did the company commanders. "I am very much pleased with my captains," he wrote in August; and confirming this judgment in September, he remarked: "I have a fine set of captains who do all they can to uphold my hands and keep down everything like disaffection."[65]

While satisfied with the progress of his companies, Cobb felt that there was need for further drill and some additional arms before the Legion could be considered ready for the field. He was taken by surprise, therefore, when orders arrived on 11 September, to report to General John Bankhead Magruder at Yorktown. The destination of the Legion had been a matter of speculation among officers and men for more than a month. Early in August the general impression was that the command would be sent to join the Troup Artillery in West Virginia. Later that month, Cobb surmised as much both to his wife and to Lieutenant Joel Barnett of the Panola Guards, who unfairly concluded that the Colonel "is not anxious to signolise [sic] himself by facing bullets, and I think he will manage to get out to Western Va[.] in the Kanawa Valley somewhere near the sulpher [sic] Springs in time to take up winter Quarters—by that time I think the Federals will be driven out by Lee and Wise[.]"[66]

In reality, Cobb was much opposed to a move in that direction. Letters from members of the Troup Artillery invariably complained of great hardship and pleaded for a change of station. Averse to sharing their plight and anxious to relieve them, Cobb promised repeatedly to have the battery transferred to his command as soon as practicable. He felt, however, that it would be very inadvisable to push the matter immediately.

---

[63]Thomas Cobb to Marion Cobb, 6 September 1861, ibid.

[64]Thomas Cobb to Marion Cobb, 10 September 1861, ibid. Captain Powell was a minister, who, in Cobb's opinion, was "a plain[,] straightforward, earnest man." Thomas Cobb to Marion Cobb, 19 August 1861, ibid. Due to age and poor health, he resigned from the Legion in June 1861. Joel C. Barnett to wife, 26 June 1861, Barnett Letters.

[65]Thomas Cobb to Marion Cobb, 19 August, 12 September 1861, Thomas R. R. Cobb Collection. Cobb was subsequently forced to modify this view.

[66]Joel C. Barnett to wife, 20, 21 August 1861, Barnett Letters; Thomas Cobb to Marion Cobb, 20 August, 11 September 1861, Thomas R. R. Cobb Collection.

> I am sorry for the boys . . . for I know they have a hard time. I am resolved to have them, but *fear* to *remind* the Secty. of his promise now, lest to comply with it, he orders me *to join them*. So soon as I receive orders, I shall insist on the promise . . . that they shall join me, and I am well satisfied I can thus relieve them.[67]

The receipt of orders on 11 September, might have solved Cobb's dilemma had it not been for the meddling of Judge Lumpkin, who objected to the removal of the Troup Artillery from West Virginia while there was any possibility of a battle, apparently on the ground that such a withdrawal would weaken the Confederate position in that region. Greatly embarrassed by his father-in-law's attitude, he explained to his wife that he was honor bound to ask for the artillery at once, "because I promised the boys I would do so and I get messages from them daily to this effect." But, he added, "I shall not press it as I would have done because your father seems so much opposed to their moving."[68]

Calling at the war office on 13 September, Cobb found Walker amenable to his request and later that day so informed his wife.

> I reminded the Secty. of War today of his promise about the troup artillery. He remembered it promptly and agreed at once to comply with it and order them to join me, but asked me to wait until he could order another artillery company to join Genl. Lee. This I promptly consented to do as it would give time for a fight if there was to be one, while it secured me the boys during the winter. I trust this arrangement will satisfy your father, while it enables me fully to comply with my promises to the boys.[69]

Seemingly assured of having the Troup Artillery with him in the not too distant future, Cobb turned his attention to the task of preparing the Legion for the movement to Yorktown. Stopping at the ordnance department before returning to camp, he inquired about some weapons which Ordnance Chief Josiah Gorgas had promised him for several weeks. Told by Gorgas that they were no longer available, Cobb lost his temper and

---

[67]Thomas Cobb to Marion Cobb, 2 September 1861, Thomas R. R. Cobb Collection.

[68]Thomas Cobb to Marion Cobb, 11 September 1861, ibid. Judge Lumpkin's interest in the Troup Artillery stemmed from the fact that two of his sons, a grandson, and two grandnephews were members of the battery.

[69]Thomas Cobb to Marion Cobb, 14, [13] September 1861, ibid.

"gave him a little plain talk which," he declared, "I think he will remember for some time."[70]

In the meantime, news of the impending move to the Peninsula had spread through the Legion and was greeted with enthusiasm. "We have had a stirring day in the camp," Cobb reported on the twelfth. "Everybody is excited at the prospect of going away, and so anxious are our sick men not to be left that there was a considerable decrease on the sick list today."[71]

The health of his troops was one of the primary reasons for Cobb's eagerness to leave Richmond. The Legion had been fortunate enough to escape serious and widespread illnesses longer than most of the regiments in surrounding encampments, but in late August the number of diarrhea cases began to mount, a measles epidemic broke out, and several instances of typhoid fever were diagnosed. Only fifty-seven men were reported ill on the twenty-ninth, whereas approximately four times that many were on the sick list by 8 September. Cobb attributed the increase to the pestilential location of his camp, which Lieutenant Barnett described as "a perfect stink hole," and to a want of personal hygiene among the men. "I have done all I could to keep my men healthy," he complained, "but they will be imprudent in spite of me and would be filthy if I let them alone."[72] Although the shift to Yorktown did not ensure cleanliness, it did remove the Legion from the disease-ridden Richmond fairgrounds.

Early on the morning of 15 September, a Sunday much to Cobb's regret, the cavalry battalion and nineteen baggage wagons departed for the Peninsula with instructions to proceed via Williamsburg to a site near Yorktown, which Lieutenant Colonel Garnett had been sent ahead to select. At 3:30 A. M. the following day, reveille sounded for the infantry companies, and by 7:00 A. M. they had broken camp and marched three miles to the railroad depot, where a waiting train transported them to West Point on the York River. From West Point they traveled by

---

[70]Ibid.

[71]Thomas Cobb to Marion Cobb, 12 September 1861, ibid.

[72]Thomas Cobb to Marion Cobb, 8 September 1861, ibid.; Joel C. Barnett to wife, 31 August, 19 September 1861, Barnett Letters.

steamer, arriving in the rain at Yorktown about 5:00 P. M.[73] While Garnett directed the infantry units to their encampment, Cobb remained behind to supervise the unloading of baggage until 11:00 that night. "I then rode out alone," he recorded, "and found my way in the dark and rain, challenged every five minutes by sentinels and got to the camp when [where] the drenched men were putting up tents at random. I went to bed supperless about one o'clock."[74]

In the morning, Cobb surveyed his new camp closely for the first time. It was situated in an open field near the York River, approximately two miles below Yorktown and within three hundred yards of the house in which Cornwallis met Washington to sign the articles of capitulation in 1781. "I look with reverence at it," wrote Cobb, "and feel as if I was on classic ground."[75] Not inappropriately, he named the site occupied by the Legion "Camp Washington."

During the next three days, Cobb reestablished the regular routine, reconnoitered his position, and expressed gratification over the way in which his infantry battalion had carried out its first major military movement. It had been accomplished promptly and with a minimum of confusion. "I never saw men work better or under worse auspices," he wrote.[76] The only disturbing factor was the failure of the cavalry to arrive on schedule. Rumor had it that the column had been halted in Williamsburg for an indefinite period by order of General Magruder, "thus dividing and destroying my command," exclaimed Cobb, "before I have well gotten it organized. I am determined not to submit to such an imposition and shall appeal to the president if necessary, to protect me from the outrage."[77]

A congressman as well as a colonel, he obviously had no qualms about employing political influence to countermand the orders of his imme-

---

[73]Thomas Cobb to Marion Cobb, 15, 17 September 1861, Thomas R. R. Cobb Collection; Joel C. Barnett to Annie, 19 September 1861, Barnett Letters; John A. Cobb to Mary Ann Cobb, 15 September 1861, Howell Cobb Collection.

[74]Thomas Cobb to Marion Cobb, 17 September 1861, Thomas R. R. Cobb Collection.

[75]Ibid.

[76]Ibid.

[77]Thomas Cobb to Marion Cobb, 19 September 1861, ibid.

diate superior, nor did he consider the fact that the president had burdens enough without being bothered by such a relatively unimportant demand, especially when it involved the prerogative of a field commander. This was not to be the last time that Cobb threatened to use his governmental connections to modify ordinary army routine.

On 20 September, accompanied by Captain Knight of the Panola Guards, Cobb set out to locate the missing companies and to insist upon their return. After riding a mile in the direction of Williamsburg, he encountered the cavalry, which Magruder had detained for two days and then released without explanation. Cobb was delighted. "All came in good health and fine spirits," he rejoiced. "I feel very much relieved and am much more buoyant in my spirits today. The tents are all pitched now and we make quite a fine appearance."[78]

Unlike their commander, the cavalry officers had not been particularly annoyed by the inexplicable delay in Williamsburg and, upon reporting to "Camp Washington," spoke highly of Magruder's character. When the general came to Yorktown on 21 September, Cobb paid his respects and was admittedly impressed by the man's appearance and personality. Yet, there were certain things about Magruder that troubled and even infuriated him, one of which was a seeming penchant for Sunday parades. Bad weather cancelled one such parade on the twenty-second, but on the twenty-ninth the Legion and five other regiments were called out for a general review. "It was our hour for preaching but I was compelled to obey," raged Cobb.

> We had to . . . march a mile to the parade ground. It took them an hour and a half to get through the Review, and I thought then we would be dismissed, but to my amazement and grief the old "fuss and feathers" kept my men till four o'clock (six hours) in a Brigade Drill. I was angry to sinfulness. It nearly killed some of them, just out from the measles and broke us all down, to gratify his peacock pride. And all this on Sunday. Heaven-daring, God defying sin. He had the right to order and I was bound to obey, but I had a prayer-meeting tonight, and did not hesitate to express my strong reprobation of such God-less infidelity. . . . I intend to appeal to headquarters against this wanton desecration of the Sabbath. If I fail there I shall move in

[78]Thomas Cobb to Marion Cobb, 20 September 1861, ibid. See also Thomas Cobb to Howell Cobb, 20 September 1861, Howell Cobb Collection.

> congress on the subject and if I fail there, I shall resign for I had rather live under Lincoln than go to the Devil and carry all my men with me.[79]

In light of this outburst, reaffirming the intense evangelical nature of his religious convictions, it is rather amazing to find him writing within two months that "infractions of God's day do not oppress me as much as they should and . . . I am gradually becoming habituated to the idea that a military necessity overrides all our accustomed ideas."[80]

Besides being incensed at Sunday drill, Cobb doubted the wisdom of Magruder's military plans. At their first meeting, the general had been very voluble and had disclosed his intention to attack Newport News at the tip of the Peninsula as soon as the *Merrimac* had dispersed the Federal blockading fleet. Privately skeptical, Cobb could not perceive how such an offensive would give the Confederates a permanent advantage or shorten the war. "This would be a bloody work," he said, "and I confess to me seems an unnecessary waste of life. Time may develop other views on the subject."[81]

Time also improved his opinion of Magruder, whose ingratiating manner was hard to resist. Constantly flattered by the general, Cobb became increasingly fond of his commander and before the end of October was praising him unreservedly. "He is a fine officer, and in heart a noble man. He works day and night, and does not receive half the credit for which he is entitled." And, Cobb further observed, "His plans for the defence of the Penninsula [sic] are Capital. . . . I know of no officer in the service, who with the same means has done so much and I know of none for whom the Government has done so little."[82]

---

[79]Thomas Cobb to Marion Cobb, 29 September 1861, Thomas R. R. Cobb Collection.

[80]Thomas Cobb to Marion Cobb, 10 November 1861, ibid.

[81]Thomas Cobb to Marion Cobb, 25 September 1861, ibid. Cobb did not make his objections known to Magruder at this time, but he subsequently intimated his opposition to an assault on Newport News. "I told Genl. Magruder he could count on my legion for any enterprise which would promote the public cause, but at the same time I desired not to rush into any useless expedition which could be productive of no good." Thomas Cobb to Marion Cobb, 10 October 1861, ibid.

[82]Thomas Cobb to Marion Cobb, 26 October 1861, ibid.

His rapport with Magruder made it all the easier to enlist the general's support in obtaining the transfer of the Troup Artillery, the members of which were still pleading to be relieved. Magruder submitted a request for the battery on 8 October, one week after Cobb received word from Secretary Walker that the company could not be withdrawn from West Virginia for another two weeks. This was not an unreasonable delay, for it had been generally understood since mid-September that the artillery would not join the Legion for thirty days, and Cobb willingly acquiecsed in the War Department's decision.[83]

His attempt to pursue a consistent course of action in this matter while simultaneously satisfying all the parties concerned was again complicated by his father-in-law's incomprehensible and utterly exasperating attitude. "In one letter you tell me your father does not wish them moved from Western Virginia," Cobb replied to his wife,

> and I consent for them to remain for two or three weeks longer. In another you say . . . he wants them with me. A letter from Ed [Lumpkin] at the same time begs me to claim them. I write for them and insist on my claim. Now comes this letter saying your Father wishes them to return to Georgia. I shall not interfere if Gov. Brown claims their return, but I cannot ask it. My whole course has been based on the *unity* and *integrity* of my legion. I cannot ask for it to be severed and destroyed. I will be silent. I can do no more.[84]

Cobb maintained his silence until the middle of October, at which time he reopened correspondence with the war department on the subject of the Troup Artillery and followed with a letter to General Robert E. Lee. "*I will have the company* or raise a row. Depend upon that," he vowed.[85] Nothing quite so drastic was required. A note from General Lee arrived on 12 November, indicating that the battery would be transferred shortly, and on the twenty-second, Cobb saw the official

---

[83]Thomas Cobb to Marion Cobb, 1 October 1861, ibid.; *Official Records*, series 1, vol. 4, p. 674.

[84]Thomas Cobb to Marion Cobb, 5 October 1861, Thomas R. R. Cobb Collection.

[85]Thomas Cobb to Marion Cobb, 2 November 1861, ibid. See also Thomas Cobb to Marion Cobb, 15, 25 October 1861, ibid.; Thomas Cobb to Robert E. Lee, 19 October 1861, Robert E. Lee Papers, Virginia Historical Society, Richmond, Virginia.

dispatch ordering the Troup Artillery to Yorktown. Hence, he informed his wife, "this matter is settled at last."[86]

Long before the artillery reported for duty, the Georgia Legion had moved to a new position. On 3 October, Magruder issued an order arranging his troops in line of defense across the Peninsula and instructing them to construct winter quarters. The Legion was to be held in reserve at Cockletown, a ramshackle, crossroad village approximately seven miles south of Yorktown. Cobb had been expecting the order, which was promulgated on 6 October, for several days, and, though the thought of spending the winter in the vicinity of this "miserable little hole" was repugnant to him, he welcomed the opportunity to get his men out of their tents and into huts before the onset of cold weather.[87]

Escorted by his company commanders, Cobb rode out on 8 October, to find a suitable camp site. A pine forest about two miles from Cockletown and several miles to the rear of Magruder's first line of defense was chosen for this purpose, and two days later the Legion was marched to the new location, called "Camp Marion." The movement was made in the rain, and because he "felt sorry to see the poor fellows trudging through the mud and water," Cobb permitted each man to have a ration of whiskey that night.[88] Strong drink for medicinal use was not at variance with his moral code; taken for pleasure it was intolerable.

On the second day in "Camp Marion," while his men continued to clear the woods and trim pine logs for their winter shelters, Cobb scouted his right flank in a radius of twenty-five miles and returned in the late afternoon convinced that the enemy could not trap him on the James River side of the Peninsula. That night he was awakened by a courier with a message from Magruder indicating that the Federals would probably

---

[86]Thomas Cobb to Marion Cobb, 12, 22 November 1861, Thomas R. R. Cobb Collection; *Official Records*, series 1, vol. 51, pt. 2, p. 382; J. P. Benjamin to Robert E. Lee, 15 October 1861, Robert E. Lee to Thomas Cobb, 26 October 1861, Lee Papers.

[87]*Official Records*, series 1, vol. 4, pp. 668-70; Thomas Cobb to Marion Cobb, 24, 26, 28 September, 1, 5, 6 October 1861, Thomas R. R. Cobb Collection. The line ran from Young's Mill, near the mouth of Deep Creek, on the extreme right, to the Poquosin River, on the left.

[88]Thomas Cobb to Marion Cobb, 8, 10 October 1861, Thomas R. R. Cobb Collection.

advance from Fort Monroe and Newport News in the morning. He was directed to detach two cavalry companies to cooperate with Confederate forces at Young's Mill, under the command of General Lafayette McLaws, and to move the rest of Legion to the main line of defense.[89]

With laudable dispatch, Cobb carried out his orders, and for a day and night his troops bivouacked in the open awaiting the approach of the enemy. On the morning of the fourteenth, they returned to camp, without so much as a glimpse of a Federal soldier.[90] This was the first of many false alarms emanating from Magruder's headquarters, which soon earned him a well-deserved reputation for excitability and fostered unfounded charges of drunkenness.[91]

Cobb learned quickly to accept these frequent alerts as a mere inconvenience; nonetheless, they prompted him to examine his defensive capabilities more closely. Between the Legion and the front line there were a few pickets and a mile to the left a regiment of cavalry; otherwise, Cobb's nearest support was seven miles away at Yorktown, where, in his judgment, he would be compelled to retreat if the enemy attacked in force. Hoping to preclude the necessity of such a withdrawal, he ordered the entire Legion to strengthen and extend some breastworks located about a mile below "Camp Marion." This project, requiring four days of hard

---

[89]Thomas Cobb to Marion Cobb, 12, 14 October 1861, ibid.; *Official Records*, series 1, vol. 4, pp. 677-79.

[90]T. P. Stovall's Richmond Hussars and Benjamin C. Yancey's Fulton Dragoons were the companies detailed to support McLaws, who had been instructed to move forward and ambush the Federals below Young's Mill. Stovall advanced to within seven miles of Newport News; then, with a small detachment, he advanced another five miles before encountering a company of Union troops. Fired upon, he was forced to retreat, and the expedition ended without further incident. Joel C. Barnett to wife, 15 October 1861, Barnett Letters; R. H. L. Clack to James J. Clack, 20 October 1861, Clack Letters; Thomas Cobb to Marion Cobb, 14 October 1861, Thomas R. R. Cobb Collection.

[91]Thomas and Howell Cobb both denied, emphatically and repeatedly, that Magruder was guilty of drunkenness. Thomas Cobb to Marion Cobb, 21 September 1861, 9 January 1862, Thomas R. R. Cobb Collection; Lamar Cobb to John B. Lamar, 23 October 1861, Howell Cobb to Mary Ann Cobb, 1 January 1861 [1862], Howell Cobb Collection. The Legion was called out so often to man the forward defenses that Lieutenant Barnett mistakenly assumed that Magruder was "only drilling the Army . . . & learning them the localities & roads." Joel C. Barnett to wife, 21 October 1861, Barnett Letters.

labor, together with the construction of a short military road, daily drill, and constant alarms, brought the building of winter quarters almost to a standstill. As a result, it was December before the huts were finally completed.[92]

In the final analysis, the problem of keeping his officers content and the difficulties inherent in commanding a legion type of organization proved infinitely more troublesome to Cobb than did the Federals, who posed no immediate threat to his position or to any part of Magruder's Army of the Peninsula. The Legion had been on the Peninsula barely a week when Cobb found himself besieged by officers seeking furloughs. "All sorts of excuses are formed and I am 'bedevilled' almost out of my patience," he complained. "I shall have to let them go, if Genl. Magruder will give his consent. Some arrangement must be made for winter clothing for the men, and on this plea most of them base their applications."[93]

A number of officers brought their families to live in Richmond or near the encampment, where they could visit them nightly, and others were planning to do the same. "Several times we have been ordered out and the officers were away," noted Cobb, who tolerated the situation, and even encouraged it, until the privilege was abused. He then curtailed absences from camp to two a week. The rule was not unjust, but it was resented. Captain Lawton was so offended, in fact, that he talked of

---

[92]Joel C. Barnett to wife, 3 November, 30 December 1861, Barnett Letters; R. H. L. Clack to James J. Clack, 1 December 1861, Clack Letters; Thomas Cobb to Marion Cobb, 22, 27, 28, 31 October, 1 November, 17 December 1861, Thomas R. R. Cobb Collection.

[93]Thomas Cobb to Marion Cobb, 23 September 1861, Thomas R. R. Cobb Collection. Magruder granted permission, and Cobb authorized his captains to appoint an officer from every company to acquire clothing. Captains Glenn, Lamar, and Powell chose themselves. Thomas Cobb to Marion Cobb, 28 September 1861, ibid. Five weeks later, Captain Knight also departed on leave supposedly to carry out the same assignment. Barnett, who despised Knight, declared that "Ordinarily there would not be anything in this, but Genl Magruder has given a positive order against all furlough untill the 1st January . . . [and] it looks a little unmanly, selfish, & unsoldierlike to make such an excuse to evade a positive order. Col. C. would not have allowed it in my opinion but the Capt had been in ill humor for more than a week & to get rid of him (I presume) *ordered* him home to look after clothing for [the] cmpy[.]" Joel C. Barnett to wife, 3 November 1861, Barnett Letters.

resigning. "This has made me the more resolute," remarked Cobb, "for these men will have to learn (and the sooner the better) that I am firm as I am kind."[94]

Nor was this all. Late in October, Cobb was called upon to settle a potentially explosive quarrel between Captain Yancey of the Fulton Dragoons and Major Young and, at the same time, to come to grips with the bitter enmity that existed between his infantry and cavalry battalions.[95] "I have more than double trouble with my Legion," he revealed,

> because of the rivalry between mounted and footmen of which I had no conception prior to coming into camp. It requires all of my tact and patience to keep them all harmonious. Each Corps suspects me of favoring the other, and it is only by the strictest justice I can manage them. I am well satisfied with my success so far, but if I ever go into the field again I will never undertake a mixed corps.[96]

Considering his subsequent quarrel with the war department over maintaining the Legion intact, it should be stressed that Cobb himself acknowledged the impracticality of this type of formation. "*My great mistake*," he emphasized, "was combining Cavalry and Infantry together. There is no congenial feeling between them but rather a repulsion. Hence constant jars and threatened collisions. Moreover I have more than double labor."[97] His "double labor" included, for example, the gathering of hay and fodder, which was evidently in short supply on the Peninsula. "I am annoyed . . . to get food for my 400 horses," he repeatedly declared.

---

[94]Thomas Cobb to Marion Cobb, 16 October 1861, Thomas R. R. Cobb Collection.

[95]Benjamin Yancey to Major P. M. B. Young, 24 October 1861, Thos. R. R. Cobb to Benjamin Yancey, 25 October 1861, P. M. B. Young to Benjamin Yancey, 26 October 1861, Benjamin C. Yancey Papers, microfilm copy, Southern Historical Collection, University of North Carolina Library.

[96]Thomas Cobb to Marion Cobb, 27 October 1861, Thomas R. R. Collection.

[97]Thomas Cobb to Marion Cobb, 2 November 1861, ibid. "It taxes all my time and energy to attend to one regiment," declared Howell Cobb. "I really feel sorry for Tom whose labors are more than double of mine from the fact that he has both cavalry and infantry in his legion." Howell Cobb to Mary Ann Cobb, 1 November 1861, Howell Cobb Collection.

"The horses look very badly. The captains and men growl, while I am working day and night."[98]

It must not be assumed that Cobb was the only member of the command putting forth an effort or that all his officers were uncooperative.[99] However, it did appear that many were more concerned with their own comfort and advancement than with the welfare of the Legion, and Cobb was very close to the truth in pointing out that a "single imprudence on my part would create discord and confusion."[100] The "discord and confusion," which he was trying to hold in check, emerged in late November and early December as a direct result of two events over which he had no control—the death of Major Bagley, and the promotion of Lieutenant Colonel Garnett.

On 9 November, the Legion and two other regiments, under the personal command of General Magruder, began a twelve day foraging expedition in the neighborhood of Big Bethel. On the night of the twelfth, Cobb obtained permission to return to "Camp Marion" to visit the sick and, at Magruder's request, delivered dispatches to other encampments. During his absence, the Legion's infantry battalion was ordered in the direction of Newport News to lay an ambuscade, and, according to Lieutenant Barnett, the proximity of the enemy made everyone nervous, officers and men alike. The next morning, some of the soldiers mistook two Virginia pickets for Federals and opened fire. Caught in the fusillade, Major Bagley was killed and Captain Morris slightly wounded.[101]

---

[98]Thomas Cobb to Marion Cobb, 23 September 1861, Thomas R. R. Cobb Collection.

[99]For instance, his commissary officer, Captain Terrell Lampkin, was very diligent and efficient. Thomas Cobb to Marion Cobb, 8 November 1861, ibid. Moreover, from Lieutenant Barnett's description of his duties, it would appear that most of the officers were as busy as Cobb. The Lieutenant wrote: "Battalion drill in the morning—Compy drill in the evening—attending roll call, morning & evening—getting the Surgeon to attend our sick—Moving our tents—attending to getting pine poles for huts after drill & answering questions, & settling complaints has kept me quite buisy [sic]. . . . I thought that my time was more cut up than anyone else but I find that Mr. McH[enry] complains of the same also Mr. Porter the Minister." Joel C. Barnett to wife 18 October 1861, Barnett Letters.

[100]Thomas Cobb to Marion Cobb, 2 November 1861, Thomas R. R. Cobb Collection.

[101]Thomas Cobb to Marion Cobb, 9, 12 November 1861, ibid.; Joel C. Barnett to wife, 14 November 1861, Barnett Letters. *Official Records*, series 1, vol. 4, p. 598. A private was also wounded, and Lieutenant Colonel Garnett's horse was shot from under him.

Cobb was appalled by the accident, and, though genuinely distressed by Bagley's death, he could not resist a parting reference to the Major's character. "Poor Bagley was the worst prepared man in the legion for death. He is gone. Peace to his ashes. Silence for his shortcomings."[102]

The foraging expedition ended on 20 November, and by then Cobb had already decided not to replace Bagley, whose death, he explained, "raised a stew about his successor, almost every Captain aspiring to the place."[103] A day later his decision was nullified by the astounding information that Garnett had been commissioned a brigadier general. "I think Davis meant this as a lick for me," he conjectured pettishly. "Well, thank God, I have patriotism enough to despise his malice and still work for my country. But here I am without a single field officer."[104] Deprived of all senior officers at one time, it was inexpedient for him to attend the fifth session of the Confederate Congress until the vacancies were filled.

On 21 November, he announced his intention to elevate Young to the rank of lieutenant colonel and, perhaps to avoid the appearance of favoritism, granted his captains the right to nominate the infantry and cavalry majors. Although fairly certain that Knight would be chosen to command the infantry battalion, he was not in the least disappointed when the captains unanimously elected Jefferson M. Lamar for the post. Cobb had been acquainted with this young man before the war and, since coming into camp, had singled him out for frequent praise. "Jeff Lamar . . . aids me very much and has one of the best companies of quiet young gentlemen I ever saw," he asserted.[105] "He is a first rate man and does all he can to assist me in the management of the legion."[106]

The cavalry officers, meanwhile, were unable to reach an agreement and urged Cobb to make the selection for them. He promptly named Benjamin C. Yancey (whom he considered gentlemanly, courteous, and

---

[102]Thomas Cobb to Marion Cobb, 13 November 1861, Thomas R. R. Cobb Collection.

[103]Thomas Cobb to Marion Cobb, 22 November 1861, ibid.

[104]Ibid. Major Young of the cavalry had gone on sick leave between the dates of Bagley's death and Garnett's promotion.

[105]Thomas Cobb to Marion Cobb, 19 August 1861, ibid.

[106]Thomas Cobb to Marion Cobb, 29 August 1861, ibid.

longwinded) as cavalry major, placed him in charge of the Legion, and departed for Richmond.[107] The choice was manifestly fair, yet dissensions of the worst sort developed, dissensions which undermined the morale of the entire Legion and which were never completely eradicated.

Unaware of the discontent, Cobb took his seat in the Provisional Congress on 26 November, where he served as an avowed spokesman for the army. Since early September, he had been criticized, publicly and privately, for holding a congressional post as well as a military commission. Much of the criticism was based on the false premise that he had been receiving a double salary, when, in fact, he accepted only a colonel's pay after 28 August, the date his commission was confirmed. "I abandoned a practice worth at least seven thousand dollars *per annum*," he pointed out to his critics, "and have received as Congressman and Colonel for more than a year's service a little over one thousand dollars."[108] The allegations persisted, nonetheless, and no doubt increased his desire to resign from Congress. He refrained from doing so, he claimed, only because "All the officers here protest. . . . They say I can do the army so much good by speaking from my own experience and observation."[109] That his Georgia constituents were entitled to a full time representative seems not to have been considered, albeit such a thought may have been implicit in his absolute refusal to run for election to the Permanent Congress.

Cobb subsequently submitted various proposals designed to strengthen the recruitment program of the Confederacy, but in late November he was more interested in returning home than in being a spokesman for either the people of Georgia or the military. Thus, before debate began in December on the controversial Furlough and Bounty Bill, a measure vitally affecting the organization of the army, he left for a brief leave of absence in Athens, where his comments on the course of the war were to cause a local furor.

---

[107]Thomas Cobb to Marion Cobb, 1 October, 26 November 1861, ibid. The appointments of Yancey, Lamar, and Young were confirmed by the Confederate Congress on 29 November 1861. *Confederage Journal*, 1: 508.

[108]*Southern Banner*, 4 September, 2 April 1862.

[109]Thomas Cobb to Marion Cobb, 14 October 1861, Thomas R. R. Cobb Collection.

CHAPTER 9

Confederate General

Top photograph:
View of the left wing of Thomas R. R. Cobb's home on Prince Avenue, Athens, Georgia
Bottom photograph:
Right wing of the Cobb home

During the early part of December 1861, Cobb enjoyed his first furlough in nearly four months. Speaking at a so-called soldiers' prayer meeting in Athens on the fourth, he upset his audience by warning that the Confederacy could not depend upon European assistance to win the war or upon former friends in the northern states but "That... help must come from God" and "To Him alone we must look."[1]

A number of citizens, Colonel David Barrow foremost among them, feared that his remarks might foster defeatism and perhaps encourage the formation of a reconstruction party in Athens. They urged him, therefore, to adopt a less pessimistic tone in his next lecture. Cobb acceded to their wishes, for he was decidely not a friend of reconstruction. Invited by the Reverend Nathan Hoyt to address the congregation of the First Presbyterian Church on Sunday, 8 December, he cast aside his former solemnity and spoke confidently of the magnificent resources of the Confederacy. God, he concluded, was on the side of the South and would not let it go down in defeat.[2] Having lifted the spirits of his

---

[1]Mary Ann Cobb to son, 8 December 1861, Howell Cobb Collection.

[2]Ibid.; *Southern Banner*, 11 December 1861.

townsmen, Cobb left for Virginia on Monday, the ninth, and reached Richmond at noon on the thirteenth. The Troup Artillery arrived in the city at about the same time and was ordered to move in sections to "Camp Marion."

Returning to camp ahead of the battery, Cobb expected to find the Legion in a somewhat disorganized state, but he was quite unprepared for the chaotic situation that confronted him. "Nothing done since I left," he exclaimed, "no drills, no work, no discipline, no cordiality." Some of the captains, he continued, "were ready to growl at me for the appointment of Majors. I regret to say that the man most petted and indulged by me in the Legion (Captain Knight) was at the bottom of the dissatisfaction."[3]

Discipline and military routine were quickly reestablished in the camp. "It will be weeks before I can get everything working to my notion," Cobb declared, "but I am convinced the disaffection is very partial, the mal-contents are all coming in and giving in and I apprehend no sort of trouble or ill-feeling."[4] Captain Knight, for one, apologized for his behavior and was thus restored to the good graces of his colonel, who again asserted that "I think the whole trouble arising from the appointment is passed and my mind is much relieved."[5]

His optimism was premature. Captain T. P. Stovall still felt that he, rather than Yancey, should have been promoted to major of the cavalry. Openly airing his grievances, he spoke often of resigning from the Legion and caused no little discontent among his men. Not until 5 February 1862, was Cobb able to report that the "Stovall matter" was under control, and even then there were indications that, if ignored again, the captain would carry through his threat to resign.[6]

Before Stovall had been temporarily placated, Cobb encountered sullen hostility from his cavalry major, who had failed ignominously in his attempt to keep order in the Legion during the colonel's brief absence.

---

[3]Thomas Cobb to Marion Cobb, 14 December 1861, Thomas R. R. Cobb Collection.

[4]Ibid.

[5]Thomas Cobb to Marion Cobb, 16 December 1861, ibid.

[6]Thomas Cobb to Marion Cobb, 5 February 1862, ibid.; Radford C. Rhodes to Alexander H. Stephens, 29 December 1861, John Jenkins to Alexander H. Stephens, 9 February 1862, Stephens Papers, Library of Congress; Pope Barrow to Nellie, 6 February 1862, Barrow Papers.

"Yancey had done his best," acknowledged the latter upon his return to camp in December, "but he is a slow coach."[7] The Major sensed, perhaps, that Cobb was not entirely pleased with his management of the command and was no doubt cognizant of the fact that not a few of the troops were exceedingly happy and relieved when the colonel resumed control of the camp. Possibly wounded pride was the explanation for his grim mood. "He says but little," Cobb noted, "but is evidently estranged from me and seeks to throw every obstacle in my way. I am treating him with kindness but firmness."[8]

William G. Delony, the efficient, handsome, auburn haired captain of the Georgia Troopers from Athens, was disgruntled, too. He claimed not to care that Yancey had been promoted over him but was angered at the reasons assigned for the decision, namely, "age, position, and other attainments," and so indicated in a coldly polite interview with the colonel. "He is 'surprised' that I am not satisfied," Delony reported to his wife, "and I am surprised that he is surprised which is about the sum and substance of our conversation."[9]

Conflicts within the Troup Artillery compounded Cobb's difficulties. The battery had been in camp barely four days when Lieutenant H. H. Carlton, in a drunken rage, "cursed" and "threatened to kill" Captain Marcellus Stanley.[10] Although the lieutenant was clearly in the wrong, his insubordination reflected a general antagonism toward the captain, who, because of poor health and unpopularity, was on the verge of resigning his commission. "There is more trouble and dissension among the Artillery than any where else," complained Cobb. "Expecting Stanley to resign, parties and cliques have grown up and I feel daily the bad

---

[7]Thomas Cobb to Marion Cobb, 14 December 1861, Thomas R. R. Cobb Collection.

[8]Thomas Cobb to Marion Cobb, 1 January 1862, ibid.

[9]William Delony to Rosa, 31 December 1861, William G. Delony Papers, University of Georgia Libraries.

[10]Thomas Cobb to Marion Cobb, 19 December 1861, Thomas R. R. Cobb Collection; Pope Barrow to parents, 19 December 1861, Barrow Papers.

results."[11] In his opinion, Stanley was an outstanding officer, whose resignation at this juncture would create further factionalism in the company. "It will ruin the company," he emphasized.[12]

In spite of Yancey's uncooperative attitude, Stovall's continuing petulance, Deloney's pique, and problems with the Troup Artillery, Cobb insisted that the "most *cordial* good feeling prevails in all the Legion among the officers. Captain Deloney was the last with the 'pouts' and he has become very agreeable. As to my appointments I am satisfied I did right and have no reason to regret my action in regard to anyone of them."[13] Rumors to the contrary, he stoutly denied, branding them "pure fabrication." The supposed amicability was only on the surface, however, and was only maintained by Cobb's presence in camp, thus tending to bear out his contention that "*nobody but myself can manage this Legion and keep everything* harmonious."[14]

These deplorable frictions coincided with a period of alarm on the Peninsula. General Magruder had persuaded himself that a massive Federal offensive against his position was imminent. Forty thousand enemy troops, he reported, had been concentrated at Fort Monroe and Newport News and would attack as soon as a fleet, carrying additional forces, arrived from Annapolis. The war department, now headed by Judah P. Benjamin, tersely discounted his exaggerated warning. "It is not believed that any such forces as are represented to you can possibly be within the enemy's line," replied the secretary. Moreover, "We have no news whatever of any fleet . . . threatening your department."[15]

Persisting in his delusion, Magruder cancelled furloughs, called for reenforcements, issued dramatic battle orders, and signaled innumerable

[11]Thomas Cobb to Marion Cobb, 27 December 1861, Thomas R. R. Cobb Collection. Of Captain Stanley, Carlton had earlier written: "I never was so much deceived in a man in all my life. I don't suppose there is a more indifferent Capt[.] in the Confederate service. The men all dislike him and would gladly see him resign. I do sometimes think he is crazy." H. H. Carlton to George, 4 October 1861, Carlton-Newton-Mell Collection.

[12]Thomas Cobb to Marion Cobb, 9 January 1862, Thomas R. R. Cobb Collection.

[13]Ibid.

[14]Thomas Cobb to Marion Cobb, 2 November 1861, ibid. See also Pope [Barrow] to father, 18 January 1862, Barrow Papers.

[15]*Official Records*, ser. 1, vol 4, pp. 707-708, 712-13, 717.

pre-dawn alerts, which resulted in nothing more tangible than the unnecessary exposure of his army to rain and sleet. Along with most of the officers and men of the Legion, Cobb shared the war department's skepticism. "I do not see the remotest prospect of a fight here," he wrote. "Magruder is still apprehensive, but I cannot think he has cause."[16] Several days later, in response to an urgent dispatch from Magruder, Cobb galloped eight miles to headquarters, where, he related, "I found the general in full expectation of an attack on Yorktown by a fleet from Annapolis tonight and his business with me was merely to instruct me what to do in such an event. I think it is all stuff."[17] He regretted to say that the "old fellow injures himself with his men by his unending alarms," but, he added, "They do him injustice by doubting his courage. He is a brave and good officer. His fault is running off after one idea. He loses sight of everything else till he rides his hobby to death."[18]

While it was possible to dismiss Magruder's fears of a winter campaign as the figment of an excitable imagination, it was not improbable that the Federals would launch a major offensive to capture Richmond in the spring of 1862. This probability presented the Confederacy with a crucial problem. The enlistment of a substantial portion of the army was due to expire in March and April, and, unless these troops could be retained in service, a military disaster might ensue.

The Furlough and Bounty Act had been passed in December 1861, to solve this dilemma. By offering a bounty of fifty dollars and a leave of sixty days to all twelve months' volunteers who agreed to reenlist for three years or the duration of the war, the Congress had hoped to

[16]Thomas Cobb to Marion Cobb, 14 December 1861, Thomas R. R. Cobb Collection. Many others agreed with Cobb, including Lieutenant Pope Barrow of the Troup Artillery, who asserted: "Genl. Magruder . . . is certainly the most excitable man I ever saw. . . . He imagines every two or three weeks that the Yankees are right on him and then his whole army is turned topsy turvy to prepare to receive them." Pope Barrow to parents, 19 December 1861, Barrow Papers. For similar views see R. H. L. Clack to James J. Clack, 9 January 1862, Clack Letters; Joel C. Barnett to wife, 12 January 1862, Barnett Letters; *Southern Banner*, 15 January 1862, containing correspondence from an enlisted man in the Troup Artillery.

[17]Thomas Cobb to Marion Cobb, 19 December 1861, Thomas R. R. Cobb Collection.

[18]Thomas Cobb to Marion Cobb, 20 December 1861, ibid.

stimulate reenlistments. Despite these and other inducements, volunteers seemed reluctant to commit themselves to further service. The Troup Artillery was a case in point. The company was scheduled to be released from active duty in April 1861, and its members were badly divided on the issue of reenlisting for the war. If some decision were not reached soon, the battery would be lost to the Legion at the beginning of an important campaign. The alternatives were to recruit and train replacements at once, without waiting for the men to decide whether to extend their enlistments, or else to force them by law to remain in the army. Additional legislation to offset the anticipated loss of twelve months' volunteers and to fill ranks thinned by disease and battle was thus imperative.

In common with other Confederate officials, Cobb was deeply concerned about the recruitment question. "I confess the future is enveloped with clouds impenetrable to my eyes," he declared. "The worst symptom to me is the indisposition of the 12 Mos. men to re-enlist."[19] At the urging of Assistant Secretary of State William M. Browne, he set out for Richmond on 11 January 1862, to take part in congressional debates on the subject of enlarging the army and to transact some pressing business relating to the Legion. "My presence here is deemed so important by Mr. Hunter, Mr. Memminger and other friends of the army that I feel as if I ought to stay if I can," he wrote on the day after his arrival.

> I find the Government much alarmed about recruiting the army for next Spring's campaign, and it is well they are so. We are in a very critical condition and it has been a hard matter to wake up the President to see and feel it. How can this be best done? is the absorbing question of Congress and hence the great desire to have us who are daily connected with the army in their deliberations.[20]

At that moment, Congress was heatedly discussing a bill to increase the size of the army by granting bounties and other benefits (similar to those contained in the Furlough and Bounty Act) to new volunteers, who were willing to be mustered into the service for three years or the war. Cobb took an immediate interest in the measure and tried to impress his

---

[19]Thomas Cobb to Marion Cobb, 30 December 1861, ibid.

[20]Thomas Cobb to Marion Cobb, 12 January 1862, ibid.

views on the members of Congress. After two days of debate, his patience began to wear thin. "Till one o'clock last night or rather this morning I was without one moment I could call my own," he complained.

> Congress was in the midst of legislation on a military bill about which they knew nothing and were not disposed to listen to those who did. Stephens was philosophying [sic] largely and with oracular consequence while a good many old fogies shook wise heads and wondered at his eloquence. In short, my wife, I am bending every energy to save the country, by saving the army from ridiculous legislation.[21]

Precisely which provisions in the bill he objected to is not clear, but, when appointed to a special committee of five to reconsider the measure, he was able to modify it to his liking and to obtain its final passage. "Thank God! Thank God!" he exclaimed. "I have done good work today. We passed a most important army bill, which friends say would not have gone through without my presence . . . and I hope during the week to perfect all the work for which I came."[22]

Self-satisfied though he was, Cobb realized that this act alone probably would not raise sufficient troops to fend effectively against a powerful enemy thrust. "I am very much troubled about the state of the country," he asserted once more.

> The spring will find our enemies with a large and well disciplined army ready to advance upon us, whereas four fifths of ours are twelve months men every one of whom will return home before he enlists again for the war. How are our lines to be filled? Will the people at home enlist? I fear not. What are we to do? These questions are puzzling the wisest heads. I found Congress hugging the delusion that the 12 mos. men would re-enlist. I think I have opened their eyes somewhat, and the President's also.[23]

Sentiment for conscription, the most logical solution to the manpower problem, had not yet crystalized. As Cobb pointed out to his wife in early February, "The idea of forcing the 12 mos men to enlist never entered the head of any sensible man. I pledge you my word I never hear a suggestion of such a course in Congress or in Richmond."[24] When

---

[21]Thomas Cobb to Marion Cobb, 14 January 1862, ibid.

[22]Thomas Cobb to Marion Cobb, 15 January 1862, ibid.; *Confederate Journal*, 1: 667-75, 695.

[23]Thomas Cobb to Marion Cobb, 17 January 1862, Thomas R. R. Cobb Collection.

[24]Thomas Cobb to Marion Cobb, 8 February 1862, ibid.

Congress finally did resort to forcible enlistment in April, he condemned the conscription act as "an infamous outrage on the 12 mos. men." There was "a military necessity for it," he admitted,

> but *that necessity was caused by the imbecility of the government.* Davis and his toadies laughed at me when I told them the men would not reenlist under the bounty act, and urged upon them more active preparations for the spring campaign. Now Davis comes to Congress and says "we are ruined unless you force the 12 mos. men to remain." What a commentary upon his administration.[25]

It was one thing to perceive an obvious problem and quite another to provide a workable remedy. Cobb had done the former but not the latter, nor, for that matter, had any of his colleagues. Indeed, Congress enacted a mass of military measures in January and February 1862, including laws sponsored and supported by Cobb, all of which were difficult to administer and interpret and none of which prevented a shortage of troops. "Every conceivable means of securing men was adopted, save that of compulsion," notes an authority on the subject.[26] Short of recommending coercive legislation at this juncture, there was apparently nothing else that Davis or the Congress could have done to meet the forthcoming enemy onslaught. Cobb's criticism of the president was, therefore, unwarranted, and it was more of a commentary on his own character than on the conduct of the administration.

On 23 January, the last of several bills introduced by Cobb was signed into law.[27] A week later, while preparing to rejoin the Legion, he learned that the president was planning to veto a recently passed furlough bill. "If he does, his friends will hear some plain talk," he promised.[28] And on the day the veto message was delivered, he reiterated his intention to oppose it.[29]

In the judgment of Jefferson Davis, the furlough bill endangered the security of the Confederacy. "At this crisis," he explained,

---

[25]Thomas Cobb to Marion Cobb 24 April 1862, ibid.

[26]Albert B. Moore, *Conscription and Conflict in the Confederacy* (New York: Hillary House Publishers, Ltd., 1963), p. 8.

[27]*Confederate Journal*, 1: 698.

[28]Thomas Cobb to Marion Cobb, 30 January 1862, Thomas R. R. Cobb Collection.

[29]Thomas Cobb to Marion Cobb, 1 February 1862, ibid.

> without any check or control by commanding generals, 5 per cent of their effective forces would be withdrawn under the provisions of this bill. With conflicts impending against an enemy greatly our superior in numbers, our safety is dependent on keeping in the field every effective man that can be furnished with a weapon; this bill, therefore, it seems to me, is most inopportunely presented.[30]

The logic of the president's argument was unassailable. The veto stood; and, for all Cobb's dire threats, there appears to have been no serious move to override it.

Throughout the latter part of the fifth session of Congress, Cobb professed a patriotic desire to sustain the administration in this period of extreme emergency and claimed to be a more conscientious supporter of its policies than many of the president's avowed friends. "Dissension now is death," he declared. "I must not put a feather's weight upon a Government which hardly bears up . . . under the burden which its ill-advised officers are daily heaping upon it."[31]

In view of this, his decision to "condemn boldly his [the president's] errors and to uphold him generously when he is right" was somewhat contradictory. In private, he seldom, if ever, upheld Davis but condemned him often as "an obstinate stupid fool."[32] His public statements, though much less severe, were sharp enough to mark him as an opponent of the administration. "You know," he reminded his wife, "how earnestly I have striven to sustain the Prest. . . . , but I declare I am compelled to oppose him every day until I am now recognized as being of the opposition."[33]

Reserving his most vicious verbal cuts for Secretary of War Judah P. Benjamin, he assassinated the man's character and censured his management of the war department publicly as well as privately. "A grander rascal than this Jew dog Benjamin, I do not believe lives in this Confeder-

---

[30]James D. Richardson, ed., *The Messages and Papers of the Confederacy*, 2 vols. (Nashville: United States Publishing Company, 1905), 1: 164.

[31]Thomas Cobb to Marion Cobb, 24, 30 January 1862, Thomas R. R. Cobb Collection.

[32]Thomas Cobb to Marion Cobb, 24 January, 1 February 1862, ibid.

[33]Thomas Cobb to Marion Cobb, 1 February 1862, ibid. Yet, when Alexander H. Stephens criticized Davis, Cobb was infuriated. The vice president, he asserted, "is openly opposing the administration and trying to build up an opposition party. He is demagoguing low down." Thomas Cobb to Marion Cobb, 12 January 1862, ibid. See also Thomas Cobb to Marion Cobb, 24 January 1862, ibid.

acy," he snarled. He "is a mean low sycophantic dodging Jew."[34] In his hatred for Benjamin, he listened to and repeated the vilest gossip about the secretary's marital relations and concluded sanctimoniously that "God rules . . . and will use even such an unbelieving Jew for the promotion of His holy and just purposes."[35] Policy differences might account, in part, for Cobb's constant attacks on Secretary Benjamin and President Davis, but only in part. Personal factors were also involved. In the final analysis, they provide the best explanation for his malicious attitude.

To begin with, Cobb bitterly resented the fact that he and his brother, Howell, had been passed over for promotion. In his opinion, the slight was deliberate. Particularly was he irritated by the president's seeming preference for West Point officers. "Davis," he exclaimed, "is a monomaniac about West Point. He thinks it will 'make a whistle of a pig tail.' " Consequently, he rued the president's power to appoint generals and insisted that "*right there* is our greatest trouble now.[36]

A second and closely related factor underlying Cobb's vindictiveness was the failure of Davis and Benjamin to act promptly on his project to enlarge the Legion. This scheme had grown out of the extraordinary demands imposed upon him by the peculiar nature of his command. A combined force of infantry and cavalry, as Cobb had frequently pointed out, doubled the difficulties of its commander; the addition of an artillery company trebled them. His brother, Howell, and Lieutenant Pope Barrow of the Troup Artillery both corroborated that his duties were aggravating and exhausting. "He is the same energetic man here that he is at home," testified the latter. "He has vexations and trials that would run a nervous man crazy."[37] Worried about his brother's health, Howell Cobb predicted that,

---

[34]Thomas Cobb to Marion Cobb, 26 January, 1 February 1862, ibid.

[35]Thomas Cobb to Marion Cobb, 15, 26 January 1862, ibid.

[36]Thomas Cobb to Marion Cobb, 14, 24 January 1862, ibid. Howell Cobb, Robert Toombs, and Alexander H. Stephens all harbored similar prejudices against the president's West Point appointments. See Howell Cobb to Mary Ann Cobb, 25 January 1862, Howell Cobb Collection; Robert Toombs to Alexander H. Stephens, [30] September 1861, Phillips, ed., *Correspondence*, p. 577; Johnston and Browne, *Life of Stephens*, p. 414.

[37]Pope [Barrow] to father, 18 January 1862, Barrow Papers.

> unless he can make some arrangement to be relieved from a part of his labors it will wear him out—This I hope he will be able to do—but like myself he is no particular favorite with the Government and what would readily be done for some others is not so easily effected for him.[38]

In an effort to relieve some of the strain, Howell Cobb consulted twice with Magruder and sent a letter to Secretary Memminger requesting his brother's promotion to brigadier general and offering to add his own regiment to the Legion in order to form the requisite brigade. Discovering what his elder brother had in mind, Thomas Cobb protested on the ground that "enemies would glory in my promotion over his head."[39] To this argument, Howell replied: "Your objections are not good. I don't care a d—n about military promotion."[40] Nonetheless, Thomas Cobb had already decided that his acceptance of a higher commission would depend upon the fulfillment of two conditions: first, the prior advancement of his brother and, secondly, "that the Legion should be increased to a Brigade . . . and that I should continue to command it."[41]

His conditions were incredible, and the president would have been justified in rejecting them. However, when Cobb formally broached the idea of an enlarged Legion in mid-December 1861, Davis seemed amenable to the project. Nothing definite was agreed to, but Cobb left the meeting feeling rather encouraged. "If Mr. Davis will only carry out his promise intimated to me to raise my Legion to a Brigade," he wrote, "he would move a mountain load off my shoulders. Then each regiment would have its own Colonel who would have to meet all the annoyances now heaped upon me. My responsibilities would be greater, but I could bear that, if I could be relieved of these petty troubles."[42]

During a second interview with the president on 14 January 1862, Cobb was told to submit his proposals in writing for further study. Complying with these instructions, he drafted a plan, which envisioned a Legion of five thousand men—one regiment of cavalry, four regiments of

---

[38]Howell Cobb to Mary Ann Cobb, 1 November 1861, Howell Cobb Collection.

[39]Thomas Cobb to Marion Cobb, 4 November 1861, Thomas Cobb Collection.

[40]Howell Cobb to Thomas Cobb, 14 November 1861, ibid.

[41]Thomas Cobb to Marion Cobb, 4 November 1861, ibid.

[42]Thomas Cobb to Marion Cobb, 14 December 1861, ibid.

infantry, and a battalion of artillery. Since the Troup Artillery was due to be mustered out of the service near the end of April, two batteries instead of one would have to be recruited. According to the plan, the Troup Artillery was to be discharged as soon as it could train one of the existing infantry companies as a replacement. The second battery was to be raised in Georgia, and both were to be ready for action by 15 April.[43]

After presenting his plan to Davis, Cobb waited impatiently for some word of approval. "The President is still silent on my proposition," he wrote on 23 January, "and I am determined not to press it any more. If he does not appreciate my ability to serve the country in this way, my self respect will not allow me to urge it upon him."[44] For the next three weeks, hardly a day went by without an angry outburst concerning the delay. "Davis has treated Howell like a dog and me with the utmost indifference," he raged. "I have given the President *the conditions on which I will accept*. He dallies and higgles about it, until I am disgusted."[45] Holding the secretary of war equally to blame, he commented contemptuously that "I *do not speak to Benjamin* and have denounced him as a dirty dog. The consequence is that my hands . . . are hampered for the balance of the war. . . . I have no doubt that I have finally settled the question of the increase of the Legion."[46]

Hearing nothing further from the president, Cobb returned to "Camp Marion" on 3 February, to be greeted by the cheers of his men, a torchlight procession, and the music of an eighteen-piece Legion band, which had been recently organized under the direction of Dr. E. A. Wurm on leave from his duties at the Lucy Cobb Institute. News of his intention to increase the command to brigade strength and to release the Troup Artillery ahead of time had preceded him to the Peninsula by several days. Lieutenant Joel Barnett, for example, accurately reported the substance of the plan as early as 27 January, and Anderson Reese, a private in the Troup Artillery, announced in a letter to the *Southern Banner* that members of the battery "have been on the *qui vive* for the last ten days. . . .

[43]Thomas Cobb to Marion Cobb, 14 January 1862, ibid.

[44]Thomas Cobb to Marion Cobb, 23 January 1862, ibid.

[45]Thomas Cobb to Marion Cobb, 27 January 1862, ibid.

[46]Thomas Cobb to Marion Cobb, 1 February 1862, ibid.

They have heard that it is the intention of the 'powers that be' to disband them sometime during this month."[47]

Although his project had not yet received Davis' sanction, Cobb rode to Yorktown shortly after his arrival from Richmond to secure Magruder's consent to the early discharge of the battery. "I am trying hard to have the artillery mustered out," he remarked, "and think I shall succeed in less than a fortnight."[48] At the same time, Captain Knight's Panola Guards were selected to replace the Troup Artillery and began four hours of daily battery drill. Knight's company progressed so well that Cobb hoped to gain the release of Stanley's men before the end of February. His hopes were dashed, however, by a telegraphic message from Magruder cancelling the departure of all troops from his department. This dispatch prompted Cobb to surmise that the capture of Roanoke Island on the eighth by a Federal force under Ambrose Burnside had frightened Magruder into believing that the enemy might attempt a landing on the Peninsula preparatory to an attack on Richmond.[49]

This unexpected development was followed by the even more unexpected intelligence that his brother, Howell, had at last been promoted to brigadier general. "It is tardy justice," he wrote. "It removes one great difficulty in my way of increasing my legion, for I determined that I never would rank Howell, as long as Davis vented his spite on him by withholding what every one felt was due him."[50] The final stumbling block was eliminated shortly thereafter, or so he thought, when the president endorsed his proposal to enlarge the Legion.

---

[47]Joel C. Barnett to wife, 27 January 1862, Barnett Letters; *Southern Banner*, 19 February 1862. Reese's letter was dated 8 February. Lieutenant Frank Pope of the Troup Artillery also mentioned that among the officers and men there was "a general impression . . . that the Company would be . . . Mustered out . . . during this month." Frank Pope to Col. David Barrow, 2 February 1862, Barrow Papers. See also Benjamin Mell to father, 30 January 1862, Carlton-Newton-Mell Collection; B. E. Yerby to father, 31 January 1862, Yerby Letters; T. A. Barrow to father, 30 January 1862, Barrow Papers.

[48]Thomas Cobb to Marion Cobb, 5 February 1862, Thomas R. R. Cobb Collection; Pope [Barrow] to Nellie, 6 February 1862, Barrow Papers.

[49]Thomas Cobb to Marion Cobb, 18 [10?] February 1862, Thomas R. R. Cobb Collection; Pope Barrow to sister, 11 February 1862, Barrow Papers; Joel C. Barnett to wife, 12 February 1862, Barnett Letters.

[50]Thomas Cobb to Marion Cobb, 13 February 1862, Thomas R. R. Cobb Collection.

On 15 February, Cobb applied for a furlough in order to raise the regiments for his new command. At first, Magruder denied him permission to leave because of "the present uncertainty as to the movements of the enemy."[51] He subsequently relented, but refused absolutely to allow the discharge of the Troup Artillery, which continued in service pending the termination of its tour of duty in late April.

On the morning of 19 February, Cobb left for Athens with verbal instructions from Davis to forward all regiments recruited to General Albert Sidney Johnston, whose army had suffered twin setbacks at forts Henry and Donelson on the sixth and sixteenth. Cobb presumed, of course, that the Legion was soon to be transferred to the Georgia-Tennessee theater of operations, where it would be merged with the new regiments to form a brigade under his command. Later he would discover how mistaken this assumption was.

Arriving in Athens on the evening of the twenty-first, Cobb spent the ensuing two weeks trying to recruit the required five thousand troops. To facilitate enlistments, he placed an advertisement in the *Southern Banner* appealing to the patriotism of all "true Men" and directing them to gather in Atlanta, where they were to be mustered into service and organized as regiments to "operate on the Southern line—EITHER IN GEORGIA, TENNESSEE, OR CAROLINA" as part of the enlarged Legion. He also made arrangements for a second artillery company and called on Governor Joseph E. Brown for assistance. The governor agreed to furnish a number of regiments from the quota assigned to the state by a Confederate law, which Cobb himself had introduced.[52] Sensing an opportunity for advancement, two of Cobb's captains, W. J. Lawton and C. A. McDaniel, obtained permission from Judah P. Benjamin to return to Georgia to raise regiments for service in the newly expanded Legion.[53] By the end of his leave Cobb had practically accomplished his mission.

---

[51]Thomas Cobb to Marion Cobb, 16 February 1862, ibid.

[52]*Southern Banner*, 26 February 1862; *Official Records*, ser. 4, vol. 1, p. 1013; Benjamin C. Yancey to wife, 23 February 1862, Yancey Papers; Geo. T. Barnes to Alexander H. Stephens, 25 April 1862, Stephens Papers, Library of Congress; *Confederate Journal*, 1: 675, 698; Thomas Cobb to Marion Cobb, 8 February 1862, Thomas Cobb to Jefferson Davis, 18 March 1862, Thomas R. R. Cobb Collection; *Southern Watchman*, 12, 19 March 1862. The recruitment law authorized the president "to call upon the several states for troops to serve for three years or during the war."

[53]The possibility of promotion occurred to others as well. A private in T. P. Stovall's company sought Vice President Stephens' assistance in securing the rank of lieutenant.

During his absence from the Peninsula, the Georgia Legion and four other regiments had been placed in the Second Brigade under the command of Howell Cobb. Early in March, this brigade and that of Brigadier General George W. Randolph were ordered to defend the strategic rail junction of Suffolk, Virginia, against a possible attack by Burnside's expedition, which had moved from Roanoke Island to the North Carolina mainland. If Suffolk fell, Norfolk, twenty-two miles to the northeast, would be exposed along with the entire right flank of Magruder's Army of the Peninsula.[54]

Notified of the movement by telegraph, Thomas Cobb rejoined the Legion on the night of 10 March. "My men were happy to see me," he reported, "and I find *it is well* that I came to them. No great trouble but everything in confusion."[55] In the morning, he reconnoitered the approaches to his position and by nightfall of the following day had restored order and routine in his camp. "I feel much more competent now," he wrote, "to discharge my duty in the event of a battle."[56]

When the enemy failed to make an appearance, Cobb made a quick trip to Richmond to complete his plans for enlarging the Legion. Unable to see the president immediately, he conversed with his friend William M. Browne, who informed him that "Davis was backing out."[57] The accuracy of the information was confirmed by the president on the morning of the seventeenth. "I found to my great mortification that Brown[e] was right," Cobb explained to his wife.

Since "my Col . . . is on the eve of increasing his Legion to a larger number," he wrote, "[I] thought you might use your influence in my behalf." John Jenkins to Alexander H. Stephens, 9 February 1862, Stephens Papers, Library of Congress.

[54]*Official Records*, ser. 1, vol. 9, pp. 44-45, 51-53, 57-59.

[55]Thomas Cobb to Marion Cobb, 11 March 1862, Thomas R. R. Cobb Collection. According to William G. Delony, the Georgia Troopers lost all their mess equipment due to poor leadership on the part of Major Yancey. See William Delony to Rosa, 19 March 1862, Delony Papers.

[56]Thomas Cobb to Marion Cobb, 12 March 1862, Thomas R. R. Cobb Collection.

[57]Thomas Cobb to Marion Cobb, 3 April 1862, ibid. By this time Cobb had aroused the expectations of officers and men alike by intimating strongly that the Legion would soon be expanded and sent to Tennessee via Georgia. Samuel A. Burney to wife, 11 March 1862, Burney Letters; William J. Rheney to mother, 18 March 1862, Rheney Letters; B. E. Yerby to grandpa, 11 March 1862, Yerby Letters; William Delony to Rosa, 16 March 1862, Delony Papers.

> He [Davis] pretends (and I will not doubt his honesty) that he never expected me to command any but one of the regiments, and of course I cannot press on him to give me a higher commission. Mortifying as it is, I am compelled to disband the troops I have raised and to continue my old legion. I think it due to myself to publish to the people of Georgia the reasons of my action and I have prepared a letter to the President setting forth the facts. This I shall publish in the Georgia papers.[58]

The "facts," as he outlined them, revealed that the subject of military promotion had been mentioned only twice during his several conversations with the president and both times in an ambiguous and "almost jocose" manner. Consequently, Cobb might very easily have misinterpreted the intent behind the president's remarks.[59] Davis, on the other hand, does not appear to have been entirely candid with the Georgia colonel. Without question, he had authorized him to raise regiments for incorporation in a brigade, and it was certainly justifiable for Cobb to conclude that he was to be the commander.

In the gloomiest of moods, Cobb left the city early on the morning of 18 March, to return to Suffolk. Before his departure, Browne, Memminger, and R. M. T. Hunter had all promised to intercede in his behalf and persuaded him to delay publication of his open letter until they could act. He also had a powerful ally in General George Randolph, who had been designated to succeed Benjamin as head of the war department. "The new Secty. of War . . . is a great friend of mine," he claimed, "and will do anything he can to carry out my wishes. I believe he esteems me as highly as Genl. Magruder did and this was *beyond* my merits."[60]

Despite the assurance of support from influential friends, Cobb looked for "the meanest conduct from Davis."[61] Still, there was a bare

---

[58]Thomas Cobb to Marion Cobb, 18 [17] March 1861, Thomas R. R. Cobb Collection. In a letter to Governor Brown, Davis stated explicitly that he had "never authorized him [Cobb] to increase his command to 5,000 men" and had "steadily refused to augment any legion beyond a colonel's command." Jefferson Davis to Joseph E. Brown, 7 April 1862, Felix Hargrett Typescript.

[59]Thomas Cobb to President Davis, 18 March 1861, Thomas R. R. Cobb Collection.

[60]Thomas Cobb to Marion Cobb, 19 March 1862, ibid. Nominated on 17 March, Randolph assumed office about a week later. Benjamin, meanwhile, had moved to the state department to replace Hunter, who had resigned to serve in the Confederate Senate. See Patrick, *Davis and His Cabinet*, pp. 101-102, 122-23.

[61]Thomas Cobb to Marion Cobb, 18 March 1862, Thomas R. R. Cobb Collection.

possibility that the president might change his mind, and, for that reason, the Georgia colonel continued to withhold his letter from print and sent Major Yancey to Atlanta to take charge of recruits whose number swelled daily. Indeed, his principal embarrassment was an inability to respond firmly to the growing demand for admission to the Legion. Because of "the silence of my friends in Richmond," he grumbled, "I am constrained to keep still and evade inquiries until I do hear. This annoys and sometimes mortifys [sic] me."[62]

While Cobb awaited the final decision concerning his scheme to augment the Legion, the Second Brigade was ordered to Goldsboro, North Carolina, approximately 120 miles southwest of Suffolk, to help protect the railroad at that point from Burnside's expedition, which had captured New Bern on the fourteenth. Cobb's cavalry companies moved out of camp on 20 March, just ahead of a dispatch ordering the Legion to return to the Peninsula. The order was issued at the instigation of Magruder, who, fearful of being overwhelmed, had fallen back to his second line of defense and called for reenforcements. Forewarned, Cobb had sped his cavalry on its way to avoid compliance with the order. "My men would rather have been drafted and every tenth man hung," than to go back to the mud and tedium of the Peninsula, he declared. The ruse worked, for Magruder was informed that the dispatch had arrived in Suffolk too late to stop the Legion and that an Alabama regiment was to be forwarded to him instead.[63]

The Troup Artillery went by rail to Goldsboro on the twenty-first, but train transportation was not available for the Legion's infantry battalion until the night of the twenty-third. The journey to North Carolina was "most unpleasant," related Cobb upon reaching his destination the next day. "All night long my men had to sit in the cold air on platform cars and without a thing to eat. At Weldon I determined to give all . . . a drink of whiskey, and after much trouble succeeded in buying some."[64]

---

[62]Thomas Cobb to Marion Cobb, 28 March 1862, ibid.

[63]*Official Records*, ser. 1, vol. 9, pp. 50-52, 58, 393-94, 396, 449-54; Thomas Cobb to Marion Cobb, 20 March 1862, Thomas R. R. Cobb Collection.

[64]Thomas Cobb to Marion Cobb, 24 March 1862, Thomas R. R. Cobb Collection.

By the late afternoon of 24 March, the Legion had moved into position along the rail line leading from Goldsboro to New Bern, and there it remained for nearly two weeks. To Cobb, the prospect of a battle in this vicinity seemed relatively remote. "There are no indications of an advance by the enemy," he wrote, "and my men begin to speak despondently of the chances of a fight here."[65] Several days later, he noted that all signs pointed to the Peninsula as the real scene of conflict. His observation was not without substance. Confederate forces under General Joseph E. Johnston were already being withdrawn from the Rapidan-Rappahannock region of northern Virginia and reconcentrated around Yorktown in order to check General George B. McClellan, who had landed a large Federal army at Fort Monroe. To bolster the defense further, Howell Cobb's Second Brigade was ordered to rejoin Magruder, and by the night of 6 April, the movement back to the Peninsula had been completed.[66]

In the morning the Legion and other elements of the Second Brigade were thrown into position behind the Warwick River, which separated the contending armies, and which had been widened at various points by the construction of thick dams. The Confederate line followed the course of this stream from Wynn's Mill, near the redoubts of Yorktown, to Lee's Mill and then swung northwestwardly in the direction of Mulberry Point on the James River. To the left of Lee's Mill and in the rear of what was known as Dam Number Two, the infantry battalion of Cobb's Legion and a six-pound howitzer belonging to the Troup Artillery were stationed. A section of this battery, composed of two guns, and the rest of the Second Brigade were posted two miles further up river at Dam Number One, while a fourth cannon, also part of the Troup Artillery, was placed in position at Wynn's Mill.[67] The mounted wing of the Legion had been left at Goldsboro under the command of Lieutenant Colonel Young. "I did not bring the cavalry here," Cobb explained, "because there is no use for them. They would only be couriers and their horses would suffer."[68]

---

[65]Thomas Cobb to Marion Cobb, 26 March 1862, ibid.

[66]Thomas Cobb to Marion Cobb, 1 April 1862, ibid.; Joel C. Barnett to wife, 7 April 1862, Barnett Letters.

[67]Joel C. Barnett to wife, 7 April 1862, Barnett Letters; Thomas Cobb to Marion Cobb, 10 April 1862, Thomas R. R. Cobb Collection.

[68]Thomas Cobb to Marion Cobb, 28 April 1862, Thomas R. R. Cobb Collection.

From the day of its arrival on the Peninsula, the Legion was constantly reminded of the enemy's proximity by the sound of distant band music, by the sight of smoke from opposing campfires, and by almost daily skirmishing on the picket line. To be ready for the Federal assault, Cobb kept his men hard at work digging entrenchments. Full of confidence, he proclaimed his belief that whenever McClellan did attack "*we will repulse him* and if we do we shall make another Manassas route of it."[69]

Amidst these defensive preparations, Cobb received a communication from Secretary of War Randolph, dated 9 April, which contained a final decision on his plan to enlarge the Legion. His request to command a brigade of all arms was permanently denied. Instead, he was authorized to double the size of his cavalry and retain the present formation or to raise both the infantry and cavalry battalions to regimental strength and disband the Legion. The attachment of a second artillery company was also disallowed. In conclusion, Randolph advised him to "inform the gentlemen in Georgia expecting to join your legion that the legionary formation is found to be so inconvenient that the Department no longer authorizes it, and that the exigencies of the service render it impossible for them to be united with you."[70]

In effect, Cobb had been offered a threefold choice: command of a cavalry regiment, command of an infantry regiment, or retention of a somewhat larger Legion. Bitterly disappointed, he chose the latter alternative and ordered Major Yancey to bring the cavalry recruits from Atlanta to Goldsboro, where they were supposed to be united with the other companies of his mounted battalion.

His reaction to the President's decision was predictable. Davis, he exclaimed, "*has deliberately violated his agreement with me*, giving as a reason his objection to *Legionary* formations. This reason I know to be *false*."[71] The real motive behind the president's "perfidy towards me," he averred, was an unwillingness to promote two brothers to the rank of

---

[69]Thomas Cobb to Marion Cobb, 10 April 1862, ibid.

[70]*Official Records*, ser. 4, vol. 1, p. 1052. This letter conformed generally to the explanation given to Governor Brown by President Davis two days earlier. See Jefferson Davis to Joseph E. Brown, 7 April 1862, Felix-Hargrett Typescript.

[71]Thomas Cobb to Marion Cobb, 11 April 1862, Thomas R. R. Cobb Collection.

brigadier general.[72] Friends in Richmond had brought this to his attention a week earlier, and Randolph subsequently insinuated the same thing in a private letter, which Cobb mailed to his wife along with certain other correspondence. This evidence, he contended, "vindicates my course and my character" by demonstrating that the "President's conduct to me has been *infamous*." However, "I do not wish my friends to abuse him in the present state of affairs."[73] Presumably, this consideration also kept him from publishing his open letter to the president.

Whatever the motives of Davis, the official explanation for rejecting the plan was perfectly valid. The Legion was an unwieldy formation, difficult to coordinate, and practically impossible to commit to battle as a single unit. Cobb's own experience in commanding such a force was proof enough of this. During every major military movement thus far, his cavalry companies had been required to travel independently of the main body and in the most recent move had been left behind at Goldsboro because they could not operate effectively on the Peninsula. Even if the battalion had been transferred to the Yorktown-Warwick line, it would have been detached from the rest of the command to perform courier, scout, and picket duties, thereby impairing the integrity of the Legion.

The Troup Artillery only aggravated the situation. As Cobb himself admitted, "*An Artillery Co. is a drag upon me*. In an action they must act separately. . . . At other times they merely increase my trouble."[74] Since a regimental sized Legion was so cumbersome, it was logical for the war department to assume that a brigade of this kind would be utterly unmanageable and contrary to the organizational requirements of the army.

Besides being disgruntled over the defeat of his pet scheme, Cobb was rather perplexed by the failure of the Troup Artillery to reenlist for the duration of the war. As recently as 31 March, while encamped at Goldsboro, he had put the issue squarely before the battery and was disgusted to find that "*not one* single man would agree to re-enlist."[75] He must have

---

[72]Thomas Cobb to Marion Cobb, 28 April 1862, ibid.

[73]Thomas Cobb to Marion Cobb, 11 April 1862, ibid.

[74]Thomas Cobb to Marion Cobb, 13 April 1862, ibid.

[75]Thomas Cobb to Marion Cobb, 31 March 1862, ibid.; Anderson W. Reese to Alexander H. Stephens, 28 March 1862, Stephens Papers, Library of Congress.

anticipated something of this sort, for a number of replacements from the neighborhood of Athens had been recruited previously and were expected to report for duty any day. Their non-arrival in April irked him to such an extent that he was "tempted to disband them altogether and turn the guns over to the Government when the present Co. is discharged."[76]

On 16 April, only eight days before the enlistment of the Troup Artillery was due to expire, Congress passed the first conscription act, which, although Cobb failed to realize it at the time, solved his dilemma. The law obligated all men between the ages of eighteen and thirty-five to military service for a period of three years, including the twelve months' volunteers, who were granted bounties, furloughs, and the right to elect new officers. As indicated elsewhere, Cobb denounced the act and predicted serious repercussions. "I fear almost a mutiny in some regiments," he asserted. Yet he detected no disturbance among the members of his battery. "They are very much worried by this iniquitous conscription," he wrote, "but are behaving well."[77]

In accord with the provisions of the conscription act, the Troup Artillery reorganized on 29 April. Three of the old officers refused to run for reelection, and of the two who did, one was defeated. The loss of these leaders, the demoralized state of the company, and a lack of confidence in the new captain, H. H. Carlton, reenforced Cobb's desire to get rid of the battery. He kept it, he claimed, only because two of his young relatives were still serving in the ranks. "In all the 12 mos. regts. the same thing is occurring," he observed. In brief, "The conscript act is working wretchedly."[78]

In spite of its many shortcomings, the conscription act probably saved a sizeable portion of the Confederate Army from near disintegration in the spring and early summer of 1862.[79] Modifying his harsh estimate of the law, Cobb conceded on 1 May, that "re-organization of the

---

[76]*Southern Banner*, 30 April, 14 May 1862; Thomas Cobb to Marion Cobb, 27 March, 13 April 1862, Thomas R. R. Cobb Collection.

[77]Thomas Cobb to Marion Cobb, 24, 28 April 1862, Thomas R. R. Cobb Collection.

[78]Thomas Cobb to Marion Cobb, 29 April 1862, ibid.; Benjamin Mell to father, 1 May 1862, Carlton-Newton-Mell Collection.

[79]Moore, *Conscription and Conflict*, p. 14, relates that the enlistment of 148 regiments of twelve months' volunteers was about to elapse.

12 mo. regiments under the conscription act . . . *is working better than we feared*, as far as dissatisfaction is concerned. The regiments generally look upon it as a necessity and submit quietly." He clung to the conviction, however, that the clause permitting the election of new officers was disruptive. The men, he remarked, "have defeated almost *every good* officer and elected privates and corporals to their places, who have been electioneering by promises to favor them and have loose discipline."[80] No matter how chaotic conditions might have become in other units, discipline did not break down in the Troup Artillery. Carlton proved himself a capable officer, and by the end of May, Cobb reported that recruits from Athens had arrived and that the company as a whole was performing efficiently.[81]

In the meantime, the military situation on the Peninsula had undergone a change. On the morning of 16 April, two weeks prior to the departure of most of Cobb's original artillery officers, the Federals opened a sustained barrage on Dam Number One. Two guns of the Troup Artillery were stationed at this point, but only the six-pound howitzer directed by Lieutenant Frank Pope could be brought to bear. The other gun commanded by Lieutenant Edward Lumpkin had been placed so awkardly that it was unable to reply effectively. About 3:30 P.M. enemy forces attempted to cross the Warwick River and were met by elements of the Second Brigade. "The assault of the Yankees," Cobb later reported, "was daring and brave and . . . repeated." After a sharp engagement, the Federals fell back, and by dark the battle of Lee's Mill or Dam Number One had ended.[82]

Occupying positions in the area of Dam Number Two, the Legion's infantry battalion was not directly involved in the encounter. Nevertheless, Cobb was greatly affected by the battle. "I cannot describe to you the sensations I experienced," he imparted to his wife the following night.

> I was never cooler or calmer or less excited in my life, nor do I think I ever had my heart more earnestly submissive to God's Will. My Legion was stationed on the extreme right of the line and was never

---

[80]Thomas Cobb to Marion Cobb, 1 May 1862, Thomas R. R. Cobb Collection.

[81]Thomas Cobb to Marion Cobb, 20, 23 May, 5 June 1862, ibid.

[82]Thomas Cobb to Marion Cobb, 17 April 1862, ibid; *Official Records*, ser. 1, vol. 11, pt. 1, pp. 416-19; *Southern Banner*, 30 April 1862.

> in the thickest of the fight. In fact we were most of the time exposed only to random shots. For four hours the battle raged without intermission and the roar of the artillery and thunder roll of the musketry exceeded all my anticipation or imagination. I never saw men cooler than mine were. At once the whole line wavered except the Legion and for a few moments my feelings were agonizing, but Howell rode along the lines and rallied them, and in ten minutes or less order was restored.[83]

For the rest of the month of April, the Legion was subject to long dreary hours in the trenches, sniper fire, and occasional shelling from an enemy battery. "It is astonishing," marveled Cobb, "how we get used to everything. When we first came here, the sound of a skirmish brought every man to his arms. Today . . . my men did not stop their axes and spades, while a brisk fire was kept up across the creek not five hundred yards distant."[84] How long this state of affairs would continue, he had no way of knowing. "General Johnston is very taciturn," he noted, and "keeps his own counsel . . . so that I do not know when I may be ordered either to cross over for an attack or to commence a retreat."[85]

Johnston had been arguing for a withdrawal since 14 April. In his opinion, the Yorktown-Warwick River line was indefensible against long range Federal artillery, gunboats, and the mass of troops that McClellan had concentrated along the Confederate front. Holding a similar view, Cobb concluded that once McClellan "opens by land and water on Yorktown that place is *obliged to fall*." Thus, when orders were received on 1 May, to retire to Williamsburg, he endorsed them with the comment that "This retreat is . . . delicate and dangerous. . . . But I approve of it, because I am satisfied Yorktown cannot hold out."[86]

Characterized by confusion and delay, the movement to Williamsburg was completed by 4 May. From Williamsburg the Legion pushed on through rain and mud to Baltimore Crossroads, where it halted on the tenth and bivouacked for five days.[87] Before leaving Dam Number Two,

---

[83]Thomas Cobb to Marion Cobb, 17 April 1862, Thomas R. R. Cobb Collection.

[84]Thomas Cobb to Marion Cobb, 28 April 1862, ibid. "We hear a great deal of fireing [sic] day & night," recorded Lieutenant Barnett, "so we pay but little attention to it. . . ." Joel C. Barnett to wife, 21 April 1862, Barnett Letters.

[85]Thomas Cobb to Marion Cobb, 21 April 1862, Thomas R. R. Cobb Collection.

[86]Thomas Cobb to Marion Cobb, [30 April], 1 May 1862, ibid.

[87]Thomas Cobb to Marion Cobb, 1, 10 May 1862, ibid.; Joel C. Barnett to wife, 13 May 1862, Barnett Letters.

Cobb had discovered, much to his irritation, that his mounted battalion had been sent to Guiney's Station, near Fredericksburg, in which vicinity it was currently operating under Lieutenant Colonel Young. The battalion had departed Goldsboro prior to the arrival of the new cavalry companies from Atlanta, and according to latest report, they were in Richmond in a disorganized condition.

Taking advantage of the pause in the march, Cobb rode to the capital on the night of the eleventh, to locate his recruits and to demand the reunification of his command. In both respects his efforts were futile. The recruits were not in the city as reported, and his request for the return of the cavalry from Guiney's Station was turned aside. "The Prest. and Genl. Lee treated my application to reunite my legion with great nonchalance," he complained, "and replied to every argument and appeal with the reason of 'Military Necessity.' "[88]

Unable to accomplish anything in Richmond, Cobb left Adjutant John C. Rutherford behind to await the appearance of Major Yancey with the new cavalry companies and rode back to the infantry encampment on the night of the twelfth. Exhausted by hard riding and loss of sleep, he was in no mood to accept the division of his command with equanimity. "I believe the government is determined to separate my battalions permanently," he charged.

> Lee denies it but I see the cloven foot of Davis' persecution sticking out. I am quietly waiting events and have resolved upon my course as soon as I have sufficient evidence. *I will not be reduced to a Major's command and shall certainly resign* as soon as the villainy is completed.[89]

Before dawn on 15 May, the Legion was again on the march and by nightfall on the seventeenth had camped within one mile of Richmond. By then, two of the new cavalry companies had reached the city, and the others were expected momentarily. But this good news was offset by two items of discouraging information. First, there were no arms and few saddles immediately available for the mounted recruits, and secondly, Major Yancey planned to resign from the Legion. Feeling frustrated, Cobb wrote out his resignation and vowed to his wife on the eighteenth

---

[88]Thomas Cobb to Marion Cobb, 12 May 1862, Thomas R. R. Cobb Collection.

[89]Thomas Cobb to Marion Cobb, 13 May 1862, ibid.

that he intended to transmit it to the war department the following day. "I shall come home to organize a guerrilla force to act independently of this despicable government," he told her.[90]

His determination to give up command of the Legion was actually less firm than his letters implied. Between 19 May, when his resignation was to have been submitted, and 23 May, the rest of his cavalry recruits reported and were gradually supplied with arms and saddles. Furthermore, after conferring with General Johnston, he was persuaded that a temporary division of the Legion was essential. "I cannot say that Genl. Johnston is wrong," he admitted to his wife,

> and yet I do feel that but little consideration is paid to me. I am organizing and arming the five new companies and shall have them in camp in a few days. Genl. Lee wishes to send them also to Fredericksburg, but I protested and he yielded. I don't know what to do, and shall wait anxiously to see what your good judgment will suggest.[91]

Her advice, which was to withhold the resignation and remain with the Legion, coincided with his present inclination. "*I cannot give up my infantry*," he decided. "They are more devoted to me than the cavalry. I will hold on to both and toil on and struggle on till this miserable war is ended."[92]

The fact that his cavalry battalion was about to be reunified undoubtedly helped to seal this decision. All of the new companies had reported to camp by the twenty-sixth, and the older units had been ordered to rejoin the Legion on the thirty-first. "As soon as I get the Battalion together," Cobb declared, "I shall organize it thoroughly. I shall do the same with the infantry and then whenever separated I shall choose the one with which I shall go."[93]

That the two battalions would be separated from time to time was the import of a special order, dated 28 May, which placed the cavalry of Cobb's, Wade Hampton's, and Henry A. Wise's legions under the command of General J. E. B. Stuart. Since the cavalry might be detached for

---

[90]Thomas Cobb to Marion Cobb, 18 May 1862, ibid.

[91]Thomas Cobb to Marion Cobb, 22 May 1862, ibid.

[92]Thomas Cobb to Marion Cobb, 30 May 1862, ibid.

[93]Ibid.

picket duty, raids, or reconnaissance missions at any instant, Cobb felt that each of his battalions should be organized as independent commands and that each should be allowed the same number of field and staff officers. Permission to duplicate officers was granted and the process of reorganization began.[94] Lieutenant Colonel P. M. B. Young was retained in grade and assigned permanently to the cavalry, which he was then commanding. Major Yancey's resignation two weeks earlier had already created a controversy among the cavalry officers over his replacement. Captain Stovall, who had been aggrieved before at not being promoted, pressed his claim hard. But, when Captain Delony was given equal consideration, he resigned in a huff. Stovall "has acted like a dirty dog," asserted Cobb, and hence "Delony becomes Major" by default.[95]

Delony was by no means grateful to Cobb for his new position. The Colonel, he felt, had neither helped nor hindered his promotion. "Cobb has been very polite and very kind and very obliging," he acknowledged, "but I cannot for my life feel towards him as I would wish." Given a choice, he would have preferred to see the cavalry separated from the infantry on a permanent basis under Young (with whom he was "perfectly satisfied"), but ventured the opinion that "Cobb . . . is too ambitious ever to give up either and the consequence is that we will be always trammelled in our movements."[96]

---

[94]*Official Records*, ser. 1, vol. 11, pt. 3, pp. 558, 582. Cobb had been authorized to appoint a commissary officer and a quartermaster for the cavalry as early as 13 May. His brother-in-law, Miller Lumpkin, was promoted to the former post, and a young man named Benjamin C. Crane from Athens was appointed to the latter. Thomas Cobb to Marion Cobb, 13, 14, 18 May 1862, Thomas R. R. Cobb Collection.

[95]Thomas Cobb to Marion Cobb, 28, 30 May 1862, Thomas R. R. Cobb Collection. William Delony to Rosa, 6, 9 June 1862, Delony Papers. The resignation of Stovall and the promotion of Delony touched off a contest among their lieutenants for the two vacancies, as usual, with resulting ill-will. See William Delony to Rosa, 6, 17 June 1862, ibid.; Ella Gertrude (Clanton) Thomas, Journal, September 1862, p. 88, Perkins Library, Duke University. W. J. Lawton, one of the four original cavalry officers, was no longer with the Legion. It will be recalled that in March he had been permitted to raise a regiment for service in the enlarged Legion proposed by Cobb. When that plan was rejected, Lawton had been sent to join Nathan Bedford Forrest in Tennessee. Relations between Cobb and his former captain had never been good, and long after the latter's transfer, Cobb bore a grudge against him. "Lawton acted like a hypocritical dog to me," he stated in late July, after hearing of Forrest's raid on Murfreesboro, Tennessee. "*He won't fight* and when the truth comes out he had nothing at all to do with the fight at Murfreesboro." Thomas Cobb to Marion Cobb, 29 July 1862, Thomas R. R. Cobb Collection.

[96]William Delony to Rosa, 20 June 1862, Delony Papers.

In selecting a lieutenant colonel for the infantry battalion, Cobb mulled over three possibilities: his brother-in-law, Luther J. Glenn, commander of the Stephens' Rifles; Jefferson M. Lamar, the infantry major; and Captain G. B. Knight of the Panola Guards, for whom he had always had a high regard. "Glenn would like to be Lt. Colonel of the infantry," he confided, "and *I wish he could be.* He is the *best officer* I have in the legion. But by promotion he is not entitled to it, and by election he would create enemies to seek it. Hence he frankly tells me not to look to him at all."[97] The choice was now narrowed to either Lamar or Knight. Although the former was first in line for promotion, Cobb appointed the latter and explained that it was "done with Jeff's full approbation, and Glenn's also."[98] Lamar continued to hold the rank of infantry major.

The reorganization of the Legion had taken more than a week, during which time the command had occupied three different encampments and missed a major engagement at Seven Pines or Fair Oaks Station. On 23 May, eight days before the battle began, it had moved to the Mechanicsville Bridge, which spanned the Chickahominy River about five miles northeast of Richmond. Two days later, Cobb's men were redeployed a mile below the bridge, and from this new location the Georgia colonel could see Federal "troops [part of McClellan's right wing] passing *down* the river on the other side, as if they intended to attack *below* our position. I am more convinced than ever," he stated, "that they will never attack us *here*."[99] The attack, when it came, was initiated by Confederate General Joseph E. Johnston, who assailed the enemy six miles east of Richmond at the convergence of the Williamsburg and Nine Mile roads.

On the day of the attack, 31 May, the Legion (minus the cavalry) was marching slowly in the direction of Seven Pines. Throughout the second day of battle the march continued, and at sunrise on 2 June, Cobb's command encamped at Mrs. Christian's Farm several miles from the scene of the conflict. By then, the action was over, having closed indecisively on the first.[100] During the engagement, Johnston had been

[97]Thomas Cobb to Marion Cobb, 2 June 1862, Thomas R. R. Cobb Collection.

[98]Thomas Cobb to Marion Cobb, 7 June 1862, ibid.

[99]Thomas Cobb to Marion Cobb, 26 May 1862, ibid.

[100]Thomas Cobb to Marion Cobb, 2 June 1862, ibid. Howell Cobb's Second Brigade, to which the Legion was attached, and all other regiments in Magruder's division had been

seriously wounded and was superseded by General Robert E. Lee, who was to lead the Army of Northern Virginia until its surrender at Appomattox Court House two years and ten months later.

Except for digging earthworks and making two uneventful advances toward the front, the Legion remained inactive at Mrs. Christian's Farm for the next eleven days. Twice in that period Cobb visited his cavalry battalion, which was posted five miles away near Brook Church. To cover this distance regularly was not only inconvenient but physically wearing. Consequently, on 7 June, Cobb again requested the unification of his command. The reply, drafted by R. H. Chilton, Lee's Assistant Adjutant-General, was prompt, positive, and barely polite. "It is deemed necessary in the operations about Richmond," he wrote, "that the cavalry should be kept upon the flanks of the army." Because the mounted arm was numerically weak, a concentration of forces was imperative, and such concentration had been carried out "for the supposed good of the service, not from personal considerations." Moreover, "It must be apparent that your cavalry can be much more usefully employed where it is than it could be . . . with your Legion in its present position behind the Chickahominy, where there would be no field for its operations."[101]

The explanation was certainly reasonable from a military point of view, but Cobb's vanity was hurt. He confessed to his wife,

> that my situation in the army is most mortifying to my pride. I am really a colonel *without a command*, for my Battalions being separated, the Lt. Col of each legitimately should command it. True I have kept command of my infantry, but an Army Officer would have held himself degraded in my position. *I will not resign*. Your good counsel convinced me on that point. Still I chafe under this injustice and long for an opportunity to expose the malignant persecution with which Davis and his minions have followed me.[102]

On 12 June, the Second Brigade—temporarily commanded by Thomas Cobb, while his brother negotiated prisoner exchanges—moved two miles further east to Burnt Tavern on the Nine Mile Road, thus widening

---

held in reserve. See Douglas S. Freeman, *Lee's Lieutenants. A Study in Command*, 3 vols. (New York: Charles Scribner's Sons, 1942), 1: 226, 252-53, 259. Hereinafter cited as Freeman, *Lee's Lieutenants*.

[101]*Official Records*, ser. 1, vol. 11, pt. 3, pp. 581-82.

[102]Thomas Cobb to Marion Cobb, 8 June 1862, Jackson Scrapbook.

the gap between the Legion's infantry and cavalry. Nevertheless, Cobb rode back and forth trying to maintain contact with both battalions. "The truth is," he lamented, "I am absent so much from my men . . . that they are becoming weaned away from me. They do not manifest that pleasure at my coming or that regret at my going, which they once did and it wounds and annoys me."[103]

Tired and depressed, Cobb developed what was tantamount to a persecution complex. Davis despised him, he was sure, and "Lee hates me . . . and sneers whenever my name is mentioned with approbation."[104] Convinced that his cavalry was assigned most of the picket duty, he expressed no elation over Stuart's famous "Ride around McClellan" (12-15 June) but was incensed that his men had not been allowed to participate in the raid. "In other words," he grumbled, "we were doing the dirty work and the *gentlemen* doing nothing were placed forward . . . where eclat or honor were to be obtained."[105] "I am heartily sick of this life of mine and am begging now to have my legion sent away to some other field where 'military necessity' will not keep me in this position. I asked to be sent to Chattanooga."[106]

His plea for a transfer to Tennessee was turned down as was an earlier request to serve in the Shenandoah Valley under General Thomas J. Jackson, whom he admired greatly both as a devout Calvinist and a victorious military leader. At the moment, Lee had need of every available man. For the past two or three weeks, he had been evolving a plan to relieve the pressure on Richmond and drive the enemy back to Harrison's Landing on the James River or else destroy him completely. His strategy was to strike McClellan's exposed right flank, lying north of the Chickahominy, and roll it down the river. The battle plan was extremely complicated, and much hinged on the timely arrival of "Stonewall" Jackson's Valley Division. Jackson was expected to turn the strong Federal position at Beaver Dam Creek. This maneuver was to be the signal for the divisions of D. H. Hill, A. P. Hill, and James Longstreet to cross

---

[103]Thomas Cobb to Marion Cobb, 19 June 1862, Thomas R. R. Cobb Collection.

[104]Thomas Cobb to Marion Cobb, 17 June 1862, ibid.

[105]Thomas Cobb to Marion Cobb, 20 June 1862, ibid.

[106]Thomas Cobb to Marion Cobb, 19 June 1862, ibid. Delony also thought the Legion cavalry was doing the "dirty work." William Delony to Rosa, 17 June 1862, Delony Papers.

the Chickahominy and force the enemy out of Mechanicsville and away from Beaver Dam Creek. As the Confederate movement gained momentum, it was hoped that the Federals would be driven through the Gaines Mill-Cold Harbor area and beyond the York River Railroad, which led to the Union supply base at the White House. Thus would McClellan be cut off from his main source of supply on the York and crushed, theoretically, against the James River. The role of Stuart's command, embracing the cavalry of Cobb's Georgia Legion, was to cover Jackson's left as he approached Beaver Dam and to assist in the advance, damaging the enemy at every opportunity.[107]

Being a mere colonel, of which he was keenly conscious, Cobb was not informed of Lee's plan of action, but he was aware that an attack was imminent and guessed of Jackson's coming. "Something is brewing *certainly*," he observed on 21 June. And three days later, he again reported: "A general battle cannot be postponed many days." In the event of a fight, he related further, "My cavalry and infantry will both be engaged in all . . . probability and probably fifteen or more miles apart. I cannot be with both and with which to go has been my trouble. My present determination is to go with the cavalry."[108]

Cobb was at the cavalry camp on the twenty-fifth, when he was suddenly ordered to join General Stuart on the Brook Turnpike, which ran due north of Richmond. Obeying with alacrity, he met the general at the appointed place and formed his men in a column with four other mounted units. That night, the column, personally commanded by Stuart, rendezvoused with Jackson's division near Ashland, fourteen miles further north. Lee's offensive, the so-called Seven Days' campaign, was about to begin.[109]

At dawn on the twenty-sixth, Stuart's command rode eastward, crossed the Virginia Central Railroad, and then turned south, keeping

---

[107]Thomas Cobb to Marion Cobb, 13, 20 June 1862, Thomas R. R. Cobb Collection; Douglas S. Freeman, *R. E. Lee. A Biography*, 4 vols. (New York: Charles Scribner's Sons, 1934), 2: 108-21. Hereinafter cited as Freeman, *Lee.* Clifford Dowdey and Louis H. Manarin, eds., *The Wartime Papers of R. E. Lee* (Boston: Little, Brown and Company, 1961), pp. 198-200.

[108]Thomas Cobb to Marion Cobb, 21, 24 June 1862, Thomas R. R. Cobb Collection.

[109]Unless otherwise indicated, the movements of the Georgia Legion between 25 June and 6 July, are based upon Cobb's report in *Official Records*, ser. 1, vol. 11, pt. 2, pp. 524-25.

well to the left of Jackson's line of march. The day passed without incident, but on the afternoon of the twenty-seventh, the cavalry reached the field at Cold Harbor just as the battle was coming to a close. Caught in the open, Cobb's troops were fired upon by hidden Union batteries, "the shells striking under their horses and exploding over their heads." Promptly and sensibly, Cobb withdrew them behind the protection of a hill before any casualties resulted.

The next day, as the column proceeded toward the York River Railroad, a squadron of the Georgia Legion, led by Major William Delony, galloped ahead to Dispatch Station, routed a handful of Federal defenders, and severed enemy communications with the White House.[110] When the main body of Confederate riders came up, the command swung eastward in the direction of McClellan's base, which had been set afire to prevent the capture of supplies, and bivouacked that night not far from the burning depot.

On the twenty-ninth, Cobb took a detachment to Tunstall's Station, demolished some track and rolling stock, and rejoined Stuart's column at the White House. In the morning, one of the colonel's squadrons was left to finish the work of destruction, while the rest of the command hastened to the Chickahominy River to block the lower bridges in case McClellan attempted to use them as a line of retreat. As the cavalry watched the river crossings, Lee's infantry divisions fought hotly contested engagements at Frayser's Farm (30 June) and Malvern Hill (1 July), which resulted in heavy casualties but forced the Federal Army to seek refuge at Harrison's Landing under the cover of Union gunboats.

When it became apparent that McClellan was withdrawing to the James rather than the Chickahominy, Cobb was ordered to assume a position on the River Road, between Malvern Hill and Harrison's Landing, where he could intercept enemy stragglers. On 3 July, after posting his men in the woods skirting the road, which were shelled regularly by gunboats, he notified his wife that the campaign had almost ended. "We have had a hard time," he related.

---

[110]"The only *two* charges made by cavalry during these battles were made my mine," Cobb recorded later, this one by Delony and another by Captain Gilbert J. Wright, Lawton's successor. Thomas Cobb to Marion Cobb, 8 July 1862, Thomas R. R. Cobb Collection; William Delony to Rosa, 29 June 1862, Delony Papers.

> Sometimes we have been without a morsel to eat for 36 hours and *all the time nothing but what we capture* from the enemy. So it has been a feast or famine, with us all the while. I have eaten raw meat to satisfy hunger. Our horses have fared the same way.[111]

For the ensuing three days, the Legion's mounted companies apprehended dozens of stragglers and collected hundreds of abandoned horses, mules, weapons, and a substantial quantity of ammunition. The biggest prize was lost, however. Intelligence had reached Cobb on 3 July, that a large number of Federal wagons, guarded by two regiments of infantry, a battery of artillery, and five hundred cavalry, were still on the road from Malvern Hill and might be captured. "My . . . battalion," he wrote, "is on picket tonight watching them. We have possession of the road *below* them and will have no trouble except from the gunboats, which command the river road on which it is retreating."[112] Couriers were sent in search of Lee and Stuart to convey the information and to obtain reenforcements. No help came on the fourth. On the morning of the fifth, Cobb still had "great hopes of capturing their entire wagon train."[113] But, reenforcements again failed to appear, and the Federals escaped unmolested to Harrison's Landing.

The following day, the Confederate Army belatedly arrived in force. Hemmed in by infantrymen, Cobb moved his camp one mile to Carter's Mill, where he received an order from Stuart assigning one of his squadrons to another location. He complied, but not without complaint. "I will send the Squadron as directed . . . ," he responded, but,

> At the same time I respectfully protest . . . against this order[.] I am forced to keep an entire Squadron on picket on the River Road. I have but *three* with me. To place *two* on picket every day renders it impossible for me to relieve them, and even when the Squadron from the White House returns, my men must stand picket every other night.
>
> Is it desired that I shall have no command whatever with me?[114]

Stuart had no such desire. In fact, he cited the Georgia colonel in his official report as a leader of "zeal and ability" with a "capacity for higher

---

[111]Thomas Cobb to Marion Cobb, 3 July 1862, Thomas R. R. Cobb Collection.

[112]Ibid.

[113]Thomas Cobb to Marion Cobb, 5 July 1862, ibid.

[114]Thomas Cobb to Capt. Fitzhugh, 6 July 1862, Stiles Correspondence.

trusts."[115] Cobb did not repay the compliment. "In my lat[e] tour with Stuart," he complained, "I was left to do all the dirty and hard work on the way, while his old West Point friends (the two Lees) [Fitzhugh and William H. F. Lee] were assigned every desirable position along the route." Nor had Lee's conduct of the Seven Days' battle altered his opinion of the general's character. "Genl. Lee has not the first feeling of a gentleman," he averred. "He is a fine officer I have no doubt and is entitled to the credit of planning the late campaign, but he is haughty and boorish and supercilious in his bearing and is particularly so to me. . . ."[116]

Not only was he discontent with his immediate superiors, but he soon became dissatisfied with the actions of some of his subordinates. On 7 July, at the urging of his brother, who had fallen ill, Cobb assumed command of the Second Brigade, encamped near Malvern Hill, and thus, for the first time in weeks, had an opportunity to inspect his infantry battalion.[117] During the recent campaign, these companies, though marched to the limit of endurance and fired on twice, had not been involved in a single assault. Casualties, therefore, were practically nonexistent; yet, there were problems, especially with the quality of leadership in the Legion. Captain Morris of the Poythress Volunteers was old and, as Cobb had long ago discovered, a poor soldier. Captain Camak of the Mell Volunteers was also "proving to be a poor officer," in his judgment. He "drinks excessively and is not with his company half his time. I am losing patience with him." The greatest disappointment, however, was Lieutenant Colonel Knight. He had brawled with one of his officers over the ownership of a tent fly, and the two had to be pulled apart by onlookers. Whether Cobb ever knew of the incident or not, he was displeased with Knight's management of the battalion and, in mid-July, accepted his resignation.[118] Jefferson M. Lamar was thereupon promoted to lieutenant

---

[115]*Official Records*, ser. 1, vol. 11, pt. 2, p. 522.

[116]Thomas Cobb to Marion Cobb, 11 July 1862, Thomas R. R. Cobb Collection.

[117]Thomas Cobb to Marion Cobb, 8 July 1862, ibid.; Howell Cobb to Mary Ann Cobb, 7 July 1862, Howell Cobb Collection. When he failed to recover his health after resting in Richmond for several days, Howell Cobb returned to Georgia to recuperate.

[118]Thomas Cobb to Marion Cobb, 18 July 1862, Thomas R. R. Cobb Collection; Joel C. Barnett to wife, 26 June, 1862, Barnett Letters.

colonel, and Glenn became the new infantry major. The former, Cobb asserted, "is a much better officer" than Knight.[119]

By the end of August 1862, resignations and promotions had taken a heavy toll of Cobb's officers. Of the twelve original captains—infantry, artillery, and cavalry—only Thomas U. Camak still remained in command of his company. A similar loss was evident among the lieutenants, and, in September, when the Legion was finally committed to battle, the attrition rate increased.[120]

Worries of this sort, together with his ceaseless brooding about alleged mistreatment at the hand of Davis, Lee, and Stuart, plus the added responsibilities of brigade command, affected Cobb's nerves. He smoked excessively, lost weight, and was simply unable to function with his usual vigor. "I am very weary . . . ," he informed his mother.

> I have been in a continu[al] state of unpleasant exci[te]ment for more than a y[ear] [.] It has worn out my min[d] [and] wasted away my body. . . [,] broken down my spiri[t] and tried severely my Christ[ian] principle and faith. I lo[ng] to be out of it—to be at home once more.[121]

Between 7 July and 8 August 1862, the Second Brigade changed camps several times and participated in a minor expedition to drive the Federals from Malvern Hill, which they had reoccupied on 5 August and held until the night of the sixth. After retaking the hill on the morning of

---

[119]Thomas Cobb to Marion Cobb, 27 July 1862, Thomas R. R. Cobb Collection. He was annoyed, however, that Lamar had brought his wife to live next to the camp. "Col. Lamar will be of no service to me now," he snapped.

[120]Delony, Lamar, and Glenn were promoted within the Legion. The resignations of Stovall, Yancey, Lawton, Knight, and Stanley have been mentioned previously. Like Lawton, Captain McDaniel had raised a regiment for Cobb's proposed brigade, but when that scheme fell through, he was ordered to East Tennessee at the head of the Forty-first Georgia. Captain Powell of the Tom Cobb Invincibles resigned on the eve of the Seven Days' campaign because of age and ill health. In August, Captain Morris also resigned, perhaps for the same reason.

[121]Thomas Cobb to Sarah R. Cobb, 19 July 1862, Jackson Scrapbook. For his mental and physical state, Cobb blamed Davis primarily. "I will not conceal from you that I am not well today," he wrote to his wife. "I have no positive disease but I find myself losing strength with my flesh. . . . The *physical* labor, I could have borne easily. It has been my *mental annoyance*, and Davis has been the arch-fiend in the matter. I need the *rest of home*. . . ." Three days later, he declared: "If the war lasts much longer I expect my degredation [sic] will satisfy the malice of even Jefferson Davis." Thomas Cobb to Marion Cobb, 30 July, 2 August 1862, Thomas R. R. Cobb Collection.

the seventh, without opposition, Lee withdrew most of his troops to the vicinity of Richmond. The Second Brigade was left in a forward position, however, and, on the eighth, was ordered to move to a high bluff overlooking the James River at Deep Bottom, from which point it could harass Union gunboats on the water below.

"It is a beautiful place to fortify and excellent to defend," Cobb reported.

> I am well pleased at the prospect of having a chance to show my engineering skill and *as I will have an independent command* . . . I like the chance exceedingly. In two weeks, *if they will let me alone,* I will be ready to fight the Monitor. I feel as if it was the first time I had a chance to show what I can do.[122]

In a happier mood than he had been in months, Cobb stopped complaining, gained weight, and began displaying much of his former vitality. Contributing to his exuberance was the expectation of a thirty-day furlough as soon as his brother returned from Georgia. "I have pushed my work here, so that there might be no reason for detaining me," he notified his wife. "In fact, by Monday night [18 August] I shall finish it. And then home-sweet-home!"[123]

Surrendering the brigade to his brother on the nineteenth, Cobb departed for Athens, where he was to remain until 11 September. During his absence, Lee's army defeated Federal forces under General John Pope at Second Manassas and invaded Maryland. News of the former event, and a letter from his brother, describing an "inhuman march" imposed on the Legion by Confederate General D. H. Hill, made it impossible for Cobb to relax. According to his sister-in-law, he was so upset that "if he gets no news tomorrow [8 September] of a satisfactory character he will leave for Virginia."[124]

Despite his anxiety, Cobb stayed in Athens four more days before leaving for Virginia. Arriving in Richmond, he was told that the Legion was somewhere near Harper's Ferry, and, on the seventeenth, he set out to find it. After traveling by rail to Staunton, he encountered exasperating

---

[122]Thomas Cobb to Marion Cobb, 8 August 1862, Thomas R. R. Cobb Collection.

[123]Thomas Cobb to Marion Cobb, 16 August 1862, ibid.

[124]Howell Cobb to Mary Ann Cobb, 29 August 1862, Mary Ann Cobb to Howell Cobb, 7 September 1862, Howell Cobb Collection.

delays. "We reached here safely tonight," he wrote, "but the horses are still behind and will not be here until tomorrow at noon." When the train came with the mounts, it brought no saddles. "My leave of absence expires today," Cobb exclaimed on the nineteenth, "and yet here I am still wasting time at this place. The telegraph would not work last night and we could send no message for our saddles. I am restless and anxiously looking for the train to see if they will come."[125]

His impatience was increased by reports of battles at Boonsborough (South Mountain) on 14 September and at Sharpsburg on the seventeenth. "I must be off," he wrote. "To sit here idle, while the decisive battles of the war are fought will never do."[126] Apparently he was not aware of the nearly disastrous engagement at Crampton's Gap (14 September), in which his Legion had received its first real test under fire. Of this, he would learn soon enough.

Leaving Staunton on the twentieth, Cobb traveled to Winchester and finally rejoined his infantry battalion two miles south of Martinsburg, Virginia, on the twenty-fourth. "I reached here today," he related, "having been thirteen days on the road from home and five days on horseback since I left Staunton. My whole journey has been a sad one and my meeting with the legion today has cast a deeper gloom over me. Their faces are still overcast, although they tried to be cheerful and seemed happy to see me."[127] Casualties had been heavy; how many troops had been killed, wounded, or captured, Cobb was never able to determine exactly. Whatever the number, they were, in his opinion, "the flower of my battalion, my best and truest men, never sick, never off duty, always ready."[128] The loss of Lieutenant Colonel Jefferson Lamar, who died of a

---

[125]Thomas Cobb to Marion Cobb, 17, 19 September 1862, Thomas R. R. Cobb Collection.

[126]Thomas Cobb to Marion Cobb, 19 September 1862, ibid.

[127]Thomas Cobb to Marion Cobb, 24 September 1862, ibid.

[128]Thomas Cobb to Marion Cobb, 29 September 1862, ibid. In September and again in November, he estimated that fifty had been killed, seventy-five or more wounded, and approximately fifty taken prisoner. Thomas Cobb to Marion Cobb, 29 September, 9 November 1862, ibid. Official figures varied considerably. For these see *Official Records*, ser. 1, vol. 19, pt. 1, pp. 812, 817-18, 824, 861-62. The initial casualty reports were exaggerated due to the fact that many of the men became separated from their units during the battle and were presumed to be permanently lost. See Howell Cobb to Mary Ann Cobb, 17 September 1862, Howell Cobb Collection; Joel C. Barnett to wife, 17 September 1862, Barnett Letters.

groin wound on the field of battle, grieved him the most. "Poor Jeff," he wrote, "The more I think of him, the deeper is my grief. He was so purehearted and nobleminded and looked forward to so much happiness and seemed to me to deserve it so richly, that his death is one of the inscrutable providences of God."[129]

The foremost task facing Cobb upon his return was to reorganize and reequip his shattered command. "One third are without shoes and more without a blanket. Not a dozen of them have a change of clothes. Many of them without guns," and "None of us have a tent," he declared. "Never were poor fellows in greater need. I have met with little success as yet but shall not stop until I do something for them."[130]

The Troup Artillery, which had lost one of its guns, and the cavalry were in little better shape. The latter was operating at half strength, partly because of casualties but in larger part because of jaded horses. It had also been deprived temporarily of the leadership of Lieutenant Colonel Young, who had sustained a painful leg wound. In his absence, Major Delony had assumed control of the mounted battalion and, in Cobb's judgment, it could not have been in more capable hands. Delony "is an excellent officer," he remarked, "and I much prefer leaving my men in his command to Col. Young's."[131]

The lieutenant colonel had been commended by Lee in August for "courage and efficiency" and was cited again in October for conspicuous gallantry during the Maryland campaign. His talents were further recognized in November by a promotion to colonel of cavalry. Not a word of praise was uttered by Cobb, however. Hearing a rumor that Young had received the rank of ordnance colonel and would be transferred out of the Legion, he commented: "I should not regret it, if it be true."[132] This growing dislike for his chief cavalry officer had manifested itself on previous occasions. In July, for example, he had been ready to credit an unverified report that Young was drunk on duty. "If I can get proof," he

---

[129]Thomas Cobb to Marion Cobb, 2 October 1862, Thomas R. R. Cobb Collection. Glenn was eventually promoted to lieutenant colonel of infantry, and Camak, who had been captured, was appointed major in November, after being paroled and exchanged.

[130]Thomas Cobb to Marion Cobb, 26 September 1862, ibid.

[131]Thomas Cobb to Marion Cobb, 20 October 1862, ibid.

[132]Thomas Cobb to Marion Cobb, 20 October 1862, ibid.; *Official Records*, ser. 1, vol. 11, pt. 3, p. 660, vol. 19, pt. 1, p. 824; Warner, *Generals in Gray*, p. 348.

had threatened, "I shall have him cashiered."[133] Yet, when told by several officers that Delony "was drinking a great deal," he merely stated that "It has disturbed me very much," and "I don't know what to do about it."[134]

In the meantime, the Confederate Army had fallen back to the outskirts of Winchester and, on the twenty-ninth, established a line of defense within six miles of the town. On that date, Cobb moved his headquarters to the cavalry camp for the first time since his arrival from Georgia. "I never saw the men so happy to see me," he boasted.

> They beg me never to leave them again, and if possible to get us all ordered to Georgia for the winter. I am making an effort to have this done and were it anybody but myself it would be done. But Davis delights to thwart me so much I doubt capitally if he allows it, should Genl. Lee order it.[135]

Shortly thereafter, Cobb called at the headquarters of General Lee and found him "exceedingly kind and complimentary." Lee agreed to transfer the Legion to Georgia at the conclusion of the current campaign and advised the colonel to mount the entire command and increase it to two full regiments. Cobb was ecstatic. He announced the good news to his men and wrote to his wife that an order, signed by Lee and endorsed by Generals Hampton, Stuart, Longstreet, and McLaws, had been drawn authorizing the change of duty station. "So that," he rejoiced, "before 1st January next I am assured I shall have my command re-united and returned to Georgia."[136] He was especially pleased at the prospect of no longer being "over-shadowed and lost in a huge army." Instead, "I shall have some chance for independent thought and action."[137]

On 6 October, Cobb dispatched his adjutant, John C. Rutherford, to Richmond to secure Secretary Randolph's approval for the transfer. It

---

[133]Thomas Cobb to Marion Cobb, 15 July 1862, Thomas R. R. Cobb Collection.

[134]Thomas Cobb to Marion Cobb, 25 October 1862, ibid. Cobb's objection to the lieutenant colonel was shared by Major Delony and others. Although favorably inclined toward Young in July, Delony had developed an antipathy for the man and within six months denounced him as indecisive, "childish and unmanly." William Delony to Rosa, 15 July 1862, 22 January 1863, Delony Letters. See also Holland, *P. M. B. Young*, pp. 68-69.

[135]Thomas Cobb to Marion Cobb, 29 September 1862, Thomas R. R. Cobb Collection.

[136]Thomas Cobb to Marion Cobb, 4 October 1862, ibid. "The idea of going to Georgia," according to Major Delony, "has made the men crazy and nothing else is now thought of." William Delony to Rosa, 6 October 1862, Delony Papers.

[137]Thomas Cobb to Marion Cobb, 15 October 1862, Thomas R. R. Cobb Collection.

was subsequently given as well as permission to implement Lee's suggestion about mounting the infantry and increasing both battalions to regiments.[138] Seldom in his military career had Cobb been more contented. He became less critical of his superiors, and some of his bitterness seemed to evaporate. Toward Lee, in particular, his attitude underwent a remarkable transformation. The general, he declared, "has taken pains to show and express his confidence in me as an officer and personally has been as kind as I could ask or desire.[139]

On 15 October, Cobb was ordered to take command of the Second Brigade once more. His brother had been granted a furlough to attend to private affairs and left camp the following morning. Within two weeks of his departure, Howell Cobb was directed to report to General P. G. T. Beauregard for a new assignment, and by November he had arranged for the transfer of his staff to Georgia.[140] In this manner, Thomas Cobb inherited permanent control of the brigade, which entitled him to the rank of brigadier general.

In the past, various officers had expressed the view that the Georgia colonel was long overdue for promotion and that the administration was wrong in ignoring him. This view became even more prevalent in October, when he assumed the responsibilities of a brigadier. General William Barksdale of Mississippi bluntly announced, for example, that it was "a d—n shame" and that "such was the opinion of every officer in McLaws Division. . . ."[141] It was Lee, however, who was instrumental in obtaining Cobb's promotion. The general recommended him for the grade of brigadier general on 27 October, and the commission was promulgated on 6 November.[142]

---

[138]Thomas Cobb to Marion Cobb, 6 October 1862, C. C. Jones, collector, *Autograph Letters and Portraits of Signers of the Constitution of the Confederate States*, Perkins Library, Duke University; H. H. Carlton to father, 7 October 1862, Carlton-Newton-Mell Collection; Thomas Cobb to Marion Cobb, 15, 20 October 1862, Thomas R. R. Cobb Collection.

[139]Thomas Cobb to Marion Cobb, 15 October 1862, Thomas R. R. Cobb Collection.

[140]Thomas Cobb to Marion Cobb, 14, 15, 16 October 1862, ibid.; Horace Montgomery, *Howell Cobb's Confederate Career* (Tuscaloosa: Confederate Publishing Company, Inc. 1959), p. 76.

[141]Thomas Cobb to Marion Cobb, 18 October 1862, Thomas R. R. Cobb Collection. See also Pope Barrow to father, 9 October 1862, Barrow Papers.

[142]*Official Records*, ser. 1, vol. 19, pt. 2, pp. 683, 699. "Tardy Justice!" commented Howell Cobb upon learning the news. "I hope he will accept—as he ought in justice to the

Before this action became official, word of it circulated among the members of the Legion, who worried that the colonel's advancement might cancel the plan to return to Georgia. "A camp rumor that I was appointed general over this brigade in Howell's place has annoyed my men a good deal," he observed, "but I have told them *I would not accept it, if tendered to me,* and that Davis would see me dead before he would tender it. These assurances have quieted their anxiety in a great measure."[143]

Although Cobb did not refuse the commission, he did attempt to appease his men by withholding his acceptance for several days to be sure that nothing would interfere with the Legion's transfer that winter. To celebrate the promotion, his newly appointed staff prepared a sumptuous meal and surprised him with it on the afternoon of 15 November. Expecting to dine on the usual bread and beef, he was startled to see roast turkey, stewed and fried oysters, pickles, preserves, potatoes, pastry, and pound cake. "I was very much gratified," he confided to his wife, "and told them truly that this manifestation gave me much more sincere pleasure than the promotion itself."[144]

By this time, the Army of Northern Virginia had left Winchester. On 1 November, it reached Front Royal and by the fifth had marched to Culpeper Court House, where it encamped until the eighteenth. From Culpeper, General James Longstreet's Corps, embracing Thomas Cobb's Brigade, pushed on to Fredericksburg to contest the approach of General Ambrose Burnside's Army of the Potomac and, on the nineteenth, began occupying the high ground west of town.

The Confederate line of defense paralleled the Rappahannock River. On the extreme left was R. H. Anderson's Division. To the right of Anderson, the command of General Lafayette McLaws, including Cobb's Brigade, stretched from Marye's Heights to a point just beyond Howison's Hill. Posted on the right of McLaws were the divisions of George E. Pickett and John B. Hood, and later General "Stonewall" Jackson's Corps was placed in position to the right of Longstreet's line.[145]

---

country—but I fear he may not." Howell Cobb to Mary Ann Cobb, 10 November 1862, Howell Cobb Collection.

[143]Thomas Cobb to Marion Cobb, 5 November 1862, Thomas R. R. Cobb Collection.

[144]Thomas Cobb to Marion Cobb, 15 November 1862, ibid.

[145]*Official Records*, ser. 1, vol. 21, pp. 568-69.

Cobb's Brigade, composed of the Sixteenth and Twenty-fourth Georgia Regiments, the Fifteenth North Carolina, and the Georgia Legion (infantry), was located near the top of Howison's Hill on a site named "Camp Jeannie" in honor of the wife of the Reverend R. K. Porter, who had served as chaplain of the Legion since the beginning of the war. Satisfied with the location, Cobb confidently announced:

> I think my Brigade can whip ten thousand of them attacking us in front. We have a magnificent position, the best perhaps on the line. I have no idea the Yankees will ever dare to attack us. They may try to flank, but my own opinion is they are making a feint here and will cross lower down at Urbana or Port Royal if they cross at all. Evidently a large army is in front of us. We hear their drums and bands plainly and my blood boils whenever I hear them. To a Righteous God I look for protection.[146]

At dark on 26 November, Cobb's Brigade went on picket duty in Fredericksburg for two days. Returning to "Camp Jeannie" on the twenty-ninth, he discovered that Phillips' Legion was to be attached to his command and that the Eighteenth Georgia Regiment was to replace the Fifteenth North Carolina. "This makes my entire command *Georgians*," he recorded, "and increases my strength slightly. Still I dislike to give up the N. C. Regt[.] who have been with us during so many trials. The officers and men of the Regiment are very reluctant to leave me which is very gratifying."[147]

With his brigade reconstituted, Cobb put his men to work constructing earthen defenses. Much impressed by the stoutness of these entrenchments, General William Pendleton, chief of Confederate artillery, decided to locate a large thirty-pound parrot gun in one of the emplacements and instructed Cobb to throw up five additional redoubts to the right and rear of the Howison House. This assignment the Georgia brigadier carried out with his "accustomed intelligence and energy."[148]

---

[146]Thomas Cobb to Marion Cobb, 29 November 1862, Thomas R. R. Cobb Collection.

[147]Thomas Cobb to Marion Cobb, 29 November 1862, Thomas R. R. Cobb Papers, Perkins Library, Duke University; *Official Records*, ser. 1, vol. 21, p. 538.

[148]*Official Records*, ser. 1, vol. 21, p. 564; Thomas Cobb to Marion Cobb, 2 December 1862, Thomas R. R. Cobb Collection. According to the guide book of the Fredericksburg National Military Park, the Howison Hill redoubt "is the largest and best preserved battery position in the park."

On the night of 4 December, Cobb was again on picket duty with his brigade. Relieved the next evening, he marched the men back to their tents in a snow storm. "Very thankful we are that we did not have to stand picket all night," he commented.[149] The frigid weather continued through the eighth, leading him to believe that if the cold "lasts for a week longer it must close this campaign," and then, he added, "I shall ask to be sent to Georgia."[150]

While doubting that the Federals would attack any time soon, if at all, Cobb, nonetheless, wrote his wife to reassure her that he would not needlessly endanger his life. "Do not be uneasy about my being 'rash,'" he told her.

> The bubble of reputation cannot drag me into folly. God helping me, I hope to do my duty when called upon, trusting the consequences to Him. I look for, hope for, and ask for no reward but peace and a clear conscience. I go on picket tomorrow again and hence cannot write regularly.[151]

The following morning, 11 December, under cover of a dense fog, Federal engineers extended floating bridges over the Rappahannock. At the time, Barksdale's Mississippi Brigade was guarding the river bank from Fredericksburg to Deep Run and could not be withdrawn. It harrassed the enemy pontoniers throughout the day, while Cobb waited in reserve. Eventually, one of his regiments, the Sixteenth Georgia, was hastened forward to support the Mississippians at Deep Run, where the Federal bridge builders were making rapid progress.

After dark, Barksdale's tired troops, having been subjected to hours of heavy bombardment, retreated from the town and crossed a broad, open plain to a sunken road at the foot of Marye's Heights, where they were relieved by Cobb's Brigade (minus the Sixteenth Georgia). Defensively, this was a strong position, protected in front by a sturdy stone wall, which had been reenforced with dirt, and from above by massed batteries, which could play on the field below. That night Cobb deployed his regiments in the sunken road behind the wall in preparation for the action to come.[152]

149Thomas Cobb to Marion Cobb, 6 December 1862, Thomas R. R. Cobb Collection.

150Thomas Cobb to Marion Cobb, 8 December 1862, ibid.

151Thomas Cobb to Marion Cobb, 10 December 1862, ibid.

152Freeman, *Lee's Lieutenants*, 2: 333-38; *Official Records*, ser. 1, vol. 21, pp. 579-80, 599, 607. The Georgia Legion was apparently posted elsewhere, for it was not listed as one

At noon on 13 December, the anticipated attack began. Overhead the Confederate artillery opened on the advancing Federals and blew gaping holes in their lines. Full of determination and courage, Cobb watched the Union troops approach. Holding his men in check until the enemy was within easy range, he ordered a volley, which, in conjunction with the murderous cannon fire from the heights, caused Burnside's forces to break and retreat.

The first Union assault had been repulsed, but a second attack was being formed on the plain below the stone wall. During the lull, Cobb stood behind a house located on the line of battle in conference with General John R. Cooke and a group of officers. A random shell exploded against the building killing Cooke and wounding several others. Shrapnel struck Cobb in the thigh and knocked him to the ground. Fully conscious and perfectly calm, he asked for a tourniquet to stem the flow of blood spurting from a severed artery. Carried to the rear by stretcher-bearers, he was transferred to an ambulance and taken to a field hospital where Dr. John T. Gilmore, chief surgeon of McLaws' Division, worked frantically to stop the bleeding. His efforts failed. Suffering from severe shock, Cobb lapsed into a coma and died a few minutes later, his head cradled in the arms of the Reverend R. K. Porter, his friend and chaplain. Dead at thirty-nine, Thomas Cobb had given his life in defense of southern nationalism.[153]

---

of the units behind the wall. Indirect evidence to support this is contained in a newspaper account of the battle which reports casualties in all of Cobb's regiments except the Legion. See *Southern Watchman*, 31 December 1862. See also W. H. Kilpatrick to J. C. Newton, 25 January 1862 [1863], Letters from Confederate Soldiers, 1860-1865, vol. 2, Georgia Department of Archives and History, in which it is stated that the Legion was not with Cobb but supporting the artillery.

[153]For the details of the battle and Cobb's death see *Official Records*, ser. 1, vol. 21, pp. 555, 564, 570, 580, 582, 588-90, 608, 625-26; *Southern Banner*, 17, 24 December 1862, 14 January 1863; *Southern Watchman*, 31 December 1862; Robert U. Johnson and Clarence C. Buel, eds., *Battles and Leaders of the Civil War*, 4 vols. (reprint ed., New York: Thomas Yoseloff, 1956), 3: 94; E. J. Eldridge to Dr. E. D. Newton, 2 April [186?], Carlton-Newton-Mell Collection; J. H. Lumpkin to Dearest, 30 December 1862, Joseph Henry Lumpkin Papers; William Delony to Rosa, 17 December 1862, Delony Papers. Most accounts relate that Cobb was wounded during a later assault. Evidence to the contrary is marshalled in Freeman, *Lee's Lieutenants*, 2: 361-62. Freeman errs, however, in stating that Cooke was hit atop Marye's Heights instead of in the road with Cobb.

CHAPTER 10

Epilogue

Relatively recent photograph of the Lucy Cobb Institute
(date unknown)

A train bearing the body of Thomas R. R. Cobb and an escort composed of the Reverend R. K. Porter, Charles M. and Edward Lumpkin, John C. Rutherford, and Jesse, Cobb's black body servant,who had been with him since the beginning of the war, arrived in Athens, Georgia, on 18 December 1862. A delegation of citizens met them at the Georgia Railroad Depot and accompanied the remains to the family residence on Prince Avenue.[1]

The following day, 19 December, every shop in town closed down and hundreds of citizens turned out for the most elaborate funeral in the history of Clarke County. Services were conducted at the First Presbyterian Church by the Reverend Nathan Hoyt assisted by Chaplain Porter and the local Methodist minister. From the church a long and carefully organized procession consisting of clergymen, pallbearers, family, relatives, and Jesse, Confederate soldiers and officers, members of the bench and bar, faculty and trustees of the University of Georgia and Lucy Cobb

[1]*Southern Banner*, 24 December 1862. In Augusta, Georgia, where a change of trains was necessary, Cobb's body was drawn in a hearse through the streets of the city to the toll of church bells and laid in state at the city hall under a guard of honor before being sent on to Athens. *Confederate Union*, 30 December 1862.

Institute, town officials, the Masonic lodge in regalia, the Athens fire company in uniform, and citizens afoot and in carriages wound to the top of Oconee Hill Cemetery, where Cobb was laid to rest in a grave beside his deceased children—two infant sons and his beloved daughter Lucy.[2]

Tributes to his memory appeared in newspapers around the state; the trustees of the University of Georgia passed resolutions recalling in glowing terms his past services to education; and his immediate military superiors, McLaws, Longstreet, and Lee, submitted reports praising his dedication to duty. Letters of condolence followed. In a personal note to Howell Cobb, General Lee wrote:

> I beg leave to express my sympathy in your great sorrow. Your noble and gallant brother has met a soldier's death, and God grant that this army and our country may never be called upon again to mourn so great a sacrifice.
>
> Of his merits, his lofty intellect, his genius, his accomplishments, his professional fame, and above all his true Christian character, I need not speak to you, who knew him so intimately and well. But as a patriot and soldier, his death has left a gap in the army which his military aptitude and skill renders it hard to fill. [3]

But it was A. O. Bacon, a former student of the Lumpkin Law School, who perhaps best expressed the mood of Cobb's friends, relatives, and admirers. "Genl [.] Cobb," he exclaimed to Pope Barrow,

> What shall I say of him! I want to see you and talk about him for I cant write my thoughts and feelings. High indeed would have been the price of the victory at Fredericksburg if none other had fallen—Georgia, in his death, sustained the greatest loss which has yet befallen her. Considered in every relation of life he was truly the greatest man I ever met and few countries can boast his equal—I yield to no man in my admiration of him."[4]

Cobb had now been elevated to the pantheon of Confederate war heroes. His faults soon forgotten, he was lionized for his virtues, and his defense of the stone wall below Marye's Heights became celebrated. Echoing

---

[2]*Southern Banner*, 24 December 1862. The children had been disinterred from the yard of Cobb's home on Prince Avenue and placed in the family plot on Oconee Hill. J. H. Lumpkin to Dearest, 30 December 1862, Joseph Henry Lumpkin Papers.

[3]*Official Records*, ser. 1, vol. 21, pp. 1067-68. Also printed in *Southern Banner*, 11 February 1863.

[4]A. O. Bacon to Pope [Barrow], 3 January 1863, Barrow Papers.

Lee's tribute to the Georgian, Douglas Southall Freeman wrote in later years that "Thomas R. R. Cobb . . . gave fully to his new Brigade the high abilities with which he was credited."[5] And no less an authority on Georgia history than E. Merton Coulter asserted that Cobb was "one of the ablest men in the state's history."[6]

There were detractors, of course, most notably the Stephens brothers, who claimed to like Cobb personally but who considered him a busybody and privately denigrated his legal work as vast in quantity but lacking in quality.[7] Yet, even they admitted that much of what he accomplished was worthwhile and publicly joined in singing his praises.[8] Indeed, it was Alexander H. Stephens who planted the notion in the minds of historians that Cobb favored temporary secession as a prelude to reconstructing the Union on "better terms" and that, in pressing this "one idea," he "did more . . . in carrying the State out, than . . . all others combined."[9] Actually reconstruction of the Union on any terms was the antithesis of Cobb's position.

Without swallowing the eulogies and latter-day acclamation whole, it is still possible to argue that Thomas Cobb's achievements over a brief life span of thirty-nine years (and a professional career of twenty) were both creditable and historically significant. In the field of education he founded the Lucy Cobb Institute, which lasted into the twentieth century, worked for a better state university open to all classes of people, and helped lay the foundation for a public school system. Also, he was primarily responsible for organizing on a permanent basis an up-to-date law school—the Lumpkin Law School—as part of the University of Georgia, the establishment of which was a step toward ensuring higher standards in the legal profession. His performance as reporter of the Georgia Supreme Court (1849-1857) compared favorably with that of reporters elsewhere in the nation; his legacy here included fifteen volumes of decisions, *A General*

---

[5]Freeman, *Lee's Lieutenants*, 2: 328.

[6]Coulter, *Georgia History*, p. 294.

[7]Alexander H. Stephens to Linton Stephens, 16 January 1863, Stephens Correspondence.

[8]See, for example, the laudatory sketch in Stephens, *Constitutional View*, 2: 333-35.

[9]Ibid., p. 321. See also Paul Escott, *After Secession. Jefferson Davis and the Failure of Confederate Nationalism* (Baton Rouge: Louisiana State University Press, 1978), p. 26.

Digested Index to Georgia Reports, and a *Supreme Court Manual* on rules and appeal procedures. Of greater importance were his efforts at codification. His *Digest* (1851) satisfied a need long and deeply felt by lawyers, judges, and justices of the peace in Georgia, and his unique contribution to the *Georgia Code* (1861-1863) was recognized by the bench and bar in his own day and after. Long before David Dudley Field codified the substantive common law in New York, Cobb had done it in Georgia. Unfortunately, the Civil War prevented publicity of the fact; hence when Field finally drafted a civil code containing common law doctrines, he was unaware of Cobb's earlier successes in this regard.[10]

From the point of view of the historian of southern society, Cobb's most interesting legal publication was his *Inquiry into the Law of Negro Slavery* (1858). This massively documented compendium of proslavery argumentation was something of a pioneering venture. Except for George M. Stroud's *Sketch of the Law of Slavery*, which Cobb dismissed, perhaps unfairly, as a mere "Abolitionist pamphlet," no other work on the legal aspects of slavery had been published. John C. Hurd's exhaustive, two volume *Freedom and Bondage in the United States*, rebutting some of Cobb's contentions about interstate comity, appeared later.[11] *The Law of Negro Slavery* exemplified perfectly the central theme of southern nationalism—slavery as a positive good—and it advanced both the racial and patriarchal strains of the proslavery argument. Cobb leaned more toward the former than the latter but refused to be drawn into the race plurality debate, and, in the end, used virtually every theory then current to justify the institution of slavery. Not surprisingly, his book has been a prime source for historians of southern ideology.[12]

If the defense of slavery was the main feature distinguishing the South from the North, it was not the only one. Concerning southern

---

[10]Smith, "First Codification," p. 448.

[11]Cobb, *Law of Slavery*, p. ix; *American Law Register*, 9: 448; Johnson and Malone, eds., *Dictionary of American Biography*, 7: 423.

[12]Jenkins, *Proslavery Thought*, pp. 107-55, 173-207, 244-75, passim, relies most heavily on Cobb's work but others have drawn upon it as well. For some of the others see, Frederickson, *Black Image*, pp. 58, 62, 83; Finkelman, *Imperfect Union*, p. 331; Degler, *Place Over Time*, p. 91; Johnson, *Patriarchal Republic*, p. 141; Robert Brent Toplin, "Between Black and White: Attitudes Toward Southern Mulattoes, 1830-1861," *Journal of Southern History* 45 (May 1979), p. 191; Jack P. Maddox, Jr. "Proslavery Millennialism: Social Eschatology in Antebellum Southern Calvinism," *American Quarterly* 31 (Spring 1979), pp. 54-55. Hereinafter cited as Maddox, "Proslavery Millennialism."

evangelicals Anne Loveland writes: "The belief in the sovereignty and omnipotence of God and the dependence of man informed the whole of their thinking, and more than any other single element, contributed to the distinctiveness of southern evangelical thought in the nineteenth century."[13] Cobb manifested southern evangelicalism in every sense. He accepted the idea that slavery had a Biblical basis; urged the moral reformation of individuals yet remained restrained on the subject of social reform; and shared with other revivalists a Calvinistic view of human nature. His evangelical precepts, combined with a proslavery ideology and an incredibly ubiquitous involvement in the legal, religious, educational, social, and political affairs of the time, made him a truly representative southerner, one who exhibited the distinctiveness, or "limited distinctiveness," of the antebellum South.[14] The extent of his representativeness is suggested by the wide variety of interpretations which historians have imposed upon his words and deeds. One author implies that he was a millennialist, another calls him a "Georgia frontiersman," still another sees him as a spokesman for herrenvolk democracy, and yet another claims that he was the leader of a slaveholding patriarchal minority.[15]

Born on a plantation and raised in an upcountry town where he encountered people from every social strata, related by blood to a Democratic politician and by marriage to a Whig judge, influenced by a Baptist mother and a Presbyterian wife, and drawn by a superior intellect toward a life of contemplation and scholarship but driven by a restless temperament into championing innumerable causes, Cobb mirrored much of

[13]Loveland, *Southern Evangelicals*, p. 265.

[14]On the question of whether the South was wholly or partially distinctive see Degler, *Place Over Time*. It should be remembered that Cobb's manifold interests—the Presbyterian Church, the Prayer Meeting Revival of 1858, temperance, Sabbath observance, common schools, Sunday schools, codification, and greater professionalism in the practice of law—were national in scope. Thus, if Cobb was not exactly in the American mainstream, he was not totally divorced from it either. Even in the palmiest days of southern nationalism he clung to vestiges of his former unionism by proposing to name the Confederacy the "Republic of Washington" and by modeling the new constitution on the old.

[15]Maddox, "Proslavery Millennialism," p. 54-55; McCardell, *Idea of a Southern Nation*, p. 234; Frederickson, *Black Image*, p. 62; Johnson, *Patriarchal Republic*, pp. 124-27, 137-39, 163-65, 174-75.

southern life and thought and articulated the attitudes of a substantial cross section of the Georgia population.

One attitude that was typically Georgian was a devotion to the Union. At the beginning of the 1850s Cobb (and for that matter most southerners) supported sectional compromise and berated fire-eaters with as much acerbity as they did abolitionists for endangering the nation. His unionism, of course, always had a southern tinge to it; preservation (not expansion) of slavery, coupled with interstate comity on slave transit in the North, was the sine qua non of sectional harmony. Gradually, during the decade of controversy over slavery, Cobb's Union sentiments eroded and all the elements of his southern nationalism emerged. The election of Lincoln was simply the episode which brought the elements together. By 1860 Cobb was a thoroughgoing and uncompromising southern nationalist committed to a revolutionary movement for independence.

The formation of the Confederate States of America, following hard in wake of the secession crusade (that is, the revolutionary movement), represented the culmination of his short-lived dream of separate southern nationhood. Not only did he play a major role in constructing the Confederacy but, in framing a new constitution incorporating the first comprehensive bill of rights in Georgia's history, he practically fathered, in the opinion of one historian, a second revolution in his native state. The exact nature of that revolution, however, is a matter of debate. Insofar as Cobb is concerned, it was probably not the sort of revolution Michael Johnson talks about, a revolution to secure political and social control for conservative aristocrats. On the contrary, it had distinctly democratic overtones, or at least Cobb's contribution to it did.[16]

Ironically, Cobb was no happier, indeed less happy, living in the Confederacy than he had been in the old Union. His experience in the Confederate Congress was disillusioning. The give-and-take of politics eluded him altogether, and he complained constantly about governmental incompetence, nepotism, and the absence of patriotism. One is reminded here again of Ronald Formisano's commentary on "Men who had a strong tendency toward devotionalism": they lacked "organizational malleability" and the "knack for compromise" and, hence, were unable to work patiently in harness with others. Politics, then, was no

[16]Lee, *Confederate Constitutions*, p. 148; Johnson, *Patriarchal Republic*, pp. 124-27.

more Cobb's cup of tea in 1861 than it had been in 1843 when he declared: "I see the cup is sparkling, but the dregs I must drink with it . . . are misery [,] disappointment [,] & hate."[17]

His stint in the military was equally frustrating. Irked by his subordinate role, he longed for higher command. "In the Army no man *thinks* but the head," he told his wife, "and if a man below has a head and allows it to think, he must either wear himself out fruitlessly or else by talking, get his name famous as a disorganizing brawler. *I am disgusted with the Military* unless I could be *the thinking part myself*."[18]

Cobb was not without the attributes of a good officer. He had courage, physical stamina, quickness of mind, a sense of duty, and a concern for the welfare of his troops. Moreover, he carried out orders with precision, invariably scouted the terrain around his position to determine its strengths and weaknesses, maintained discipline, and, though often at odds with his subalterns, enjoyed the respect of his men. His primary problem came with the nature of the organization he recruited. The legion type formation was so unwieldy and ineffective that the war department rightly ruled it obsolete. Thus, from the outset of the war, Cobb's command was frequently divided into component parts out of military necessity, causing its colonel to rail against personal mistreatment. Once given command of a normal brigade, Cobb's difficulties seemed less complex and his attitude improved. Eventually his leadership merits were recognized and rewarded by promotion to brigadier general, but untimely death prevented him from demonstrating fully the extent of his military capabilities.

As with all public figures, Thomas Cobb tasted, at one time or another, a measure of sweet success and bitter failure. He helped to shape the events of his day and, in turn, was shaped by them. If he lacked true greatness in any field of endeavor, he was by no means commonplace. In many respects his life was unusual; but, in the last analysis, what makes it interesting and historically significant is not uniqueness but the degree to which it reflected the mood and trends of antebellum southern society.

---

[17]Formisano, "Antipartyism and the Second Party System," pp. 685-86; Thomas Cobb to Marion Lumpkin, 14 December [1843], Jackson Scrapbook.

[18]Thomas Cobb to Marion Cobb, 7 June 1862, Thomas R. R. Cobb Collection.

His life's journey from planter's son to Confederate general, from southern unionist to southern nationalist personified southern distinctiveness at every point.

Bibliography

Manuscript Sources

University of Georgia Libraries, Athens, Georgia
David C. Barrow Papers
Baber-Blackshear Collection
Joseph E. Brown Papers—Felix Hargrett Typescript
Carlton-Newton-Mell Collection
Thomas Carr Collection
Howell Cobb Collection
Cobb-Erwin-Lamar Collection
Thomas R. R. Cobb Collection
Telamon Cuyler Collection
William G. Delony Collection
Harden-Jackson-Carithers Collection
Crawford W. Long Collection
Joseph Henry Lumpkin Papers
Wilson Lumpkin Papers
Patrick Hues Mell Collection
Prince Papers
Keith Read Collection

Perkins Library, Duke University, Durham, North Carolina
Joseph E. Brown Manuscripts
Thomas R. R. Cobb Papers
J. D. B. DeBow Manuscripts
Edward Harden Manuscripts
Seaborn Jones Papers
Herschel V. Johnson Manuscripts

E. A. Nisbet Manuscripts
William H. Seward Papers
Alexander H. Stephens Manuscripts
Weir-Boyd Letters

Southern Historical Collection, University of North Carolina, Chapel Hill, North Carolina
James T. Harrison Papers
Jackson-Prince Papers
Lafayette McLaws Papers
Christopher G. Memminger Papers (microfilm)
William Porcher Miles Papers
William Letcher Mitchell Papers
Alexander H. Stephens Correspondence (microfilm)
Benjamin C. Yancey Papers

Georgia Department of Archives and History, Atlanta, Georgia
Joel Crawford Barnett Letters (microfilm)
Samuel A. Burney Letters (microfilm)
R. H. L. Clack Letters (microfilm)
Thomas R. R. Cobb folder, Original Manuscripts File #2
Thomas R. R. Cobb folder, Box 3 (Correspondence to Governor Brown), Georgia Adjutant General Records
Confederate War Letters of Private B. E. Yerby (typescript)
Henry Rootes Jackson Scrapbook (microfilm)
J. C. Nunn Correspondence, C. S. A. Letters (microfilm)
William J. Rheney Letters (microfilm)
John Henly Smith Letterbook, 1859-1860

Emory University Library, Atlanta, Georgia
Alexander H. Stephens Papers

Library of Congress, Manuscripts Division, Washington, D. C.
Robert J. Breckinridge Papers
Alexander H. Stephens Papers

Henry E. Huntington Library and Art Gallery, San Marino, California
Joseph C. Stiles Correspondence

The Virginia Historical Society, Richmond, Virginia
Robert E. Lee Papers

The Historical Society of Pennsylvania, Philadelphia, Pennsylvania
Simon Gratz Collection

First Presbyterian Church of Athens, Georgia
Ms. Letter, Thomas R. R. Cobb to Pupils of the Presbyterian Sunday School, 4 July 1858
A. L. Hull, "A Historical Sketch of the Sunday-School of the First Presbyterian Church of Athens"

Letters in Private Collections
Ms. Letters, Thomas R. R. Cobb to Howell Cobb, in the possession of Dr. E. Merton Coulter, Athens, Georgia

Ms. Letter, Thomas R. R. Cobb to Joseph H. Lumpkin, 5 January 1842, in the possession of Miss Callie Hull, Washington, D. C.

Newspapers

Athenian (Athens, Georgia), 1827.

Confederate Union (Milledgeville, Georgia), 1862.

Daily Chronicle & Sentinel (Augusta, Georgia), 1860-1861.

Daily Columbus Enquirer (Columbus, Georgia), 1858-1863.

Daily Richmond Examiner (Richmond, Virginia), 1861.

Gazette of the State of Georgia (Savannah, Georgia), 1783-1788.

Georgia Journal and Messenger (Macon, Georgia), 1858-1860.

Louisville Gazette (Louisville, Georgia), 1799-1803.

Montgomery Weekly Advertiser (Montgomery, Alabama), 1860.

Montgomery Weekly Mail (Montgomery, Alabama), 1861-1862.

Montgomery Weekly Post (Montgomery, Alabama), 1861-1862.

New York Herald (New York, New York), 1858-1859.

New York Times (New York, New York), 1858-1859.

New York Tribune (New York, New York), 1858-1859.

Richmond Enquirer (Richmond, Virginia), 1861-1863.

Rome Tri-Weekly Courier (Rome, Georgia), 1861.

Southern Banner (Athens, Georgia), 1833-1864.

Southern Confederacy (Milledgeville, Georgia), 1861-1862.

Southern Enterprise (Thomasville, Georgia), 1860-1861.

Southern Federal Union (Milledgeville, Georgia), 1861.

Southern Recorder (Milledgeville, Georgia), 1847-1849-1850, 1855-1864.

Southern Presbyterian (Columbia, South Carolina), 1861.

Southern Watchman (Athens, Georgia), 1857-1863.

Weekly Constitutionalist (Augusta, Georgia), 1859.

Collected Letters, Diaries, Memoirs, Autobiographies, Reminiscences

Armes, William D., ed. *The Autobiography of Joseph L. LeConte.* New York: D. Appleton and Company, 1903.

Andrews, Garnett. *Reminiscences of an Old Georgia Lawyer.* Atlanta: Franklin Steam Printing House, 1870.

"Thomas Bragg Diary, 1861-1862," microfilm, Southern Historical Collection, University of North Carolina Library, Chapel Hill, North Carolina.

Chesnut, Mary Boykin. *A Diary from Dixie.* Edited by Ben Ames Williams. Boston: Houghton Mifflin Company, 1949.

"Civil War Diary, 1861-1863 of Charles J. McDonald Conaway [Connaway]," Georgia Department of Archives and History, Atlanta, Georgia.

Dowdey, Clifford and Manarin, Louis H., Eds. *The Wartime Papers of R. E. Lee.* Boston: Little, Brown and Company, 1961.

Hillyer, Junius, "Memoirs of the Early Life and Times of Judge Junius Hillyer," Hillyer Papers, University of Georgia Libraries, Athens, Georgia.

Jones, Charles Colcock, collector. *Autograph Letters and Portraits of Signers of the Confederate States*, Perkins Library, Duke University, Durham, North Carolina.

Means, Alexander. *Diary of 1861.* Edited by Ross H. McLean. Emory University Publications Sources and Reprints, ser. 6, no. 1. Atlanta: Emory University, 1959.

Myers, Robert Manson, ed. *The Children of Pride. A True Story of Georgia and the Civil War.* New Haven: Yale University Press, 1972.

Phillips, Ulrich, B., ed. *The Correspondence of Robert Toombs, Alexander H. Stephens, and Howell Cobb*, in American Historical Association, *Annual Report*, 1911, vol. 2 (Washington, D. C., 1913).

Rawick, George P., ed. *The American Slave. A Composite Autobiography. Georgia Narratives.* Vol. 12. 1941. Second reprint ed. Westport, CT: Greenwood Publishing Company, 1974.

Shryock, Richard H. "Letters of Richard D. Arnold, M. D., 1808-1817," in *Historical Papers,* ser. 15, Trinity College Historical Society. Durham NC: Duke University Press, 1925.

Thomas, Ella Gertrude (Clanton), "Journal, 1861-1864," Perkins Library, Duke University, Durham, North Carolina.

Wiley, Bell I. Ed. *Letters of Warren Akin: Confederate Congressman.* Athens GA: University of Georgia Press, 1959.

Wylie, Lollie, Belle, ed. *Memoirs of Judge Richard H. Clark.* Atlanta: Franklin Printing and Publishing Company, 1898.

Periodicals, Pamphlets, Memorials, Theses, Dissertations

Almand, Bond. "The Preparation and Adoption of the Code of 1863." *Georgia Bar Journal* 14 (1951-1952).

Barrow, Phyllis. "A History of Lucy Cobb Institute." Master's thesis, University of Georgia, 1951.

Clark, Richard H. "The History of the First Georgia Code." *Georgia Bar Association Reports* 7 (1890).

"Cobb or Cobbs Family." *William and Mary College Quarterly* 19 (1910).

Cobb, Thomas R. R. *Educational Wants of Georgia, An Address Delivered Before the Society of the Alumni of Franklin College, At Its Annual Meeting.* Athens GA: Reynolds, and Bro., 1857.

Cobb, Thomas R. R. "Memorial to the General Assembly of Georgia, 1849," Emory University Library, Atlanta, Georgia.

Cory, Earl Wallace. "Temperance and Prohibition in Ante-Bellum Georgia." Master's thesis, University of Georgia, 1961.

Coulter, E. Merton. "Slavery and Freedom in Athens, Georgia, 1860-1866." *The Georgia Historical Quarterly* 49 (1965).

Coulter, E. Merton. "William D. Martin and the School He Endowed: Martin Institute." *The Georgia Historical Quarterly* 50 (1966).

Coulter, E. Merton. "Why John and Joseph LeConte Left the University of Georgia, 1855-1856." *The Georgia Historical Quarterly* 53 (1969).

Davis, J. Treadwell. "The Presbyterians and the Sectional Conflict." *The Southern Quarterly* 8 (1960).

Donald, David. "The Proslavery Argument Reconsidered." *The Journal of Southern History.* 37 (1971).

Ezell, John S. "A Southern Education for Southrons." *The Journal of Southern History 17 (1951).*

Faust, Drew Gilpin. "Evangelicalism and the Meaning of the Proslavery Argument: The Reverend Thornton Stringfellow of Virginia." *The Virginia Magazine of History and Biography.* 85 (1977).

Formisano, Ronald. "Political Character, Antipartyism and the Second Party System." *American Quarterly.* 21 (1969).

"Genealogy." *The Virginia Magazine of History and Biography* 4 (1896). *Georgia University Magazine* 8 (1855).

Goode, John. "The Confederate Congress." *The Conservative Review. A Quarterly* 4 (1900).

Greene, Helen Ione. "Politics in Georgia, 1830-1854." Ph.D. dissertation, University of Chicago, 1945.

Huffman, Frank J., Jr. "Town and Country in the South, 1850-1880: A Comparison of Urban and Rural Social Structures." *The South Atlantic Quarterly* 76 (1977).

Hull, A. L. "The Making of the Confederate Constitution." *Publications of the Southern History Association* 9 (1905).

Johnson, Michael P. "A New Look at the Popular Vote For Delegates to the Georgia Secession Convention." *The Georgia Historical Quarterly* 56 (1972).

Jones, James Allison. "History of the First Presbyterian Church of Athens." Master's thesis, University of Georgia, 1949.

Lamar, Joseph R. "Georgia Law Books." *Georgia Bar Association Annual Report* (1898).

Maddox, Jack P., Jr. "Proslavery Millennialism: Social Eschatology in Antebellum Southern Calvinism." *American Quarterly* 31 (1979).

May, Robert E. "John A. Quitman and His Slaves: Reconciling Slave Resistance with the Proslavery Defense." *The Journal of Southern History* 46 (1980).

McCash, William B. "Thomas Cobb and the Codification of Georgia Law." *The Georgia Historical Quarterly* 62 (1978).

McCash, William B. "Thomas R. R. Cobb and the 'Better Terms' Argument." *The Georgia Historical Quarterly* 60 (1976).

McCrary, Royce C. "Georgia Politics and the Mexican War." *The Georgia Historical Quarterly* 60 (1976).

McMurray, Richard, ed. "One Man, One Vote—1860 Style." *The Georgia Historical Quarterly* 53 (1969).

Montgomery, Horace. "The Two Howell Cobbs: A Case of Mistaken Identity." *The Journal of Southern History* 28 (1962).

Morris, Sylvanus. "The Lumpkin Law School." *Georgia Law Review* 1.

Morrow, Ralph E. "The Proslavery Argument Revisited." *Mississippi Valley Historical Review* 48 (1961).

Nadelhaft, Jerome. "The Somerset Case and Slavery: Myth, Reality, and Repercussions." *Journal of Negro History* 51 (1966).

Pessen, Edward. "How Different from Each Other were the Antebellum North and South?" *The American Historical Review* 85 (1980).

Ringold, May Spencer. "Robert Newman Gourdin and the '1860 Association.' " *The Georgia Historical Quarterly* 55 (1971).

Robinson, William M., Jr. "A New Deal in Constitutions." *The Journal of Southern History* 4 (1938).

Simpson, John Eddins. "A Biography of Howell Cobb, 1815-1861." Ph.D. dissertation, University of Georgia, 1971.

Smith, Marion. "The First Codification of the Substantive Common Law." Reprint. *Tulane Law Review* 4 (1930).

Sumner, Ellen Louise. "Unionism in Georgia, 1860-1861." Master's thesis, University of Georgia, 1960.

Surrency, Erwin C. "Law Reports in the United States." *The American Journal of Legal History* 25 (1981).

Surrency, Erwin C. "The First American Criminal Code: The Georgia Code of 1816." *The Georgia Historical Quarterly* 64 (1979).

Welters, Barbara. "The Cult of True Womanhood: 1820-1860." *American Quarterly* 18 (1966).

Public Records

Annual Report of the Comptroller General of the State of Georgia Made to the Governor, 1846-1860. Places and dates of publication vary.

Acts of the General Assembly of the State of Georgia, 1841-1854, 1858-1861. Places and dates of publication vary.

Candler, Allen D., comp. *The Colonial Records of the State of Georgia.* 26 vols. Atlanta: Franklin Printing and Publishing Company, 1904-1916.

Candler, Allen D., comp. *The Confederate Records of the State of Georgia.* 6 vols. Atlanta: Franklin Printing and Publishing Company, 1909-1911.

Candler, Allen D., comp. *The Revolutionary Records of the State of Georgia.* 3 vols. Atlanta: Franklin-Turner Company, 1908.

Clarke County, Georgia, "Court of Ordinary, Wills," vols. C and D.

Clarke County, Georgia, "Tax Digests," 1841-1863.

Clark, R. H., Cobb, T. R. R., and Irwin D., codifiers. *The Code of the State of Georgia.* Atlanta: John H. Seals, 1861.

Cobb, T. R. R. *The Supreme Court Manual: Containing The Organic Law of the Court, With Notes of the Decisions Thereon; The Rules of the Court, With Notes of the Court Thereon; Together With Forms and Directions for Bringing Up Cases.* Athens GA: Gazette Job Establishment, 1949.

Cobb, Thomas R. R., comp. *A Digest of the Statute Laws of the State of Georgia, in Force Prior to the Session of the General Assembly of 1851, With Explanatory Notes and References; And Also, With Notes, Giving the Exposition of the Statutes, by the Supreme Court of the State; Together With An Appendix* Athens GA: Christy, Kelsea & Burke, 1851.

"Executive Department Minutes of the State of Georgia, 1843-1859," Georgia Department of Archives and History, Atlanta, Georgia.

Jefferson County, Georgia, "Court of Ordinary, Minutes," Books A-B, 1801-1818.

Jefferson County, Georgia, "Court of Ordinary, Wills," Book A.

Jefferson County, Georgia, "Inferior Court Minutes," Books 1-11, 1796-1858.

Journal of the Congress of the Confederate States of America, 1861-1865. 7 vols. Washington: Government Printing Office, 1904-1905.

Journal of the House of Representatives of the State of Georgia, 1807-1815, 1849-1854, 1858-1861. Places, dates, and publishers vary.

Journal of the Senate of the State of Georgia, 1842-1849, 1858-1861. Places, dates, and publishers vary.

National Archives Microfilm Publications. Microcopy No. 266. Compiled Service Records of Confederate Soldiers Who Served in Organizations from the State of Georgia. Cobb's Legion. Microfilm copies in Georgia Department of Archives and History.

Prince, Oliver H., comp. *A Digest of the Laws of the State of Georgia; Containing All Statutes and the Substance of All Resolutions of a General and Public Nature, and Now in Force, Which Have Been Passed in This State, Previous to the Session of the General Assembly of Dec. 1837. With Occasional Explanatory Notes, and Connecting References. To Which is Added An Appendix* Second edition. Athens GA: Oliver H. Prince, Publisher, 1837.

Reports of Cases in Law and Equity Argued and Determined in the Supreme Court of the State of Georgia, 1846-1859. Atlanta: The Franklin Printing and Publishing Company, 1900-1906. Reprint. Vols. 1-24. Cases variously reported by James M. Kelly, Thomas R. R. Cobb, and B. Y. Martin.

Richardson, James D., ed. *A Compilation of the Messages and Papers of the Confederacy. Including the Diplomatic Correspondence of 1861-1865.* 2 vols. Nashville: United States Publishing Company, 1905.

The War of the Rebellion Records: A Compilation of the Official Record of the Union and Confederate Armies. 128 vols. Washington, DC: Government Printing Office, 1880-1901.

University of Georgia Records

"A weekly record of absentees from church prayers recitations together with all fines imposed by the faculty of Franklin College Beginning Jany 1834."

Catalogue of the Officers and Students of Franklin College, University of Georgia. 1838-1841, 1860-1861.

Catalogue of the Trustees, Officers, Alumni and Matriculates of the University of Georgia, from 1785 to 1901. With a Historical Sketch by A. L. Hull. Athens GA: E. D. Stone Press, 1901.

"Minutes of the Board of Trustees of the University of Georgia, 1835-1871." Vols. 3-4.

"Minutes of the Faculty of Franklin College," 1836-1873.

"Minutes of the Phi Kappa Society," 1835-1885.

"Minutes of the proceedings of the Prudential Committee of the Board of Trustees of Franklin College," 1834-1857.

"Prospectus, University of Georgia, Law Department, June 1, 1859."

Books

Alexander, Thomas B., and Beringer, Richard E. *The Anatomy of the Confederate Congress.* Nashville: Vanderbilt University Press, 1972.

Avery, I. W. *The History of the State of Georgia from 1850 to 1881, Embracing the Three Important Epochs: The Decade Before the War of 1861-65; The War; The Period of Reconstruction, with Portraits of the Leading Public Men of This Era.* New York: Brown and Derby, Publishers, 1881.

Biographical Directory of the American Congress 1774-1961. The Continental Congress September 5, 1774, to October 21, 1788. The Congress of the United States from the First to the Eighty-sixth Congress March 4, 1789, to January 3, 1961, inclusive. Washington DC: Government Printing Office, 1961.

Boogher, Elbert W. G. *Secondary Education in Georgia, 1732-1858.* Philadelphia: N.p., 1933.

Boykin, Samuel, ed. *A Memorial Volume of the Hon. Howell Cobb of Georgia.* Philadelphia: J. B. Lippincott and Company, 1870.

Brooks, Robert Preston. *The University of Georgia Under Sixteen Administrations 1785-1955.* Athens GA: The University of Georgia Press, 1956.

Brown, Herbert Ross. *The Sentimental Novel in America 1789-1860.* New York: Pageant Books, Inc., 1959.

Bryan T. Conn. *Confederate Georgia.* Athens GA: University of Georgia Press, 1953.

Capers, Gerald M. *Stephen A. Douglas. Defender of the Union.* Boston: Little, Brown and Company, 1959.

Capers, Henry D. *The Life and Times of C. G. Memminger.* Richmond: Everett Waddy Company, Publishers, 1893.

Cobb, Thomas R. R. *An Inquiry into the Law of Negro Slavery in the United States of America to which is prefixed, An Historical Sketch of Slavery.* Philadelphia: T. and J. W. Johnson and Company, 1858.

Cody, L. L. *The Lumpkin Family of Georgia.* Macon GA: N.p., 1928.

Coulter, E. Merton. *Georgia: A Short History.* Revised edition. Chapel Hill NC: The University of North Carolina Press, 1947.

Coulter, E. Merton. *College Life in the Old South.* Athens GA: The University of Georgia Press, 1951.

Coulter, E. Merton. *The Confederate States of America 1861-1865.* Baton Rouge: Louisiana State University Press, 1950.

Coulter, E. Merton. *Lost Generation: The Life and Death of James Barrow, C. S. A.* Tuscaloosa AL: Confederate Publishing Company, Inc., 1956.

Coulter, E. Merton. *John Jacobus Flournoy: Champion of the Common Man in the Antebellum South.* Savannah GA: The Georgia Historical Society, 1942.

Coulter, E. Merton. *William Montague Browne: Versatile Anglo-Irish American, 1823-1883.* Athens GA: University of Georgia Press, 1967.

Craven, Avery O. *The Growth of Southern Nationalism 1848-1861.* Baton Rouge: Louisiana State University Press, 1953.

Craven, Avery O. *The Coming of the Civil War.* Chicago: The University of Chicago Press, 1957.

Degler, Carl N. *Place Over Time. The Continuity of Southern Distinctiveness.* Baton Rouge: Louisiana State University Press, 1977.

DeVoto, Bernard. *The Year of Decision 1846.* Boston: Houghton Mifflin Company, Sentry Edition, 1961.

Dumond, Dwight L. *The Secession Movement 1860-1861.* New York: Macmillan Company, 1931.

Dumond, Dwight L., ed. *Southern Editorials on Secession.* 1931. Reprint. Gloucester MA: Peter Smith, 1964.

Faust, Drew Gilpin, ed. *The Ideology of Slavery. Proslavery Thought in the Antebellum South, 1830-1860.* Baton Rouge: Louisiana State University Press, 1981.

Fielder, Herbert. *A Sketch of the Life and Times and Speeches of Joseph E. Brown.* Springfield MA: Press of Springfield Printing Company, 1883.

Finkelman, Paul. *An Imperfect Union. Slavery, Federalism, and Comity.* Chapel Hill NC: The University of North Carolina Press, 1981.

Flippin, Percy Scott, *Herschel V. Johnson of Georgia. State Rights Unionist.* Richmond: Press of the Dietz Printing Company, Publishers, 1931.

Frederickson, George M. *The Black Image in the White Mind. The Debate on Afro-American Character and Destiny, 1817-1914.* New York: Harper & Row, Publishers, 1971.

Freeman, Douglas S. *Lee's Lieutenants: A Study in Command.* Three volumes. New York: Charles Scribner's Sons, 1942.

Freeman, Douglas S. *R. E. Lee: A Biography.* Four volumes. New York: Charles Scribner's Sons, 1934.

Genonese, Eugene. *The Political Economy of Slavery: Studies in the Economy and Society of the Slave South.* New York: Random House, 1965; Vintage ed., 1967.

Grice, Warren. *The Georgia Bench and Bar. The Development of Georgia's Judicial System.* Macon GA: The J. W. Burke Company, 1931.

Haar, Charles M., ed. *The Golden Age of American Law.* New York: G. Braziller, 1965.

Hamilton, Holman. *Prologue to Conflict: The Crisis and Compromise of 1850.* New York: W. W. Norton and Company, Inc., Norton Library, 1966.

Harris, John B., ed. *A History of the Supreme Court of Georgia.* Macon GA: J. W. Burke Company, 1948.

Hill, Louise B. *Joseph E. Brown and the Confederacy.* Chapel Hill NC: The University of North Carolina Press, 1939.

Hill, Samuel S., Jr. *The South and North in American Religion.* Athens GA: The University of Georgia Press, 1980.

Holland, Lynwood M. *Pierce M. B. Young: The Warwick of the South.* Athens GA: University of Georgia Press, 1964.

Hull, A. L. *Annals of Athens, Georgia 1801-1901 With an Introductory Sketch by Dr. Henry Hull.* Athens GA: Banner Job Office, 1906.

Hurd, John C. *The Law of Freedom and Bondage in the United States.* Two volumes. Reprint. New York: Negro Universities Press, 1968.

Hynds, Ernest C. *Antebellum Athens and Clarke County*, Athens GA: University of Georgia Press, 1974.

Jenkins, William S. *Pro-Slavery Thought in the Old South.* Reprint. Gloucester MA: Peter Smith, 1960.

Johnson, Allen and Malone, Dumas, eds. *Dictionary of American Biography.* Twenty vols. New York: Charles Scribner's Sons, 1930.

Johnson, Michael P. *Toward a Patriarchal Republic. The Secession of Georgia.* Baton Rouge: Louisiana State University Press, 1977.

Johnson, Robert U. and Buel, Clarence C., eds. *Battles and Leaders of the Civil War.* Four volumes. Reprint. New York: Thomas Yoseloff, 1956.

Johnson, Zachary Taylor. *The Political Policies of Howell Cobb.* Nashville: George Peabody College for Teachers, 1929.

Johnston, Richard M. and Browne, William H. *Life of Alexander H. Stephens.* Philadelphia: J. B. Lippincott and Company, 1878.

Klein, Philip S. *President James Buchanan: A Biography.* University Park: The Pennsylvania State University Press, 1962.

Knight, Lucian Lamar. "Genealogy of the Knight, Walton, Woodson, Lamar, Daniel, Benning, Cobb, Jackson, Grant and Other Georgia Families. Including Biographies of Many Distinguished Members." Bound, typed volume in the Library of Congress, Washington DC.

Lee, Charles Robert, Jr. *The Confederate Constitutions.* Chapel Hill NC: The University of North Carolina Press, 1963.

Lewis, David E. *Report on Public Education with Appendixes Giving Statistics of School Returns, and Other Documents on the Subject.* Milledgeville GA: Boughton, Nisbet and Barnes, State Printers, 1860.

Loveland, Anne C. *Southern Evangelicals and the Social Order 1800-1860.* Baton Rouge: Louisiana State University Press, 1980.

Mathews, Donald G. *Religion in the Old South.* Chicago: University of Chicago Press, 1977.

McCardell, John. *The Idea of a Southern Nation. Southern Nationalists and Southern Nationalism.* New York: W. W. Norton & Company, 1979.

McElreath, Walter. *A Treatise on the Constitution of Georgia Giving the Origin, History and Development of the Fundamental Law of the State, with all Constitutional Documents Containing Such Law.* Atlanta: N. p., 1912.

McLoughlin, William G., Jr. *Modern Revivalism: Charles G. Finney to Billy Graham.* New York: The Ronald Press, 1959.

McLoughlin, William G., Jr. *Revivals, Awakenings, and Reform. An Essay on Religion and Social Change in America, 1607-1977.* Chicago: University of Chicago Press, 1978.

Meade, Robert D. *Judah P. Benjamin: Confederate Statesman.* New York: Oxford University Press, 1943.

Mell, R. H., Jr. *The Life of Patrick Hues Mell.* Louisville KY: Baptist Book Concern, 1895.

Miller, Stephen F. *The Bench and Bar of Georgia: Memoirs and Sketches. With an Appendix, Containing a Court Roll from 1790 to 1857, etc.* Two volumes. Philadelphia: J. B. Lippincott and Company, 1858.

Minutes of the General Assembly of the Presbyterian Church in the United States of America with an Appendix. Vol. 15. Philadelphia: Presbyterian Board of Publication, 1858.

Minutes of the Synod of Georgia at their Fifteenth Annual Session. Atlanta: Franklin Printing House, 1859.

Montgomery, Horace. *Cracker Parties.* Baton Rouge: Louisiana State University Press, 1950.

Montgomery, Horace, ed. *Georgians in Profile: Historical Essays in Honor of Ellis Merton Coulter.* Athens GA: University of Georgia Press, 1958.

Montgomery, Horace. *Howell Cobb's Confederate Career.* Tuscaloosa AL: Confederate Publishing Company, Inc., 1959.

Moore, Albert B. *Conscription and Conflict in the Confederacy.* New York: Hillary House Publishers LTD, 1963.

Nichols, Roy. *Franklin Pierce: Young Hickory of the Granite Hills.* Philadelphia: University of Pennsylvania Press, 1958.

Nichols, Roy. *The Disruption of American Democracy.* New York: The Macmillan Company, 1948.

Northen, William F., ed. *Men of Mark in Georgia. A Complete and Elaborate History of the State from its settlement to the present time, chiefly told in biographies and autobiographies of the most eminent men of each period of Georgia's progress and development.* Six volumes. Atlanta: A. B. Caldwell, Publisher, 1911.

Orr, Dorothy. *A History of Education in Georgia.* Chapel Hill NC: The University of North Carolina Press, 1950.

Parks, Joseph H. *Joseph E. Brown of Georgia.* Baton Rouge: Louisiana State University Press, 1977.

Partick, Rembert W. *Jefferson Davis and His Cabinet.* Baton Rouge: Louisiana State University Press, 1944.

Pearce, Haywood J., Jr. *Benjamin H. Hill: Secession and Reconstruction.* Chicago: The University of Chicago Press, 1928.

Phillips, Ulrich B. *Georgia and States Rights. A Study of the Political History of Georgia from the Revolution to the Civil War, with Particular Regard to Federal Relations.* Washington DC: Government Printing Office, 1902.

Phillips, Ulrich B. *The Life of Robert Toombs.* New York: The Macmillan Company, 1913.

Pound, Roscoe. *The Formative Era of American Law.* Boston: Little Brown and Company, 1938.

Roberts, L. E. "Sectional Factors in the Movement for Legislative Reapportionment and Reduction in Georgia 1777-1860." *Studies in Georgia History and Government.* Edited by J. C. Bonner and L. E. Roberts. Athens GA: University of Georgia Press, 1940.

Saye, Albert B. *A Constitutional History of Georgia 1732-1945.* Athens GA: University of Georgia Press, 1948.

Scomp, H. A. *King Alcohol in the Realm of King Cotton. Or A History of the Liquor Traffic and of the Temperance Movement in Georgia from 1733 to 1887.* N. p.: Press of the Blakely Printing Company, 1888.

Scott, Anne Firor. *The Southern Lady from Pedestal to Politics 1830-1930.* Chicago: The University of Chicago Press, 1970.

Sell, E. S. *History of the State Normal School.* Athens GA: N. p., 1923.

Sellers, Charles G., Jr., ed. *The Southerner as American.* Chapel Hill NC: The University of North Carolina Press, 1960.

Shryock, R. H. *Georgia and the Union in 1850.* Durham NC: Duke University Press, 1926.

Silver, James W. *Confederate Morale and Church Propaganda.* 1957. Reprint. Gloucester MA: Peter Smith, 1964.

Smith, H. Shelton. *In His Image, But . . . Racism in Southern Religion 1780-1910.* Durham NC: Duke University Press, 1972.

Smith, Timothy. *Revivalism and Social Reform in Mid-Nineteenth Century America.* New York: Abingdon Press, 1957.

Stackpole, Edward J. *Drama on the Rappahannock. The Fredericksburg Campaign.* Harrisburg: Military Service Publishing Company, 1957.

Stacy, James. *A History of the Presbyterian Church in Georgia.* Atlanta: Westminster Company, n. d.

Stephens, Alexander H. *A Constitutional View of the Late War Between the States: Its Causes, Character, Conduct, and Results.* Two volumes. Philadelphia: National Publishing Company, 1868-1870.

Thomas, Emory M. *The Confederate Nation 1861-1865.* New York: Harper & Row Publishers, 1979.

Thomas, Z. V. *History of Jefferson County.* Macon GA: J. W. Burke Company, 1927.

Vander Velde, Lewis G. *The Presbyterian Churches and the Federal Union 1861-1869.* Cambridge: Harvard University Press, 1932.

Ware, Ethel K. *A Constitutional History of Georgia.* New York: Columbia University Press, 1947.

Warren, Charles. *A History of the American Bar.* Boston: Little, Brown and Company, 1911.

Whan, Vorin E., Jr. *Fiasco at Fredericksburg.* State College: The Pennsylvania University Press, 1961.

White, Henry Alexander. *Southern Presbyterian Leaders.* New York: The Neale Publishing Company, 1911.

Yearns, Wilfred B. *The Confederate Congress.* Athens GA: The University of Georgia Press, 1960.

Wooster, Ralph A. *The Secession Conventions of the South.* Princeton NJ: Princeton University Press, 1962.

Index

THOMAS R. R. COBB:
THE MAKING OF A SOUTHERN NATIONALIST

Designed by Haywood Ellis
Typography designed by Janet Middlebrooks

Composition by Omni Composition Services, Macon, Georgia
typeset in Garamond (text) and Univers Bold Condensed (heads)
on an Addressograph/Multigraph Comp/Set phototypesetter 5404,
and paginated on an A/M Comp/Set 4510.

Production specifications:
text paper—60 pound Warren's Olde Style
endpapers—80 pound Warren's Olde Style
cover (on .088 boards)—James River Kivar 9 6-338 Firenze
dust jacket—100 pound enamel, printed three colors (PMS 422 grey,
PMS 302 blue, and black) and varnished.

Printing (offset lithography) by Omnipress of Macon, Inc., Macon, Georgia
Binding by John H. Dekker and Sons, Inc., Grand Rapids, Michigan